THE MIND OF THE SOUTH

THE MIND
OF
THE SOUTH

W. J. Cash

WITH AN INTRODUCTION BY
DENIS BROGAN

THAMES AND HUDSON · LONDON

To

MY MOTHER & FATHER

First published in Great Britain in 1971 by
Thames and Hudson Ltd, London

Printed in Great Britain by Stephen Austin and Sons Ltd,
Caxton Hill, Hertford

ISBN 0 500 53006 8

CONTENTS

INTRODUCTION

By DENIS BROGAN

HABENT SUA FATA LIBELLI: "Books have their own destiny." This sagacious Roman proverb is exemplified in the history of this very remarkable book, *The Mind of the South*. For it must be remembered that the first edition was published in 1941, and although it had a *succès de scandale*, and more than that, in that year the American mind was turning rapidly away from the problems of the South to the problems of the world. The great European war, which became a great world war, was to alter the South with very great speed. For example, it greatly increased Negro emigration to the North; it poured a great deal of Federal capital into the South; it broke down a great many Southern taboos; and it accelerated the industrialization of the South, to which Cash had paid far too little attention. In this sense, *The Mind of the South* was going out of date almost as soon as it was published, and a good many of the critics of the book assumed that many of Cash's harsh judgments on his native section were not so much wrong as irrelevant to the New South that was being given a forced-draft development by the importation of Northern capital and the creation of a new industrial world. To go back to the South today, to Houston, Atlanta, Birmingham (Alabama), is to go back to a region which has greatly changed, in most ways for the better, since 1941, not to speak of, say, 1901. But some of the optimism with which this forced-draft growth of the South during the Second World War was welcomed was a shallow optimism. The political structure of the South has not yet been reformed, and the political leaders of the South are, many of them, almost if not quite as backward as were those when Cash wrote his famous tract. *The Mind of the South* illuminates a great deal in the South of 1970 as well as in the South of 1941, and deserves re-publication.

The book was the work of a very distinguished, young, Southern journalist, and it irritated most people in the South, although it irritated them for different reasons. It irritated the naïve devotees of the Southern cavalier legend. It irritated even more the passionate devotees of Southern evangelistic religion. True, there were Southern Baptists who had many of the views of W. J. Cash, but they were hardly representative Southern Baptists. Its comparative indifference or hostility to the new business oligarchs of the South irritated the Babbitts of Atlanta, still more of Birmingham, Alabama. A great many Southerners did believe that much of what Cash said was true and relevant, but could not forgive him for saying it, especially as the numerous enemies of the Old Confederacy in the North found weapons in it to puncture the absurd pride (as they saw it) of the Southern communities.

In many ways, Cash's book recalls the famous *antebellum* book of Hinton Rowan Helper, *The Impending Crisis of the South.* Each book was resented, and more than resented, for its attack on the established ethos and the established illusions of the South. But Helper himself was an almost revolutionary force, since in calling for the reconsideration of the plantation economy in the South, he was moved, not by any sympathy with the slaves, but by anger against the plantation oligarchy which, he thought, was betraying Southern interests. In many ways, Helper was right, but his book is bitter, passionate, and he was not a man to inspire much affection or, perhaps, in the long run much respect. Cash's book has much in common with Helper's, but it also differs in very important ways. Cash was a much more amiable man than Helper, and his criticism of the South was not as narrow, egoistic, and unattractively militant. He disliked a great deal in the Establishment of the South in the period just before the Second World War, as Helper had disliked it in the period just before the outbreak of " the War between the States." But the South in which Cash grew up was a good deal more civilized and a good deal more a part of the modern world than the South in which Helper grew up, and the dilemmas and dangers threatening the peace of the South in 1941, serious as they were, were not nearly as serious as those which led to the great catastrophe of the Civil war.

But the *succès de scandale* of Cash's book in the long run did his reputation harm. He might have moderated his criticism and improved his scholarly apparatus if he had not died so soon, but he was vulnerable to reasonable criticism, especially from the increasingly important and competent academic community of the Old Confederacy. It was no light matter to have the University of North Carolina critical of the rhetorical, vehement, and often unscholarly picture of Southern life which Cash had produced. Indeed, Cash's book suggests some of his own serious intellectual limitations. He was not nearly as much a pioneer as he seemed to think. He pays service to people like John Spencer Bassett and to some of the historians who were beginning to revise Southern history, but on the whole he takes a traditional view of some of the most bitterly debated aspects of Southern history as it is seen by scholars. He would have been both surprised and horrified to see Southerners writing appreciative studies of the merits of Reconstruction, and perhaps stressing the fact that the liberation of the South from " Northern tyranny " was not an unmixed benefit. Even a very learned and acute Southern historian like David Potter, arguing with great ingenuity and scholarship that perhaps the price of freeing the slaves in the Civil War was excessively high for everybody, was not defending the traditional view of Reconstruction or the traditional view of the origins of " The War." Indeed, David Potter presents a most brilliant defence against the common charge that Lincoln provoked the Civil War deliberately, and that the attack on Fort Sumter was rather like the French answer to the Hohenzollern candidature in Spain in 1870.

Then, Cash was describing a South that was changing under his eyes, changing far more rapidly than he realized, or at any rate than he recounts. Cash's South is still mainly the "cotton kingdom." Its main business is agricultural, its ethos still that of the county courthouse, even if the great plantation houses of Southern fiction and, in part, of Southern fact were, as Cash points out, disappearing or passing into the hands of total strangers. He would have appreciated the irony of one Southern university seat where the most magnificent Southern mansion, looking just like a set from *Gone with the Wind*, was built by an extremely successful dentist shortly before the outbreak of the Second World War. And although there are allusions to the growth of urban life and to the coming of the new road system, of the automobile, of industry, this work is in some ways as archaic a picture as that once popular sentimentalization of the South, Page's *Red Rock*. Although Cash was too good a journalist and too observant a resident of the South to fall for the neo-agrarianism of the Nashville school, he still had nostalgia, not only for the days "Before the War," but for the South that might have come into existence and had a happier history but for the catastrophe of the Civil War; for Cash, despite the rage he caused in many Confederate breasts, was himself a very patriotic Southerner.

Indeed, one of the least satisfactory features of his book is his rather simple Southern patriotism. He is still fighting the battle of the iniquities of the tariff which was, of course, an exploitation of the cotton economy of the South (and was also an exploitation of the cereal economy of the North-West). His allusions to Reconstruction are naïve in their simple allocation of guilt and innocence. That the Southern leadership asked for what it got, that it missed its chance of making a successful adjustment to Northern victory after the murder of Lincoln, was ignored.

It is possible, of course, that today one is unjust to Cash by being ironically sceptical about his account of the horrors of Reconstruction, indeed of the horrors of " the War between the States." We have seen very much greater horrors today. There was a good deal of plundering by Sherman's troops, a good deal of deliberate devastation by Sheridan's troops in the Valley of Virginia. But to anyone who saw Berlin immediately after the end of the Second World War, or, indeed, Rotterdam, the oft repeated story of the horrors of destruction wrought in the South seems highly exaggerated. The American Civil War was, on both sides, by the standards of our terrible century, a very humane performance indeed. After all, the post-Hiroshima world can hardly take too seriously the destruction of some manor houses or even the nearly complete destruction of the new city of Atlanta.

The performance of the North was not edifying; but if you consider the terrible losses the North suffered, if you consider the degree to which, in Europe, such an unsuccessful rebellion would have been punished with savagery, the North seems magnanimous by European standards, not only by comparison with Nazi standards, but even by English standards, for after one of the greatest civil wars in history, which cost the victorious side greater casualties in proportion to the population than either Great Britian or the United States suffered in the two Great Wars, the absence of vindictive punishment was re-markable. There was only one Southern official hanged for the mismanagement, to put it politely, of a great prison camp, and he was a German immigrant. This could be contrasted not only with the horrors of German and, indeed, of Russian perfor-mances in the Second World War or the more diabolical horrors of the atom bomb, but with the savagery of the repression of a very minor revolt in Dublin in Easter week 1916. But Southern tradition, noticing the impoverishment of the South, which was genuine, and unwilling to blame many of its sorrows on its own political follies, not only the follies of starting the war,

but the follies of its reaction to the victors' authority, was itself
and is often today one of the most serious handicaps which the
rapidly evolving South has to suffer. That Cash has such a naïve
and totally black picture of Reconstuction is a significant piece
of evidence of the degree to which the South lived on legend,
and it might be said that Cash himself knew the part, and the
disastrous part, that mere legend played in Southern life without
appreciating the fact that he was himself, in a very serious way,
a victim of it.

One last weakness in *The Mind of the South*, more and more
obvious today, is the almost complete neglect of the Negroes.
" The South " is the white South. Cash considers the rights and
wrongs of the freedmen hardly more than a Spartiate would
have done. He disliked many forms of Southern demagogy.
But this is a white man's picture of a white man's problem. One
of the greatest changes in the South, and a change for the better,
is the reluctant admission (largely, of course, under Northern
pressure) of the Negroes into the American body politic.

But these criticisms do not destroy the great value of Cash's
book. That with so much first-hand knowledge of the South he
made these mistakes is revealing in itself. But he also very often
makes extremely perspicacious criticisms of Southern society.
He was very largely free of some of the most popular and dangerous Southern illusions. He did not believe that there had been
a great aristocratic culture in the South; even in Virginia, the
number of people who were like Jefferson was quite small. He
was comparatively free from what has been called " gone-with-
the-windery." He knew and stressed the very great educational
needs of the South. He did not like most of the manifestations
of popular religion in the South, and I think it may be said that
most of his criticisms are justified and most of them are not
overstated. It is not his positive criticisms, but his omissions
which one can note today, reflecting that the American South,
for all its drawbacks, problems, and illusions, is a far more
civilized, a far more " contemporary " society than it was in

Cash's lifetime — which ended not very long ago. Politicians like Governor Maddox of Georgia' or ex-Governor Wallace of Alabama are superior to former politicians like Bilbo of Mississippi and "Cotton Ed" Smith of South Carolina. Political leadership in the South today, either by genuine conviction or for tactical reasons, is better mannered and formally more humane and enlightened than it was even as late as 1941. Even Senator Eastland is less of an archaic monument like Ozymandias of Egypt than he was twenty years ago. This is not saying much, but it is saying something.

But the great merit of Cash's book, which makes a great deal of academic criticism irrelevant to its purpose, is the degree to which it gives to the outsider a feeling of understanding for what can be called the Southern temperament. It may be a matter of climate, and certainly to be in the Deep South in summer under the high, noble skies of Alabama is to realize that one is not in, for example, Iowa or Massachusetts. But in fact most Southern states — even Alabama, even Mississippi — are more civilized, more humane, and more promising than they were when Cash was writing. It is, indeed, partly because Cash was so much a child of Southern origin, and suffered in many ways from that fact, that his book is so valuable, for here is a highly intelligent and experienced resident and critic of the South who yet cannot shake himself free from some of its most dangerous illusions. But the advantages of Cash's devotion to his Section and his highly critical attitude to many aspects of Southern life (indeed, to most aspects, of Southern life) make his book not merely what the French call a *document pour servir*, but a living document today. Perhaps the main difference between Cash's South and the South of today is that one can say of the modern South with Goethe, "Zwei Seelen wohnen, ach! in meiner Brust." Even as late as 1940, in a great part of the South only one soul, and not a highly edifying one, dwelt in the Southern body politic.

Academics rightly criticize many of the scholarly defects of

Cash's highly impressionistic book. The state of the political economy of the South required a more competent statistical basis than Cash provides for it or, indeed, probably thought was necessary. One can be irritated (as I have been in re-reading this book again for the third or fourth time since it was first published) by pretentious pieces of historical nonsense, like the use of the term " proto-Dorian." There is a great deal too much of historical rhetoric, and there is none of the detailed yet controlled statistical study of Southern society, mainly centred in the University of North Carolina which Cash greatly admired but did not imitate. No one for a moment would think of comparing Cash with, for example, Howard Odum or David Potter. But the merits very much outweigh the defects. That a great deal of the South in 1970 can still be illuminated by Cash's possibly over-rhetorical sermon is important. For it is a sermon. Some of it is, of course, a very unkind sermon. The attempt of Southern states to build up variations of Sinclair Lewis's Zenith City are possibly pathetic. But since Cash wrote, of course, there have grown up great Southern cities that, for good or evil, are quite like Minneapolis–St Paul.

In many other ways, the South has immensely improved. If there is violence in the South, there is also violence in the North: it is an old American habit. The gains of the Negro in the South have been real. The whole region is, in the ordinary sense of the word, far more " advanced " than it was when Cash wrote, and the worst of the economic scars, caused not only by Reconstruction but by a great deal of Southern folly, have healed. To go back, for example, to a city like Columbia, South Carolina, which I first saw over forty years ago, is to go into a new world. Columbia is not Athens, Greece, but it is not Athens, Georgia, either, and one could point out a whole series of Southern towns which are beginning to be real cities, and the growth of a critical, sophisticated (in a good sense of the word) bourgeoisie has given the South, what it never had before (with the exception of New Orleans), real cities, in many ways more attractive and in some ways more promising than a good many Northern cities.

The steady flow of Negroes to the North has at any rate reduced the terror of the Southern whites that they could be overwhelmed by a Negro majority. No state is now in that danger, if it was ever a danger. Southern education still suffers from the comparative poverty of the region, from the great arrears that remain to be made up, and from the survival of attitudes of which the anti-evolution trial in Dayton, Tennessee, in 1925 was the most dramatic example. Of course, there are relapses. After all, the enlightened or, at any rate, immensely wealthy state of California is fighting the battle today for a place for the theory of evolution in the public schools! There are moments when one suspects that Orange County, California, is more backward in most important ways than any county of the Deep South. The much greater spread of literacy and depth of literacy is having very visible and encouraging results. There are, of course, powerful, selfish, and possibly shortsighted leaders of the Southern economy who are perfectly ready to encourage the political ambitions of demagogues whom they despise, just as we have old Etonian leaders of the Orange Order in Ulster. We have wealthy, well educated, and in many ways humane and intelligent magnates who yet find it quite easy to live politically with people like Governor Maddox and ex-Governor Wallace. It is perhaps a pity that Huey Long was assassinated because he was a much more remarkable man than, and a far superior demagogue to, the man of the brief and scarifying picture of him painted by Cash!

And there is one great change in the South which Cash would have ironically appreciated. There are moments in reading this book at which one is inclined to say of the title, *The Mind of the South,* something like the famous description of snakes in Iceland, " there are no snakes in Iceland." At moments, the South of which Cash was writing could be described as mindless. This is no longer true. The South has entered into the modern

world, and if it has a great deal of ground to make up, not all of
the modern world is something to be blindly imitated or admired.
There are aspects of Southern society which are much more
amiable and civilized than those of the North, an amiability and
civilization visible among Blacks and Whites though perhaps
more visible among the Blacks who have been trained to compulsory politeness. The rancour that Cash felt at the manners of
" uppity Niggers " was a natural if rather disagreeable reaction
in him. Today the clashes in the South are more serious than the
right to sit at the counter in ice cream parlours or, indeed, to be
received as guests in the Governor's mansion in South Carolina.
There is much more light visible in the modern South than there
was in Cash's time, although he notes, sometimes unconsciously,
a growing civilization, sophistication and scepticism, all of
which Cash would have welcomed, and to whose growth he
did, in some degree, contribute by his famous tract.

Whatever pedantic or even scholarly criticisms may be made
of Cash as a historian, he was a brilliant observer, and above all
he could convey his own critical love for the South as well as
his horror at some of the manifestations of the less edifying
aspects of Southern civilization. No one who remembers the
South (as I do) as it was well over forty years ago, can doubt
that it is vastly more civilized today than it was in the days of
President Coolidge, and if its growing pains are agonizing, they
are growing pains all the same, and among the people who sowed
the seeds of growth was W. J. Cash. This is a sermon to his
countrymen which, consciously or unconsciously, a great many
people in the South have listened to and absorbed.

Yet it is, of course, painfully true that a great deal of Cash's
epistle to his countrymen has not been absorbed in the more
backward parts of the South, in rural Alabama or even in rural
Texas. It is also true that the ruling class in the South has not
lived up to its responsibilities, and even so powerful and opulent
a corporation as the Coca-Cola Company has only very recently
begun to accept its social obligations. And because the South

has become much more industrialized, the things that Cash does not deal with seem to us overwhelmingly important. Nevertheless, behind the façade of the new cities of the South lies still a great deal of the *damnosa hereditas* of the old slave system and of the long and depressing political history of the South since the Northern victory. So that in 1970 *The Mind of the South* is still highly relevant, and since so much of the old South has survived even the immense revolution experienced during the Second World War and after, it is possible that many of the criticisms of Cash's book which were academically fashionable between 1941 and now, seem exaggerated and, in a sense, too optimistic. The best compliment one can pay to Cash is to read him carefully and sympathetically, and hope that the optimism of his critics will be fully justified. It has not been justified completely yet.

11 *August* 1970   D.W.B.

PREVIEW TO UNDERSTANDING

THERE exists among us by ordinary — both North and South — a profound conviction that the South is another land, sharply differentiated from the rest of the American nation, and exhibiting within itself a remarkable homogeneity.

As to what its singularity may consist in, there is, of course, much conflict of opinion, and especially between Northerner and Southerner. But that it is different and that it is solid.— on these things nearly everybody is agreed. Now and then, to be sure, there have arisen people, usually journalists or professors, to tell us that it is all a figment of the imagination, that the South really exists only as a geographical division of the United States and is distinguishable from New England or the Middle West only by such matters as the greater heat and the presence of a larger body of Negroes. Nobody, however, has ever taken them seriously. And rightly.

For the popular conviction is indubitably accurate: the South is, in Allen Tate's phrase, " Uncle Sam's other province." And when Carl Carmer said of Alabama that " The Congo is not more different from Massachusetts or Kansas or California," he fashioned a hyperbole which is applicable in one measure or another to the entire section.

This is not to suggest that the land does not display an enormous diversity within its borders. Anyone may see that it does simply by riding along any of the great new motor roads which spread across it — through brisk towns with tall white buildings in Nebraska Gothic; through smart suburbs, with their faces newly washed; through industrial and Negro slums, medieval in dirt and squalor and wretchedness, in all but redeeming beauty; past sleepy old hamlets and wide fields and black men singing their sad songs in the cotton, past log cabin and high grave houses, past hill and swamp and plain. . . . The distance from Charleston to Birmingham is in some respects measurable only in sidereal terms, as is the distance from the Great Smokies to Lake Pontchartrain. And Howard Odum has demonstrated that the economic and social difference between the Southeastern and Southwestern states is so great and growing that they have begun to deserve to be treated, for many purposes, as separate regions.

Nevertheless, if it can be said there are many Souths, the fact remains that there is also one South. That is to say, it is easy to trace throughout the region (roughly delimited by the boundaries of the former Confederate States of America, but shading over into some of the border states, notably Kentucky, also) a fairly definite mental pattern, associated with a fairly definite social pattern — a complex of established relationships and habits of thought, sentiments, prejudices, standards and values, and associations of ideas, which, if it is not common strictly to every group of white people in the South, is still common in one appreciable measure or another, and in some part or another, to all but relatively negligible ones.

It is no product of Cloud-Cuckoo-Town, of course, but proceeds from the common American heritage, and many of its elements are readily recognizable as being simply variations on the primary American theme. To imagine it existing outside this continent would be quite impossible. But for all that, the peculiar history of the South has so greatly modified it from the general American norm that, when viewed as a whole, it decisively justifies the notion that the country is — not quite a nation within a nation, but the next thing to it.

To understand it, it is necessary to know the story of its development. And the best way to begin that story, I think, is by disabusing our minds of two correlated legends — those of the Old and the New Souths.

What the Old South of the legend in its classical form was like is more or less familiar to everyone. It was a sort of stage piece out of the eighteenth century, wherein gesturing gentlemen move soft-spokenly against a background of rose gardens and dueling grounds, through always gallant deeds, and lovely ladies, in far-thingales, never for a moment lost that exquisite remoteness which has been the dream of all men and the possession of none. Its social pattern was manorial, its civilization that of the Cavalier, its ruling class an aristocracy coextensive with the planter group — men often entitled to quarter the royal arms of St. George and St. Andrew on their shields, and in every case descended from the old gentlefolk who for many centuries had made up the ruling classes of Europe.

They dwelt in large and stately mansions, preferably white and with columns and Grecian entablature. Their estates were feudal baronies, their slaves quite too numerous ever to be counted, and their social life a thing of Old World splendor and delicacy. What had really happened here, indeed, was that the gentlemanly idea, driven from England by Cromwell, had taken refuge in the South and fashioned for itself a world to its heart's desire: a world singularly polished and mellow and poised, wholly dominated by ideals of honor and chivalry and *noblesse* — all those sentiments and values and habits of action which used to be, especially in Walter Scott, invariably assigned to the gentleman born and the Cavalier.

Beneath these was a vague race lumped together indiscriminately as the poor whites — very often, in fact, as the "white-trash." These people belonged in the main to a physically inferior type, having sprung for the most part from the convict servants, re-demptioners, and debtors of old Virginia and Georgia, with a sprinkling of the most unsuccessful sort of European peasants and farm laborers and the dregs of the European town slums. And so, of course, the gulf between them and the master classes was impassable, and their ideas and feelings did not enter into the make-up of the prevailing Southern civilization.

But in the legend of the New South the Old South is supposed to have been destroyed by the Civil War and the thirty years that followed it, to have been swept both socially and mentally into the limbo of things that were and are not, to give place to a society which has been rapidly and increasingly industrialized and modernized both in body and in mind — which now, indeed, save for a few quaint survivals and gentle sentimentalities and a few shocking and inexplicable brutalities such as lynching, is almost as industrialized and modernized in its outlook as the North. Such an idea is obviously inconsistent with the general assumption of the South's great difference, but paradox is the essence of popular thinking, and millions — even in the South itself — placidly believe in both notions.

These legends, however, bear little relation to reality. There was an Old South, to be sure, but it was another thing than this. And there is a New South. Industrialization and commercialization have greatly modified the land, including its ideology, as we shall see in due course. Nevertheless, the extent of the change and of the break between the Old South that was and the South of our time has been vastly exaggerated. The South, one might say, is a tree with many age rings, with its limbs and trunk bent and twisted by all the winds of the years, but with its tap root in the Old South. Or, better still, it is like one of those churches one sees in England. The façade and towers, the windows and clerestory, all the exterior and superstructure are late Gothic of one sort or another, but look into its nave, its aisles, and its choir and you find the old mighty Norman arches of the twelfth century. And if you look into its crypt, you may even find stones cut by Saxon, brick made by Roman hands.

The mind of the section, that is, is continuous with the past. And its primary form is determined not nearly so much by industry as by the purely agricultural conditions of that past. So far from being modernized, in many ways it has actually always marched away, as to this day it continues to do, from the present toward the past.

It follows, therefore, that to get at its nature we shall have first of all to examine into the question of exactly what the Old South was really like.

BOOK ONE

The Mind of the South

ITS ORIGIN AND DEVELOPMENT IN THE OLD SOUTH

CHAPTER I

OF TIME AND FRONTIERS

Nobody of any considerable information, of course, any longer believes in the legend of the Old South precisely as, for purposes of relief, I have sketched it in my introduction. Nobody can. For during the last twenty-five years the historians, grown more sober since the days when John Fiske could dispense with discretion and import whole fleets packed to the bowsprits with Prince Rupert's men, have been steadily heaping up a mass of evidence that actual Cavaliers or even near-Cavaliers were rare among Southern settlers.

And indeed, even though no such body of evidence existed, the thing would still be obvious. Men of position and power, men who are adjusted to their environment, men who find life bearable in their accustomed place — such men do not embark on frail ships for a dismal frontier where savages prowl and slay, and living is a grim and laborious ordeal. The laborer, faced with starvation; the debtor, anxious to get out of jail; the apprentice, reckless, eager for a fling at adventure, and even more eager to escape his master; the peasant, weary of the exactions of milord; the small landowner and shopkeeper, faced with bankruptcy and hopeful of a fortune in tobacco; the neurotic, haunted by failure and despair; and once in a blue moon some wealthy bourgeois, smarting under the snubs of a haughty aristocracy and fancying himself in the role of a princeling in the wilderness — all these will go. But your fat and moneyed squire, your gentleman of rank and connection, your Cavalier who is welcome in the drawing-rooms of London — almost never. Not even, as a rule, if there is a price on his head, for across the Channel is France, and the odds are that Cromwell can't last.

But though, in view of such considerations, nobody any longer holds to the Cavalier thesis in its overt form, it remains true that the popular mind still clings to it in essence. Explicit or implicit in most considerations of the land, and despite a gathering tendency on the part of the more advanced among the professional historians, and lately even on the part of popular writers, to cast doubt on it, the assumption persists that the great South of the first half of the nineteenth century — the South which fought the Civil War — was the home of a genuine and fully realized aristocracy, coextensive and identical with the ruling class, the planters; and sharply set apart from the common people, still pretty often lumped indiscriminately together as the poor whites, not only by economic condition but also by the far vaster gulf of a different blood and a different (and long and solidly established) heritage.

To suppose this, however, is to ignore the frontier and that *sine qua non* of aristocracy everywhere — the dimension of time. And to ignore the frontier and time in setting up a conception of the social state of the Old South is to abandon reality. For the history of this South throughout a very great part of the period from the opening of the nineteenth century to the Civil War (in the South beyond the Mississippi until long after that war) is mainly the history of the roll of frontier upon frontier — and on to the frontier beyond.

Prior to the close of the Revolutionary period the great South, as such, has little history. Two hundred years had run since John Smith had saved Jamestown, but the land which was to become the cotton kingdom was still more wilderness than not. In Virginia — in the Northern Neck, all along the tidewater, spreading inland along the banks of the James, the York, the Rappahannock, flinging thinly across the redlands to the valley of the Shenandoah, echoing remotely about the dangerous water of Albemarle — in South Carolina and Georgia — along a sliver of swamp country running from Charleston to Georgetown and Savannah — and in and around Hispano-Gallic New Orleans, there was something which could be called effective settlement and societal organization.

Here, indeed, there was a genuine, if small, aristocracy. Here was all that in aftertime was to give color to the legend of the Old South. Here were silver and carriages and courtliness and manner. Here were great houses — not as great as we are sometimes told, but still great houses: the Shirleys, the Westovers, the Stratfords. Here were the names that were some time to flash with swords and grow tall in thunder — the Lees, the Stuarts, and the Beauregards. Charleston, called the most brilliant of American cities by Crèvecœur, played a miniature London, with overtones of La Rochelle, to a small squirarchy of the rice plantations. In Virginia great earls played at Lord Bountiful, dispensing stately hospitality to every passer-by — to the barge captain on his way down the river, to the slaver who had this morning put into the inlet with a cargo of likely Fulah boys, to the wandering Yankee peddling his platitudinous wooden nutmeg, and to other great earls, who came, with their ladies, in canopied boats or in coach and six with liveried outriders. New Orleans was a pageant of dandies and coxcombs, and all the swamplands could show a social life of a considerable pretension.

2

It is well, however, to remember a thing or two about even these Virginians. (For brevity's sake, I shall treat only of the typical case of the Virginians, and shall hereafter generally apply the term as embracing all these little clumps of colonial aristocracy in the lowlands.) It is well to remember not only that they were not generally Cavaliers in their origin but also that they did not spring up to be aristocrats in a day. The two hundred years since Jamestown must not be forgotten. It is necessary to conceive Virginia as beginning very much as New England began — as emerging by slow stages from a primitive backwoods community, made up primarily of farmers and laborers. Undoubtedly there was a sprinkling of gentlemen of a sort — minor squires, younger sons of minor squires, or adventurers who had got themselves a crest, a fine coat, and title to huge slices of the country. And probably some considerable part of the aristocrats at the end of the Revolution are to be explained as stemming from these bright-plumed birds. It is certain that the great body of them cannot be so explained.

The odds were heavy against such gentlemen — against any gentlemen at all, for that matter. The land had to be wrested from the forest and the intractable red man. It was a harsh and bloody task, wholly unsuited to the talents which won applause in the neighborhood of Rotten Row and Covent Garden, or even in Hants or the West Riding. Leadership, for the great part, passed inevitably to rough and ready hands. While milord tarried at dice or languidly directed his even more languid workmen, his horny-palmed neighbors increasingly wrung profits from the earth, got themselves into position to extend their holdings, to send to England for redemptioners and convict servants in order to extend them still further, rose steadily toward equality with him, attained it, passed him, were presently buying up his bankrupt remains.

The very redemptioners and convict servants were apt to fare better than the gentleman. These are the people, of course, who are commonly said to explain the poor whites of the Old South, and so of our own time. It is generally held of them that they were uniformly shiftless or criminal, and that these characters, being inherent in the germ plasm, were handed on to their progeny, with the result that the whole body of them continually sank lower and lower in the social scale. The notion has the support of practically all the standard histories of the United States, as for example those of John Bach McMaster and James Ford Rhodes. But, as Professor G. W. Dyer, of Vanderbilt University, has pointed out in his monograph, *Democracy in the South before the Civil War,* it has little support in the known facts.

In the first place, there is no convincing evidence that, as a body, they came of congenitally inferior stock. If some of the convicts were thieves or cutthroats or prostitutes, then some of them were also mere political prisoners, and so, ironically, may very well have represented as good blood as there was in Virginia. Perhaps the majority were simply debtors. As for the redemptioners, the greater number of them seem to have been mere children or adolescents, lured from home by professional crimps or outright kidnapped. It is likely enough, to be sure, that most of them were still to be classed as laborers or the children of laborers; but it is an open question whether this involves any actual inferiority, and certainly it involved no practical inferiority in this frontier society.

On the contrary. Most of them were freed while still in their twenties. Every freeman was entitled to a headright of fifty acres. Unclaimed lands remained plentiful in even the earliest-settled areas until long after the importation of bound servants had died out before slavery. And to cap it all, tobacco prices rose steadily. Thus, given precisely those qualities of physical energy and dogged application which, in the absence of degeneracy, are pre-eminently the heritage of the laborer, the former redemptioner (or convict, for that matter) was very likely to do what so many other men of his same general stamp were doing all about him: steadily to build up his capital and become a man of substance and respect. There is abundant evidence that the thing did so happen. Adam Thoroughgood, who got to be the greatest planter in Norfolk, entered the colony as an indentured servant. Dozens of others who began in the same status are known to have become justices of the peace, vestrymen, and officers of the militia — positions reserved, of course, for gentlemen. And more than one established instance bears out *Moll Flanders*.

In sum, it is clear that distinctions were immensely supple, and that the test of a gentleman in seventeenth-century Virginia was what the test of a gentleman is likely to be in any rough young society — the possession of a sufficient property.

Aristocracy in any real sense did not develop until after the passage of a hundred years — until after 1700. From the foundations carefully built up by his father and grandfather, a Carter, a Page, a Shirley began to tower decisively above the ruck of farmers, pyramided his holdings in land and slaves, squeezed out his smaller neighbors and relegated them to the remote Shenandoah, abandoned his story-and-a-half house for his new " hall," sent his sons to William and Mary and afterward to the English universities or the law schools in London. These sons brought back the manners of the Georges and more developed and subtle notions of class. And the sons of these in turn began to think of themselves as true aristocrats and to be accepted as such by those about them — to set themselves consciously to the elaboration and propagation of a tradition.

But even here the matter must not be conceived too rigidly, or as having taken place very extensively. The number of those who had moved the whole way into aristocracy even by the time of the Revolution was small. Most of the Virginians who counted themselves gentlemen were still, in reality, hardly more than superior farmers. Many great property-holders were still almost, if not quite, illiterate. Life in the greater part of the country was still more crude than not. The frontier still lent its tang to the manners of even the most advanced, all the young men who were presently to rule the Republic having been more or less shaped by it. And, as the emergence of Jeffersonian democracy from exactly this milieu testifies, rank had not generally hardened into caste.

3

But this Virginia was not the great South. By paradox, it was not even all of Virginia. It was a narrow world, confined to the areas where tobacco, rice, and indigo could profitably be grown on a large scale — to a relatively negligible fraction, that is, of the Southern country. All the rest, at the close of the Revolution, was still in the frontier or semi-frontier stage. Here were no baronies, no plantations, and no manors. And here was no aristocracy nor any fully established distinction save that eternal one between man and man.

In the vast backcountry of the seaboard states, there lived unchanged the pioneer breed — the unsuccessful and the restless from the older regions; the homespun Scotch-Irish, dogged out of Pennsylvania and Maryland by poverty and the love of freedom; pious Moravian brothers, as poor as they were pious; stolid Lutheran peasants from northern Germany; ragged, throat-slitting Highlanders, lusting for elbow-room and still singing hotly of Bonnie Prince Charlie; all that generally unpretentious and often hard-bitten crew which, from about 1740, had been slowly filling up the region. Houses, almost without exception, were cabins of logs. Farms were clearings, on which was grown enough corn to meet the grower's needs, and perhaps a little tobacco which once a year was " rolled " down to a landing on a navigable stream. Roads and trade hardly yet existed. Life had but ceased to be a business of Indian fighting. It was still largely a matter of coon-hunting, of " painter " tales and hard drinking.

Westward, Boone had barely yesterday blazed his trail. Kentucky and Tennessee were just opening up. And southward of the Nashville basin, the great Mississippi Valley, all that country which was to be Alabama, Mississippi, western Georgia, and northern Louisiana, was still mainly a wasteland, given over to the noble savage and peripatetic traders with an itch for adventure and a taste for squaw seraglios.

Then the Yankee, Eli Whitney, interested himself in the problem of extracting the seed from a recalcitrant fiber, and cotton was on its way to be king. The despised backcountry was coming into its own — but slowly at first. Cotton would release the plantation from the narrow confines of the coastlands and the tobacco belt, and stamp it as the reigning pattern on all the country. Cotton would end stagnation, beat back the wilderness, mow the forest, pour black men and plows and mules along the Yazoo and the Arkansas, spin out the railroad, freight the yellow waters of the Mississippi with panting stern-wheelers — in brief, create the great

South. But not in a day. It was necessary to wait until the gin could be proved a success, until experience had shown that the uplands of Carolina and Georgia were pregnant with wealth, until the rumor was abroad in the world that the blacklands of the valley constituted a new El Dorado.

It was 1800 before the advance of the plantation was really under way, and even then the pace was not too swift. The physical difficulties to be overcome were enormous. And beyond the mountains the first American was still a dismaying problem. It was necessary to wait until Andrew Jackson and the men of Tennessee could finally crush him. 1810 came and went, the battle of New Orleans was fought and won, and it was actually 1820 before the plantation was fully on the march, striding over the hills of Carolina to Mississippi — 1820 before the tide of immigration was in full sweep about the base of the Appalachians.

From 1820 to 1860 is but forty years — a little more than the span of a single generation. The whole period from the invention of the cotton gin to the outbreak of the Civil War is less than seventy years — the lifetime of a single man. Yet it was wholly within the longer of these periods, and mainly within the shorter, that the development and growth of the great South took place. Men who, as children, had heard the war-whoop of the Cherokee in the Carolina backwoods lived to hear the guns at Vicksburg. And thousands of other men who had looked upon Alabama when it was still a wilderness and upon Mississippi when it was still a stubborn jungle, lived to fight — and to fight well, too — in the ranks of the Confederate armies.

The inference is plain. It is impossible to conceive the great South as being, on the whole, more than a few steps removed from the frontier stage at the beginning of the Civil War. It is imperative, indeed, to conceive it as having remained more or less fully in the frontier stage for a great part — maybe the greater part — of its antebellum history. However rapidly the plantation might advance, however much the slave might smooth the way, it is obvious that the mere physical process of subduing the vast territory

which was involved, the essential frontier process of wresting a
stable foothold from a hostile environment, must have consumed
most of the years down to 1840.

It is plain, too, in the light of these things, that if one is to maintain that the ruling class of the great South was really an aristocracy, one must suppose either that it somehow rose up from the
frontier and got to be such in forty or fifty years at best, or that
it represented an extension of the Virginia aristocracy — that
these Virginians (using the term for all the old colonial groups,
mind you) migrated in great numbers to the new regions, and are
to be taken as accounting for most of the great estates which presently grew up from cotton.

4

But, concerning this last, what we have seen about the im-
probability of the Cavalier's immigration from England to the
American wilderness is exactly applicable. The Virginia aristocrat
was notoriously a gregarious soul, loving to ride into Richmond
or Norfolk for the day or to have himself rowed over to the house
of a neighbor for an evening at wine and cards, fond of balls, of
races, of whatever brought men and women together under relatively urbane conditions. But the new country was a particularly
unpleasant and lonely one. One's nearest neighbor might be half
a county away. Few towns grew up in the wake of the plantation's
advance, and those which did were generally frowzy clumps of
grocery-shacks and revolting grog-shops.

Moreover, the Virginia gentleman was accustomed to a comparatively aged and mellow world, in which matters were nicely adjusted with a view to his comfort. Like every aristocrat, he required above all things a fixed background, the sense of absolute
security and repose which proceeds from an environment which
moves in well-worn grooves, and in which change occurs rarely
and never abruptly. The new country, however, was full of the

ringing of axes and the acrid smoke of new-grounds. Whirl was its king. From day to day it put on a new face. Landmarks were likely to vanish overnight. Life there simply could not be — not yet — a certain, settled thing, to be taken with easy, insouciant grace.

Add the fact that the gentry of the Old Dominion who survived the wave of bankruptcies which followed the abolition of entail and primogeniture usually found their income sufficient for the almost shabby manner of living which presently succeeded the old magnificence, and that the Charlestonians and the Orleannais, as bodies, prospered with a fair uniformity — add, once more, that these aristocrats were not often distinguished by any more money-lust, and it becomes somewhat difficult to believe that, even when one allows for youth and the adventure-urge, any great number of them ever voluntarily left their native heath and went to live among the woeful pines and the redbugs along the Yazoo.

Yet, first and last, a great many Virginians did go to the cotton country, of course. But most of them went out of necessity and not voluntarily. They were the bankrupts left behind by Mr. Jefferson's reforms, the owners of worn-out lands, or the too numerous sons of fathers with declining estates. Are they to be taken as mainly explaining the ruling class? To suppose it is to fly in the face of the probabilities and the evidence. For two or three generations they had lived at ease, free from the necessity for toil and free from competition. But the essence of the frontier — any frontier — is competition. And on this frontier it was competition of a particularly dismaying order — a tooth-and-claw struggle, complicated by wildcat finance and speculation. How the gentleman fared in it let one tell who was present in Alabama and Mississippi in the 1830's (I quote from the pages of Joseph Glover Baldwin's *The Flush Times,* published at New York in 1853):

"Superior to many of the settlers in elegance of manners and general intelligence, it was the weakness of the Virginian to imagine he was superior too in the essential art of being able to hold his hand and make his way in a new country, and especially such a country, and at such a time. What a mistake that was! The times were out of joint. It was hard to say whether it were more dangerous to stand still or move. . . . All the habits of his life, his taste, his associations, his education — everything, the trustingness of his disposition, his want of business qualifications, his sanguine temperament, all that was Virginian in him, made him the prey, if not of imposture, at least of unfortunate speculations. Where the keenest jockey often was bit, what chance had *he?* . . . But how could he believe it? How could he believe that that stuttering, grammarless Georgian, who had never heard of the Resolutions of '98, could beat him in a land trade? . . .

" If he made a bad bargain, how could he expect to get rid of it? He knew nothing of the elaborate machinery of ingenious chicane, such as feigning bankruptcy, fraudulent conveyances, making over to his wife, running property; and had never heard of such tricks of trade as sending out coffins to the graveyard, with negroes inside, carried off by sudden spells of imaginary disease, to be ' resurrected ' in due time, grinning, on the banks of the Brazos.

". . . He required credit and security, and of course had to stand security in return. When the crash came (the great panic of 1837, that is) . . . he fell an easy victim. They broke by neighborhoods. . . . There was one consolation — if the Virginian involved himself like a fool, he suffered himself to be sold out like a gentleman. . . . Accordingly they kept tavern and made a barter of hospitality, the only disagreeable part of which was receiving the money. . . ."

But perhaps I labor the case of the Virginia aristocrats unduly. In point of fact, they may be disposed of as a possible explanation of the ruling class of the great South on the immediate and obvious ground that there weren't enough of them. It is impossible to say precisely how numerous the South's ruling class was in 1860. Most often it is made to include all the slave-owners. Professor Dodd has argued, however, that it ought actually to include only some four or five thousand of the greater planters. Even at that it is impossible that the Virginians and all their allied aristocracies should account for them. I have no figures, but I confidently hazard the guess that the total number of families in Virginia, South Carolina, Louisiana — in all the regions of the little aristocracies — who were rationally to be reckoned as proper aristocrats came to less than five hundred — and maybe not more than half that figure. As a matter of fact, any bright Southern schoolboy can tell you offhand the names of all the important ones among them.

5

How account for the ruling class, then? Manifestly, for the great part, by the strong, the pushing, the ambitious, among the old coon-hunting population of the backcountry. The frontier was their predestined inheritance. They possessed precisely the qualities necessary to the taming of the land and the building of the cotton kingdom. The process of their rise to power was simplicity itself. Take a concrete case.

A stout young Irishman brought his bride into the Carolina upcountry about 1800. He cleared a bit of land, built a log cabin of two rooms, and sat down to the pioneer life. One winter, with several of his neighbors, he loaded a boat with whisky and the coarse woolen cloth woven by the women, and drifted down to Charleston to trade. There, remembering the fondness of his woman for a bit of beauty, he bought a handful of cotton seed, which she planted about the cabin with the wild rose and the honeysuckle — as a flower. Afterward she learned, under the tutelage of a new neighbor, to pick the seed from the fiber with her fingers and to spin it into yarn. Another winter the man drifted down the river, this time to find the half-way station of Columbia in a strange ferment. There was a new wonder in the world — the cotton gin — and the forest which had lined the banks of the stream for a thousand centuries was beginning to go down. Fires

flared red and portentous in the night — to set off an answering
fire in the breast of the Irishman.

Land in his neighborhood was to be had for fifty cents an acre.
With twenty dollars, the savings of his lifetime, he bought forty
acres and set himself to clear it. Rising long before day, he toiled
deep into the night, with his wife holding a pine torch for him
to see by. Aided by his neighbors, he piled the trunks of the trees
into great heaps and burned them, grubbed up the stumps, hacked
away the tangle of underbrush and vine, stamped out the poison
ivy and the snakes. A wandering trader sold him a horse, bony
and half-starved, for a knife, a dollar, and a gallon of whisky.
Every day now — Sundays not excepted — when the heavens allowed, and every night that the moon came, he drove the plow
into the earth, with uptorn roots bruising his shanks at every
step. Behind him came his wife with a hoe. In a few years the
land was beginning to yield cotton — richly, for the soil was fecund
with the accumulated mold of centuries. Another trip down the
river, and he brought home a mangy black slave — an old and
lazy fellow reckoned of no account in the rice-lands, but with
plenty of life in him still if you knew how to get it out. Next year
the Irishman bought fifty acres more, and the year after another
black. Five years more and he had two hundred acres and ten
Negroes. Cotton prices swung up and down sharply, but always,
whatever the return, it was almost pure velvet. For the fertility of
the soil seemed inexhaustible.

When he was forty-five, he quit work, abandoned the log house,
which had grown to six rooms, and built himself a wide-spreading
frame cottage. When he was fifty, he became a magistrate, acquired
a carriage, and built a cotton gin and a third house — a " big house "
this time. It was not, to be truthful, a very grand house really.
Built of lumber sawn on the place, it was a little crude and had
not cost above a thousand dollars, even when the marble mantel
was counted in. Essentially, it was just a box, with four rooms,
bisected by a hallway, set on four more rooms bisected by another

hallway, and a detached kitchen at the back. Wind-swept in winter, it was difficult to keep clean of vermin in summer. But it was huge, it had great columns in front, and it was eventually painted white, and so, in this land of wide fields and pinewoods it seemed very imposing.

Meantime the country around had been growing up. Other " big houses " had been built. There was a county seat now, a cluster of frame houses, stores, and " doggeries " about a red brick courthouse. A Presbyterian parson had drifted in and started an academy, as Presbyterian parsons had a habit of doing everywhere in the South — and Pompeys and Cæsars and Ciceros and Platos were multiplying both among the pickaninnies in the slave quarters and among the white children of the " big houses." The Irishman had a piano in his house, on which his daughters, taught by a vagabond German, played as well as young ladies could be expected to. One of the Irishman's sons went to the College of South Carolina, came back to grow into the chief lawyer in the county, got to be a judge, and would have been Governor if he had not died at the head of his regiment at Chancellorsville.

As a crown on his career, the old man went to the Legislature, where he was accepted by the Charleston gentlemen tolerantly and with genuine liking. He grew extremely mellow in age and liked to pass his time in company, arguing about predestination and infant damnation, proving conclusively that cotton was king and that the damyankee didn't dare do anything about it, and developing a notable taste in the local liquors. Tall and well-made, he grew whiskers after the Galway fashion — the well-kept whiteness of which contrasted very agreeably with the brick red of his complexion — donned the long-tailed coat, stove-pipe hat, and string tie of the statesmen of his period, waxed innocently pompous, and, in short, became a really striking figure of a man.

Once, going down to Columbia for the inauguration of a new Governor, he took his youngest daughter along. There she met a Charleston gentleman who was pestering her father for a loan. Her manner, formed by the Presbyterian parson, was plain but not bad, and she was very pretty. Moreover, the Charleston gentleman was decidedly in hard lines. So he married her.

When the old man finally died in 1854, he left two thousand acres, a hundred and fourteen slaves, and four cotton gins. The little newspaper which had recently set up in the county seat spoke of him as " a gentleman of the old school " and " a noble specimen of the chivalry at its best "; the Charleston papers each gave him a column; and a lordly Legaré introduced resolutions of respect into the Legislature. His wife outlived him by ten years — by her portrait a beautifully fragile old woman, and, as I have heard it said, with lovely hands, knotted and twisted just enough to give them character, and a finely transparent skin through which the blue veins showed most aristocratically.

6

Such is the epic, in little, of the rise of the ruling class in the great South. And yet — maybe I go too fast. Maybe, in fact, it is only a part of the epic. Certainly it happened like that over and over again. In many parts, as in Mississippi, it even happened, because of the almost unparalleled productivity of the soil, in accelerated tempo, and so went even further. But I suspect that something else happened, too. Behind the figure of my Irishman bulk the outlines of others, all of them fashioned from darker colors — others adumbrated in the passage I have already quoted from the old Alabama observer, Judge Baldwin, concerning the downfall of the Virginians.

Let us consider his testimony a little further. He is describing the conditions the Virginians could not meet:

" The country was just settling up. Marvelous reports had gone forth of the fertility of the virgin lands; and the productions of the soil were commanding a price remunerating to slave labor as it had never been remunerated before. Emigrants came flocking from all quarters of the Union, especially from the slave-holding States. The new country seemed to be a reservoir, and every road leading to it a vagrant stream of enterprise and adventure. Money, or what passed for money, was the only cheap thing to be had. Every cross-road and every avocation presented an opening — through which a fortune was seen by the adventurer in near perspective. Credit was a thing of course. To refuse it — if the thing was ever done — was an insult for which a bowie-knife was not too summary a means of redress. The State banks were issuing their bills by the sheet, like a patent steam printing press its issues; and no other showing was asked of the applicant for the loan than an authentication of his great distress for money. . . .

" Under this stimulating process, prices rose like smoke. Lots in obscure villages were sold at city prices; lands, bought at the minimum cost of government, were sold at from thirty to forty dollars per acre, and considered dirt cheap at that. In short, the country had got to be a full ante-type of California, in all except the gold. . . . Money got without work, by those unaccustomed to it, turned the heads of its possessors, and they spent it with a recklessness with which they had gained it. . . .

" In the fullness of time, the new era had set in — the era of the second great experiment of independence; the era, namely, of credit without capital, and enterprise without honesty. . . . The condition of society may be imagined; — vulgarity — ignorance — fussy and arrogant pretension — unmitigated rowdyism — bullying insolence, if they did not rule the hour, seemed to wield unchecked dominion. . . ."

The dim figures behind my Irishman become plainer. From the frenzied scene described here — a scene strikingly reminiscent of the Florida of a decade ago, and, indeed, of the whole United States throughout the 1920's — there emerge certain very definite personalities: the boomer, the shark, and, in teeming profusion, that typical slicker of the old backwoods, the horse-trader.

Inevitable figures, of course. In theory, the frontier is the land of equal opportunity for all. In theory, its rewards are wholly to industry, to thrift, to luck — to my Irishman. In practice, they are

just as often to cunning, to hoggery and callousness, to brutal un-
scrupulousness and downright scoundrelism. In practice, on any
frontier which holds out large prospects, and where, accordingly,
men congregate in numbers, where events move swiftly and competition is intense, there invariably arises the schemer — the creator
and manipulator of fictitious values, the adept in spurring on the
already overheated imaginations of his fellows — and, in his train,
a whole horde of lesser swindlers and cheats. And when the bankruptcies which they breed are done with, when the frontier is past
and its final rewards totaled up, these, or many of them, anyhow,
are likely to have five thousand acres where my Irishman had two
thousand.

Strictly, of course, what our observer reports here applies only
to the Mississippi Valley, but, in degrees, I think it holds good for
all the cotton country and all the great South. Everywhere, in some
measure, the advance of the plantation was accompanied by a
fevering of imagination and a surge upward in values, and everywhere the knave and the horse-trader turned these things to account. Did they, in fact, come finally to make up the greater part
of the planter class? To say that outright would be to go too far,
no doubt; but if we were to modify it to say men distinguished by
something of the same hard and coarse stamp as the horse-trader
at least, we should not perhaps be greatly wide of the truth. "Vulgarity — ignorance — fussy and arrogant pretension — unmitigated rowdyism — bullying insolence . . .": these are significant
words from one who was himself a Southerner and a patriot.

There is other evidence to the same general effect. On the eve of
the Civil War, Frederick Law Olmsted, first of all that host of
Yankee journalists who were presently to overrun the country below the Potomac, was snarling over the *nouveaux* he found about
Vicksburg, and adding:

"The farce of the vulgar rich has its foundation in Mississippi,
as in New York and Manchester, in the rapidity with which certain
values have advanced, especially that of cotton, and simultaneously,
that of cotton land and Negroes. Of course, there are men of refine-

ment and cultivation among the rich planters of Mississippi, and many highly estimable and intelligent persons outside of the wealthy class, but the number of such is smaller in proportion to that of the immoral, vulgar, and ignorant newly-rich than in any other part of the United States."

A few years earlier he had already set down an opinion but little if at all more favorable to the seaboard states of the South.

Olmsted, however, has been called prejudiced. Maybe he was. But nobody will accuse D. R. Hundley, author of *Social Relations in Our Southern States*, published at Philadelphia in 1860, of being so. A Charleston lawyer of good family, he wrote his book primarily as a defense of " the chivalry " against the attacks of Yankee critics. Yet, in the long run, his conclusions do not differ materially from those of Olmsted. For, though he is full of enthusiasm for the Southern gentlemen, he says flatly that such gentlemen were less numerous among the planters than what he calls Cotton Snobs — as he depicts them, parvenus and unprincipled boors.

In the light of all this, is it possible still to maintain that the ruling class of the great South was, in the full sense and as a whole, an aristocracy? Or that it was anything, for the great part, but the natural flower of the backcountry grown prosperous? To ask it is to answer it. There were many gentlemen in the South, as even Olmsted grants. There remained always, of course, the Virginians; for, though gradually overshadowed and swallowed up into the new master class of cotton, the little aristocracies clung tenaciously to their tradition. Moreover, what I have said about their general failure in the cotton country must not be taken to apply too absolutely. If they nowhere succeeded in large numbers, if they nowhere accounted for the majority of successes in any considerable district, some of them (some of the completely realized aristocrats and a great many more of those gentlemen farmers who had grown up beside them) did nevertheless succeed. There were few parts of the South, indeed, in which it was not possible to find two or three — occasionally a small colony — of them.

And besides these, there were everywhere, and from the beginning, other men, moving along on the level of my Irishman or scaling up to a higher type yet, to individuals and families with a heritage of education and polite breeding — men of a plain tradition, to whom personal decency and upright integrity were a matter of course. But none of these last could properly be reckoned aristocrats. Their birth was comparatively humble, and their breeding middle-class.

The ruling class as a body and in its primary aspect was merely a close clique of property — and one of which the personnel, because of the rapid clip at which estates changed hands during the era of speculation, can hardly have even approximated fixation before 1840. Its emergence to power can be exactly gauged by the emergence of Andrew Jackson — born in a log cabin in the Carolina wilderness — who first achieved political importance as its more or less explicit protagonist. It reached its bloom in Calhoun, the son of a plain and slaveless farmer of the midlands of South Carolina, and in William L. Yancey, a Carolina upcountryman who achieved fame and fortune on the Alabama frontier.

7

There remain the people who, under the classical interpretation, were lumped together as poor whites — the non-slaveholding masses of the South. Who were they? Obviously and simply, in the large and outside the oldest regions, the residue of the generally homogeneous population of the old backwoods of the eighteenth century, from which the main body of the ruling class had been selected out. The relatively and absolutely unsuccessful, the less industrious and thrifty, the less ambitious and pushing, the less cunning and lucky — the majority here as everywhere. The weaker elements which, having failed in the competition of the cotton frontier, or having perhaps never entered it, were driven back inexorably by the plantation's tendency to hog the good cotton lands into a limited number of large units, to the lands that had been adjudged as of little or no value for the growing of the staple.

But driven back in degree, of course. Thousands and ten thousands — possibly the majority — of non-slaveholders were really yeoman farmers. Some of these occupied the poorer cotton lands; but by far the greater number of them were planted on lands which, while they were reckoned as of no account for cotton, were fertile enough for other purposes. Nearly all of them enjoyed some measure of a kind of curious half-thrifty, half-shiftless prosperity — a thing of sagging rail fences, unpainted houses, and crazy barns which yet bulged with corn. And if they are to be called poor whites, then it is not at all in the ordinary connotation of the term, but only in a relative and broad sense — only as their estate is compared with that of the larger planters, and, what is more important, only as they may be thought of as being exploited, in an indirect and limited fashion, by the plantation system.

But I must pause to explain more fully what I mean by this exploitation. It involved the fact, not only that the plantation system had driven these people back to the less desirable lands, but also that it had, to a very great extent, walled them up and locked them in there — had blocked them off from escape or any considerable economic and social advance as a body. (No, not even by flight beyond the Mississippi, since the cotton planters, with their appetite for gain merely whetted by what they had already won, were presently seizing the best lands there, too — were moving out upon Arkansas and Texas armed with plentiful capital and solid battalions of slaves.) For this system, once on its feet, was a static one, the tendency of which was to hold each group rigidly in the established equilibrium.

Moreover, having driven these people back, it thereafter left them virtually out of account. Wholly dominant, possessing, for practical purposes, absolute control of government and every societal engine, it took its measures solely with an eye to its own interests — which were not the interests, clearly, of most of the non-slaveholders. Worse yet, it concerned itself but little if at all about making use of them as economic auxiliaries — as feeders of those things which the plantation had need of but did not produce in sufficient quantities. It would be nonsense, certainly, to suggest that it had no traffic with them, or that it did not, in fact, furnish them a considerable market. Nevertheless, it is true that, in following its own interests alone, it always preferred to buy a great part of its hay and corn and beef and wool from the North or the Middle West rather than go to the trouble and expense of opening up the backcountry adequately. Roads, railroads, transportation facilities generally, were provided mainly with regard to the movement of cotton. And so, though the slaveless yeomen might wax fat in the sort of primitive prosperity which consisted in having an abundance of what they themselves could produce, they could not go much further than that — were left more or less to stagnate at a level but a step or two above the pioneers.

The poor whites in the strict sense were merely the weakest elements of the old backcountry population, in whom these effects of the plantation had worked themselves out to the ultimate term; those who had been driven back farthest — back to the red hills and the sandlands and the pine barrens and the swamps — to all the marginal lands of the South; those who, because of the poorness of the soil on which they dwelt or the great inaccessibility of markets, were, as a group, most completely barred off from escape or economic and social advance. They were the people to whom the term " cracker " properly applied — the " white-trash " and " po' buckra " of the house-niggers, within the narrowest meaning of those epithets, which, however, were very far from being always used with nice discrimination.

They exhibited some diversity of condition, beginning at the bottom with a handful of Jukeses and Kallikaks, with all the classical stigmata of true degeneracy, and scaling up to, and merging at the top with, the lower type of yeoman farmer. Not a few of the more abject among them were addicted to " dirt-eating," but the habit was by no means so universal as has sometimes been claimed. Some of them were masters of hundreds of acres of a kind. Others had no claim to their spot of earth save that of the squatter.

The houses of the better sort were crude shells of frame or logs, with as many as seven or eight rooms at times. Those of the run were mere cabins or hovels, with shutters for windows, with perhaps no other door than a sack, and with chinks wide open to the wind and the rain. Very often an entire family of a dozen, male and female, adult and child, slept, cooked, ate, lived, loved, and died — had its whole indoor being — in a single room.

But whatever their diversity, their practice of agriculture was generally confined to a little lackadaisical digging — largely by the women and children — in forlorn corn-patches. The men might plow a little, hunt a little, fish a little, but mainly passed their time on their backsides in the shade of a tree, communing with their hounds and a jug of what, with a fine feeling for words, had been named " bust-head." And finally, as the very hallmark of the type, the whole pack of them exhibited, in varying measure, a distinctive physical character — a striking lankness of frame and slackness of muscle in association with a shambling gait, a boniness and misshapeliness of head and feature, a peculiar sallow swartness, or alternatively a not less peculiar and a not less sallow faded-out colorlessness of skin and hair.

This is the picture — often drawn more or less as I have drawn it here — which no doubt has given rise to the whole classical notion of the poor whites as belonging to a totally different stock from the run of Southerners and particularly from the ruling class, and which has persuaded so many eminent historians that he must be explained by the convict servants and redemptioners of old Virginia. But, quite apart from the considerations I have already urged against it, that theory can be fully disposed of by a moment's reflection on what it is one is asked to believe in order to swallow it; to wit: that some fifty thousand indentured servants set down in tidewater Virginia in the seventeenth century account in the nineteenth for at least two million crackers, scattered all the way from the Great Dismal Swamp to the Everglades and from the Atlantic to the Mississippi and beyond — that these servants and their progeny were so astoundingly inferior that through two centuries they spread over the land, past a dozen frontiers and through vast up-heavals, without ever in the slightest losing their identity, without ever marrying and intermingling with the generality, and breeding steadily only with their own.

Actually, there is nothing in the description of the cracker to give us pause — nothing which need raise any doubt that he de-rived from like sources with the mass of Southerners of whatever degree — nothing that is not readily to be explained by the life to which the plantation had driven him back and blocked him in. For this life, in its essence, was simply a progressively impoverished version of the life of the old backwoods. The forest, which had been the rock upon which that life had been built, was presently in large part destroyed by the plantation and the prevailing waste-fulness. Hence the hunter who had formerly foraged for the larder while his women hoed the corn found himself with less and less to do. Lacking lands and markets which would repay any extensive effort as a farmer, lacking any incentive which would even serve to make him aid the women at tasks which habit had fixed as ef-feminate, it was the most natural thing in the world for him to sink deeper and deeper into idleness and shiftlessness. More, the passing of the forest increasingly deprived his table of the old abundant variety which the teeming wild life had afforded. In-creasingly his diet became a monotonous and revolting affair of cornpone and the flesh of razorback hogs. And so, increasingly, he was left open to the ravages of nutritional disease (long since proved to be the cause of " dirt-eating ") and of hookworm and malaria.

Take these things, add the poorness of the houses to which his world condemned him, his ignorance of the simplest rules of sanitation, the blistering sun of the country, and apply them to the familiar physical character of that Gaelic (maybe a little Iberian) strain which dominated in so large a part of the original Southern stocks — to this physical character as it had already been modified by the backwoods into the common Southern type — and there is no more mystery about even the peculiar appearance of the cracker.

A little exaggerating here, a little blurring there, a little sagging in one place and a little upthrusting in another — and *voilà!* . . . Catch Calhoun or Jeff Davis or Abe Lincoln (whose blood stemmed from the Carolina foothill country, remember) young enough, nurse him on " bust-head," feed him hog and pone, give him twenty years of lolling — expose him to all the conditions to which the cracker was exposed — and you have it exactly.

8

The matter of the derivation of the poor white, indeed, goes further than I have yet said. Not only is it true that he sprang from the same general sources as the majority of the planters, but even that, in many cases, he sprang from identical sources — that he was related to them by the ties of family. In any given region the great planter who lived on the fertile lands along the river, the farmer on the rolling lands behind him, and the cracker on the barrens back of both were as often as not kindred. And in sections half a thousand miles apart the same connection could be traced between people of the most diverse condition.

The degree of consanguinity among the population of the old Southern backcountry was very great. As I have suggested, economic and (for all the considerable variation in original background) social distinctions hardly existed prior to the invention of the cotton gin; certainly few existed to the point of operating as an effective barrier to intermarriage. And the thin distribution of the people often made it necessary for the youth, come of marrying age, to ride abroad a considerable way for a wife. Hence by 1800 any given individual was likely to be cousin, in one degree or another, to practically everybody within a radius of thirty miles about him. And his circle of kin, of course, overlapped more or less with the next, and that in turn with the next beyond, and so on in an endless web, through the whole South.

What happened when the cotton gin tossed the plantation ferment into this situation is obvious. Given a dozen cousins — brothers, if you wish — one or two would carve out plantations at home (in the Carolinas or Georgia, say); another or two, migrating westward, might be lucky enough to do the same thing there; four or five, perhaps attempting the same goal, would make just enough headway to succeed as yeoman farmers; and the rest would either fail in the competition or, being timid and unambitious, would try the impossible feat of standing still in this world of pushing men — with the result that, by processes I need not describe, they would gradually be edged back to poorer and poorer lands. In the end, they — or the weakest and least competent of their sons — would have drifted back the whole way: would definitely have joined the ranks of the crackers. And once there, they would be more or less promptly and more or less fully forgotten by their more prosperous kinsmen.

That this is really what took place is a proposition which does not depend on mere supposition or dogmatic statement. Whoever will take the trouble to investigate a little in any county in the South — outside the areas occupied by the colonial aristocracies, at any rate — will be immediately struck by the fact that the names of people long prominent locally, people emphatically reckoned as constituting the aristocracy, are shared by all sorts and conditions of men. Stay awhile in any town of the land, and presently some gentleman native to the place will point you out a shuffling, twisted specimen, all compact of tangled hair, warts, tobacco stains, and the odor of the dung-heap, and with a grandiloquent wave of the hand and a mocking voice announce: " My cousin, Wash Venable! " What he means, of course, is what he means when he uses the same gesture and the same tone in telling you that the colored brother who attends to his spittoons is also his cousin — that you will take him seriously at your peril. What he means is that the coincidence of names is merely a little irony of God, and that the thing he says is clearly not so.

But, though he may know it only vaguely if at all, it more often than not is so just the same. It is not necessary to rest on the reflection that, while it is plausible enough that some such coincidences should arise from mere chance, it seems somehow improbable that a hundred such coincidences in the same county, ten thousand such coincidences in the South generally, can be so explained. If one gets out into the countryside where the " cousin " lives, one is pretty sure to come upon definite and concrete evidence. Maybe there will be an old woman — there nearly always is an old woman — with a memory like a Homeric bard's, capable of moving easily through a mass of names and relationships so intricate that the quantum theory is mere child's play in comparison. And scattered here and there all about the South are one-gallus genealogists, somewhat smelly old fellows with baggy pants and a capacity for butchering the king's English, but shrewd withal and, like the old woman, capable of remarkable feats of memory. From such sources one may hear the whole history of the Venables, beginning with Big John, who used to catch squirrels with his hands and whoop with laughter when they bit him, down to seventh cousin Henry's third wife and the names that had been selected for the babies that were born dead. One may discover, indeed, that the actual relationship between the mocking gentleman in the town and " Cousin Wash " is somewhat remote. But — it was not so remote in the Old South.

Perhaps there are limits beyond which this should not be pushed, but they are not narrow. I am advised by those who know Virginia better than I do that even there, if only one goes back far enough, it is often quite possible to establish such connections. And I have myself traced the origin of many of the names ensconced in the beautiful old red brick houses which dot the lovely landscape of bluegrass Kentucky to a group of families in the piedmont country of North Carolina — families which, to my personal knowledge, perfectly illustrate, in their native habitat, the account I have set down here.

CHAPTER II

OF THE MAN AT THE CENTER

I HAVE gone into the social origins of the Old South somewhat at length because they are obviously of immense significance in terms of mind. Strike the average of all that I have said, and you get as the basic Southerner, or, rather more exactly, as the core about which most Southerners of whatever degree were likely to be built, an exceedingly simple fellow — a backcountry pioneer farmer or the immediate descendant of such a farmer. A man, indeed, who, because of one, two, or more generations in the backcountry was an even more uncomplex sort than had been the original immigrants from Europe. In some respects, perhaps as simple a type as Western civilization has produced in modern times.

He had much in common with the half-wild Scotch and Irish clansmen of the seventeenth and eighteenth centuries whose blood he so often shared, and from whom, in so far as he remained the product of European influences, he mainly drew his tradition; but with the English squire to whom the legend has always assimilated him, and to whom the Southern Agrarians have recently sought to reassimilate him, not much.

True, both squire and Southerner may be properly described as agrarians. But this word "agrarian" is an extremely loose one; it may be applied to anything from the first settled life of Neolithic man, and from the culture pattern of a Russian muzhik in the time of Peter the Grand, down to, one might almost say, the rustic play of Marie Antoinette and the Duchesse du Maine. And, as a matter of fact, nothing could be more unlike the life of the English squire in its fundamental aspect than that native to the South, noth‑

ing could have differed more profoundly from the peculiar color-
ing with which the squire's world endowed his subconsciousness
than that with which the Southerner's endowed his. For the
squire's agrarianism was a highly formalized and artificial thing.
If it struck its roots in the soil, it lived and had its being only in
the medium of a consciously realized tradition — a tradition with
a great deal more of the salon than of the earth in it.

The Southerner, however, was primarily a direct product of the
soil, as the peasant of Europe is the direct product of the soil. His
way of life was his, not — John Crowe Ransom to the contrary
notwithstanding — as one " considered and authorized," not because he himself or his ancestors or his class had deliberately
chosen it as against something else, not even because it had been
tested through centuries and found to be good, but because, given
his origins, it was the most natural outcome of the conditions in
which he found himself.

The whole difference can be summed up in this: that, though
he galloped to hounds in pursuit of the fox precisely as the squire
did, it was for quite other reasons. It was not that hoary and sophisticated class tradition dictated it as the proper sport for gentlemen. It was not even, in the first place, that he knew that English
squires so behaved, and hungered to identify himself with them
by imitation, though this of course was to play a great part in con-
firming and fixing the pattern. It was simply and primarily for the
same reason that, in his youth and often into late manhood, he ran
spontaneous and unpremeditated foot-races, wrestled, drank Gargantuan quantities of raw whisky, let off wild yells, and hunted
the possum: — because the thing was already in his mores when
he emerged from the backwoods, because on the frontier it was
the obvious thing to do, because he was a hot, stout fellow, full of
blood and reared to outdoor activity, because of a primitive and
naïve zest for the pursuit in hand.

I do not forget the Virginians and their artificializing influence.
I shall have, indeed, presently to report our Southerner as developing a striking self-consciousness and as growing somewhat more

complex. But this is what he almost invariably was in the begin-. ning, and what he remained at bottom right down to the end. This simple, rustic figure is the true center from which the Old South proceeded — the frame about which the conditions of the plantation threw up the whole structure of the Southern mind.

2

Inevitably, then, the dominant trait of this mind was an intense individualism — in its way, perhaps the most intense individualism the world has seen since the Italian Renaissance and its men of " terrible fury." The simple man in general invariably tends to be an individualist. Everywhere and invariably his fundamental attitude is purely personal — and purely self-asserting. Only in old, complex, aristocratic societies — in most societies — this tendency in him is likely to be sadly cramped and restricted in its possible development. The close-pressing throng of his fellow men, rigid class distinctions, the yoke of law and government, economic imperatives — all these bear upon him with crushing weight and confine his individualistic activities to a very narrow space indeed. Any genuine scope is possible only to those in the topmost levels of such a society — and even in their case it is not too wide. Even they, for all their prerogatives, cannot really escape the shackles; for against their privileges is usually set off a body of unavoidable obligations — nay, obligations often inhere in the privileges themselves.

Our Southerner, however, was remarkably free from such limits. In so far as he was of the blood of the Scotch and the Irish he had perhaps never been so much subject to them as men of other European groups. But in any case, and whatever his original derivations, the frontier had loosened his bonds as completely as it is possible to imagine them being loosed for man in a social state. The thin distribution of the population over vast reaches of country, the virtual absence of distinctions, and of law and government save in their most rudimentary stages, the fact that at every turn a man was thrown back wholly upon his own resources — all these combined to give his native individualism the widest scope and to spur it on to headlong growth.

And what the frontier had begun, the world which succeeded it — that world which was the creation of the plantation — was admirably calculated to preserve and even greatly to extend. For, to begin with, one of the effects of the plantation system was to perpetuate essentially frontier conditions long after their normal period had run — to freeze solid many of the aspects of the old backwoods which had operated for individualism in the first place. Thus, by drawing the best lands into a relatively few large units, it effectually shooed away the ambitious and desirable immigrant — completely blocked off immigration, in fact — and so carried over and fixed as a permanent feature of the Old South that thin distribution of population which had been the matrix of the back-country pattern. Now, as before, and despite the striking gregariousness which had long been growing up in counterbalance, the Southerner, whoever and wherever he was, would be likely to be much alone. Or if not strictly alone, then companied only by his slaves and members of his own family, to all of whom his individual will would stand as imperial law.

Again, the plantation tended to find its center in itself: to be an independent social unit, a self-contained and largely self-sufficient little world of its own. In its beginnings, to be sure, it often required some degree of communal effort, particularly if the would-be planter had few or no slaves. But once the forest was cut and the stumps grubbed up, once the seed were in a few times and the harvest home a few times, once he had a Negro or two actually at work — once the plantation was properly carved out and on its way, then the world might go hang. The great part of everything he needed could be and was grown or manufactured on the place, and the rest could be, and, as I have said, often was, imported from the North. Thus, freed from any particular dependence on his neighbors, the planter, as he got his hand in at mastering the slave, would wax continually in lordly self-certainty. More and more, as time went on, he would come to front the world from his borders like a Gael chieftain from his rock-ringed glen, wholly content with his autonomy and jealously guardful that nothing should encroach upon it.

And what is true of the planter is true also, *mutatis mutandis,* for the poorer whites under this plantation order. The farmers and the crackers were in their own way self-sufficient too — as fiercely careful of their prerogatives of ownership, as jealous of their sway over their puny domains, as the grandest lord. No man felt or acknowledged any primary dependence on his fellows, save perhaps in the matter of human sympathy and entertainment — always a pressing one in a wide and lonely land.

The upshot of this is obvious. It made powerfully against the development of law and government beyond the limits imposed by the tradition of the old backcountry. There was in that tradition, of course, a decided feeling that some measure of law and government was necessary. When the Southern backlandsman moved out into the new cotton country west of the Appalachians, he immediately set up the machinery of the State, just as his fathers before him had done in the regions east of the mountains; everywhere he built his courthouse almost before he built anything else. And here in the South, as in all places in all times, the State, once established, inevitably asserted its inherent tendency to growth, to reach out and engross power.

But against this was the fact that the tradition contained also, and as its ruling element, an intense distrust of, and, indeed, downright aversion to, any actual exercise of authority beyond the barest minimum essential to the existence of the social organism. This feeling, common to the American backcountryman in general, had, in truth, reached its apogee in the Southern coon-hunter. On the eve of the Revolution he was refusing to pay, not only the special taxes levied by the Crown but also — very usually at least — any taxes at all. Hence it fell out in this plantation world that, if the State grew, it grew with remarkable slowness. The South never developed any such compact and effective unit of government as the New England town. Its very counties were merely huge, sprawling hunks of territory, with almost no internal principle of cohesion. And to the last day before the Civil War, the land remained by far the most poorly policed section of the nation.

3

If the yoke of law and government weighed but lightly, so also did that of class. Prior to the last ten or fifteen years before Secession, the Old South may be said, in truth, to have been nearly innocent of the notion of class in any rigid and complete sense. And even when the notion did come into use, it was always something for philosophers bent on rationalizing an economic system to bandy about rather than something which was really an integral part of Southern thinking in general.

Here, manifestly, I do not infer that the Old South was ever egalitarian, as, say, the U.S.S.R. is egalitarian, or that the back-country's lack of distinctions was brought over into the plantation order without modification. From what I have already recorded, from the reports of every contemporary observer, it is clear that, from an early time, there was a great deal of snobbish feeling; that an overweening pride in the possession of rich lands and slaves, and contempt for those who lacked them, quickly got to be commonplaces; and that the *nouveaux,* fired by the example of the Virginians and their high pride of birth and breeding, were eagerly engaged in heaping distinction upon distinction and establishing themselves in the role of proper gentlemen. Nowhere else in America, indeed, not forgetting even Boston, would class awareness in a certain very narrow sense figure so largely in the private thinking of the master group. And not only in the private thinking of the master group, for that matter. Everybody in the South was aware of, and habitually thought and spoke in terms of, a division of society into Big Men and Little Men, with strict reference to property, power, and the claim to gentility.

Nevertheless, the Southerner's primary approach to his world was not through the idea of class. He never really got around in his subconsciousness to thinking of himself as being, before all else, a member of a caste, with interests and purposes in conflict with the interests and purposes of other castes. And certainly he never felt even the premonitory twinges of class awareness in the full sense — of that state in which the concept of society as divided into rigid layers and orders burrows into the very tissues of the brain and becomes the irresistible magnetic pole for one's deepest loyalties and hates, the all-potent determiner of one's whole ideological and emotional pattern. Rather, he saw with essentially naïve, direct, and personal eyes. Rather, his world, as he beheld it, remained always, in its basic aspect, a simple aggregation of human units, of self-contained and self-sufficient entities, whose grouping along class lines, though it might and would count tremendously in many ways, was yet not a first thing.

Perhaps this will seem amazing in view of what I have already said about the effect of the plantation system in driving back and blocking up poor white and farmer. That might have been expected to generate resentment and even hate — to set off class conflict and make class feeling a prevailing emotion. Yet when one carefully examines the whole of the curious situation which existed in the plantation world, there is nothing amazing here.

The groundwork in this case as elsewhere, it must be borne firmly in mind, was the tradition of the backcountry and the more or less fresh — the never entirely obliterated — remembrance of the community of origins: factors operating, of course, for the preservation of the old basic democratic feeling. It is perfectly plain, indeed, that if, being a poor white or a farmer, you knew that your planter neighbor was a kinsman, you were normally going to find it as difficult to hate him as to think of him as being made of fundamentally different stuff from yourself — a " shining one " begotten by God for the express purpose of ruling you. You might defer to him as a rich man, and you might often feel spite and envy; but to get on to genuine class feeling toward him you would have to have an extraordinarily vivid sense of brutal and intolerable wrong, or something equally compulsive.

Similarly, if you were a planter, and recalled that you had played about a cabin as a boy, that as a youth you had hunted the possum with that slouching fellow passing there, or danced the reel with the girl who had grown unbelievably into the poke-bonneted, sun-faded woman yonder (had maybe kissed her on that moon-burning, unutterable, lost night when you rode away to New Orleans with Andy Jackson), why, the chances were that, for all your forgetfulness when your ambition was involved, for all your pride in your Negroes, and your doctrinaire contempt for incompetence, there was still at the bottom of you a considerable community of feeling with these people — that, in truth, it would unconsciously dominate you and keep class awareness from penetrating below your surface and into the marrow of your bones, so long as those below did not rouse to a sense of wrong and begin to strike back.

But now behold with what precision the plantation conspired — and quite without the intervention of feeble human wit — to see that this sense of wrong did not develop.

4

In the first place, if the plantation system had robbed the common Southern white of much, it had not, you will observe, robbed him completely. Since it was based on Negro slavery, and since Negro slavery was a vastly wasteful system and could be made to pay only on rich soils, it had practically everywhere, as I have implied, left him some sort of land and hence some sort of subsistence. And in doing that, it had exempted him from all direct exploitation, specifically waived all claim to his labor (for the excellent reason, of course, that it had no use for it), and left his independence totally unimpaired. So long, indeed, as the "peculiar institution" prevailed, he might rest here forever, secure in the knowledge that his estate in this respect would never grow worse — after his fashion, as completely a free agent as the greatest planter of the country.

In this regard, it seems to me, the Old South was one of the most remarkable societies which ever existed in the world. Was there ever another instance of a country in which the relation of master and man arose, negligible exceptions aside, only with reference to a special alien group — in which virtually the whole body of the natives who had failed economically got off fully from the servitude that, in one form or another, has almost universally been the penalty of such failure — in which they were *parked,* as it were, and left to go to the devil in the absolute enjoyment of their liberty?

Again, if the Southern social order had blocked in the common Southerner, it had yet not sealed up the exit entirely. If he could not escape *en masse,* he could nevertheless escape as an individual. Always it was possible for the strong, craving lads who still thrust up from the old sturdy root-stock to make their way out and on: to compete with the established planters for the lands of the Southwest, or even — so close to the frontier stage did the whole country remain, so little was the static tendency realized, so numerous were the bankruptcies, with such relative frequency did many estates go on changing hands, and above all, perhaps, so open an opportunity did the profession of law afford — to carve out wealth and honor in the very oldest regions. Thus, of the eight governors of Virginia from 1841 to 1861, only one was born a gentleman, two began their careers by hiring out as plow-hands, and another (the son of a village butcher) as a tailor.

But in their going these emergent ones naturally carried away with them practically the whole effective stock of those qualities which might have generated resentment and rebellion. Those who were left behind were the simplest of the simple men of this country — those who were inclined to accept whatever the day brought forth as in the nature of things — those whose vague ambition, though it might surge up in dreams now and then, was too weak ever to rise to a consistent lust for plantations and slaves, or anything else requiring an extended exercise of will — those who, sensing their own inadequacy, expected and were content with little.

Moreover, they were in general those in whom the frontier tradition was likely to run strongest; which is to say that they were often almost indifferent, even in their dreams, to the possession of plantations and slaves and to the distinctions which such possessions set up. For it is characteristic of the frontier tradition everywhere that it places no such value on wealth and rank as they command in an old and stable society. Great personal courage, unusual physical powers, the ability to drink a quart of whisky or to lose the whole of one's capital on the turn of a card without the quiver of a muscle — these are at least as important as possessions, and infinitely more important than heraldic crests. In the South, if your neighbor overshadowed you in the number of his slaves, you could outshoot him or outfiddle him, and in your own eyes, and in those of many of your fellows, remain essentially as good a man as he.

Once more, the escape of the strong served potently to perpetuate in the weak the belief that opportunity was still wholly free and unlimited. Seeing the success of these, and recalling obscurely that somewhere out there beyond the horizon were fertile lands to be had for the taking, it was the easiest thing for men steeped in the tradition of the frontier to harbor the comfortable, the immensely soothing, faith that if only they chose . . . that if only they chose . . .

But all these considerations are in some sense only negative. And there was in fact a very positive factor at work in the situation. If the plantation had introduced distinctions of wealth and rank among the men of the old backcountry, and, in doing so, had perhaps offended against the ego of the common white, it had also, you will remember, introduced that other vastly ego-warming and ego-expanding distinction between the white man and the black.

Robbing him and degrading him in so many ways, it yet, by singular irony, had simultaneously elevated this common white to a position comparable to that of, say, the Doric knight of ancient Sparta. Not only was he not exploited directly, he was himself made by extension a member of the dominant class — was lodged solidly on a tremendous superiority, which, however much the blacks in the " big house " might sneer at him, and however much their masters might privately agree with them, he could never publicly lose. Come what might, he would always be a white man. And before that vast and capacious distinction, all others were foreshortened, dwarfed, and all but obliterated.

The grand outcome was the almost complete disappearance of economic and social focus on the part of the masses. One simply did not have to get on in this world in order to achieve security, independence, or value in one's own estimation and in that of one's fellows.

Hence it happened that pressure never developed within the enclosing walls thrown up by the plantation, that not one in a thousand of the enclosed ever even remotely apprehended the existence of such walls. And so it happened, finally, that the old basic feeling of democracy was preserved practically intact.

5

But I am leaping ahead too rapidly? I am too easily slurring over that narrow class consciousness and that land-and-slave snobbery which I have myself laid down as marked characteristics of the master class? Granted all that I have said, these would still remain — and, remaining, would intolerably wound such men as these common whites — men who, by token of the very things I have predicated of them, by token of their possession of land and independence, by token of their memory of common origin with the planters, would be fiercely self-assertive and sensitive and inordinately resentful of slights and snubs — would be sufficient by themselves to propel such men headlong into class awareness and hate?

So it might seem. But to understand what actually took place here, we must recall again how close the Old South always was to the frontier in time, how late it was before the flux of land-grabbing and fortune-building began to yield place to crystallization, before the planter group or any other acquired even proximate fixity of personnel and character. For this clearly means that distinctions were to the last more in the process of becoming than realized, that such rigidity as they possessed resided more in the concept than in the application.

They might determine, these distinctions, whom one would marry or whom one would have in for dinner, but never with quite the strictness that the legend of the Old South has led us to expect. Behind the normal inclination of property to ally itself only with property, behind the convention that rank must wed only with rank, the backcountry heritage often showed through. Planters very commonly intermarried with yeomen, and alliances between planters and people who were pretty definitely reckoned poor whites were not unheard of. Fully three-quarters of the planters were accustomed to having their farmer neighbors and cousins at their boards now and then; nor was it any rare thing for a great man with political ambitions to seize on a dozen crackers at a camp-meeting or a party rally and bear them off to his home to sleep on his best beds and make merry with his best liquor — or anyhow his second-best liquor. And in all save the oldest districts and the haughtiest of the "big houses," the line at parties and dances was drawn, with discrimination of course, but with scarcely more discrimination than one would normally expect in a farmer community anywhere.

But there was something more important yet, something that I perhaps begin already to suggest. The very marrow of this tradition of the backcountry to which I have referred so often, of the feeling which was basic in the Southern situation, was a sort of immense kindliness and easiness — the kindliness and easiness of men who have long lived together on the same general plane, who have common memories, and who are more or less conscious of the ties of blood. And now, at the exact moment when distinctions were springing up, when land-and-slave pride and the snob spirit were swelling into being, this kindliness and easiness were flowing over to join forces with other factors which I shall discuss presently, to give rise to — to serve as the essential kernel of — the famous Southern manner.

In sober fact, we shall find as we go along that this manner had more than one fault, and was not, as it was practiced by the generality, so altogether lovely as we have been told. But for all that, it served wonderfully for a balance wheel in the Southern social world and so as a barrier against the development of bitterness.

If the common white was scorned, yet that scorn was so attenuated and softened in its passage down through the universal medium of this manner, struck at last so obliquely upon his ego, that it glanced off harmless. When he frequented public gatherings, what he encountered would seldom be naked hauteur. Rather, there would nearly always be a fine gentleman to lay a familiar hand on his shoulder, to inquire by name after the members of his family, maybe to buy him a drink, certainly to rally him on some boasted weakness or treasured misadventure, and to come around eventually to confiding in a hushed voice that that damned nigger-loving scoundrel Garrison, in Boston — in short, to patronize him in such fashion that to his simple eyes he seemed not to be patronized at all but actually deferred to, to send him home, not sullen and vindictive, but glowing with the sense of participation in the common brotherhood of white men.

To sum up, the working code of the Old South, the code which really governed most relations between the classes, was exactly adapted to the exigencies of the Southern order — was adapted above all to the old basic democracy of feeling — was itself, in its peculiar way, simply an embodiment of that feeling. If the common white, with the backcountry hot within him, was likely to carry a haughtiness like that of the Spanish peasant underneath his slouch, very well, so far from challenging and trampling on that, his planter neighbors in effect allowed it, gave it boundless room — nay, even encouraged it and invited it on to growth.

6

In the social situation which I outline here, we have a factor of the first importance for the entire Southern pattern — one which, as we shall see, reached out and wove itself into the Southern mind at many points, and which gave rise, and continues to this day to give rise, to the most striking consequences.

But nowhere was its effect more marked than in the field of that individualism which, as the reader may have forgotten by this time, is the point with which we were immediately engaged. For not only did it do the obvious thing of expanding and extending that individualism in mere quantitative fashion, not only did it provide the perfect ground for the growth of the fundamental Jeffersonian philosophy far beyond anything the rest of the nation was to see — it did even more. In focusing the old backcountry pride upon the ideas of superiority to the Negro and the peerage of white men, and thereby (fully in the masses, and in some basic manner even in the planters) divorcing it from the necessity for achievement, it inevitably shifted emphasis back upon and lent new impulsion to the purely personal and *puerile* attitude which distinguishes the frontier outlook everywhere.

And when to that was added the natural effect on the planters of virtually unlimited sway over their bondsmen, and the natural effect on the common whites of the example of these planters, it eventuated in this: that the individualism of the plantation world would be one which, like that of the backcountry before it, would be far too much concerned with bald, immediate, unsupported assertion of the ego, which placed too great stress on the inviolability of personal whim, and which was full of the chip-on-shoulder swagger and brag of a boy — one, in brief, of which the essence was the boast, voiced or not, on the part of every Southerner, that he would knock hell out of whoever dared to cross him.

This character is of the utmost significance. For its corollary was the perpetuation and acceleration of the tendency to violence which had grown up in the Southern backwoods as it naturally grows up on all frontiers. Other factors, some of which we shall glance at later on, played their part in perpetuating and elaborating this pattern, too. But none was more decisive than this one. However careful they might be to walk softly, such men as these of the South were bound to come often into conflict. And being what they were — simple, direct, and immensely personal — and their world being what it was — conflict with them could only mean immediate physical clashing, could only mean fisticuffs, the gouging ring, and knife and gun play.

Nor was it only private violence that was thus perpetuated. The Southerner's fundamental approach carried over into the realm of public offenses as well. What the direct willfulness of his individualism demanded, when confronted by a crime that aroused his anger, was immediate satisfaction for itself — catharsis for personal passion in the spectacle of a body dancing at the end of a rope or writhing in the fire — now, within the hour — and not some ponderous abstract justice in a problematic tomorrow. And so, in this world of ineffective social control, the tradition of vigilante action, which normally lives and dies with the frontier, not only survived but grew so steadily that already long before the Civil War and long before hatred for the black man had begun to play any direct part in the pattern (of more than three hundred persons said to have been hanged or burned by mobs between 1840 and 1860, less than ten per cent were Negroes) the South had become peculiarly the home of lynching.

But if I show you Southern individualism as eventuating in violence, if I imply that the pride which was its root was in some sense puerile, I am very far from suggesting that it ought to be held in contempt. For it reached its ultimate incarnation in the Confederate soldier.

To the end of his service this soldier could not be disciplined. He slouched. He would never learn to salute in the brisk fashion so dear to the hearts of the professors of mass murder. His " Cap'n " and his " Gin'ral " were likely to pass his lips with a grin — were charged always with easy, unstudied familiarity. He could and did find it in himself to jeer openly and unabashed in the face of Stonewall Jackson when that austere Presbyterian captain rode along his lines. And down to the final day at Appomattox his officers knew that the way to get him to execute an order without malingering was to flatter and to jest, never to command too brusquely and forthrightly. And yet — and yet — and by virtue of precisely these unsoldierly qualities, he was, as no one will care to deny, one of the world's very finest fighting men.

Allow what you will for *esprit de corps,* for this or for that, the thing that sent him swinging up the slope at Gettysburg on that celebrated, gallant afternoon was before all else nothing more or less than the thing which elsewhere accounted for his violence — was nothing more or less than his conviction, the conviction of every farmer among what was essentially only a band of farmers, that nothing living could cross him and get away with it.

7

But already, by implication, I have been taking you deep into the territory of a second great Southern characteristic which deserves to be examined thoroughly in its own right. I mean the tendency toward unreality, toward romanticism, and, in intimate relation with that, toward hedonism. And rightly to understand this tendency, we cannot begin better than by returning upon the simple figure which I have posed as the center about which the Southern pattern would be built.

A common impression to the contrary notwithstanding, the simple man in general rarely has any considerable capacity for the real. What is ordinarily taken for realism in him is in fact only a sort of biological pragmatism — an intuitive faculty of the practical, like that exhibited by those astounding wasps and bees celebrated by Jean-Henri Fabre — born of the circumstance that he has nearly everywhere and always been the driven slave of the belly, and confined to the narrow sphere of interests and activities marked out by the struggle for mere animal existence.

Relax that drive a little, let him escape a little from this struggle, and the true tenor of his nature promptly appears: he stands before us, has always stood before us in such circumstances, as a romantic and a hedonist. And this, indeed, inheres in the very terms of the equation. To say that he is simple is to say in effect that he necessarily lacks the complexity of mind, the knowledge, and, above all, the habit of skepticism essential to any generally realistic attitude. It is to say that he is inevitably driven back upon imagination, that his world-construction is bound to be mainly a product of fantasy, and that his credulity is limited only by his capacity for conjuring up the unbelievable. And it is to say also that he is the child-man, that the primitive stuff of humanity lies very close to the surface in him, that he likes naïvely to play, to expand his ego, his senses, his emotions, that he will accept what pleases him and reject what does not, and that in general he will prefer the extravagant, the flashing, and the brightly colored — in a word, that he displays the whole catalogue of qualities we mean by romanticism and hedonism.

What is thus true of the simple man in general was perhaps even more definitely true of the Southern frontiersman by the time of the coming of the plantation. In the half century and more since he had first begun to enter the backcountry, there had gone on a slow but steady sloughing off of much of even that simple heritage which he had brought from Europe. Ideas that had drifted obscurely within his ken in the old countries faded out here and were lost; his slim stock of knowledge continually dwindled; in time by far the greater number of him were literally in the intellectual status of Lula Vollmer's old mountain woman of our time, who knew of France only that it was " somers yan side of Asheville." And if this plainly does not apply to the better sort, if some of those with the best backgrounds managed heroically to preserve and pass on much, yet they too often lost ground.

It is possible, however, to be more explicit than this. Certain factors which made for a quite positive ripening were in operation here. Thus, there was the unaccustomed freedom of the new country, the glad relief of escape from the European strait-jacket, the vague sense of bright, unlimited vistas opening upon the future. Despite the unquestionable harshness of the life he led, the Southern pioneer (like his congeners elsewhere on the American frontier and in every new country) early began to exhibit a kind of mounting exultancy, which issued in a tendency to frisk and cavort, to posture, to play the slashing hell of a fellow — a notable expansion of the ego testifying at once to his rising individualism and the burgeoning of the romantic and hedonistic spirit.

Moreover, there was the influence of the Southern physical world — itself a sort of cosmic conspiracy against reality in favor of romance. The country is one of extravagant colors, of proliferating foliage and bloom, of flooding yellow sunlight, and, above all perhaps, of haze. Pale blue fogs hang above the valleys in the morning, the atmosphere smokes faintly at midday, and through the long slow afternoon cloud-stacks tower from the horizon and the earth-heat quivers upward through the iridescent air, blurring every outline and rendering every object vague and problematical. I know that winter comes to the land, certainly. I know there are days when the color and the haze are stripped away and the real stands up in drab and depressing harshness. But these things pass and are forgotten.

The dominant mood, the mood that lingers in the memory, is one of well-nigh drunken reverie — of a hush that seems all the deeper for the far-away mourning of the hounds and the far-away crying of the doves — of such sweet and inexorable opiates as the rich odors of hot earth and pinewood and the perfume of the magnolia in bloom — of soft languor creeping through the blood and mounting surely to the brain. . . . It is a mood, in sum, in which directed thinking is all but impossible, a mood in which the mind yields almost perforce to drift and in which the imagination holds unchecked sway, a mood in which nothing any more seems improbable save the puny inadequateness of fact, nothing incredible save the bareness of truth.

But I must tell you also that the sequel to this mood is invariably a thunderstorm. For days — for weeks, it may be — the land lies thus in reverie, and then . . .

The pattern is profoundly significant — was to enter deeply into the blood and bone of the South — had already entered deeply therein, we may believe, by the time of the coming of the plantation.

8

But all this was as nothing compared to the influence which the conditions created by the plantation were to exert. For here, indeed, reality would retreat to the farthest verge; here, as a corollary to things I have already told you, the very drive of the belly would recede and recede until it operated on our Southerner as gently as it has ever operated on mortal man outside some idyllic Pacific island paradise.

In this world he was to have freedom from labor beyond the wildest dream of the European peasant and the New England farmer wrestling with a meager soil in a bitter, unfriendly climate. If he were a planter, then he — whose ancestors, in likelihood, had for many generations won their daily bread under the primitive curse — found himself free from every necessity of toil, free from all but the grateful tasks of supervision and mastery, free to play the lord at dignified ease. If he were a plain farmer, with few slaves or none, then there was the fact that the growing of cotton (or of corn, for that matter) in this country required no more than three or four months of labor in the year. And finally, if he were a poor white strictly, that was to have to work least of all.

As he escaped toil, so also he escaped that other bane of the European peasant and the Yankee farmer: the haunting specter of want. He would never go actually hungry; for the possession of some sort of land and hence some sort of subsistence, you will recall, was almost universal. And even if, through some mischance, his own larder was empty, a kindly neighborhood communism, brought over from the backcountry, saw to it that he was fed, and without harrowing his dignity on the rack of formalized charity. Shelter could be no problem in a land in which pinewoods remained always a nuisance, to be disposed of by wholesale burning. If winter came, it never came so sternly that it could not be banished from the draftiest of huts by a few casual faggots. As for clothing, the little that was wanted need never be ragged, unless, and by exception, his women were lazy; it was too easy for them to grow a bit of cotton for spinning, or even to help themselves to the nearest field of a planter.

In the absolute, certainly, there was much of privation and down-right misery in the lot of the poor white, and often in that of the yeoman farmer as well. But these people did not contemplate absolutes. They continued always to reckon their estate in terms established on the frontier. As they themselves would have phrased it from the depths of a great complacency, they found it " tol'able, thankee, tol'able."

But in this complacency itself, of course, we return directly upon the handiwork of the plantation; the loss of social and economic focus on the part of the masses, the divorce of pride from the idea of effort and achievement — the whole complex of extraordinary results proceeding from the curious combination of forces at play in this world.

And that this complex constituted a tragic descent into unreality on the part of these masses I need hardly tell you. Nothing is plainer than that, out of every sensible consideration of his own interest, the common white of the South ought early to have developed some decided awareness of his true position. For these walls which bound him in were very real: they not only barred him off from any advance *en masse;* they also, slowly, obscurely, but certainly and constantly, involved his degradation.

But if this was so, it is also to be noted that the loss of social and economic focus carried his escape from the drive of the belly forward to its ultimate term. His leisure was, as it were, *reamed out.* If he did not come, as has sometimes been charged against him, actually to hold labor as such in contempt (the heritage of the frontier and his laborious European fathers was too potent in him for that; all he ever really despised was " nigger work " — work that smacked of servility or work in gangs under the orders of a boss), he did nevertheless wax vastly indifferent to it, as something in which there was no point. And his energies were freed almost entirely for other ends.

The plantation, however, involved even more than these things. As we know, it had fetched in the Negro. But the Negro is notoriously one of the world's greatest romantics and one of the world's greatest hedonists. I am well aware that, when it is a question of adapting himself to necessity, he is sometimes capable of a remarkable realism. But in the main he is a creature of grandiloquent imagination, of facile emotion, and, above everything else under heaven, of enjoyment.

And in this society in which the infant son of the planter was commonly suckled by a black mammy, in which gray old black men were his most loved story-tellers, in which black stalwarts were among the chiefest heroes and mentors of his boyhood, and in which his usual, often practically his only, companions until he was past the age of puberty were the black boys (and girls) of the plantation — in this society in which by far the greater number of white boys of whatever degree were more or less shaped by such companionship, and in which nearly the whole body of whites, young and old, had constantly before their eyes the example, had constantly in their ears the accent, of the Negro, the relationship between the two groups was, by the second generation at least, nothing less than organic. Negro entered into white man as profoundly as white man entered into Negro — subtly influencing every gesture, every word, every emotion and idea, every attitude.

9

The outcome had all the inevitability of natural law.

In that void of pointless leisure which was his, the poor white turned his energies almost wholly to elaborating the old backcountry pattern of amusement and distinction — became (though it is shocking to say it) one of the most complete romantics and one of the most complete hedonists ever recorded.

To stand on his head in a bar, to toss down a pint of raw whisky at a gulp, to fiddle and dance all night, to bite off the nose or gouge out the eye of a favorite enemy, to fight harder and love harder than the next man, to be known eventually far and wide as a hell of a fellow — such would be his focus. To lie on his back for days and weeks, storing power as the air he breathed stores power under the sun of August, and then to explode, as that air explodes in a thunderstorm, in a violent outburst of emotion — in such fashion would he make life not only tolerable but infinitely sweet.

And what is true of the poor white was true in a fashion of the planter and yeoman farmer as well. In the planter, certainly, the pattern was profoundly modified and disguised by influences which we shall consider more fully later on. And among the more thrifty sort of farmers it was softened and deprived of much of its crude power, not only because they had never so completely lost social and economic focus as the true poor white, not only because they were naturally eager to follow the example of their richer neighbors, but also because the notions of decorum involved in the lower-middle-class heritage from Europe persisted in them with even greater strength than they persisted in the planter.

But the basic fact remains. In every rank men lolled much on their verandas or under their oaks, sat much on fences, dreaming. In every rank they exhibited a striking tendency to build up legends about themselves and to translate these legends into explosive action — to perform with a high, histrionic flourish, and to strive for celebrity as the dashing blade. In every rank they were much concerned with seeing the ponies run, with hearing the band, with making love, with dancing, with extravagant play. And in every rank the essential element about which this arose was the same simple frontier inheritance which the poor white was elaborating so naïvely.

Such is the primary picture. But I must not leave the theme without calling your attention specifically to the stimulation of the tendency to violence which these things obviously involved. Nor must I leave it without pointing to two significant patterns which grew up in the closest association with this romanticism and hedonism and served it as channels of discharge.

The first of these is the Southern fondness for rhetoric. A gorgeous, primitive art, addressed to the autonomic system and not to the encephalon, rhetoric is of course dear to the heart of the simple man everywhere. In its purest and most natural form, oratory, it flourishes wherever he forgathers — and particularly in every new land where bonds are loosed and imagination is vaulting. It flourished over the whole American country in these days of continental expansion, as it has rarely flourished elsewhere at any time.

But in the South, to recapitulate, there was the rising flood of romanticism and hedonism clamoring for expression, and in the South there was the daily impact upon the white man of the example of the Negro, concerning whom nothing is so certain as his remarkable tendency to seize on lovely words, to roll them in his throat, to heap them in redundant profusion one upon another until meaning vanishes and there is nothing left but the sweet, canorous drunkenness of sound, nothing but the play of primitive rhythm upon the secret springs of emotion. Thus rhetoric flourished here far beyond even its American average; it early became a passion — and not only a passion but a primary standard of judgment, the *sine qua non* of leadership. The greatest man would be the man who could best wield it.

But to speak of the love of rhetoric, of oratory, is at once to suggest the love of politics. The two, in fact, were inseparable. Hand in hand they emerged from the frontier tradition, flourished over the swelling territory of the young Republic of the West, and grew into romantic Southern passions.

Of politics, however, it may be objected that I am assuming too much — that, *per se,* it has nothing to do with romanticism and hedonism, and that a conspicuous concern with it might well be the very hallmark of realism. Let us grant it. Let us say that, in the so-called democracies of our Western world at least, one of the proper functions of politics is the resolution of essential conflict in interest among groups and classes. Then the fact stands fast: from such a realistic content the politics of the South was in a peculiarly thorough fashion barred away.

For the end result of all the blindness and complacency bred in the masses by physical and social conditions was the thing which is commonly and somewhat inaccurately called the paternalism of the Old South. I call the term inaccurate because its almost inevitable connotation is the relationship of Roman *patron* and *client;* it suggests, with a force that has led to much confusion, that there existed on the one hand an essential dependence, and on the other a prescriptive right — that it operated through command and obedience and rested finally on compulsion. But, as what we have already seen adequately indicates, there was, in truth, none of this here. The actual fact was simply that, unaware of any primary conflict in interest, and seeing the planter not as an antagonist but as an old friend or kinsman, the common white naturally fell into the habit of honoring him as *primus inter pares,* of deferring to his knowledge and judgment, of consulting him on every occasion, and of looking to him for leadership and opinion — and, above all, for opinion in politics.

Thus the politics of the Old South was a theater for the play of the purely personal, the purely romantic, and the purely hedonistic. It was an arena wherein one great champion confronted another or a dozen, and sought to outdo them in rhetoric and splendid gesturing. It swept back the loneliness of the land, it brought men together under torches, it filled them with the contagious power of the crowd, it unleashed emotion and set it to leaping and dancing, it caught the very meanest man up out of his own tiny legend into the gorgeous fabric of the legend of this or that great hero.

But the only real interest which was ever involved in it was that of the planter. And even in his case the romantic and hedonistic element would grow so potent, so preponderant, that eventually it would bear him outside the orbit of his true interest, would swing him headlong, perhaps against his own more sober judgment, into the disaster of the Civil War.

10

It is to our simple generic figure that we must look also for primary understanding of the South's religious pattern. The legend, of course, has always had it that the land was Anglican — or at least that the ruling class was predominantly so. But in fact there were less than sixty thousand Episcopalians in the South at the outbreak of the Civil War, and these by no means included the body of the planters. Anglicanism was confined almost entirely to the seaboard districts inhabited by the old aristocracies of colonial days. Here and there it passed over into the cotton country, here and there was to be found a little clump of planters gathered about a St. John's-in-the-Wood or a St. Michael's-in-the-Wilderness. But this was the exception and not the rule.

There was a time, to be sure — the period of the ascendancy of the Virginians — when what may be called the Anglican spirit, meaning a fairly easy tolerance in religious matters, was, in sharp contrast to New England, the prevailing rule in the South. There was even a time when atheism and French deism were pretty common both in the older regions and in the backcountry. In 1819 Mr. Jefferson could set up his university on a foundation that, though it was not " godless," as was charged against it, was still remarkable for religious freedom. And Dr. Thomas Cooper, rejected as too skeptical by even this university, could find refuge in the presidency of the College of South Carolina, and at Columbia, first of all places in America, openly apply the so-called Higher Criticism to the Bible.

But this would not and could not last. If the simple backcountry-man who was to inherit the great South might sometimes, in his early isolation and engrossment with physical problems, lapse into indifference; if, in the first exuberant self-confidence born of the escape from traditional bonds, he might even be tempted into going all the way, into casting off bonds of every description, into throwing down gods as well as kings — yet, in the long run, he would have to retreat.

As I have said, his chief blood-strain was likely to be the Celtic — of all Western strains the most susceptible to suggestions of the supernatural. Even when he was a sort of native pagan, knowing little of the Bible and hooting contemptuously at parsons, he was nevertheless at bottom religious. Ancestral phobias grappled him toward the old center, and immemorial awes, drawn in with his mother's milk, whispered imperative warning in his ears.

And of the intellectual baggage which he had brought from Europe and managed to preserve on the frontier, the core and the bulk consisted of the Protestant theology of the sixteenth century and the Dissenting moral code of the seventeenth. If he was a hedonist, then, and however paradoxical it may sound, he was also likely to be a Puritan. The sense of sin, if obscured, continued to move darkly in him at every time — not so darkly, not so savagely, not so relentlessly as in the New Englander, it may be, but with conviction nevertheless. The world he knew, the hot sting of the sun in his blood, the sidelong glance of the all-complaisant Negro woman — all these impelled him irresistibly to joy. But even as he danced, and even though he had sloughed off all formal religion, his thoughts were with the piper and his fee.

With this heritage, moreover, the physical world sometimes

joined hands. If the dominant mood is one of sultry reverie, the land is capable of other and more somber moods. There are days when the booming of the wind in the pines is like the audible rushing of time — when the sad knowledge of the grave stirs in the subconsciousness and bends the spirit to melancholy; days when the questions that have no answers must insinuate themselves into the minds of the least analytical of men. And there are other days — in July and August — when the nerves wilt under the terrific impact of sun and humidity, and even the soundest grow a bit neurotic; days saturnine and bilious and full of heavy foreboding. And there are those days, too, when the earth whimpers in dread, when the lightning clicks in awful concatenation with continuous thunder, and hurricanes break forth with semi-tropical fury; days when this land which, in its dominant mood, wraps its children in soft illusion, strips them naked before terror.

Nor was it only the physical world. His leisure left the Southerner free to brood as well as to dream — to exaggerate his fears as well as his hopes. And if for practical purposes it is true that he was likely to be complacently content with his lot, and even though it was the lot of white-trash, it is yet not perfectly true. Vaguely, the loneliness of the country, the ennui of long, burning, empty days, a hundred half-perceived miseries, ate into him and filled him with nebulous discontent and obscure longing. Like all men everywhere, he hungered cloudily after a better and a happier world. And if, as was so often the case, this hunger could not move him to toil and battle for the realization of the vision here and now, it could and did impel him to the pursuit of the world beyond the world — could and did combine with everything within and without him to bear him to the sanctuary of religion.

But not to the sanctuary of Anglicanism, surely. An exotic in America which established itself only under royal patronage, it was not simple and vivid enough. Its God " without body, parts, or passions " is an abstraction for intellectuals. It is priestly. It politely ignores hell and talks mellifluously of a God of Love. Its methods, begotten in the relaxing atmosphere of England and refined through centuries, are the methods of understatement. It regards emotion as a kind of moral smallpox.

What our Southerner required, on the other hand, was a faith as simple and emotional as himself. A faith to draw men together in hordes, to terrify them with Apocalyptic rhetoric, to cast them into the pit, rescue them, and at last bring them shouting into the fold of Grace. A faith, not of liturgy and prayer book, but of primitive frenzy and the blood sacrifice — often of fits and jerks and barks. The God demanded was an anthropomorphic God — the Jehovah of the Old Testament: a God who might be seen, a God who *had* been seen. A passionate, whimsical tyrant, to be trembled before, but whose favor was the sweeter for that. A personal God, a God for the individualist, a God whose representatives were not silken priests but preachers risen from the people themselves.

What was demanded here, in other words, was the God and the faith of the Methodists and the Baptists, and the Presbyterians. These personal and often extravagant sects, sweeping the entire American country with their revivals in the first half of the nineteenth century, achieved their greatest success in the personal and extravagant South. And not only among the masses. Fully nine-tenths of the new planters — of the men who were to be masters of the great South — were, and, despite some tendency to fall away to Anglicanism as more high-toned, continued to be, numbered among their adherents.

II

But the spirit of these sects, of course, was essentially Hebraic — their ideal theocratic. And it was characteristic of them all that they asserted, and that their communicants unquestioningly believed, the voice of their ministers to be literally the voice of God.

Thus, as the *nouveaux* came to power, this spirit and this ideal

came to power also, and the evangelical ministers armored all too
often in ignorance and bitter fanaticism, virtually always in a
rigid narrowness of outlook, entered upon that long career of always growing and generally inept sway over public affairs, over the
whole mind of the South, which was one day to flower in Bishop
Cannon. By the time Andrew Jackson had got to be President, the
old easy tolerance was quite dead. Skepticism of any sort in religion was anathema, and lack of frenetic zeal was being set down
for heresy. Before long a Presbyterian minister, named Thornwell, raised a clamor against the " infidelity " of Dr. Cooper, whose
pupil he had sometime been, and got the old man turned out of his
post and himself elected in his place. And by 1850 almost every
non-Anglican seminary of any importance in the South, save only
the University of Virginia, was in the hands of evangelical faculties.

The triumph of the evangelical sects also naturally involved the
establishment of the Puritan ideal. From the first great revivals
onward, the official moral philosophy of the South moved steadily
toward the position of that of the Massachusetts Bay Colony. Adherence was demanded, and, with the exception of a handful of
recalcitrant colonial aristocrats and stubborn sinners, willingly and
even enthusiastically given, to a code that was increasingly Mosaic
in its sternness.

And this, mind, coincidentally with the growth of that curious
Southern hedonism which was its antithesis. The two streams
could and would flow forward side by side, and with a minimum
of conflict. The Southerner's frolic humor, his continual violation
of his strict precepts in action, might serve constantly to exacerbate
the sense of sin in him, to keep his zest for absolution always at
white heat, to make him humbly amenable to the public proposals
of his preachers, acquiescent in their demands for the incessant extension of their rule; his Puritanism might at a pinch move him to
outlaw the beloved fiddle from the church as an instrument of
Satan, would indeed lead him habitually to regard pleasure as in
its very nature *verboten*. Yet, in the long run, he succeeded in unit-
ing the two incompatible tendencies in his single person, without

ever allowing them to come into open and decisive contention.

Hypocrisy? Far from it. There was much of Tartarin in this Southerner, but nothing of Tartufe. His Puritanism was no mere mask put on from cold calculation, but as essential a part of him as his hedonism. And his combination of the two was without conscious imposture. One might say with much truth that it proceeded from a fundamental split in his psyche, from a sort of social schizophrenia. One may say more simply and more safely that it was all part and parcel of that naïve capacity for unreality which was characteristic of him.

CHAPTER III

OF AN IDEAL AND CONFLICT

So far, for purposes of perspective, I have dealt with the mind of the Old South in oversimplified terms, touching but lightly or not at all on two important complicating influences which must be thought of as operating on the Southerner concurrently with the rest. I mean the presence of the Virginians — the colonial gentry — and the conflict with the Yankee.

With the emergence of the new order of planters, as I have before suggested, the old aristocracies largely lost overt political and social power in the South. Here and there they might struggle on as local Whig leaders, might sometimes, in the revolutions of national politics, seem to be almost within grasp of their old sway again. But on the whole, they were gradually reduced to the role of a powerless minority, or, more accurately, became merely a lesser segment of the new ruling class. Nine-tenths of the men who would direct the affairs of the Confederate government, like nine-tenths of the men who would officer its armies, would be, not colonial aristocrats, but new people.

But, by an irony of circumstances, as their power declined, the general influence of these aristocracies was in some fashion increased. In colonial days the backcountry, sharply set apart from the plantation economy and consenting only sullenly to be ruled by them, had been colored by them hardly at all. But now — .

What they had been in their palmiest days, and what they largely remained, represented the achievement on a small scale of the goal to which all the forces of the newer South were slowly converging. If the backcountryman turned planter was plainly no aristocrat, he yet had his feet firmly planted on a road that logically led to aristocracy. And the presence of these old realized clumps of gentry served to bring that fact, which otherwise would scarcely have been perceived, clearly into the foreground of consciousness. Inevitably, therefore, they became the model for social aspiration.

The *nouveaux* would not, in fact, be content merely to imitate, merely to aspire, to struggle toward aristocracy through the long reaches of time, but wherever there was a sufficient property, they would themselves immediately set up for aristocrats on their own account.

Thus baldly put, it seems a feat in unreality impossible to human vanity at its most romantic limit. And so it might have been, indeed, if it had not been for the great whip of the conflict with the Yankee.

That conflict, as has been said before me, was inevitable. And not only for the reasons known to every reader of American history, but finally and fundamentally for the reason that it is not the nature of the human animal in the mass willingly to suffer difference — that he sees in it always a challenge to his universal illusion of being the chosen son of heaven, and so an intolerable affront to his ego, to be put down at any cost in treasure and blood.

But in this inevitable conflict the South was steadily driven back upon the defensive. It had begun with the control of the national government in its hands, but even there it lost ground so surely and so rapidly that it early became plain that it was but a matter of time before the Yankee would win to undisputed sway in the Congress and do his will with the tariff. Worse yet, running counter, as we have seen, to the stream of its time, and, above all, running counter to the moral notions of that time in embracing slavery at the hour when the rest of the West was decisively giving it up, it had to stand against the whole weight of the world's question and even of the world's frown.

And, worst of all, there was the fact that the South itself definitely shared in these moral notions — in its secret heart always carried a powerful and uneasy sense of the essential rightness of the nineteenth century's position on slavery. The evangelical religious sects had all begun by denouncing it, and were still muttering over it as late as the early 1830's. Of the 130 abolition societies established before 1827 by Lundy, the forerunner of Garrison, more than a hundred, with four-fifths of the total membership, were in the South. And in the days of their sway the old colonial gentry had been so disturbed by the institution that numbers of them had followed the lead of Christopher Gadsden of South Carolina and Thomas Jefferson in pronouncing it an insufferable crime. In the State of Virginia itself, as is well known, they had twice come close to abolishing it.

This Old South, in short, was a society beset by the specters of defeat, of shame, of guilt — a society driven by the need to bolster its morale, to nerve its arm against waxing odds, to justify itself in its own eyes and in those of the world. Hence a large part — in a way, the very largest part — of its history from the day that Garrison began to thunder in Boston is the history of its efforts to achieve that end, and characteristically by means of romantic fictions.

2

And of all these fictions, the most inevitable and obviously indicated was just that one which we know today as the legend of the Old South — the legend of which the backbone is, of course, precisely the assumption that every planter was in the most rigid sense of the word a gentleman.

Enabling the South to wrap itself in contemptuous superiority, to sneer down the Yankee as low-bred, crass, and money-grubbing, and even to beget in his bourgeois soul a kind of secret and envious awe, it was a nearly perfect defense-mechanism. And the stage was magnificently set for its acceptance. For the Yankee, accustomed by long habit and the myopia usual in such cases to thinking of the South purely in terms of its nearest and for so many years most important part, Virginia, had the association of plantation and aristocrat fixed in his mind with axiomatic force; he invariably assumed the second term of the equation when he thought of the first. And what was true of the Yankee was equally true of the world in general, which received the body of its impressions of the South directly from him.

Nor was this all. It was for the principal Western nations, as is commonly known, an age of nostalgia. An age in which, underneath all the optimistic trumpeting for the Future, all the solemn self-congratulation on Progress, there was an intense revulsion against the ugliness of the new industrialism and the drab monotony of the new rule of money-bags miscalled democracy, and a yearning back toward the colorfulness and the more or less imaginary glory of the aristocratic and purely agricultural past. An age which, producing such various phenomena of dissatisfaction as the reaction which began with Chateaubriand and flowered in Joseph de Maistre, the romanticism of Byron and the Blue Flower, the bitter tirades of John Ruskin, and the transcendental outpourings of Coleridge, Carlyle, and Emerson, found perhaps the most perfect expression for this part of its spirit in the cardboard medievalism of the Scotch novels. It was an age, in other words, of which it may be truthfully said, I think (and however paradoxical it may seem, I include Yankeedom in the allegation), that it was not only ready but eager to believe in the Southern legend — that it fell with a certain distinct gladness on this last purely agricultural land of the West as a sort of projection ground for its own dreams of a vanished golden time.

Of the many noted foreigners who traveled or sojourned in the land in the years between 1820 and 1860 — men and women often famous among other things for their experience and shrewdness in the analysis of alien peoples — only Fanny Kemble ever seriously doubted the accuracy of the account embodied in the legend. And the North itself always exhibited a curious Janus-faced attitude; at the same time when its newspapers and its orators, led by the *Liberator,* were damning the South with unction and zeal, it was also writing and reading histories which derived every planter from Cavalier noblemen, and novels which not only accepted the legend but embroidered it. Nor was this, as you might suspect, only by way of setting up a better target for democratic hate; for many of the novels showed an odd reluctance to employ dark colors in the rendering of concrete planters. Even Mrs. Stowe, when she created her most notable villain, must make him, not a Southern plantation master at all, but a Yankee come South to be an overseer!

But with the stars in their courses thus conspiring for the legend, with the South's need imperiously calling for it, it followed that simple perception of interest (a perception that lay always outside the field of consciousness, no doubt, but which was none the less real and effective) and common loyalty wholly suppressed the sneers with which the Virginians might otherwise have been expected to overwhelm the aspiration of the *nouveaux* to become aristocrats at a swoop.

3

And so, in the last analysis, it was really not difficult in the least for the *nouveaux* with the compulsion of the South's need operating upon them perhaps even more potently than upon the Virginians, and with the same habitual association between plantation and aristocrat which the Yankee and the world exhibited, fixed solidly in their minds also to achieve their sweep into the unreal. Pretense? The word is almost a misnomer in the premises. In the romantic simplicity of their thought-processes, they seem to have believed for conscious purposes that in acquiring rich lands and Negroes they did somehow automatically become aristocrats.

Did it belong to aristocrats to have splendid ancestors — to come down in old line from the masters of the earth? Genealogy would at once become an obsession, informed with all the old frontier inheritance of brag. If they were of English descent, then their forebears had infallibly ridden, not only with Rupert at Naseby, but also with William at Senlac; if Scotch or Scotch-Irish, they were invariably clansmen of the chieftain's family, and usually connections, often direct descendants, of the royal blood — of the Bruce and Kenneth McAlpin; if plain Irish, they stemmed from Brian Boru. As for the Germans, I quote you, with a change of names, from the actual genealogical record of a family of upcountry Carolina: "Hans Muller, who was a carpenter by trade and the son of Max Muller, who was the son of a Hamburg merchant and the daughter of a German emperor, immigrated in 1742 and settled in . . ."

One thing which must be borne in mind is that very often there existed in fact or tradition some slight basis on which to erect these claims. If the Southern immigrants were drawn almost entirely from the masses and lower to middle class of Europe, it is to be remembered that in old societies like those of Europe such long-lost and shadowy patents of distinction as that one which Parson Tringham dug up for John Durbeyfield and his unhappy daughter Tess are, and were, common enough among the masses. Indeed, in view of Davenport's argument that all men of English blood are at least thirtieth cousins, and the well-known calculations of Henry Adams, Malthus, and Blackstone, it may be that, if the inquiry is carried back far enough, they are practically universal. Certainly, failing even this, the Southerners had always the justification of a coincidence in names. And it is the very measure of their simplicity and their capacity for romance that they could construct the most elaborate and showy pedigrees on no better foundation in the conviction of truth.

So innocent was the thing, in fact, that quite often it was done without putting away the memory of the artisans, the *petit bourgeois,* the coon-hunting pioneers, who were their actual fathers. The genealogical record I have quoted, with its naïve juxtaposition of carpenter and emperor's daughter, is the essential type of hundreds of such genealogies. And more than a few of the lesser planters, in at least the more primitive regions, continued to the end, and at the same time they were elaborating their lineage, to practice, with more or less conscientious thrift, as millers, wheelwrights, harness-makers, or — and here we are no longer necessarily confined to the lesser sort — to trade in horseflesh.

So it went. Was it the part of aristocrats in the nineteenth century also to exhibit a noble culture? Was this an essential part of the legend with which the Yankee was to be put in his place? The *nouveaux,* the Virginians, all the South in fact, would join in asseverating and believing, that Southern culture outran not merely the Yankee's but even that of mankind as a whole, represented perhaps (they did sometimes seem to interpolate a barely perceptible perhaps) the highest level ever attained.

Ultimately, indeed, the powers of candid belief engendered in the South by need and exercise, the will to the expansion of the legend, carried it beyond the measure originally set by the presence of the Virginians — swept these Virginians themselves beyond that measure, too. And even Walter Scott was bodily taken over by the South and incorporated into the Southern people's vision of themselves. If it is not strictly true that, as H. J. Eckenrode has it, his novels (which one Yankee bookseller said he sent below the Potomac by the trainload) " gave the South its social ideal," it is unquestionable that they did become the inspiration for such extravaganzas as the *opéra bouffe* title of " the chivalry," by which the ruling class, including the Virginians, habitually designated itself.

4

But in the course of this account I have occasionally spoken of " the South " or " the whole South," and the reader may be wondering if I mean to imply that the common whites are to be thought of as having had some more than passive relationship to the developments I have been describing. That is what I do mean.

To understand this properly we shall have to begin by noting that it was the conflict with the Yankee which really created the concept of the South as something more than a matter of geography, as an object of patriotism, in the minds of the Southerners. Before that fateful engagement opened, they had been patriots, but only to their local communes and to their various states. So little had they been aware of any common bond of affection and pride, indeed, that often the hallmark of their patriotism had been an implacable antagonism toward the states which immediately adjoined their own, a notable example being the ancient feud of North Carolina with Virginia on the one side, and with South Carolina on the other. Nor was this feeling ever to die out. Merely, it would be rapidly balanced by rising loyalty to the new-conceived and greater entity — a loyalty that obviously had superior sanction in interest, and all the fierce vitality bred by resistance to open attack.

And in this loyalty the common white participated as fully as any other Southerner. If he had no worth-while interest at stake in slavery, if his real interest ran the other way about, he did nevertheless have that, to him, dear treasure of his superiority as a white man, which had been conferred on him by slavery; and so was as determined to keep the black man in chains, saw in the offensive of the Yankee as great a danger to himself, as the angriest planter. Moreover, this struggle against the Yankee and the surging emotion of patriotism it set off provided a perfect focus for his romantic and hedonistic instincts and for his love of self-assertion and battle — a chance to posture and charge and be the dashing fellow.

Add up his blindness to his real interests, his lack of class feeling and of social and economic focus, and you arrive, with the precision of a formula in mathematics, at the solid South. You can understand how farmer and white-trash were welded into an extraordinary and positive unity of passion and purpose with the planter — how it was that, when Hinton Helper (author of *The Impending Crisis of the South,* published at New York in 1857) and others began at last on the eve of the Civil War to point out the wrongs of the common white and to seek to arouse him to recognizing them, they could get no response; how, on the contrary, when the guns spoke at Sumter, the masses sprang to arms, with the famous hunting yell soaring in their throats; how, against ever mounting odds and in the face of terrible privations, the South could hold its ranks firm even in the long gloom of the closing years of the war, fight its magnificent fight, and yield only when its man power was definitely spent.

The implications here are extensive. But what concerns us now is that this solidification of feeling and interest in the South involved the final development of the paternalistic pattern (although the term is more than half wrong, I use it for the sake of convenience). Yeoman and cracker turned to the planter, waited eagerly upon his signal as to what to think and do, not only for the reasons I have already set down but also, and even more cogently, because he was their obviously indicated captain in the great common cause. " The stupid and sequacious masses, the white victims of slavery . . . believe whatever the slaveholders tell them; and thus are cajoled into the notion that they are the freest, happiest, and most intelligent people in the world," wrote the bitter Helper, gazing in baffled anger upon the scene.

There you have it, then. Seeing always from within the frame of Southern unity, the common white, as a matter of course, gave eager credence to and took pride in the legend of aristocracy which was so valuable to the defense of the land. He went farther, in fact, and, by an easy psychological process which is in evidence wherever men group themselves about captains, pretty completely assimilated his own ego to the latter's — felt his planter neighbor's new splendor as being in some fashion his also.

His participation in the legend went even further yet. Though nothing is more certain than their innocence of conscious duplicity, one who did not know them might have said that these planter captains of his were studying with Machiavellian cunning to dazzle and manipulate him. For continually, from every stump, platform, and editorial sanctum, they gave him on the one hand the Yankee — as cowardly, avaricious, boorish, half Pantaloon and half Shylock — and on the other the Southerner — as polished, brave, generous, magnificent, wholly the stately aristocrat, fit to

cow a dozen Yankees with the power of his eye and a cane—
gave him these with the delicate implication that this Southerner
was somehow any Southerner at random.

5

So we come finally to the obvious question: What was the effect
on the Southern pattern of all this, apart from its overt meaning?
In imitating the Virginians and setting up for aristocrats on their
own account, how greatly were the new cotton planters modified?
How far did the tradition of the Virginians, the standards of aristocracy, really enter into them? What was the influence on the
common white of the legend, and his enthusiastic adherence to it?

Let us begin with the matter of manner; for manner, of course,
was the badge and ensign of the aristocratic claim, and it was in
this that, striking on the congenial soil of the old backcountry
kindliness and easiness in personal relations, the model of the
Virginians achieved its happiest effect on the new planters. One
must not suppose, surely, that the manner of these planters ever
became identical with that of the colonial aristocrats. At its best
it was essentially simpler, less formal and highly finished; often
the homespun of the frontier showed through; and yet at its best
it did capture much of the beautiful courtesy and dignity and
gesturing grace of its exemplar — did body forth, in measure, the
same sense of pageantry, and seem to move, as it were, with stately
tread and in the rustling of silken robes, to the sound of far-away
trumpets forever heralding the charge. In its highest and most
favorable aspect, in sum, it was a manner not unworthy of aristoc·
racy — a manner which was perhaps a good deal better than many
genuine aristocracies have been able to show.

But there was a flaw in it. In so far as it was aristocratic, it was
ultimately not an emanation from the proper substance of the men
who wore it, but only a fine garment put on from outside. If they
could wrap themselves in it with seeming ease and assurance, if

they could convince themselves for conscious purposes that they were in sober fact aristocrats and wore it by right, they nevertheless could not endow their subconsciousness with the aristocrat's experience — with the calm certainty, bred of that experience, which is the aristocratic manner's essential warrant. In their inmost being they carried nearly always, I think, an uneasy sensation of inadequacy for their role. And so often the loveliness of their manner was marred by a certain more or less heavy condescension — a too obvious desire (reported directly or by implication by Olmsted, Fanny Kemble, the patriotic Hundley, and the wholly friendly J. H. Ingraham) to drive home the perception of their rank and value. And if this condescension was relatively inoffensive at home and among their familiars and loyal admirers, it could be, and often was, overbearing and brutal when confronted by the unknown quantity of a stranger, or by any person who might be suspected of challenging or doubting or even of failing to be sufficiently impressed by their claims.

Moreover, it must be borne in mind that the general assertion of aristocracy had naturally played a great part in reinforcing the land-and-slave pride, in heightening the concern with the class idea in the narrow sense, which produced, at its worst, the Cotton Snobs who aroused the anger and contempt of Olmsted and Hundley. And in the hands of these — at one and the same time the least adequate to aristocracy and the most determined to have its glory for their own — the planter manner was frequently torn from the simplicity which was its only true sanction, and subjected to grotesque exaggeration. Its beauty vanished under such pomposity, such insistent and extravagant lady-and-gentleman grandness as one expects to find only in the pages of some servant-girl romance; or, lacking this, in a preciousness so simpering and so nice or, again, so loftily supercilious that one might decline to believe in it if it had not been set down by the soberest observers.

Turning from the planters to the common whites, we find manner still definitely affected by the Virginia model and the aristocratic ideal. Indeed, I am not sure that the most fortunate result of all in this field is not to be found in the case of the better sort of those yeoman farmers who stood between the planters and the true poor whites. It did not go so far; there was no magnificence of sword and plume here, as there was no claim to personal aristocracy. But therein lay its strength. These men took from aristocracy as much as, and no more than, could be made to fit with their own homespun qualities; and so what they took they made solidly their own, without any sense of inadequacy to haunt them into gaucherie. The result was a kindly courtesy, a level-eyed pride, an easy quietness, a barely perceptible flourish, of bearing, which, for all its obvious angularity and fundamental plainness, was one of the finest things the Old South produced.

And something of the same kind can be said of the poor white himself. All the way down the line there was a softening and gentling of the heritage of the backwoods. In every degree the masses took on, under their slouch, a sort of unkempt politeness and ease of port, which rendered them definitely superior, in respect of manner, to their peers in the rest of the country.

6

From manner we pass naturally to the notions of honor and decorum, of what is proper and becoming to the gentleman, which constitute the deeper essence of aristocracy. Indeed, the most obvious result here passes over eventually into the realm of manner — or, at any rate, *manners* — in the broadest sense.

Encountering in the new planters the pride of the backcountry and the romanticism and hedonism which we have seen, these gentlemanly concepts — themselves a distillation from the age-long pride and romance of Western man, of course — fused with and intensified them, contributed very greatly to rounding out and fixing the pattern of the personal and the extravagant. And at the same time they served to bring into that pattern a certain discipline, to bend its native uncouthness, its frontier swagger, to seemliness and investment in established forms. Thus, for example, among these planters the tradition of fisticuffs, the gouging ring, and unregulated knife and gun play tended rapidly, from the hour of their emergence, to reincarnate itself in the starched and elaborate etiquette of the code duello, though the latter commonly underwent a considerable simplification in the process and never became universally and fully established.

There is a passage in Judge Baldwin's account of Sargeant Prentiss of Mississippi which is illuminating in this general connection:

"Instant in resentment, and bitter in his animosities, yet magnanimous to forgive when reparation had been made. . . . There was no littleness about him. Even toward an avowed enemy he was open and manly, and bore himself with a sort of antique courtesy and knightly hostility, in which self-respect mingled with respect for his foe, except when contempt was mixed with hatred, and then no words can convey any sense of the intensity of his scorn. . . .

"Even in the vices of Prentiss, there was magnificence and brilliance imposing in a high degree. When he treated, it was a mass entertainment. On one occasion he chartered the theatre for the special gratification of his friends — the public generally. He bet thousands on the turn of a card and witnessed the success or failure of the wager with the nonchalance of a Mexican monte-player, or, as was most usual, with the light humor of a Spanish muleteer. He broke a faro-bank by the nerve with which he laid his large bets, and by exciting the passions of the veteran dealer, or awed him into honesty by the flame of his strong and steady eye.

"Attachment to his friends was a passion. It was a part of the loyalty to the honorable and chivalric. . . . He never deserted a friend. His confidence knew no bounds . . . scorned all considerations of prudence and policy. He made his friends' quarrels his own . . . would put his name on the back of their paper, without looking at the face of it, and gave his *carte blanche,* if needed, by the quire. . . .

"Sent to jail for fighting in the courthouse, he made the walls of the prison resound with unaccustomed shouts of merriment and revelry. Starting to fight a duel, he laid down his hand at poker, to resume it with a smile when he returned, and went on the field laughing with his friends, as to a picnic. Yet no one knew better the proprieties of life than himself — when to put off levity and treat grave subjects and persons with proper respect. . . ."

That, if I mistake not, is the nearly perfect measure of what happened when the tradition of aristocracy met and married with the tradition of the backwoods. It contains at once the iron man of the frontier, the wild boisterousness of the backlandsman at play, and something, a great deal in fact, of such sweepingly splendid fellows as Mr. Richard Steele and Mr. Richard Brinsley Sheridan and Mr. Charles James Fox — contains them so integrally and inseparably that it is impossible to say where the one ends and the other begins.

It is an overdrawn and idealized measure, yes. But that in itself is significant. Prentiss was a native Yankee, studying to get on as a politician in the deep South, and making such a success of it that it was said of him he might have any office in the gift of his constituents for the nod of his head. And his portrait-maker, Baldwin, a Southerner of the best type, was scarcely less successful at the same trade. Do I need to add that the politician universally succeeds in the measure in which he is able to embody, in deeds or in words, the essence, not of what his clients are strictly, but of their dream of themselves?

Here, in brief, was the thing that most planters, in the unpuritanical half of their characters at least, liked to fancy themselves to be, and that they more or less seriously saw themselves as being. And so here was the thing that, after an imperfect human fashion but in a really striking degree, a handful of the best endowed, the least trammeled by Puritanism, the most generous and bold and romantic by nature, actually came to be. Here was the thing that, if, in the long run, it had to reckon with the tough fibre, the horse-trading instincts, and the coarseness of grain native to self-made men in general, yet did enter into and become the stamp, to an appreciable extent, of the body of these masters of the South.

But I must not seem to confine its influence to the planters alone. Farmer and cracker admired and shared more than vicariously in this ideal — shall we call it? — created by the impact of the aristocratic idea on the romantic pattern. It determined the shape of those long, lazy, wishful day-dreams, those mirages from an unwilled and non-existent future, in which they saw themselves performing in splendor and moving in grandeur. And its concept of honor, of something inviolable and precious in the ego, to be protected against stain at every cost, and imposing definite standards of conduct, drifted down to them — to the best of the yeomen in a form simpler but not less good, perhaps sometimes even better, than that in which it was held by the generality of planters; to the poor white in the most indistinct and primitive shape — to draw their pride to a finer point yet, to reinforce and complicate such notions of " the thing to do " as they already possessed, and to propel them along their way of posturing and violence.

I speak of violence. One of the notable results of the spread of the idea of honor, indeed, was an increase in the tendency to violence throughout the social scale. Everybody, high and low, was rendered more techy. And with the duel almost rigidly bound to that techiness at the top, everybody's course was fatally mapped out. These men of the South would go on growing in their practice of violence in one form or another, not only because of the reasons at which we have already looked but also because of the feeling, fixed by social example, that it was the only quite correct, the only really decent, relief for wounded honor — the only one which did not imply some subtle derogation, some dulling and retracting of the fine edge of pride, some indefinable but intolerable loss of caste and manly face.

Moreover, this honor complex and the rising popularity of the duel reacted on law and government — was a strong factor in blocking the normal growth of the police power. As is well known, the laws of most of the states either openly or tacitly countenanced the formal *affaire,* and in none of them was a killing in such a brush likely to bring forth more than perfunctory indictment. And the common murderer who had slain his man in a personal quarrel and with some appearance of a fair fight, some regard for a few amenities, need not fear the indignity of hanging. If the jury was not certain to call it self-defense, the worst verdict he had to expect was manslaughter.

7

But the conception of honor and decorum we have seen at work here is a fundamentally narrow and incomplete one. The ideas of rigid personal integrity in one's dealings with one's fellows and of *noblesse oblige* and chivalry in the widest sense — of the obligation to be not only just but more than just, of the obligation, above all, to the most tender concern for the welfare and happiness of the weak and powerless — these ideas, representing the highest product of aristocracy, and constituting perhaps its only real justification in the modern world, are only imperfectly adumbrated or are missing altogether. Is that to say that they are to be dismissed as having had no ponderable influence on the mind of the great South? Far from it. I have merely wished to emphasize the fact that it was the narrow and egotistic conception of honor which fitted most easily into the Southern pattern and which therefore went furthest toward establishing itself fully.

In truth, the new cotton planters seized upon the ideas of aristocratic probity and *noblesse* with zeal, and professed them with heartiness. And believed in their own professions. No group of people anywhere, indeed, ever more constantly represented to themselves and to the world that they were absolutely under the domination of these ideas and the Christian virtues, to which they wedded them; no group ever more completely contracted the habit of referring every act to these motives, of performing even the most commonplace of deeds only to the accompaniment of solemn protestations of selfless devotion; and no group was ever more convinced that it was all so.

What is more, the masses about them were convinced that it was true also — accepted these planters as being the soul of honor and social responsibility. (We look once more into the machinery of the pattern of paternalism.) More yet, the masses were themselves impregnated with something of the same thing. The habit of noble profession, of accounting for every move in terms of fealty to the social good, to standards that were essentially both aristocratic and Christian in the best sense, and of the most impenetrable conviction that it was strictly so, passed down through the whole of Southern society and became a characteristic Southern trait.

But the measure of reality underneath is not hard to come at. Wherever these notions of integrity and *noblesse* encountered the simple tradition of uprightness which I have mentioned as belonging inherently to such men as the old Irishman whose story I have recited — and such men were to be found not only among the planters but in the yeoman-farmer class too — the result was extremely impressive. This primitive uprightness was ripened, expanded, brought to issue in a great cleanness and decency, a wholly admirable rectitude, which is one of the most pleasant things that ever grew up on American soil.

In the hands of men of this stamp the convention, thrown up on the wave of high profession, that no one but a cur beat, starved, or overdrove his slaves became a living rule of daily conduct; a standard so binding as to generate contempt for whoever violated it. Occasionally, indeed, these notions of aristocratic honor acted with a particularly strong sense of the moral indefensibility of slavery and an uncommon honesty in Christianity to propel such a man to the great gesture of renunciation — forthright manumission. And others were prompted to the lesser gesture of liberation after a given term of years.

Just as striking was the attitude generated in this sort of man toward trade — the repugnance to anything which smacked of deception and chicane. Sometimes it even combined with a kind of snobbishness to set up a scorn for trade of any kind, as being in its very nature incurably mean. More usually, and more rationally, it brought forth such finely scrupulous actions as that of my old Irishman, who used to sell his corn at a certain fixed (and low) figure regardless of the market, scorning to take advantage of scarcity and the need of his neighbors, waiting peacefully through years for his pay, and, failing of it altogether, finding an excuse for the culprit in the saying: " Poor fellow, he never had any luck. He would have paid me if he could have." Or, again, such a splendid if not uncanny attitude as that of an old Scot, the Irishman's neighbor, who, having money to lend, lent it always on the borrower's bare oral promise to repay, despising mortgages and notes as inventions of the devil to betray the feet and weigh down the wings of the naturally candid spirit of man.

And so I might go on indefinitely listing the effects of the notion of honor on these men. But I really need to mention only one more: As part and parcel of their spirit, they developed a real and often tremendous sense of obligation (I speak mainly of the planters among them now, of course) to the common whites about them — a feeling that they were bound to go beyond the kindness of the old backcountry, to set them an impeccable example of conduct and sentiment, to advise them correctly, to get them out of trouble when they got in, to hold them up to the highest possible moral and intellectual level in this world, and somehow to get them through the gates of jasper at last. Thus that old Irishman, in addition to making impossible trades in which various shiftless souls acquired hams, flour, and other concrete goods in return for certain vague promises concerning the delivery of a fish or a deer or sassafras roots for tea in the spring, in addition to scandalously abusing his powers as a magistrate on the side of mercy, and in addition to financing the activities of three or four parsons, used also, in his latest days, to keep a free school on his place, manned by an ex-blacksmith with a great authority in his fist and a bowing acquaintance with the three R's, to which the boys and girls of the neighborhood who were too poor to attend the Presbyterian academy were all but literally compelled to come.

But when all this is said, we come back to the fact that the men to whom it applies, those to whom it can be made to apply in degree, were the best. In the majority of the planters the notions of integrity and *noblesse oblige* did not make any great progress toward dissolving out the hard core native to the commoner sort of fellow who has shouldered his way up in the world. The most that would be achieved here (and, with the necessary changes, this applies to the masses also) would be some softening of the surface, a slight expansion of the frontier tendency to kindness, perhaps, and a disposition to embrace whatever, without interfering with interest, gave opportunity to the love of high profession, whatever was presented in the name of the common welfare.

To be noticed, too, is that, even at the best and fullest, the idea of social responsibility which grew up in the South remained always a narrow and purely personal one. The defect here was fundamental in the primary model. The Virginians themselves, if they had long since become truly aristocratic, had nevertheless never got beyond that brutal individualism — and for all the Jeffersonian glorification of the idea, it *was* brutal as it worked out in the plantation world — which was the heritage of the frontier: that individualism which, while willing enough to ameliorate the specific instance, relentlessly laid down as its basic social postulate the doctrine that every man was completely and wholly responsible for himself.

I have before painted the common white as being immensely complacent. But the planters — both *nouveaux* and Virginian — if anything, outdid him. The individualistic outlook, the lack of class pressure from below, their position as captains against the Yankee, the whole paternalistic pattern in fact, the complete otherworldliness of the prevailing religious feeling, and, in the *nouveaux*, the very conviction that they were already fully developed aristocrats — all this, combining with their natural unrealism of temperament, bred in them a thoroughgoing self-satisfaction, the most complete blindness to the true facts of their world.

And so, even when they were most sincere in their sense of responsibility to the masses, they began, with an ingenuousness that might have been incredible elsewhere, by assuming their own interest as the true interest of the common white also — gave him advice, told him what to think, from that standpoint. Outside of two or three exceptions, such as William Gregg of South Carolina, hardly any Southerner of the master class ever even slightly apprehended that the general shiftlessness and degradation of the masses was a social product. Hardly one, in truth, ever concerned himself about the systematic raising of the economic and social level of these masses. And if occasional men like my Irishman kept free schools for their neighborhoods, these same men would take the lead in indignantly rejecting the Yankee idea of universal free schools maintained at the public charge — would condemn the run of Southern whites to grow up in illiteracy and animal ignorance in the calm conviction of acting entirely for the public good.

8

Let us go back now to the conflict with the Yankee, for we have by no means seen all its results yet. There are those extensive implications I have referred to as being involved in its solidification of the South. If this solidification was in some sense an effect of the prevailing absence of class antagonism, if it could have arisen only from that ground, it was also an integrally determining factor for that absence, struck down and eliminated whatever beginnings of such feeling may have been spawning in Southern breasts, and finally and decisively confirmed the pattern. And in doing this it of course played a great part in fixing and expanding the intensely individualistic outlook.

Moreover, it was this solidification before the Yankee, the universal concentration of Southerners on the will to victory in the struggle for mastery, that brought to full development the Southern passion for politics and rhetoric. Politics, it goes without saying, was the battlefield on which the contest would be waged for the thirty years before the ultimate resort to arms. And politics was also, so to speak, the temple wherein men entered to participate in the mysteries of the common brotherhood of white men, to partake of the holy sacrament of Southern loyalty and hate. And the shining sword of battle, the bread and wine — if I may be permitted to carry out the theological figure — through which men became one flesh with the Logos, was, of course, rhetoric, a rhetoric that every day became less and less a form of speech strictly and more and more a direct instrument of emotioń, like music.

Within this frame of politics and rhetoric the hammer and thrust of the Yankee inevitably did something else, too: It called forth that final term of Southern extravagance, that significant type of people's captain, the fire-eating orator and mob-master. Let us take good care to understand him. It is easy to think of him, to think of a William Yancey or a Barnwell Rhett, as having been a mere poseur and a conscious demagogue. But it is no more true of him than of his congeners on the military side, the dramatic cavalry captains of the Civil War. As surely as these, he was a normal and ingenuous evocation from the character of a whole people — under fire. And if he gave the masses gasconade and bluster, if he had them to understand that any Southerner at random was equal to whipping a whole squad of Yankees, he did it not out of mere calculation or irresponsibility, but because the solidity of the South operated upon him to fill him with a wonderful sense of vicarious power, because it seemed to him, as it seemed to every one of his roaring hearers, to be a mere statement of fact.

More notable yet was the influence of conflict and solidification upon the religious pattern. Under its influence, God began rapidly to be distinctly a tribal God. He remained Jehovah, certainly. As time went on, indeed, He became more purely Jehovah — the stern, simple, direct, God of the Old Testament, with elements of the Apocalypse added, the God of battles and the flaming sword, and of the pale horsemen and the winepress of blood. A severe, almost primitive, naïveté of belief and feeling got to be the fashion, sweeping back even such sophistication of religion as was already growing up, and penetrating gradually almost into the very strongholds of the Virginians themselves. If the falling of the stars in 1833 could still be interpreted rationally by the more enlightened sort of evangelical ministers, there were not many non-Anglican pulpits left in the South in 1857 which did not see the passage of Donati's great comet as a herald of the imminent outpouring of divine wrath. And not every Anglican church was immune to intimations of the kind.

But nobody intimated or suspected that this wrath might possibly pour upon the South itself. The South, men said and did not doubt, was peculiarly Christian; probably, indeed, it was the last great bulwark of Christianity. From the pulpit the word went forth that infidelity and a new paganism masking under the name of Science were sweeping the world. From pulpit and hustings ran the dark suggestion that the God of the Yankee was not God at all but Antichrist loosed at last from the pit. The coming war would be no mere secular contest but Armageddon, with the South standing in the role of the defender of the ark, its people as the Chosen People.

You suspect me of picturesque extravagance? Then hear the Presbyterian Dr. J. H. Thornwell declaiming in 1850, the year before his countrymen were to call him to the presidency of the College of South Carolina, from which he had some time ejected Dr. Cooper for his " infidel " views: " The parties in this conflict are not merely abolitionists and slaveholders — they are atheists, socialists, communists, red republicans, jacobins on the one side, and the friends of order and regulated freedom on the other. In one word, the world is the battleground — Christianity and atheism the combatants; and the progress of humanity the stake."

But this was not all. There was that eternal uneasiness of the South's conscience over slavery — the need to appease its own doubts before the onset of the Garrisonian attack. Well, but what if it was not really wrong, after all? Suppose, as one of the first churchmen of the South, Dr. Benjamin Palmer of New Orleans, put it, it was a " providential trust "? Really God's plan for instructing the black man in the Gospel and securing him entry into eternal bliss? Suppose the South was only the favored vessel of His will to that end? The Baptist Church, the Presbyterian Church, the Methodist Church, dominated by South-hating Yankee parsons, denied that logic? Then let them go fry in perdition, as they probably would anyhow. The South would have a Baptist Church, a Presbyterian Church, a Methodist Church of its own.

But this Southern Methodist Church would be one which was not strictly Methodist any more. For as the pressure of the Yankee increased, the whole South, including the Methodists, would move toward a position of thoroughgoing Calvinism in feeling if not in formal theology. It would never completely arrive there, to be sure. The old Arminian doctrine of Free Will — the doctrine most natural to the frontier, and most congenial in many respects to the Southern pattern generally — would retain a great deal of vitality always. God would continue to be, in considerable measure, a sort of constitutional monarch, bargaining for the allegiance of His subjects and yielding a *quid* for a *quo*. Nevertheless, everybody did come increasingly, and without regard for his traditional creed, to think and speak of Him as being primarily the imperious master of a puppet-show. Every man was in his place because He had set him there. Everything was as it was because He had ordained it so. Hence slavery, and, indeed, everything that was, was His responsibility, not the South's. So far from being evil, it was the very essence of Right. Wrong could consist only in rebellion against it. And change could come about only as He Himself produced it through His own direct acts, or — there was always room here for this — as He commanded it through the instruments of His will, the ministers.

The repercussions of this through the whole structure of Southern life and thought were extensive. But it is enough here to direct attention to the fact that, in combination with the strong other-worldliness natural to the evangelical sects, and the perhaps logically incompatible doctrine which made out the superior fortune of the planter to be Heaven's reward to superior virtue and piety, it was a signally important element for the complacency of both the masses and, as I have mentioned in passing, the master class; and that it, of course, served mightily for the increase of the power of the ministers.

9

It is in the connection of the conflict with the Yankee, again, that we can perhaps best understand the South's unusual proneness to sentimentality.

The root of the thing, obviously, was in the simple man with whom we began. It was part and parcel, in fact, with his unrealism and romanticism, and grew as they grew. It gathered force, too, from the *Zeitgeist,* of course — from the great tide of sentimentality which, rolling up slowly through the years following the French Revolution, broke over the Western world in flooding fullness with the accession of Victoria to the throne of England. Nowhere, indeed, did this Victorianism, with its false feeling, its excessive nicety, its will to the denial of the ugly, find more sympathetic acceptance than in the South.

But a factor which served more importantly for the growth of the pattern was the interaction of the Yankee's attack with the South's own qualms over slavery.

Wholly apart from the strict question of right and wrong, it is plain that slavery was inescapably brutal and ugly. Granted the existence, in the higher levels, of genuine humanity of feeling toward the bondsman; granted that, in the case of the house-servants at least, there was sometimes real affection between master and man; granted even that, at its best, the relationship here got to be gentler than it has ever been elsewhere, the stark fact remains: It rested on force. The black man occupied the position of a mere domestic animal, without will or right of his own. The lash lurked always in the background. Its open crackle could often be heard where field hands were quartered. Into the gentlest houses drifted now and then the sound of dragging chains and shackles, the bay of hounds, the report of pistols on the trail of the runaway. And, as the advertisements of the time incontestably prove, mutilation and the mark of the branding iron were pretty common.

Just as plain was the fact that the institution was brutalizing — to white men. Virtually unlimited power acted inevitably to call up, in the coarser sort of master, that sadism which lies concealed in the depths of universal human nature — bred angry impatience and a taste for cruelty for its own sake, with a strength that neither the kindliness I have so often referred to (it continued frequently to exist unimpaired side by side, and in the same man, with this other) nor notions of honor could effectually restrain. And in the common whites it bred a savage and ignoble hate for the Negro, which required only opportunity to break forth in relentless ferocity; for all their rage against the " white-trash " epithet concentrated itself on him rather than on the planters.

There it stood, then — terrible, revolting, serving as the very school of violence, and lending mordant point to the most hysterical outcries of the Yankee.

But the South could not and must not admit it, of course. It must prettify the institution and its own reactions, must begin to boast of its own Great Heart. To have heard them talk, indeed, you would have thought that the sole reason some of these planters held to slavery was love and duty to the black man, the earnest, devoted will not only to get him into heaven but also to make him happy in this world. He was a child whom somebody had to look after. More, he was in general, and despite an occasional spoiled Nat Turner, a grateful child — a contented, glad, loving child. Between the owner and the owned there was everywhere the most tender and beautiful relationship.

Mrs. Stowe did not invent the figure of Uncle Tom, nor did Christy invent that of Jim Crow — the banjo-picking, heel-flinging, hi-yi-ing happy jack of the levees and the cotton fields. All they did was to modify them a little for their purposes. In essentials, both were creations of the South — defense-mechanisms, answers to the Yankee and its own doubts, projections from its own mawkish tears and its own mawkish laughter over the black man, incarnations of its sentimentalized version of slavery. And what is worth observing also is that the Negro, with his quick, intuitive understanding of what is required of him, and his remarkable talents as a mime, caught them up and bodied them forth so convincingly that his masters were insulated against all question as to their reality — were enabled to believe in them as honestly as they believed in so many other doubtful things.

But there was another factor which was perhaps even more important for the growth of sentimentality than this: the influence of the presence of the Negro in increasing the value attaching to Southern woman. For, as perpetuator of white superiority in legitimate line, and as a creature absolutely inaccessible to the males of the inferior group, she inevitably became the focal center of the fundamental pattern of proto-Dorian pride.

Nor, in this connection, must we overlook the specific role played by the Negro woman. Torn from her tribal restraints and taught an easy complaisance for commercial reasons, she was to be had for the taking. Boys on and about the plantation inevitably learned to use her, and having acquired the habit, often continued it into manhood and even after marriage. For she was natural, and could give herself up to passion in a way impossible to wives inhibited by Puritanical training. And efforts to build up a taboo against miscegenation made little real progress. I do not mean to imply, certainly, that it was universal. There were many men in the South who rigidly abstained from such liaisons, and scorned those who indulged. Nevertheless, that they were sufficiently common is indisputable. Melville Herskovits informs us, in *The American Negro,* that:

" Instead of 80 or 85% of the American Negroes being wholly of African descent, only a little over 20% are unmixed, while almost

80% show mixture with white or American Indian. . . . Between one third and one fourth (27.3% to be exact) have American Indian ancestry."

And everything points to the conclusion that this state of affairs was already largely established by 1860. We must not overlook the fact, of course, that the Portuguese and Spanish slave-traders had been industriously engaged in bleaching the tar-brush for two centuries before the Negro was introduced into the South — nor that the Yankee has never shown himself averse to furthering the comity of nations. But, relatively speaking, the share of responsibility to be laid to these was doubtless small. Nor can the South's ruling share be dismissed as due merely to the aberrations of degraded white-trash. Every Southern community where Cuffey flourishes abounds in stories which run to the tune of " the *image,* my dear, the living *image,* of old Colonel Bascombe himself! "

But this set up conflict with domestic sentiment. And such sentiment, without regard to the influence of the Negro's presence, was even stronger in the Southerner than in the American generally. In the isolation of the plantation world the home was necessarily the center of everything; family ties acquired a strength and validity unknown in more closely settled communities; and, above all, there grew up an unusually intense affection and respect for the women of the family — for the wife and mother upon whose activities the comfort and well-being of everybody greatly depended; (yes, and even particularly in those houses with many servants; for the Negro as he developed under slavery in the South was one of the laziest and in general most untrustworthy servants ever heard of, requiring endlessly to be watched and driven).

Yet if such a woman knew that the maid in her kitchen was in reality half-sister to her own daughter, if she suspected that her husband sometimes slipped away from her bed to the arms of a mulatto wench, or even if she only knew or suspected these things of her sons or some other male of her family, why, of course she was being cruelly wounded in the sentiments she held most sacred. And even though she feigned blindness, as her convention demanded she should — even if she actually knew or suspected nothing — the guilty man, supposing he possessed any shadow of decency, must inexorably writhe in shame and an intolerable sense of impurity under her eyes.

Join to this the fact that the Yankee's hate (and maybe his envy) had not been slow to discover the opening in the Southern armor, that his favorite journals were filled with " screamers " depicting every Southerner as a Turk wallowing in lechery, and it is plain that here was a situation which was not to be tolerated.

And the only really satisfactory escape here, as in so many other instances, would be fiction. On the one hand, the convention must be set up that the thing simply did not exist, and enforced under penalty of being shot; and on the other, the woman must be compensated, the revolting suspicion in the male that he might be slipping into bestiality got rid of, by glorifying her; the Yankee must be answered by proclaiming from the housetops that Southern Virtue, so far from being inferior, was superior, not alone to the North's but to any on earth, and adducing Southern Womanhood in proof.

The upshot, in this land of spreading notions of chivalry, was downright gyneolatry. She was the South's Palladium, this Southern woman — the shield-bearing Athena gleaming whitely in the clouds, the standard for its rallying, the mystic symbol of its nationality in face of the foe. She was the lily-pure maid of Astolat and the hunting goddess of the Bœotian hill. And — she was the pitiful Mother of God. Merely to mention her was to send strong men into tears — or shouts. There was hardly a sermon that did not begin and end with tributes in her honor, hardly a brave speech that did not open and close with the clashing of shields and the flourishing of swords for her glory. At the last, I verily believe, the ranks of the Confederacy went rolling into battle in the misty conviction that it was wholly for her that they fought.

" Woman!!! The center and circumference, diameter and periphery, sine, tangent and secant of all our affections! " Such was

the toast which brought twenty great cheers from the audience at
the celebration of Georgia's one-hundredth anniversary in the
1830's.

10

Another effect of the interworking of the Yankee's attack and
slavery was the heightening of the snobbish feeling in the master
class.

I have already suggested that this feeling was made much stronger
by the development of the legend of general aristocracy; for the
reverse face of this claim to gentility and noble descent on the part
of the planters was, of course, the convention that the common
whites were " not our kind of people " — a different flesh altogether.

But now, in the last years before the Civil War, the incessant
need to justify the " peculiar institution " was to give birth to a
definite philosophy of caste. Slavery, it must be said, was not only
God's commanded order, not only the most humane order, but also
the most natural order. The natural order adverted to was not
Rousseau's, as I need not tell you, but Auguste Comte's. Professor
Dew of Virginia, Chancellor Harper of South Carolina, and their
imitators fell eagerly upon that philosopher's sociological system
and from that basis proceeded to envisage the South as on its way
to being — as bound to become on an early tomorrow — a rigid
caste society, rising tier on tier from the " mud-sill " of the happy
slave to the planter, charged with all power at the top: a society
which, according to their rhapsodies, would so ideally fit the true
nature of humanity that the whole world, witnessing its glory,
would abandon the stupid fetish of democracy and hasten to follow
suit.

As I said a good while ago, this philosophy remained always primarily one for the schoolmen and professional apologists for an
economic system; few men in the South ever understood its impli-

cations; and almost none of them assimilated it sufficiently to make it the genuine root of their thinking. Even those who loved best to strike the pose of Cato the Censor, to quote the dying words of Agricola Fusilier: " Master and man — arch and pier — arch above, pier beneath," to lampoon Mr. Jefferson as a " leveller," were really concerned only with the defense of slavery and the titillation of their vanity; they never entirely freed their subconscious minds from the old primitive democracy of outlook bequeathed by the frontier.

But the doctrine did serve once more to strengthen and expand the planter's narrow class pride, to increase his private contempt for the common whites, to ratify his complacency and harden toward arrogance the conviction which was growing up in him, as a natural result of the paternalistic habit, that it was his *right* to instruct and command — never to the point, as we know, of setting up tangible resentment and interfering with the social solidification of the land, but far enough for us to take careful cognizance of it none the less.

The final result of conflict and solidification, we have to notice, is that it turned the South toward strait-jacket conformity and made it increasingly intolerant of dissent. Perhaps, in view of Southern individualism, this seems paradoxical and even contradictory. The right to dissent, one might think, is the very sap and life of individualism. But in fact there is no real contradiction here, or none that was not inherent in the South itself.

We go back to the point that it was the individualism of extremely simple men, shaped by what were basically very simple and homogeneous conditions. The community and uniformity of origins, the nearness in time of the frontier, the failure of immigration and the growth of important towns — all these co-operated to cut men to a single pattern, and, as we have been seeing continuously, the total effect of the plantation world was to bind them to a single focus which was held with peculiar intensity.

Conformity and intolerance never became absolute in the Old South, certainly. Down to the Civil War it was possible for a man to be an open atheist or agnostic in most districts, though perhaps not in all, without suffering any greater penalty than being denounced every Sunday from the local pulpits, and subjected to the angry mutters or the intrusive warnings and jeremiads of his neighbor, the jeers and maybe the missiles of the children, when he passed among them. But when the great central nerve of slavery was touched, there was no such latitude. Let a Yankee abolitionist be caught spreading his propaganda in the land, let a Southerner speak out boldly his conviction that the North was essentially right about the institution, and he was not merely frowned on, cursed, hated; he was, in this country long inured to violence, dealt with more pointedly and personally: he was hanged or tarred or horsewhipped. At the very luckiest, he had to stand always prepared to defend himself against assault.

"I warn the abolitionists, ignorant and infatuated barbarians as they are, that if chance shall throw any of them into our hands, they may expect a felon's death," cried Congressman J. H. Hammond of South Carolina, as early as 1836 — and the overwhelming body of his countrymen cheered him hotly. The State of Georgia officially posted a reward of five thousand dollars for whoever should kidnap Garrison and fetch him within the Cracker jurisdiction to stand trial on charges of inciting the blacks to insurrection. In North Carolina a young Tarheel professor, B. S. Hedrick, was expelled from the faculty of the State University at Chapel Hill on a wave of popular rage because he was reported to have said that he would vote for John C. Frémont for President on the ground that Frémont's position on slavery was virtually identical with that of Jefferson; and his flight to the North was made imperative and swift by the roar of a mob hard upon his heels.

In all Dixie, indeed, from 1840 on, only a dozen or so men of the greatest and most impregnable position, such as Cassius Clay, of the border state of Kentucky, and Robert E. Lee, stationed in the North, would be able even mildly to express doubts about the institution in public without suffering dismaying penalty. Not even the cloth of a minister was sufficient protection. For when Daniel

Worth, of North Carolina, and John G. Fee, of Kentucky, almost alone among Southern ministers, attempted to speak out against it, Worth was jailed for a winter and had to endure an appalling stream of vituperation and insult; and the more militant Fee is said to have fallen twenty-two times a victim to mobs, and on two occasions to have been left for dead.

The habit spread in ever widening circles, poisonously. From the taboo on criticism of slavery, it was but an easy step to interpreting every criticism of the South on whatever score as disloyalty — to making such criticism so dangerous that none but a madman would risk it. And from that it was but another and just as easy — an almost inevitable — step to a state of affairs in which criticism of any sort at all was not impossible, surely, but an enterprise for bold and excitement-loving spirits alone. If it touched on any social sore point, on anything which the commonalty or their prompters, the planters, counted dear — and there were few things that did not fall under this description — the critic stood an excellent chance of being mobbed. If it touched only some person or private interest, he was likely to be waited on with a challenge or to be larruped through the streets of the courthouse village while the lounging populace looked on and grinned.

One can almost write the last chapter in the life of a newspaper editor in the Southern country at that time without making inquiry. For, from John Hampden Pleasants of the Richmond *Whig* down, the record is rich in entries of " fatally wounded in a duel," or " shot dead in the streets." On the *Vicksburg Journal,* indeed, the mortality by violence actually reached the total of five editors in thirteen years!

The natural result — seeing that really competent critics are by ordinary nervous souls — was that criticism either waxed feeble and effeminate, or, with a few salient exceptions, degenerated into an irrational and wholly personal bellow, usually dedicated to mean ends and practiced mainly by violent blackguards.

Definitely, in short, the South was *en route* to the savage ideal: to that ideal whereunder dissent and variety are completely suppressed and men become, in all their attitudes, professions, and actions, virtual replicas of one another.

II

With all these characteristics established, we are in a position to turn to the examination of the South's claim to a superior culture. Or, more correctly, since everything we have seen falls within the meaning of culture in the wide sense, to that claim in so far as it relates to culture in the narrow sense — to intellectual and æsthetic attainments.

And in this respect, it may be said without ceremony that it was perhaps the least well founded of the many poorly founded claims which the Southerners so earnestly asserted to the world and to themselves and in which they so warmly believed.

I know the proofs commonly advanced by apologists — that at the outbreak of the war the section had more colleges and students in those colleges, in proportion to population, than the North; that many planters were ready and eager to quote you Cicero or Sallust; that Charleston had a public library before Boston, and its famous St. Cecilia Society from the earliest days; that these Charlestonians, and with them the older and wealthier residents of Richmond and Norfolk and New Orleans, regularly imported the latest books from London, and brought back from the grand tour the paintings and even the statuary of this or that fashionable artist of Europe; that, in the latest days, the richest among the new planters of the deep South began to imitate these practices; that in communities like those of the Scotch Highlanders in the Cape Fear country there were Shakespeare libraries and clubs; that Langdon Cheves of South Carolina is reported by Joseph LeConte to have discussed the idea of evolution in private conversation long before *The Origin of Species;* and so on *ad infinitum.*

But such proofs come to little. Often, as they are stated, they are calculated to give a false picture of the facts. Thus, the majority of the colleges were no more than academies. And of the whole number of them perhaps the University of Virginia alone was worthy to be named in the same breath with half a dozen Yankee universities and colleges, and as time went on, even it tended to sink into a hotbed of obscurantism and a sort of fashionable club, propagating dueling, drinking, and gambling.

Thus again, the general quoting of Latin, the flourish of " Shakespeare says," so far from indicating that there was some profound and esoteric sympathy with the humanities in the South, a deliberate preference for the Great Tradition coming down from the ancients, a wide and deep acquaintance with and understanding of the authors quoted, really means only this, it seems to me: that the great body of men in the land remained continuously under the influence of the simple man's almost superstitious awe for the classics, as representing an arcanum beyond the reach of the ordinary.

And over and behind these considerations lies the fact that the South far overran the American average for (white) illiteracy — that not only the great part of masses but a considerable number of planters never learned to read and write, and that a very great segment of the latter class kept no book in their houses save only the Bible.

But put this aside. Say that the South is entitled to be judged wholly by its highest and its best. The ultimate test of every culture is its productivity. What ideas did it generate? Who were its philosophers and artists? And — perhaps the most searching test of all — what was its attitude toward these philosophers and artists? Did it recognize and nurture them when they were still struggling and unknown? Did it salute them before the world generally learned to salute them?

One almost blushes to set down the score of the Old South here. If Charleston had its St. Cecilia and its public library, there is no record that it ever added a single idea of any notable importance to the sum total of man's stock. If it imported Mrs. Radcliffe, Scott, Byron, wet from the press, it left its only novelist, William Gilmore

Simms, to find his reputation in England, and all his life snubbed him because he had no proper pedigree. If it fetched in the sleek trumpery of the schools of Van Dyck and Reynolds, of Ingres and Houdon and Flaxman, it drove its one able painter, Washington Allston (though he was born an aristocrat), to achieve his first recognition abroad and at last to settle in New England.

And Charleston is the peak. Leaving Mr. Jefferson aside, the whole South produced, not only no original philosopher but no derivative one to set beside Emerson and Thoreau; no novelist but poor Simms to measure against the Northern galaxy headed by Hawthorne and Melville and Cooper; no painter but Allston to stand in the company of Ryder and a dozen Yankees; no poet deserving the name save Poe — only half a Southerner. And Poe, for all his zeal for slavery, it despised in life as an inconsequential nobody; left him, and with him the *Southern Literary Messenger,* to starve, and claimed him at last only when his bones were whitening in Westminster churchyard.

Certainly there were men in the Old South of wide and sound learning, and with a genuine concern for ideas and, sometimes, even the arts. There were the old Jeffersons and Madisons, the Pinckneys and the Rutledges and the Henry Laurenses, and their somewhat shrunken but not always negligible descendants. Among both the scions of colonial aristocracy and the best of the newcomers, there were men for whom Langdon Cheves might stand as the archetype and Matterhorn — though we must be careful not to assume, what the apologists are continually assuming, that Cheves might just as well have written *The Origin of Species* himself, if only he had got around to it. For Darwin, of course, did not launch the idea of evolution, nor yet of the struggle for existence and the survival of the fittest. What he did was laboriously to clarify and organize, to gather and present the first concrete and convincing proof for notions that, in more or less definite form, had been the common stock of men of superior education for fifty years and more. There is no evidence that Cheves had anything original to offer; there is only evidence that he was a man of first-rate education and considerable intellectual curiosity, who knew what was being thought and said by the first minds of Europe.

To be sure, there were such men in the South: men on the plantation, in politics, in the professions, in and about the better schools, who, in one degree or another, in one way or another, were of the same general stamp as Cheves. There were even men who made original and important contributions in their fields, like Joseph LeConte himself, one of the first of American geologists; like Matthew Fontaine Maury, author of *Physical Geography of the Sea,* and hailed by Humboldt as the founder of a new science; like Audubon, the naturalist. And beneath these were others: occasional planters, lawyers, doctors, country schoolmasters, parsons, who, on a more humble scale, sincerely cared for intellectual and æsthetic values and served them as well as they might.

But in the aggregate these were hardly more than the exceptions which prove the rule — too few, too unrepresentative, and, above all, as a body themselves too sterile of results very much to alter the verdict.

In general, the intellectual and æsthetic culture of the Old South was a superficial and jejune thing, borrowed from without and worn as a political armor and a badge of rank; and hence (I call the authority of old Matthew Arnold to bear me witness) not a true culture at all.

12

This is the fact. The reason for it is not too far to seek.

If we were dealing with the cotton South alone, one might be tempted to think, indeed, that it resides wholly in the question of time, in the consideration I have emphasized, that there were but seventy years between the invention of the cotton gin and the outbreak of the Civil War. But even here the answer is hardly adequate; in view of the wealth and leisure ultimately afforded the master class, in view of the fact that the second generation had largely grown up in this wealth and leisure, one might have expected, even though this cotton South had stood quite alone, to find a greater advance, something more than the blank in production we actually find.

But we are not dealing with the cotton South alone, of course. As we have sufficiently seen, it was the Virginians, too. Here was the completed South, the South in flower — a South that, rising out of the same fundamental conditions as the great South, exhibiting, with the obvious changes, the same basic pattern, and played upon in the first half of the nineteenth century by the same forces, had enjoyed riches, rank, and a leisure perhaps unmatched elsewhere in the world, for more than a hundred years at least; a South, therefore, which, by every normal rule, ought to have progressed to a complex and important intellectual culture, to have equaled certainly, probably to have outstripped, New England in production, and to have served as a beacon to draw the newer South rapidly along the same road. And if it did none of these things, why, then, we shall have to look beyond the factor of time for a satisfactory explanation, not only of its barrenness but, to a considerable extent, of that of the great South also.

In reality, the reason is immanent, I think, in the whole of Southern life and psychology. Complexity in man is invariably the child of complexity in environment. The desire for knowledge when it passes beyond the stage of being satisfied with the most obvious answer, thought properly so called, and, above all, æsthetic concern, arise only when the surrounding world becomes sufficiently complicated to make it difficult or impossible for human energies to escape on a purely physical plane, or, at any rate, on a plane of direct activity. Always they represent, among other things, a reaching out vicariously for satisfaction of the primitive urge to exercise of muscle and nerve, and achievement of the universal will to mastery. And always, too, they feed only upon variety and change. Whence it is, no doubt, that they have never reached any notable development save in towns, and usually in great towns.

But the Southern world, you will remember, was basically an extremely uncomplex, unvaried, and unchanging one. Here economic and political organization was reduced to its simplest elements. Here were no towns to rank as more than trading posts save New Orleans, Charleston, Richmond, and Norfolk; here, perhaps, were no true towns at all, for even these four (three of which were scarcely more than overgrown villages) were rather mere depots on the road to the markets of the world, mere adjuncts to the plantation, than living entities in their own right, after the fashion of Boston and New York and Philadelphia. Here was lacking even that tremendous ferment of immigration which was so important in lending variety to the rest of the American scene. And here everywhere were wide fields and blue woods and flooding yellow sunlight. A world, in fine, in which not a single factor operated to break up the old pattern of outdoor activity laid down on the frontier, in which, on the contrary, everything conspired to perpetuate it; a world in which even the Virginian could and inevitably did discharge his energies on the purely physical plane as fully as his earliest ancestor in the land; a world in which horses, dogs, guns, not books, and ideas and art, were his normal and absorbing interests.

And if this was not enough? If his energies and his ambition demanded a wider field of action? He went, in this world at battle, inescapably into politics. To be a captain in the struggle against the Yankee, to be a Calhoun or a Brooks in Congress, or, better still, to be a Yancey or a Rhett ramping through the land with a demand for the sword — this was to be at the very heart of one's time and place, was, for the plantation youth, full of hot blood, the only desirable career. Beside it the pursuit of knowledge, the writing of books, the painting of pictures, the life of the mind, seemed an anemic and despicable business, fit only for eunuchs. " Why," growled a friend of Philip Pendleton Cooke, Virginia aristocrat and author of the well-known lyric, *Florence Vane,* " Why do you waste your time on a damned thing like poetry? A man of your position could be a useful man " — and summed it up exactly.

But it was not only the consumption of available energy in direct action. The development of a considerable intellectual culture requires, in addition to complexity of environment, certain predisposing habits of mind on the part of a people. One of these is analysis. " *L'état de dissociation des lieux communs de la morale semble en corrélation assez étroite avec le degré de la civilization intellectuelle,*" says Remy de Gourmont — and says truly. Another is hospitality to new ideas. Still another is a firm grip on reality; and in this connection I am not forgetting the kind of art which is called romantic and the more fanciful varieties of poetry; in so far as they are good, in so far as they are truly art, they also must rise ultimately from the solid earth. And, finally, there is the capacity, at least, for detachment, without which no thinker, no artist, and no scholar can do his work.

But turn back now and examine the South in the light of this. Analysis is largely the outcome of two things: the need to understand a complex environment (a consideration already disposed of) and social dissatisfaction. But, as we are aware, satisfaction was the hallmark of Southern society; masters and masses alike were sunk in the deepest complacency; nowhere was there any palpable irritation, any discontent and conflict, and so nowhere was there any tendency to question. Again, being static and unchanging, the South was, of course, an inherently conservative society — one which, under any circumstances, would have naturally been cold to new ideas as something for which it had no need or use. As for the grip on reality, we know that story fully already. Imagination there was in plenty in this land with so much of the blood of the dreamy Celt and its warm sun, but it spent itself on puerilities, on cant and twisted logic, in rodomontade and the feckless vaporings of sentimentality. And as for detachment, the South, you will recall, was, before all else, personal, an attitude which is obviously the negation of detachment. Even its love of rhetoric required the immediate and directly observable satisfactions of speech rather than the more remote ones of writing.

There is still more here. As well as having nothing to give rise to a developed intellectual culture, as well as having much that was implicitly hostile, much that served as a negative barrier, the Old

South also had much that was explicitly hostile and served as a quite positive barrier. The religious pattern will come to mind at once. Theologians have everywhere been the enemies of analysis and new ideas, and in whatever field they have appeared — feeling, quite correctly, that, once admitted, there is no setting limits to them. And in this country in which the evangelical ministers had already won to unusual sway, in which they had almost complete control of the schools, in which they had virtually no opposition, they established their iron wall with an effectiveness which went well beyond even its American average.

But the greatest force of all was the result of conflict with the Yankee. In Southern unity before the foe lay the final bulwark of every established commonplace. And the defense of slavery not only eventuated, as we have seen, in a taboo on criticism; in the same process it set up a ban on all analysis and inquiry, a terrified truculence toward every new idea, a disposition to reject every innovation out of hand and hug to the whole of the *status quo* with fanatical resolution. Detachment? In a world in which patriotism to the South was increasingly the first duty of men, in which coolness about slavery was accounted treason, it was next to impossible.

In sum, it was the total effect of Southern conditions, primary and secondary, to preserve — but let Henry Adams tell it, in the pages of the *Education,* from direct observation of Roony Lee, the son of Robert E. Lee, and other young Southerners he knew at Harvard between 1854 and 1858, who had behind them two hundred years of shaping in the pattern, and who are to be taken, as Adams infers, as the typical flower of the Old South at its highest and best:

" Tall, largely built, handsome, genial, with liberal Virginia openness toward all he liked, he [Lee] had also the Virginian habit of command. . . . For a year, at least . . . was the most popular and prominent man in his class, but then seemed slowly to drop into the background. The habit of command was not enough, and the Virginian had little else. He was simple beyond analysis; so simple that even the simple New England student could not realize him.

No one knew enough to know how ignorant he was; how child-like; how helpless before the relative complexity of a school. As an animal the Southerner seemed to have every advantage, but even as an animal he steadily lost ground.

". . . Strictly, the Southerner had no mind; he had temperament. He was not a scholar; he had no intellectual training; he could not analyze an idea, and he could not even conceive of admitting two. . . ."

There it is, then. We return to the point with which we began. It was the total effect of Southern conditions, primary and second-ary, to preserve the Southerner's original simplicity of character as it were in perpetual suspension. From first to last, and whether he was a Virginian or a *nouveau,* he did not (typically speaking) think; he felt; and discharging his feelings immediately, he de-veloped no need or desire for intellectual culture in its own right — none, at least, powerful enough to drive him past his taboos to its actual achievement.

BOOK TWO

The Mind of the South

ITS CURIOUS CAREER IN THE

MIDDLE YEARS

CHAPTER I

OF THE FRONTIER THE YANKEE MADE

THE CIVIL WAR and Reconstruction represent in their primary aspect an attempt on the part of the Yankee to achieve by force what he had failed to achieve by political means: first, a free hand in the nation for the thievish aims of the tariff gang, and secondly, and far more fundamentally, the satisfaction of the instinctive urge of men in the mass to put down whatever differs from themselves — the will to make over the South in the prevailing American image and to sweep it into the main current of the nation.

To that end, he set himself to destroy the Southern world. And at Appomattox he seemed to have succeeded. The foundation stone had been torn away in the abolition of slavery. And the land was stripped and bled white — made, indeed, a frontier once more, in that its people were once more without mastery of their environment and must begin again from the beginning to build up social and economic order out of social and economic chaos.

But the victory was, in fact, almost entirely illusory. If this war had smashed the Southern world, it had left the essential Southern mind and will — the mind and will arising from, corresponding to, and requiring this world — entirely unshaken. Rather, after the manner of defensive wars in general and particularly those fought against odds and with great stubbornness, it had operated enormously to fortify and confirm that mind and will.

The armies had brought men together from the four quarters, molding them to a common purpose for four years, teaching them more and more to say and think the same things, giving them common memories — memories transcending all that had gone before and sealed with the great seal of pain and hunger and sweat — binding man more closely to man, class more closely to class. If in that long-ago, already half-fabulous time before rebellion roared at Sumter, this South they had cheered had still perhaps seemed to them a little nebulous, it was not so any longer. They had been over the land now; had manured it with their dead, often enough with their own limbs; knew its hills and rivers and forests, its farthest man and its farthest woman; loved it with the intense love of personal acquaintance and participation, with the incalculable love which is engendered by personal suffering and sacrifice; held it for the most real of things.

Local patriotism was far from being dead in them, but nobody remembered now that they had ever gone out to die merely for Virginia or Carolina or Georgia. In their years together, a hundred control phrases, struck from the eloquent lips of their captains in the smoke and heat of battle, had burned themselves into their brains — phrases which would ever after be to them as the sounding of trumpets and the rolling of drums, to set their blood to mounting, their muscles to tensing, their eyes to stinging, to call forth in them the highest loyalties and the most active responses. And of these phrases the great master key was in every case the adjective. Southern.

Moreover, four years of fighting for the preservation of their world and their heritage, four years of measuring themselves against the Yankee in the intimate and searching contact of battle, had left these Southerners far more self-conscious than they had been before, far more aware of their differences and of the line which divided what was Southern from what was not. And upon that line all their intensified patriotism and love, all their high pride in the knowledge that they had fought a good fight and had yielded only to irresistible force, was concentrated, to issue in a determination, immensely more potent than in the past, to hold fast to their own, to maintain their divergences, to remain what they had been and were.

Nor were they to be long about putting this determination into evidence. For as soon as Andrew Johnson began to hand them back the governments of their various states, they everywhere set themselves, before everything else, to the enactment of the famous vagrancy and contract laws — everywhere, that is, struck, with characteristic directness in action, straight to the heart of their problem and sought at a stroke to set their old world whole again by restoring slavery in all but the name.

And so inevitably the Yankee, seeing his victory thus brought to nothing, came back. Came back in towering rage and hate, and shorn of all the fine notions of chivalry, the remembrance that he was after all a Christian, with which he had hitherto occasionally toyed. Came back to sit down for thirty years this time, to harry the South first with the plan called Thorough and the bayonet, and afterward with the scarcely less effective devices of political machination and perpetually impending threats. To make the frontier absolute and continual. To rob, to loot, to waste the pitiful remaining substance of this people in riot. To subvert the Southern world again and to hold it subverted. Not only to strip the Southern white man of mastery, of every legitimate instrument of mastery, to stop him more or less fully from every avenue leading to legitimate mastery, but also largely to hand over at least the seeming of that mastery to the black man.

2

And the result — well, the result in part, of course, was that the tariff gang got what it wanted — that the Republican Party had time and freedom to establish itself in the national trough so solidly that it would never really be got out again until the coming of the great depression of 1929. But for the rest — for that will to wean the South from its divergences and bring it into the flow of the nation, which, as I have said, was the most fundamental drive behind the Yankee's behavior — there is not among all the ironic results of such efforts of mass stupidity another more ironic than this.

Not Ireland nor Poland, not Finland nor Bohemia, not one of the countries which prove the truth that there is no more sure way to make a nation than the brutal oppression of an honorably defeated and disarmed people — not one of these, for all the massacres, the pillage, and the rapes to which they have so often been subjected, was ever so pointedly taken in the very core of its being as was the South. And so not one ever developed so much of fear, of rage, of indignation and resentment, of self-consciousness and patriotic passion.

For these thirty years the South was to live with unparalleled completeness under the sway of a single plexus of ideas of which the center was an ever growing concern with white superiority and an ever growing will to mastery of the Negro. And of which the circumference was a scarcely less intense and a scarcely less conscious concern with the maintenance of all that was felt to be Southern, a scarcely less militant will to yield nothing of its essential identity. For these thirty years it was to battle with unexampled fury, for the achievement of this will, the satisfaction of this obsession, and, what was obviously necessary to the purpose, the setting up again of a world which should be as nearly like the old one the Yankee had destroyed as was humanly possible.

It would not escape change, of course. The world into which it would emerge after these thirty years would be in many respects a vastly different one from that of the Old South. Conditions that had been primary under the *ancien régime* would have vanished, or at least, and already at the end of the Reconstruction period, would be in the process of vanishing. In more than one significant regard the essential social direction of the South would have been diverted and even reversed. And, as a result of the Yankee's efforts and the South's own driving necessities, the land would now bear within itself that which was eventually to be productive of even greater social changes. Nor would the Southern mind itself have by any means come off scot-free.

None the less, for immediate purposes, the Yankee was to retire from this thirty-year conflict in what amounted to abject defeat. If the world which he had to leave to the South was a changed world, it was still a world in which the first social principle of the old was preserved virtually intact: a world in which the Negro was still " mud-sill," and in which a white man, any white man, was in some sense a master. And so far from having reconstructed the Southern mind in the large and in its essential character, it was this Yankee's fate to have strengthened it almost beyond reckoning, and to have made it one of the most solidly established, one of the least *reconstructible* ever developed.

Such is the primary fact. And having looked at it, let us turn back now to follow out the story of the effect of Reconstruction more in detail, glancing, as we go, at such particular fruits of the Civil War as deserve further attention.

3

The natural corollary of what I have been saying — what is contained in it — is a very great increase in the social solidity of the South.

In turning the South into a frontier, in ruining it economically and holding it ruined, the Yankee had very largely swept away those causes of discord which, without ever making themselves distinctly and overtly felt, had been increasingly growing up in the background of the Old South. What with the vast destruction of property in the abolition of slavery, and the oppressive tax burdens laid upon wasted fields by the carpetbag governments, there were no rich left now for a Hinton Helper to cavil at. At best, there were only the land-poor — men so harried and overborne by the struggle to meet the demands made upon them, the effort merely to hold their property together, that their neighbors were more inclined to pity than to envy them.

There were few people in the South in these years who did not sometimes know actual want, fewer still to whom the mere making of a living was not a pressing problem, none who could afford luxury. Practically everybody ate poor food, wore poor clothes, and went without money from year's end to year's end.

Outward distinctions did not disappear wholly, of course. Carriages still rolled along the sand tracks and red gullies which passed for roads; the more earnest exponents of gentility and the more eager aspirants to it were marked out by the long-tailed coat — a sort of uniform of the class at the time; and the lady of the manor might still appear on great occasions in faded silk or satin. But these were tired old carriages, drawn by sad-eyed, introspective nags; these coats were worn, for glory, but far more, as every common jack knew well, because of the universal need of the gentry to hide just such patches on their pants as he himself openly exhibited; and every woman, reckoning up the age of the lady's decayed finery, could be certain that, underneath it, her petticoats were of homespun cotton as surely as those of the humblest Judy.

Along with this and the new gigantism of the Negro issue went a marked mitigation of the haughtiness which had been tending to break out more openly in the last days before the war. I do not mean, of course, that the narrow social pride of the ruling class would ever break down. Far from it, as we shall see. Nevertheless, under these new conditions — in some sense representing a retreat toward the primitive ones which had prevailed on the first frontier — and under the pressure of common need and purpose, the old kindliness which had persisted through growing snobbery underwent a great revival. The hand on the shoulder of the commoner, the inquiry after the health of Cousin Elvira and the last baby, the jests, the rallying, the stories, and, of course, the confiding reminders of the proto-Dorian bond of white men were more warm, less baldly patronizing, and more frequent than they had been for many a year now.

To be noted here also is that many of the new land-poor, the masters of the great plantation units in the Old South, inevitably failed in their struggles to hold their baronies intact and in part or in whole were sold out. But their lands went, in this world of poverty, for a song; and since this world boasted nobody able to purchase the whole of such units even at the rate of a song, their holdings were generally broken up into a number of smaller units. Which means, not only that the ownership of the better lands began to be somewhat more widely distributed, but also that the static economic and social set-up toward which the Old South had always moved without ever fully arriving at it was sharply shaken up and loosened, left less firmly established than it had been.

The way up was perhaps more fully open now, the Southern world more dynamic, than at any time since, say, 1840. It was a rocky and dangerous way; one that, in view of prevailing conditions, would in practice be open only to hard, pushing, horse-trading men. None but such as were remarkable for thrift, acumen, energy, undeviating desire for acquisition and power, and, in many cases, no great scruples as to the means; none but such as, even in the bitter days of the Civil War, had been able, either by painful toil and a single eye to gain or by such chicanery as the common manipulations of the Confederate currency, to gather and hold a little mobile capital — none but such as these would actually be able to make much use of the new opportunity, to grasp the newly available lands, carve out considerable holdings, and emerge to the ranks of the ruling class. But these would, in numbers.

And, as we have seen before now, it is precisely with such men that we have mainly to do when we consider the question of openness of opportunity in relation to the breeding of social discontent.

It is to be observed in this connection too, and finally, that it was the common white — and particularly the poor white properly so called — in whom the Yankee's activities generated the greatest terror and rage, in whom race obsession and passion for getting the Negro safely bound again in his old place were most fully developed. And that is true regardless of the fact that the master class had at stake an immediate economic interest which the masses lacked. For, if worse came to worse, the planter and, for that matter, the better sort of farmer had other effective bolsters for their essential ego than this one superiority. The cracker didn't. Let him be stripped of his proto-Dorian rank and he would be left naked, a man without status.

The upshot was a suppression of class feeling that went beyond anything that even the Old South had known — an absence of concern with the class idea in the broad sense, the like of which has probably not been seen in any other developed society of modern times. For the next thirty years — and for all the fact that they would be sadly hounded by economic and social ills — the common whites of the South would be even more completely than in the preceding thirty a people without primary economic and (as being, first of all, concerned with the improvement of their general status) social focus.

4

But involved in this, in its turn, were two other consequences which need to be signalized. One of these was that the individualism which had been so basic for the psychology of the Old South was preserved virtually intact.

Some sort of individualism would continue through this period, right down to our own time, to be the prevailing philosophy in the entire American nation, of course. But in the North it would be increasingly an individualism with a difference. Already by the time of the Civil War tangible class awareness and a vague but real notion of the general social interest had begun to confront it; already it was being subtly modified. And from the reign of Grant forward, this modification would proceed in accelerated tempo. By 1885, men were arising in the land to denounce it and to demand that it be chained. At the end of another decade they were actually beginning, however timidly, to nail on the shackles. It was being, as it were, urbanized and tamed; worse, under attack it was growing self-conscious, uneasy, unsure of its ground, falling back to the defensive; in brief, and in spite of the mask of cynical assertion under which it often attempted to hide the fact, entering slowly but certainly upon decline.

The South, on the contrary, would retain the old primitive feeling and outlook of the frontier. Southerners in 1900 would see the world in much the same terms in which their fathers had seen it in 1830; as, in its last aspect, a simple solution, an aggregation of self-contained and self-sufficient monads, each of whom was ultimately and completely responsible for himself.

The second consequence of which I have to speak was a striking extension of the so-called paternalism of the Old South: its passage in some fashion toward becoming a genuine paternalism.

We must begin here from the Civil War. Out of that ordeal by fire the masses had brought, not only a great body of memories in common with the master class, but a deep affection for these captains, a profound trust in them, a pride which was inextricably intertwined with the commoners' pride in themselves. They had tried these men under difficult circumstances and had found them bold, dashing, splendid, and, as a rule, neither overbearing nor, in the field, careless of the welfare of their following; above all, able, fit to cope with the problem in hand and to cut through to the common goal if anybody could.

Moreover, and for all the genial looseness which indubitably had characterized it, military discipline had done its work here as everywhere. Upon the common fellow the habits of following and of obedience were far more deeply engraved than they had been before. Indeed, we may go further yet. In these four years there had begun to grow up in him some palpable feeling — vague still, but distinctly going beyond anything he had exhibited previously — of the *right* of his captains, of the master class, to ordain and command.

In these captains themselves we find a cognate result. They were more set in the custom of command, much more perfectly schooled in the art of it, knew better how to handle the commoner, to steer expertly about his recalcitrance, to manipulate him without ever arousing his jealous independence. They had observed more intimately the irresponsibility which the conditions of the Old South had imprinted on the commoner — were certain now that he was inherently a child, requiring to be looked after. And, as the issue of it, were decidedly more imbued with the imperious conviction of their own right, and not only their right, but their duty, to tell the masses what to think and do.

So much for the war. But Reconstruction was, for our immediate purposes, simply an extension of that war, on lines yet more terrible and exigent. And so its effect was to hammer home the war's work, including, specifically, the essential military tone and organization.

During these thirty years the South was like nothing so much as a veteran army. The people — crackers and farmers — stood to their captains in very much the same way that, say, the troopers of Austerlitz and Marengo stood to Bonaparte and his marshals; gave them much the same idolatry, the same high faith, the same quick and sure response to suggestion; waited upon their word with the same respectful attention; were cast down by their frowns, elevated by their smiles, and, in a word, were scarcely less dependent upon the favor of their commanders for a good opinion of themselves than the most zealous trooper.

It seems a flat contradiction, no doubt — the setting of what I have just been saying side by side with the statement that the old backcountry individualism was carried forward in full integrity. And it may well be, in truth, that there is some irreducible residue of contradiction really involved. But if so, it is not of my making, but is such as resides inherently in the human mind, such, in particular, as was of the very stuff of Southern psychology. In any case, the contradiction is not so great as it sounds at the first hearing.

This will be plain enough if we turn back to fix in view once more the initial postulate from which this whole discussion advances: if we take care to remember that the same universal absorption in a single intense interest and the consequent suppression of every other focus which made possible the preservation of the ancient individualism were also the *sine qua non* of the growth in paternalism. The common Southerner's growth in the sense of the right of his captains to prescribe the public course was possible, in the last analysis, only because their prescriptions never, until the nineties at least, crossed his ego; because it never entered his head that they might conceivably run counter to his aims and desires. More accurately still, it was possible only because, like every other good Southerner, he so absolutely identified his ego with the thing called the South as to become, so to say, a perambulating South in little, and hence found in the prescriptions of his captains great expansion for his ego — associated the authority yielded the master class, not with any diminution of his individuality, but with its fullest development and expression.

5

One factor which operated for the maintenance of the individual-istic pattern in its proper character, which, indeed, made for its intensification at its very core, was the springing up to vast pro-portions of that old school of the personal, the puerile, and the swaggering: violence. In no other field was the effect of Recon-struction more marked.

As we know, race feeling had had nothing directly to do with the tendency to mob action in the Old South. So long as the Negro had been property, worth from five hundred dollars up, he had been taboo — safer from rope and faggot than any common white man, and perhaps even safer than his master himself. But with the abolition of legal slavery his immunity vanished. The economic interest of his former protectors, the master class, now stood the other way about — required that he should be promptly disabused of any illusion that his liberty was real, and confirmed in his an-cient docility. And so the road stood all but wide open to the ig-noble hate and cruel itch to take him in hand which for so long had been festering impotently in the poor whites.

In any case, and had there been no Reconstruction, the result would have been unhappy. For in the entire picture the only restraining forces to be described were the heritage of *noblesse,* of honor, of clean decency, which, in one form or another, belonged to the best men of the South, planters and farmers alike; such general distrust of violence and preference for order as had established itself in these men; and religion, in the hands of such ministers as actually had in themselves something of the spirit of the first Christian. Weak bars, plainly, to stand against economic interest and even such terror and rage as the mere abolition of slavery had left behind for everybody.

But mark now how the Yankee was heaping up the odds. In his manipulation of the unfortunate black man he was of course generating a terrible new hatred for him. Worse, he was inevitably extending this hate to the quarter where there had been no hate before: to the master class. The most superior men, with the exception of an occasional Robert E. Lee or Benjamin H. Hill, seeing their late slave strutting about full of grotesque assertions, cheap whisky, and lying dreams, feeling his elbow in their ribs, hearing his guffaw in high places, came increasingly to feel toward him very much as any cracker felt; fell increasingly under the sway of the same hunger to have their hands on him, and ease the intolerable agony of anger and fear and shaken pride in his screams.

Logically, you may say, it ought not to have been so. Ignorant and ductile, the Negro was in fact a mere passive instrument, no more to be blamed than the cudgel in the hand of a bully; and least of all by these Southerners who had always maintained, and who were now maintaining with redoubled vigor, that he was mentally an infant. But practically it would have been too much, in the heat of such a conflict, to expect even the best men anywhere to take account of this. And certainly it was too much to expect of these, unaccustomed to drawing distinctions and deeply set in their immediately personal way of seeing the world.

At the same time when the Yankee's activities were thus whipping up the pressure of hate, they were also establishing two definite sanctions for its discharge in violence. The first of these is what we may as well call the rape complex. It is a subject on which there has been much misunderstanding. Negro apologists and others bent on damning the South at any cost have, during the last decade or two, so constantly and vociferously associated the presentation of figures designed to show that no rape menace exists or ever has existed in the Southern country, with the conclusion that this rape complex is therefore a fraud, a hypocritical pretext behind which the South has always cynically and knowingly hidden mere sadism and economic interest, as to have got it very widely accepted.

In fact, the conclusion is a *non sequitur*. It is true that the actual danger of the Southern white woman's being violated by the Negro has always been comparatively small. Even in the days of Thorough itself, the chance was much less, for instance, than the chance that she would be struck by lightning. None the less (and Walter White's nearly explicit contention to the contrary notwithstanding) there were genuine cases of rape. There were other and more numerous cases of attempted rape. There were Yankee fools and scoundrels — and not all of them low-placed Yankees — to talk provocatively about the coming of a day when Negroes would take the daughters of their late masters for concubines; seeming to Southern ears to be deliberately inciting the former bondsmen to wholesale outrage. There was real fear, and in some districts even terror, on the part of the white women themselves. And there were neurotic old maids and wives, hysterical young girls, to react to all this in a fashion well enough understood now, but understood by almost nobody then.

Hence, if the actual danger was small, it was nevertheless the most natural thing in the world for the South to see it as very great, to believe in it, fully and in all honesty, as a menace requiring the most desperate measures if it was to be held off.

But this is hardly more than to scratch the surface. To get at the ultimate secret of the Southern rape complex, we need to turn back and recall the central status that Southern woman had long ago taken up in Southern emotion — her identification with the very notion of the South itself. For, with this in view, it is obvious that the assault on the South would be felt as, in some true sense, an assault on her also, and that the South would inevitably translate its whole battle into terms of her defense.

Nor is the connection here any mere vague and dubiously symbolic one. We strike back to the fact that this Southern woman's place in the Southern mind proceeded primarily from the natural tendency of the great basic pattern of pride in superiority of race to center upon her as the perpetuator of that superiority in legitimate line, and attached itself precisely, and before everything else, to her enormous remoteness from the males of the inferior group, to the absolute taboo on any sexual approach to her by the Negro. For the abolition of slavery, in destroying the rigid fixity of the black at the bottom of the scale, in throwing open to him at least the legal opportunity to advance, had inevitably opened up to the mind of every Southerner a vista at the end of which stood the overthrow of this taboo. If it was given to the black to advance at all, who could say (once more the logic of the doctrine of his inherent inferiority would not hold) that he would not one day advance the whole way and lay claim to complete equality, including, specifically, the ever crucial right of marriage?

What Southerners felt, therefore, was that any assertion of any kind on the part of the Negro constituted in a perfectly real manner an attack on the Southern woman. What they saw, more or less consciously, in the conditions of Reconstruction was a passage toward a condition for her as degrading, in their view, as rape itself. And a condition, moreover, which, logic or no logic, they infallibly thought of as being as absolutely forced upon her as rape, and hence a condition for which the term " rape " stood as truly as for the *de facto* deed.

Add explicitly what is contained in this: that, in their concern for the taboo on the white woman, there was a final concern for the right of their sons in the legitimate line, through all the generations to come, to be born to the great heritage of white men; and the record is complete. Such, I think, was the ultimate content of the

Southerners' rape complex. Such is the explanation of the fact that, from the beginning, they justified — and sincerely justified — violence toward the Negro as demanded in defense of woman, and though the offenses of by far the greater number of the victims had nothing immediately to do with sex.

The second great sanction for violence which the Yankee had created was this: that, quite apart from the woman question, and in sober reality, he had made it virtually necessary. Stripped for a decade of all control of its government, stripped for three decades of the effective use of that government to the ends it willed, the South was left with scarcely any feasible way to mastery save only this one of the use of naked force; perhaps with no other one, if we take the character of the people into account.

And here once more it was the Negro who was the obviously appointed scapegoat. For in addition to being the immediate fact at issue, he was the only really practical victim. To horsewhip, to tar, to hang a particularly obnoxious carpetbagger or scalawag, to reach even, as it happened once at Yanceyville in North Carolina, into the very carpetbag courtroom and snatch such a fellow away to the doom he deserved — all this might be very fine and satisfying, but it plainly could not be carried out on any extended scale. These men were mainly in a position to be easily protected, could be got at only at impossible risk and at the cost of certain recognition soon or late, Klan disguise or no Klan disguise; at the cost, eventually, of counter-hangings. On the other hand, to give the black man the works was just as effectually to strike Yankeedom, to serve notice of the South's will; terrifying him into frozen silence was easy; and in the world there were not bayonets enough to guard all the cabins scattered through this wide land.

Thus the bars came down with unprecedented completeness. The better men in the South, so far from feeling themselves any longer imperatively bound to restrain themselves and use their potent influence to restrain the masses, let themselves go with fury. They let their own hate run, set themselves more or less deliberately to whipping up the hate of the common whites, and often themselves led these common whites into mob action against the Negro.

6

But let me take care not to exaggerate. I must not seem to say that sentiments of *noblesse* (even toward the Negro) and of distrust of violence and too great hate were ever utterly extinguished in these best men, even as a body. Their very creation of the Ku-Klux Klan, looking primarily, of course, to efficient action, perhaps had in it always some lingering will to the retention of such control as normally inheres in semi-military organization. Certainly their quite sincere efforts to destroy this Klan in its later and more irresponsible phase testifies, among other things, to the revival of a distinct moral uneasiness, like that which had haunted the Old South in regard to slavery. And long before 1900 we find this uneasiness manifesting itself in an assiduous effort on their part to inculcate in their sons, and through them in the master class generally, a contempt for nigger-hate and nigger-hazing — to capitalize the old narrow class pride as a bar against it by setting up the convention that only white-trash indulged in it.

Yet the grand prevailing effort on both the masses and these best men themselves was very much as though none of this had been so. At the end of thirty years the South was solidly wedded to Negro-lynching because of the cumulative power of habit, obviously. But it was wedded to it far more because the dominant feeling about it (the feeling which, in time of stress, would seize control of the best almost as surely as of the sorriest cracker) was that, as an act of racial and patriotic expression, an act of chivalry, an act, indeed, having a definitely ritualistic value in respect to the entire Southern sentiment, and as an act which had had, in most concrete cases, the approbation and often the participation of the noblest and wisest of that revered generation of men which was now bending to the grave, it was not wrong but the living bone and flesh of right.

But it was not only mob violence that was perpetuated and extended. It was private violence also. And not merely for the

manifest reason that the growth of the lynching pattern had, moral
uneasiness notwithstanding, further blunted the sense of the wrong-
ness of violence in general.

For ten years the courts of the South were in such hands that no
loyal white man could hope to find justice in them as against any
Negro or any white creature of the Yankee policy; for twenty years
and longer they continued, in many quarters, to be in such hands
that such justice was at least doubtful. Hence the traditional inclination to direct action found here the same justification it had
found in the case of mob violence — the justification of necessity.

Moreover, the same combination of circumstances which had
operated to make mob violence socially desirable from the Southern viewpoint operated to make this private violence desirable also.
To smash a sassy Negro, to kill him, to do the same to a white
" nigger-lover " — this was to assert the white man's prerogative as
pointedly, to move as certainly toward getting the black man back
in his place, as to lynch. And so, to a very considerable extent, it,
too, was felt as an act of patriotism and chivalry.

The best men in the South never gave it such open and explicit
countenance as they gave to lynching, perhaps, though in the heat
of passion they often gave the example in action. Faced with an
unmistakable case of the cold-blooded murder of a Negro or a
Yankee-serving white man, or of gratuitous assault on these, they
would always respond with more or less of indignant disapproba-
tion. But, conditioned as they were, they were immensely prone
to give consent to the doctrine that a broken head or even death
was fair punishment for the sassy nigger (that is, one guilty of
any word or deed of assertion) or the " nigger-lover." They were
immensely prone and, for subconscious purposes, maybe even eager
to accept the claim, immediately put forward by every offender
who was not an utter dolt, that his violence was due to this or to
insult offered his women. And, in consequence, they were so honestly blind that it would have to be a flagrant case that would move
them to do more than merely turn away their eyes.

Save for protection given him by the Yankee-controlled courts

(a protection which, in view of the hostility and sealed lips with
which all loyal Southerners met the whole police machinery, was
hopelessly ineffective), the Negro, at least, was well-nigh as fully
exposed to private hate as to public. And with the gradual return
of the courts to Southern hands, he was to become almost open
game. For, from being places where no loyal white man could find
justice, they turned now, and naturally, into being places where no
black man would find it. In many districts, particularly in the deep
South, the killing of a Negro by a white man ceased, in practice,
even to call for legal inquiry. But wherever and whenever the
forms were still observed, the coroner or the jury was all but sure
to call it " self-defense " or " justifiable homicide," and to free the
slayer with celerity. And if any black was fantastic enough to run
to the courthouse for redress for a beating or any other wrong, he
stood a good chance (provided he was heard at all), not only of
seeing his assailant go off scot-free, but of finding the onus somehow shifted to himself, of finding himself in the dock on this or
some other count, and of ending by going away for a long time
to the county chain-gang and the mercies of persons hand-picked
for their skill in adjusting his sense of reality.

Nor did the whites reckoned as disloyal to the South entirely escape. For many years Damned Radicals, as members of the Republican Party were called, would be served in Southern courts,
not so roughly as the Negro, of course, but roughly enough in all
truth.

But this bred resentment in the black and the white pariah alike,
set up the will to retaliation, swung them, in their turn, into violence as the only way to satisfaction, as necessary in simple self-
defense, and so set up a vicious and ever widening circle.

Finally, the threshold of violence was lowered in the Reconstruction period as between loyal Southerners themselves. This would
obviously be true just as a matter of contagion. But it was true also
because, in the days when the courts were under carpetbag sway,
these Southerners naturally distrusted and hated them, not only in
cases involving Negroes and Yankee-serving whites but in all cases

whatever. Whether substantial justice could be had or not, they preferred, rather than face such offensive judges, to settle a quarrel between themselves with fist or knife or gun. And ten to twenty years of that left many of them as impatient of courts generally, as positively and fiercely opposed to any traffic with them, as the most recalcitrant of their frontier ancestors had ever been.

7

When we turn to the pattern of Southern unreality, of romanticism and what I have called hedonism, we find the story of growth to continue.

In large part this is immanent, indeed, in the things I have already been saying. Nothing is more obvious than that the whole atmosphere which prevailed from 1860 to the last march of the Red Shirts — the engagement of the best energies of the Southern people precisely at the point of passion and conflict — was perfectly calculated for the nurture of the taste for the extravagant, the intense, and the bold and flashing.

More specifically, two considerations merit attention here. One is that the Civil War and the sentimental cult of the Confederate soldier (at which we will look more closely in a moment) reacted on the Southern hero-ideal to leave it definitely military, in the grand style. I say definitely military because, of course, that ideal had always tended implicitly to find its summation in the dragoon and the lancer. But now the figure was drawn out and established in high relief. Every boy growing up in this land now had continually before his eyes the vision, and heard always in his ears the clamorous hoofbeats, of a glorious swashbuckler, compounded of Jeb Stuart, the golden-locked Pickett, and the sudden and terrible Forrest (yes, and, in some fashion, of Lord Roland and the douzepers) forever charging the cannon's mouth with the Southern battle flag. And so he demanded more imperatively than ever that those who levied on his admiration, those who aspired to lead him when he became a man, should be like that; and so more surely and more eagerly than ever he set himself to be as much like that as possible.

The nation was amazed when, in 1898, it was these young Southerners, concerning whose loyalty there had been much question, who volunteered most readily, and in fact largely filled up the armies, for the Spanish War. But there is nothing amazing about it when one understands the spirit of the Southern people.

The other matter which calls for notice is the increasingly close relationship between the pattern of violence and the Southern concept of pleasure and distinction — a relationship which is at once that of cause and that of effect.

I do not think it is true, as the South-haters have sometimes broadly insinuated, that anybody was ever lynched in the land simply because the Southerners counted it capital fun. But it is true that, from the Civil War forward, the old frolic tendency was more and more centered here, that enjoyment grew apace with practice in the business, that it figured with rising force as a very model of heroic activity, and that this feeling played a constantly expanding role in the complex.

More sinister yet was the inevitable corollary: that the old streak of brutality and cruelty began now to swell into definite sadism. From the 1880's on, as Walter White has accurately pointed out, there appears a waxing inclination to abandon such relatively mild and decent ways of dispatching the mob's victim as hanging and shooting in favor of burning, often of roasting over slow fires, after preliminary mutilations and tortures — a disposition to revel in the infliction of the most devilish and prolonged agonies.

But if the development of pleasure in violence, of sadism, and the notion that the practice of the thing was a grand way to be a hell of a fellow, probably never by itself produced a lynching, it gave rise in the field of private violence to a result equally repulsive. For here, under the social conditions I have described as making the black man practically open game, it began to generate, among both common whites and planters, a type of deliberate nigger-hazers and nigger-killers, men who not only capitalized on every shadow of excuse to kick and cuff him, to murder him, but also with malice aforethought baited him into a show of resentment in order so to serve him.

Such animals, I am glad to say, were comparatively few. Yet they were to be found in almost every locality, and they are important, both for their obvious effect on the pattern of violence itself and for their influence on the Southern hero-ideal. The growing lads of the country, reflecting prevailing sentiment in naked simplicity, and quick to see that the man who was pointed out as having slain five or eight or thirteen Negroes (I take the figures from actual cases) still walked about free, quick to penetrate the expressions of disapproval which might accompany the recital of his deeds, to evaluate the chuckles with which such recitals were too often larded, to detect the hidden note of pride and admiration — these lads inevitably tended to see such a scoundrel very much as he saw himself: as a gorgeous *beau sabreur,* hardly less splendid than the most magnificent cavalry captain.

The operation of more honorable notions, and of fear and the lack of resolution, would keep most of them, once they were grown up, from ever actually realizing the type in themselves. None the less, something of the sentiment would survive as a force at least obscurely influencing what all but the best men respected, aspired to, and really were.

8

Elsewhere the development of Southern unreality and romanticism is clear, also.

One of the most immediately striking and important changes the Civil War and Reconstruction had brought to the South was that they had irrevocably halted it in its march toward aristocracy. Before long, indeed, the movement, as we shall see more fully later, would be definitely in the other direction. The very model for it all, the Virginians, would be slipping into decay, and the master class in general would be falling back from the gains they had made in the last decades before the beginning of combat.

But at the same time the South was, of course, being continually driven more and more on the defensive. The need to justify itself in the eyes of the world and in its own and to assert its pride as against the Yankee was more imperative now than it had ever been before. Moreover, there was naturally a great aversion on the part of the individuals who made up the master class to surrender the glory which had been theirs under the *ancien régime.* And like many another people come upon evil days, the South in its entirety was filled with an immense regret and nostalgia; yearned backward toward its past with passionate longing.

And so it happened that, while the actuality of aristocracy was drawing away toward the limbo of aborted and unrealized things, the claim of its possession as an achieved and essentially indefeasible heritage, so far from being abated, was reasserted with a kind of frenzied intensity.

It was in this period that the legend of the Old South finally emerged and fully took on the form in which we know it today. With the antebellum world removed to the realm of retrospect, the shackles of reality, as so often happens in such cases, fell away from it altogether. Perpetually suspended in the great haze of memory, it hung, as it were, poised, somewhere between earth and sky, colossal, shining, and incomparably lovely — a Cloud-Cuckoo-Land wherein at last everybody who had ever laid claim to the title of planter would be metamorphosed with swift precision, beyond any lingering shade of doubt, into the breathing image of Marse Chan and Squire Effingham, and wherein life would move always in stately and noble measure through scenery out of Watteau.

From tracing themselves to the Roll of Battle Abbey, to Scotch and Irish kings, and to German emperors, many Southerners turned ultimately, in all seriousness and complete faith, to carrying their line back to such mythical personages as Brutus, the eponymous founder of Britain, and Scota, the daughter of Pharaoh, who wandered to Scotland's shores and brought that nation into being — and beyond these to the Lost Tribes of Israel! Stark Young's old gentleman who, in *River House,* was devoting his life to the establishment of this last connection, and, of course, Colonel Rudolph Musgrave, whose professional preoccupations, as recorded in *The Rivet in Grandfather's Neck,* are only comparatively less astonishing, are authentic and generic figures. In male or (more often) female incarnation, they were to be found, in these years, not only in every community, but, in one degree or another, in practically every family of any pretensions.

And in company with this went equally extravagant extensions of assertion and — let it be emphasized again — of belief concerning the power and prevalence of standards of honor and so on in the Old South, the proportions of its culture, and, in fact, all the other features of the legend.

It is worthy of note in this connection also, that the common whites came in this period to participate in the legend even more fully than they had done in the past. If they did not actually drift into thinking of their own forefathers as having been aristocrats — and they sometimes did — their identification of themselves with the master class was so close that the practical result was very much the same; that their pride did attach itself to the notion of the South's aristocratic heritage nearly as militantly as did that of any real scion of the plantation.

Nor must it be overlooked that, though the completion of the legend plainly had for one of its objects the heaping of reproach upon the Yankee, the latter, with that curious Janus-faced attitude which had always been his, nevertheless continued to accept it with great eagerness and, indeed, gave himself to the elaboration of it with renewed zeal. In Northern literature and even more in the Northern theater romantic Southern themes grew constantly in popularity, until in the 1890's they were near to dominating all others.

But the glorification of the Southern heritage, again, had certain considerable consequences, all moving, more or less, in the current of unreality. Thus, for one thing, it involved the further inflation of the tendency to the ascription of every act to the noblest motives. For another thing, it fortified and extended the complacency which had always sat over against haunting fear and uneasiness. In these years the belief that the South represented the summit of human achievement and the proper measure of mankind would lodge itself ever more solidly in the Southern credo.

Once more, this glorification had a marked influence, I think, on the fact that, at the same time when Southerners were being continually bound closer together in the broad social sense, and public haughtiness was in recession, the narrow, private pride of the old ruling class was not weakened but even distinctly enhanced. The enlarged idea of the heritage, the fact that it was bound to the past, and that therefore the charmed circle existed as a sort of closed corporation to which those who had not belonged before could not ever fully penetrate now — all this tended to widen the gulf, to erase the memory of ultimate kinship with the common whites.

Finally, and more or less in paradox with these conscious results, the increasing rift between representation and fact acted inevitably to exacerbate that subconscious sense of inadequacy which from the beginning had been the concomitant of the claim to aristocratic grandeur. And this, in turn, issued ultimately in a distinct augmentation of the tendency of the old planter manner to run to heavy patronizing when confronted by anybody who failed to be properly impressed.

9

There remain certain other patterns which require to be considered in connection with this general one of romanticism and unreality: namely, those of sentimentality, of the passion for politics, and of rhetoric.

If these Southerners had been extraordinarily prone to sentimentality in the Old South, it is probably no exaggeration to say they were to become in Reconstruction years the most sentimental people in history. Part of the impulse to growth here was communicated directly from the *Zeitgeist,* of course. For, as everyone knows, the period with which we are dealing was the heyday of that Victorianism at which we have already glanced.

But local conditions played by far the greater part. The memory of defeat in arms after a struggle so genuinely heroic as to have deserved a better end, the sense of suffering intolerable wrong under the pressure of overwhelming odds, the general drabness of life in a poverty-blighted land, the frustration of the private hopes of perhaps the majority of men in a whole generation, the heightened loyalty and the nostalgia for the past consequent upon these things — all this went to make up an atmosphere wonderfully calculated to hurry sentimentality on to acromegalic development.

The growth of the Southern legend was even more sentimental than it was grandiloquent; it moved, more powerfully even than it moved toward splendor and magnificence, toward a sort of ecstatic, teary-eyed vision of the Old South as the Happy-Happy Land. This legend is most perfectly rendered in the tone of Thomas Nelson Page's Billy as he dreams of the old plantation.

And of course the sentimentality waxed fat on the theme of the Confederate soldier and the cause for which he had fought and died. This soldier, I suggest, was in sober truth a proper subject for any people's pride. And men (Western men, at least) have everywhere and eternally sentimentalized the causes of their wars, and particularly the causes that were lost. All of them have bled for God and Womanhood and Holy Right; not one has ever died for anything so crass and unbeautiful as the preservation of slavery. But I doubt that the process has ever elsewhere been carried to the length to which it was carried in the South in this time; that ever elsewhere the laurel and the rue were so heaped upon a tomb; that ever elsewhere any soldier became so identical with Galahad, the cause for which he fought with the quest for the Sangraal.

The South's perpetual need for justifying its career, and the will to shut away more effectually the vision of its mounting hate and brutality toward the black man, entered into the equation also and bore these people yet further into the cult of the Great Southern Heart. The Old South must be made not only the happy country but the happy country especially for the Negro. The lash? A lie, sir; it had never existed. The only bonds were those of tender understanding, trust, and loyalty. And to prove it, here about us in this very hour of new freedom and bitter strife are hundreds of worn-out Uncle Toms and black mammies still clinging stubbornly to the old masters who can no longer feed them, ten thousand Jim Crows still kicking their heels and whooping for the smile of a white man. Such is the Negro, sir, when he is not corrupted by meddling fools. Hate him? My good friend, we love him dearly — and we alone, for we alone know him.

Do I again seem to satirize them for sniveling hypocrites? Then I must assure you once more that they were not. They believed in their professions here more fully than they had ever done. And they did love the thing, compounded of one part fact and three parts fiction and the black man's miming, which subsisted in their minds under the denomination of the Good Negro.

Lastly, the increased centrality of woman, added up with the fact that miscegenation, though more terrifying than it had been even in the Old South, showed little tendency to fall off despite efforts to build up standards against it, served to intensify the old interest in gyneolatry, and to produce yet more florid notions about Southern Womanhood and Southern Virtue, and so to foster yet more precious notions of modesty and decorous behavior for the Southern female to live up to.

As for the passion for politics, the tale of its immediate growth calls for little laboring. The world knows the story of the Democratic Party in the South; how, once violence had opened the way to political action, this party became the institutionalized incarnation of the will to White Supremacy. How, indeed, it ceased to be a party *in* the South and became the party *of* the South, a kind of confraternity having in its keeping the whole corpus of Southern loyalties, and so irresistibly commanding the allegiance of faithful whites that to doubt it, to question it in any detail, was *ipso facto* to stand branded as a renegade to race, to country, to God, and to Southern Womanhood. How, in a dozen major engagements and a thousand skirmishes, it hewed its way to its goal, sent the surviving carpetbaggers scuttling home to keep pub in their native slums, whipped the scalawags into repentance or defeatism, and in the end so smashed the Republican Party that, in the various states, it either ceased altogether to exist or continued to exist only as a Federal-job ring; until in the end the South was left as that curious anomaly, a so-called democratic country without an opposition party, a country in which, for practical purposes, there has been but one party from that day to this.

The world, as I say, knows this story, and its bearing for the general increase in Southern concern with politics is too obvious to require exposition. What does demand attention, however, is the further loss of reality which was involved. The destruction of the normal party system signalizes the completion of the divorce from what I have called a part of the proper business of politics — that is, the resolution of the inevitable conflict in interest between the classes, and the securing of a reasonable degree of social equity — and the arrival of the final stage of that irresponsibility which had belonged to the politics of the Old South. Bound rigidly within the single great frame by the hypnotic Negro-fixation, estopped by the necessity of unity, if the black man was to be kept in his place, from any considerable development of faction, the masses were stripped of every possibility of effectual political action for the amelioration of their estate, even (as we shall see) when they themselves should come dimly to desire it. And, contrariwise, the master class, freed from all chance of challenge or check, could and would go on more and more dealing with the governmental machinery of the South as their private property, and sink deeper into the naïve and complacent assumption of their interest as the public interest.

Thus, as the final term of the matter, emphasis was thrown back, even more completely than had been the case in the Old

South, upon the personal and the romantic. Was this candidate or that one more showy and satisfying? Did Jack or Jock offer the more thrilling representation of the South in action against the Yankee and the black man? Here, and here almost alone, would there be a field for choice.

I must not pass on from Reconstruction politics, either, without marking the fact that, as greatly perhaps as violence itself, the long training in fraud and trickery, which, as everyone knows, was a part of the campaign for mastery, acted to call out and develop in the South that most dangerous of philosophies: the philosophy that, if only the end be reckoned good, the most damnable means becomes justifiable and even glorious.

As for rhetoric, bare mention will suffice. Nothing could be plainer than that the mounting tide of passionate defense and defiance, of glorification and brag, of high profession, and of zeal for politics, which I have been describing, inevitably bore a people so given to oratory to even more striking extravaganzas in that direction, and to greater susceptibility to it.

10

The Reconstruction years left their mark upon the religious pattern of the South, too, and deeply. In New England, and to some extent all the Eastern states, the influence of the Transcendentalists and the Unitarians had already, as is common knowledge, set up a definite drift toward the general sophistication and liberalization of the old beliefs. And in the decades from 1870 to 1900, this drift, reinforced by the rapid spread of scientific ideas, would continually gather head. More or less complete and open skepticism would become an increasingly common phenomenon. And everywhere north of the Potomac and Ohio rivers piety, remaining always a mighty force, would nevertheless grow steadily more gentle, more vague, and at the same time more rational.

But in the South the movement was to the opposite quarter. For invariably when men anywhere have come upon times of great stress, when they have labored under the sense of suffering unbearable and unjust ill and there was doubt of deliverance through their own unaided effort, they have clung more closely to God and ardently reaffirmed their belief. Invariably they have tended to repudiate innovation, to cast off accretion, to return upon the more primitive faith of the past as representing a purer dispensation and a safer fortress. And if I have represented our Southerners as determined to have the mastery, yet it must be said that terror was continually threatening to seize the ascendancy, that there was in their thought a huge vein of gloomy foreboding, which trembled constantly on the verge of despair.

Streaming with this was the fact that the level of education and information in the South fell tragically in these decades. Actual illiteracy increased among the millions. But what was worse was that the state universities ceased in effect to exist for loyal whites in the Thorough period and went for long years thereafter with empty halls and skeleton faculties, and that other colleges and schools died literally by the score. Many of the men whose fathers had boasted degrees or academy training had now, in this moneyless, passion-engrossed world, to content themselves with such sketchy knowledge of the three R's as could be snatched in a few months in an occasional " old field " school. If the leadership of the Old South in its palmiest days had too often been only half-educated, even by American standards, the leadership of the land in 1890 would be scarcely better instructed and scarcely less simple in outlook than that of the first generation to emerge from the frontier.

Furthermore, the faith of the fathers was manifestly indicated as a pole for patriotic pride and a shield for the South's defense. To hold fast to it, to retreat on the ideology of the sixteenth century as embalmed in the evangelical heritage, hacking away every excrescence and sternly barring out every notion that might conceivably lead to liberalization, was, in any case, a normal part of the glorification of the past. But to do it at the same time when the

Yankee was falling away was to bolster the Southern pride ever more stoutly with the sense of being a Chosen People, to assert Southern superiority in a way which was felt to be finally decisive, and to stand forth always more unmistakably as the last great champion of the true faith in the world which, with this Yankee in the van, was plainly deserting to Satan.

For such reasons, then, it fell out inevitably that the religion of the South was brought over to the twentieth century as simple, as completely supernatural and Apocalyptic, as it had been in the earliest decades of the nineteenth, and far more rigidly held, far more pugnacious and assertive, far more impervious to change.

God, of course, became more distinctly a tribal god than ever. And yet, in His broadest aspect, He remained, of course again, the Calvinized Jehovah, master of all the living and the dead and resistless orderer of all things from the sparrow's flight to the stately pacing of the stars. Was it a little difficult to reconcile this with the idea of being a Chosen People, with the fact that " an infidel-taught band " had overcome " a Christ-taught band," that the Yankee reigned triumphant while the South wept? Not so. For is it not written that whom He loves He chastens? Did He not suffer the first Chosen People to languish in captivity, to bleed under the heel of Marduk and Ashur and Amon and Baal? No, if it was given to the Yankee still to flourish for an hour or two in his pride, yet he flourished only that the ultimate vindication and triumph of the South might be more manifest and perfect.

It was all the fixed and necessary will of the Lord; so the South must believe in order to nerve itself to endure and to hope. Nevertheless, with the ancient illogicality, there must be no chance taken with that will; it must be conciliated with redoubled care. There had been too much indifference in the Old South, too little submission to the law of Heaven as it was transmitted through the ministers, too easy a wearing of the yoke. There had been too much dancing and gaming, too much drinking and laughing, too much delight in the flesh under the amorous sun.

Instead must come the most humble and patient acceptance, the

most assiduous profession of resignation to and trust in the in-
scrutable Wisdom. What the ministers proclaimed as the divine
desire must be obeyed without question and without hesitancy,
lest the hour of the South's deliverance be fatally postponed; and
it must be so obeyed not alone by way of profession but also by way
of public conduct. In these decades the power of the evangelical
ministers, waxing conclusively prescriptive for opinion, made the
official code of the South ever more Puritanical and repressive. Save
among the moribund Virginians and the more abandoned poor
whites, the fiddle was silenced and limbs grew heavy and pompous; wine vanished from the table and alcohol became a demon to
be eschewed on pain of ruin in this world and damnation in the
next. In the end, indeed, almost the only pleasures which might
be practiced openly and without moral obloquy were those of
orgiastic religion and those of violence.

All of which means eventually that the old cleft in the Southern
psyche was still further widened. For, as I have elsewhere indicated, the essential power of the pleasure principle remained intact.
Rendered well-nigh entirely furtive and subterranean, and subli-
mated to an unhappy extent in the sinister and the hysterical, the
Southerner's primary love of play, of the convivial, nevertheless still
lived on in its own more or less innocent right, to send him sneak-
ing into the woods with his cards, forgathering with his cronies
over a jug behind the barn, slipping away over the river in the
nighttime to a cockfight or a breakdown; to bind him to his flesh-
pots behind the arras, and to break forth in queer, feverish fits of
defiance and abandon.

Hoggishness in enjoyment swelled naturally, on the principle
that taboos which overpass what is possible to human nature in a
given milieu are always the death of true restraint. And, more
curious, there came clearly into view something that had perhaps
already existed in the Old South: a tendency on the part of many
Southerners to find positive pleasure in the furtive itself, to require
secrecy and the guilty sense of sin as necessary conditions of the
highest zest. But of anything that could be properly called true

hypocrisy there was little more, I think, than before. As ever, the two currents of Puritanism and hedonism continued to flow side by side to opposite quarters, crossing often, certainly, but never to the production of an impasse, never beyond the possibility of amicable adjustment. God was stern, yes, but if one gave uncompromising allegiance to the Right, well, He knew the strength of the world and the Enemy, how sweet was profitless mirth; He would not be too hard on the sound in doctrine and the contrite.

II

The final great result of Reconstruction we have to consider in this chapter (a result which stands as a sort of summation of the things we have been seeing) is that it established what I have called the savage ideal as it had not been established in any Western people since the decay of medieval feudalism, and almost as truly as it is established today in Fascist Italy, in Nazi Germany, in Soviet Russia — and so paralyzed Southern culture at the root.

Here, under pressure of what was felt to be a matter of life and death, was that old line between what was Southern and what was not, etched, as it were, in fire and carried through every department of life. Here were the ideas and loyalties of the apotheosized past fused into the tightest coherence and endowed with all the binding emotional and intellectual power of any tribal complex of the Belgian Congo. Here was that mighty frame the Democratic Party, as potent an instrument of regimentation as any totemic society that ever existed. In a word, here, explicitly defined in every great essential, defined in feeling down to the last detail, was what one must think and say and do.

And one thought it, said it, did it, exactly as it was ordained, or one stood in pressing peril of being cast out for a damned nigger-loving scoundrel in league with the enemy. Let a man deviate from the strait way once, and by dint of much eating of meek bread he might yet win forgiveness. Let him deviate twice, three times, and men's eyes were hard and dangerous in his, women began to gather their skirts closely about them as they passed, doors that had formerly swung hospitably open slammed in his face, marriage into a decent family became difficult or impossible, the children in the village street howled and cast stones, the dogs developed an inexplicable eagerness to bite him, his creditors were likely to call in the sheriff.

Had it still been possible in the Old South to be an open atheist or skeptic without suffering any. physical penalty? Pious and patriotic drunks, riding home from a camp-meeting or a party rally, were apt now to send bullets crashing through the unbeliever's windows. And sooner or later the Klan was almost certain to pause in its routine labors long enough to teach him reverence and a proper regard for the safety of his country with a horsewhip or a coat of tar.

Tolerance, in sum, was pretty well extinguished all along the line, and conformity made a nearly universal law. Criticism, analysis, detachment, all those activities and attitudes so necessary to the healthy development of any civilization, every one of them took on the aspect of high and aggravated treason. Indeed, this is only half to state the fact, for the peculiar effect of the extraordinarily close identification of the individual with the idea of the South, and of the continually sharpening personal outlook, was this: that any questioning or doubting of the South in any respect (and in this atmosphere of boiling emotion, merely to stand aloof a little was *ipso facto* to be convicted of such questioning and doubting) was inevitably felt by each loyal Southerner as a questioning and doubting of his immediate ego. Which is to say that, being what he was, he inevitably felt it as a challenge to be resisted with all the enormous pugnacity at his disposal, as an affront to his person to be avenged with every means he could command, either alone or in collaboration with his neighbors.

Thus these activities and attitudes, from having long been difficult and dangerous, became virtually impossible. That intensely personal blackguardism to which criticism had so largely been reduced in the Old South (that blackguardism which, having once been native to all America, was rapidly dying out elsewhere in these years) continued to exist, certainly, and not only continued to exist but flourished and waxed fat as a weapon against the Yankee, a whip for the traitor, the rebel, the dissentient, a power for conformity. But of rational casting of light into the fabric of the South itself, or standing apart and examining and evaluating it in any part, of candid confession of the fact that this society, like all others, was imperfect, of honest facing of the evils which abounded — of all this there was almost nothing from the day South Carolina announced herself a sovereign power until Walter Hines Page and George Washington Cable tried it in the middle eighties — Page as editor of a weekly newspaper in North Carolina, and Cable with the publication of his book *The Silent South*. And despite the fact that both went about it more or less gingerly, the attempt brought down upon their heads such a flood of rage that they abandoned it as hopeless and removed to Yankeedom.

Nor have we done yet. Reconstruction not only did all the things I have just set down, but in the same process, as we need to observe specifically, it also completed the South's old terrified truculence toward new ideas from the outside. Here, you see, were the Civil War, Emancipation, Thorough, Equality (even Superiority) for the Negro — the whole vast effort to coerce and destroy, the entire body of the South's troubles — flowing out of Yankee civilization and the Yankee mind. Here, again, was that incalculably sensitive and fierce determination engendered in the South not to be coerced or destroyed in any essential part of its being. And so here, by an extension which would have been inevitable in any people and which was doubly inevitable in this one with its habitual incapacity for distinctions, was a propensity to see in every notion coming out of the North a menace and an abomination; to view every idea originated by the Yankee or bearing the stamp of his acceptance as containing hidden within itself the old implacable will to coerce and destroy; to repudiate him intellectually as passionately as he was repudiated politically.

And in this connection we come upon a figure which deserves some notice. I mean the Yankee schoolma'am who, in such numbers, moved down upon the unfortunate South in the train of the army of occupation, to "educate" the black man for his new place in the sun·and to furnish an example of Christian love and philanthropy to the benighted native whites. Generally horsefaced, bespectacled, and spare of frame, she was, of course, no proper intellectual, but at best a comic character, at worst a dangerous fool, playing with explosive forces which she did not understand. She had no little part in developing Southern bitterness as a whole and, along with the peripatetic Yankee journalist, contributed much to the growth of hysterical sensibility to criticism. But nowhere was her influence more important than at the point with which we are engaged.

For if she was not an intellectual, the South, with its vague standards in these matters, accepted her as such. It saw her, indeed, as a living epitome of the Yankee mind, identified her essentially with the Northern universities, took her spirit for that of the best intelligence beyond the Potomac, read in the evils springing abundantly from her meddlesome stupidity categorical proof that Northern "theory" was *in toto* altogether mad. And so she served as a distinct power in bringing Southern fear and hate to explicit focus in the purely ideological field — in setting up as definite a resistance to Yankee thought as to Yankee deeds.

12

But the ultimately decisive force in establishing this focus and this resistance was, of course, theology, and the ministers. To appreciate this fully, however, we need to pause to remember that when we say Yankee thought and the Yankee mind we are in effect saying modern thought and the modern mind.

Already far advanced in the new mechanical civilization of the West even before the Civil War, the North was, as everyone knows, to forge ahead in the post-war decades with mounting acceleration, steadily taking away the leadership from England, and progressively moving toward its ordained rank as prime exponent of it all. And as it did this, it passed also, as steadily and almost as rapidly, under the influence of that corpus of new ideas and new knowledge, that mighty expansion of man's heritage, which accompanied the growth of the mechanical civilization in Europe in the nineteenth century. In the years from 1880 to 1895 all the great Northern schools were completely made over. And by 1900 the whole of Northern thinking, properly so called, was impregnated with the new *Verstand*. By 1900 Yankeeland had definitely taken its place in the vanguard and was already becoming a chief protagonist, not of the machine alone, but of the modern intelligence as well.

But now, as I need hardly tell you, the parsons of the South regarded the growth of this modern mind with a terror which, by so much as their faith was more primitive and absolute, was even greater than that with which it was regarded by Occidental theologians generally; they saw in it simply the Faustian hell-compact, a gigantic conspiracy to crush truth out of the world, to loose the beast in man, and to strip them of their ancient sway. Determined to preserve their flocks from its contamination at any cost, they were honestly convinced, without ever so stating the proposition to themselves, that the use of any means to the purpose was justified, and even required of them by Heaven.

Long since we have observed them as they noted its first landing on the shores of the American Republic and have heard them raising the cry of " infidel " and " pagan " against Yankeedom, and proving it by the fact that this " European gangrene " was being suffered to flourish there. Long since, that is to say, we have found them quick to grasp the value of hate of the Yankee in relation to it: quick to see that, by identifying it as the peculiar property of this Yankee in America, it was possible to bring that hate fully to bear on it; to reinforce the theological fury they could stir up against the thing in its own right, with an even greater patriotic fury; in fine, to focus against it the whole mass of Southern loyalties and thus effectually to quarantine it at the Potomac.

And now, as the menace engulfed the world and swung close — why now, as the identification of Yankee and modern ideology waxed increasingly real and complete, they gave themselves with crusading energy to hammering home in the minds of their followers the notion of the two as one and inseparable, and to directing the South's fear and anger and pride to the repudiation of Yankee thought and, with it, the thought of the world.

Darwin, Huxley, Ben Butler, Sherman, Satan — all these came to figure in Southern feeling as very nearly a single person. And " infidel, atheistic, and Yankeeizing " would be a formula which, explicitly or implicitly, would be repeated ten thousand times in these years.

If it had been possible in the Old South for a Langdon Cheves to entertain the idea of evolution before the publication of *The Origin of Species,* and to make no secret of the fact that he did entertain it, he would be almost the last of his kind before 1900. When **Dr.** James Woodrow came back from studying in Europe in the 1880's and attempted to set it before his pupils at the Presbyterian theological seminary in Columbia, South Carolina, he found himself denounced from one end of the South to the other both as un-Christian and un-Southern; he was adjudged guilty of heresy by the Southern Presbyterian Church, driven out of his post at the seminary, and forced to be circumspect in order to hold another at the College of South Carolina. And when a young Yankee professor at Vanderbilt University, Alexander Winchell, ventured to think that there was probably something in the notion that man had existed before the reputed fashioning of Adam on an October morning in the year 4004 B.C., he was informed that " our people are of the opinion that such views are contrary to the plan of redemption," stripped of his office, and sent home to his native Michigan with the Tennessee Methodist Conference's denunciation of himself as an emissary of " scientific atheism " and " untamed Speculation " ringing in his ears.

But, after all, there were fewer such heretics dismissed from Southern institutions of learning in this period than from Northern ones? So there were — for the good reason that these men I name stood almost alone; that avowed champions of Darwinism simply did not develop in Southern schools in any appreciable numbers. On the one side of the matter, even first-rate minds were so tightly bound in the ruling pattern that the hospitality to novel notions normal to such minds was almost fully paralyzed. And on the other side, even if the College of South Carolina could protect Dr. Woodrow and even eventually make him its president, if another institution or two, such as Virginia and the Episcopalian Sewanee, perhaps encouraged a reasonably honest instruction in the theory, the overwhelming body of Southern schools either so frowned on it for itself or lived in such terror of popular opinion that possible heretics could not get into their faculties at all or were intimidated into keeping silent by the odds against them.

There were exceptions, of course. But such men as had the boldness of mind to break through to unequivocal acceptance of Darwin and Huxley and to saying so were naturally the sort who quickly found the road into the great Yankee universities open to them and candidly took the way of discretion. Until the turn of the century such instruction in the theory as was to be had in the Southern lyceums (it was simply not to be had in some of them) would be almost universally an essentially bootleg thing, or a thing passed over so hastily, and swathed in so many qualifications and disavowals of belief, that it was rendered almost sterile and most often either left the student's mind untouched.

And outside the schools almost the only persons in the South who would know anything about this Darwinian doctrine in these years were a small company of medical men. And these commonly indulged their curiosity with the stealthiness of a medieval alchemist about the business of wheedling the secret of the philosophers' stone out of the Fiend.

And so it went through the whole catalogue of modernity. Southerners were pioneers in this time in certain philological paths, but only in those which were far removed from any possible conflict with the prevailing ideology. And for the rest — for philology and textual criticism as applied to Holy Writ, for anthropology, ethnology, archæology, geology, comparative religion, the very findings of chemistry and physics, the effort to establish a history which should be more than a form of folk-boasting, a science of politics, economics, and sociology which should be more than a mere rationalization of the *status quo* — not one of these entered fully and generally into the curricula of Southern colleges or got more than cursory and grudging attention in any quarter, most of them in fact being flatly ignored in many; and not one of them entered to any recognizable extent into the fabric of Southern thought in the period.

Always simple in its culture, always inclined to lag, never having had within itself any very fecund principle of intellectual development, the South had now, as it were, drawn a ring about itself, as narrowly coincidental as might be with the past. Within that ring it had established a rule which inevitably crushed whatever tendency to internal growth may have appeared. And on that ring it had erected a rampart, topped in effect with a *chevaux de frise* which barred every fructifying notion from without. The result, in a world of poverty and necessary absorption in material problems, was complete stagnation.

13

There is one curious and apparently paradoxical fact here which must be considered before we leave this theme. I mean the fact that it was in this period that the South began at last to have a literature — or at least that it began to have a number of people who devoted themselves to the writing and publishing of novels, stories and sketches, and poetry.

But the actual amount of paradox involved is very small. Set Sidney Lanier to one side, say of him that, though he was both derivative and didactic, he was probably as authentically a poet as any other American of his time, Walt Whitman alone excepted; and we shall have reduced the paradox almost to the vanishing point.

We must bear in mind that it was natural for an occasional scion of the old gentlefolk of the South, faced in these lean years with the necessity of earning his own living, and finding in his temperament no taste for politics and action, to turn to writing as the solution of his personal problem. We must remember also that some of these writers had ability, and hence would perhaps have taken to the pen in any case. But when all is said and done, it seems to me that the decisive factor for the almost sudden appearance of this literature was social — that the outburst proceeded fundamentally from, and represented basically the patriotic response of the men of talent to, the absorbing need of the South to defend itself, to shore up its pride at home, and to justify itself in the eyes of the world.

In other words, what we really have in the literature of the Reconstruction era is, in its dominant aspect, a propaganda. Its novels, its sketches and stories, are essentially so many pamphlets, its poems so many handbills, concerned mainly, as is common knowledge, with the Old South, and addressed primarily to the purpose of glorifying that Old South — to the elaboration of the legend, and the conviction of both the people at home and the world outside of the truth of that legend in its fullness. Their tone is definitely polemical and forensic. Often, indeed, their form is simply that of the old rhetoric of stump and platform — the Southern oratory — brought over and set down on paper in all its native turgidity, bombast, and sentimentality; and in most cases the influence is plain.

Is this to say that this literature ought to be dismissed as entirely worthless, as having no significance whatever save as shield and buckler for the embattled South? Not so, of course. If its abrupt rise is not to be laid to any intellectual and artistic ferment, yet, for all that, here was a fateful beginning made. Here was a habit, a tradition, of some kind of writing set up. Here at last was a segment of Southern talent brought conclusively to the use of the pen. And here was example. Here were men — and women — earning a more or less adequate living by the practice of this trade, and, what is more, even winning a certain honorable status through it. True, few of their countrymen ever actually read their productions, and most of their sales and most of their fame were achieved in the North. No matter. In the nature of the case the South was increasingly moved to take a vague pride in them, to yield them the awe with which simple men view the success of incomprehensible powers, to grant them a kind of respect. Here was the channel plainly cut out for all those gifted lads who felt in their souls that they could never be elected Governor, for all those gifted lads who should come hereafter.

Moreover, there was in some of these writings, from the first, a distinct if nearly always secondary measure of literary value in the true sense. Once set at a desk with a quill, talent, in so far as it was really such, inevitably tended to assert its natural right, to bear its possessor, at any moment when he happened to be off his guard, into the detachment which is the prime necessity of the artist, to struggle against the strait-jacket of propagandizing purpose and to break out of it at every opportunity. In the case of Joel Chandler Harris it all but completely breaks clear; the secondary values seize command and become the primary ones. Plainly having in it the will to render the Old South as an idyl, *Uncle Remus* nevertheless succeeds in being an authentic creation, in catching almost without exaggeration and without false feeling a fact and a mood which actually existed. Or, again, Cable's *The Grandissimes,* so predominantly a piece of sentimental glorification that it goes mainly unread nowadays, yet had so many flashes of untrammeled insight, so many sudden lapses into realism, that his countrymen actually denounced it as a libel. And there are even passages in Thomas Nelson Page, the very forefront of propaganda, in which the advocate is all but submerged in the artist.

Propelled into the practice of letters by sociological forces, never able in these years to escape from the stultification which the dominance of a too great and too immediate patriotic bias involved, the South was yet swinging slowly and always toward a time when it should come to the use of literature more or less purely for itself. And toward the end of the period this tendency would reach definite realization in a young woman living at Number 1 Main Street at Richmond in Virginia. By 1900 Ellen Glasgow was beginning decisively to stand apart, to approach the materials of her world almost exclusively from the viewpoint of the artist.

CHAPTER II

OF QUANDARY — AND THE
BIRTH OF A DREAM

But our story of the effect of Reconstruction on the South, of the land's long struggle for mastery, is still incomplete. There remain those changes which I have announced, but have so far dealt with only casually or not at all. And to understand them fully, we need to fall back to about the year 1880 and once more take up the process of analysis.

At that period we find the South already definitely moving on the road to political mastery. Tilden has been elected President of the United States, and in order to steal the job from him in decent Christian form and without too much uproar, the tariff gang has consented to buy Southern acquiescence by withdrawing the Army. The carpetbaggers, left more or less to stand on their own bandy legs and rendered neurasthenic by haunting visions of Ku-Kluxers, are hurrying home their last consignments of loot; the more astute scalawags are beginning to take thought for cover; and Cuffey, the black man, is surrendering the dream of forty acres and a mule. The fight is not over yet, no. For twenty years to come the South must balance precariously between what is necessary to establish full sway for the Democratic Party and to divorce the Negro from the ballot, and what would inevitably bring the bayonets back again. For twenty years those perpetually impending Yankee threats will have to be circumvented with elaborate caution. Still, on the whole the advance will be certain. For all of occasional setbacks, the control of Southern government by

Southern white men will wax continually more complete and free.

None the less, mastery in any whole sense is as far from achievement as ever. If the frontier created by the Yankee's activities is beginning to give way on this political side, the case is very different on the economic side; here it is neither receding nor even remaining static, but sweeping on to ever more dismaying proportions. The jungle growth of poverty and ruin is closing on the Southern white man's clearings faster than he can make them, and threatening — as time goes on, threatening with increasing force — to stultify the gains made in the political field.

It had been obvious from the first, of course, that the South's most pressing internal need was for money. To get money, then, it had turned with absorbing passion to the extension of the only practice which, in its experience, had yielded it: the cultivation of cotton. In the years from 1875 to 1890 it would double its annual production of the staple; and in the next decade it would triple it. But so far from affording the expected relief, cotton, always fickle and dangerous, was developing now into a Fata Morgana, the pursuit of which was actually bearing the South deeper and deeper into trouble.

To grasp the fact here in its fullness, we have to notice first just where and how this increase in production was achieved. Some little part of it is explained by the opening of new lands westward of the limit reached by the plantation in the days before the war. Possibly a greater part is accounted for by the adoption here and there of more intensive methods on the old plantation lands. But the greatest part represented the calling into use of those old lands which in the antebellum South had been adjudged as of no worth for the growing of the fiber; the progressive passage of the culture into the fringes, the contained areas, and the upland borders of the original plantation country; the lands, that is, of the yeoman farmers and, to a large extent, of the poor whites.

But these lands, you will recall, were relatively, and often absolutely, poor lands. And cotton is a voracious plant. To grow it here at all would require fertilizers, and in growing quantities. Moreover, the conversion of the yeomen and the poor whites to cotton culture meant that, in greater or less measure, they ceased to be self-sufficient in food; they no longer produced provender enough at home to take care of themselves and their animals from crop to crop, and must, therefore, somehow manage to secure it from outside.

To this it is to be added also that cotton had long ago begun to exhaust even those plantation lands which had once seemed so eternally fecund; and that now perhaps the greater part of them were demanding fertilization almost as necessitously as those of the very poor whites. And on these plantation units, with from twenty-five to five hundred human mouths and half a dozen to a hundred mules to be fed from crop to crop, plantation units which had never been even remotely self-sufficient in this respect and which were still less so as time went on, the amount of aliment which had to be got from without was staggering.

2

But in the nature of the case virtually none of the farmers and none of the poor whites were in any position to finance for themselves these needs. Having to have fertilizers and food, they had to have credit. Nor was the condition of at least nine out of every ten planters any better. The financing of the plantation had always been too much for the individual planter. Even in the happiest days before the Civil War, all but the wealthiest and the most thrifty had been dependent upon the services of the cotton factor, a sort of combination banker, merchant, and sales agent located in the central markets for the staple.

Now, however, to make the circle complete, most of these great factors were bankrupt. And with them had disappeared also the whole credit machinery of the Old South. Of the few banks the region had been able to show, there was scarcely a single solvent one left. And nowhere were there sufficient aggregations of capital to set up a proper banking system anew.

To meet this situation, then, to provide the credit which had to be found, to set the farmers and the poor whites up at cotton farming, to relieve the paralysis of the plantations, there sprang into existence one of the worst systems ever developed: that of the supply merchants.

From one standpoint this system may be said to have been most admirably contrived, for it brought the available resources of the South to focus on the purpose with great effectiveness. Under it practically every man who could lay hands on from a few hundred to a few thousand dollars and persuade the wholesale houses in the North to extend him credit was soon or late borne almost irresistibly by the prospect of its rewards into establishing shop and holding himself out to supply guano and bread to two or three, a dozen, or a hundred of his neighbors, according to his resources. So thoroughly were such poor hoards of mobile capital as could be found in the South captured for the end that by the 1880's almost every crossroad was provided with at least one such banker-merchant, and every village had from two to half a score. Thus the necessary credit was achieved, as it could not, perhaps, have been achieved in any other manner.

The evil thing was the price which had to be paid. Virtual monopolists in relation to their own particular groups of clients (for though they were numerous, they were nevertheless not numerous enough, for a long time at any rate, for competition to be of any considerable importance), these new masters of Southern economics were not slow to see that it was in their power to exact whatever rate of payment they pleased. Moreover, they themselves were subjected to harsh terms by the Yankee dealers, and the risks they took were great. And so they fastened upon the unfortunate Southern cotton-grower terms which are almost without a parallel for rigor. Specifically, what he had to submit to in order to get credit from this source was the following: first, he gave a mortgage on the projected crop; next, he usually, if not strictly always, gave

a mortgage on the land on which the crop was to be grown —
often on all his lands and chattels — and finally, he undertook to
pay charges which, what with " time prices," interest rates, and so
on, commonly averaged in most districts from 40 per cent to 80
per cent.

In sum, the growing of cotton in the South was saddled with a
crushing burden, with such a burden as no agricultural product
could be expected to bear and still afford a decent return for the
producer.

But this is as yet only half the tale. Despite this handicap, the
South might still have had some hope in cotton; if only the price
of the fiber had held up to the high levels prevailing in the first
decade after the war. But of course it didn't. The swift extension
we have been looking at speedily brought on a condition bordering
upon, and often falling into, a glut in the world market. As early
as 1878 the price had dropped to ten cents. And in the next twenty
years, the general trend was fatally downward, until in 1898 it
plunged to below five cents — the lowest level in history. For all the
period from the late 1870's to the early 1900's there was not a year
in which the average return per acre was more than fifteen dollars;
and there were years in which the return for great areas of the
South was hardly more than half that.

3

The sociological and psychological consequences of this situation were varied and far-reaching. But the first thing we have to
observe is that it brings us fully into that major change at which
I have glanced already: the turning back of the South on the road
to aristocracy, and the beginning of decay, in planter and the superior sort of yeoman, of the actual content of the pattern at the
same time when the legend of its full and inalienable inheritance
was being finally elaborated.

For here, you see, was created a world in which the hard, energetic, horse-trading type of man was remorselessly indicated for survival — even more remorselessly, indeed, than in the old days when the plantation was flinging out over the backcountry, and land-speculation and wildcat finance were the prevailing order. To have any fair chance of coping with the new exigencies, that is, these Southerners were almost irresistibly summoned back upon the old backcountry heritage which had been progressively falling out of view in the last decades prior to the war.

All the elaborately built-up pattern of leisure and hedonistic *drift;* all the slow, cool, gracious and graceful gesturing of movement — which, if it had never been generally and fully established in sober reality, had nevertheless subsisted as an ideal and a tendency — was plainly marked out for abandonment as incompatible with success. And along with it, the vague largeness of outlook which was so essentially a part of the same aristocratic complex; the *magnanimity* in the old-fashioned sense of the word, with its contempt for mere money-grubbing, and its positive pride in a certain looseness of attention to affairs, in scorn for thrifty detail; the careless tolerance of inefficiency and humane aversion for the role of harsh taskmaster, which had gone so far by 1858 that Olmsted estimated that, on some plantations, a Negro did no more than a third of the work done by a hired farm-hand in New York State.

To make certain of getting the last penny of the possible returns with the fewest possible hands and the least expenditure of labor costs, and to make these meager returns perform the feat of meeting all the charges I have indicated, paying taxes, allowing for the replacement of draft animals every five or six years, maintaining the necessary equipment, and leaving something over to provide for his own family: such was the goal imperatively laid down by circumstances for the man of any considerable holdings.

And so he must give himself to business with a single-minded devotion which had not been the fashion in his country since the days when his sires wrested the earth from the forest with ax and brawn. More, if he were the greater sort of yeoman or the lesser sort of planter, then, always in the first case and very often in the latter, he must himself, along with all his sons, set hand to the plow. And whether his status was great or small, he must generally be out of bed before sun-up, pounding on the doors of his tenants, routing them out from the oldest crone to the child just able to toddle, and hurrying them into the field while the dawn was still only a promise in the east. And having got them there, he must stand over them all day, lashing them with his tongue (and sometimes with the whip itself; for, especially in the deeper South, its use on the Negro was far from having disappeared with the formal disestablishment of slavery), until darkness made further effort impossible.

But this was no more, perhaps, than barely to penetrate the essential shell of aristocracy. There was that here which went deeper and struck into the core of the gentlemanly ideal.

For even after the Southern landowner had complied with the conditions I recite, his troubles were often a long way from being solved. In many instances he was still short of the achievement of bare survival on any terms. And in what was perhaps the majority of cases, he came unavoidably to some such impasse as this: that either he was going to have to deny his children the toys they clamored for at Christmas; to turn a deaf ear to the pleas of his womenfolk for a new coat for winter, a new hat at Easter, a new piano for the parlor, a new coat of paint for the drab nakedness of the house, and, almost certainly, to son Will's ambition to go to college; to resign himself and his family to an unending prospect of accumulating shabbiness and frustrated desire — in many and many a case, indeed, actually to seeing himself reduced to sending his children to school barefoot or all but barefoot in winter, and even to setting his daughters to work in the fields like those of any European peasant or any black man — or he was going to have to trade in the need of his neighbor and to stint and cheat his laborers, the tenants and the sharecroppers.

One might have thought at first glance that the latter could hardly be done. Merely to feed and clothe and house them after any decent standard, and to make that add up to the whole of that portion of their product to which they were legally entitled — there was little room for the profits of skullduggery in this; for so it was likely to turn out naturally, and in the hands of the most honest and generous of men. But that phrase: " any decent standard," is an exceedingly elastic one, of course. And if the standard here was already the standard inherited from slavery, still, given the will, it could be made leaner yet.

The old monotonous, pellagra-and-rickets-breeding diet had at least been abundant? Strip it rigidly to fatback, molasses, and cornbread, dole it out with an ever stingier hand, and particularly in winter when there was no work to be done in the fields; blind your eyes to peaked faces, seal up your ears to hungry whines. New houses must be built now and then? Abandon altogether the standard of the old slave-cabin (which had been at best both solid and more or less tight), and take up in its place the poor white standard at its worst: upend green-pine clapboards into a flimsy box — clapboards which, drying and shrinking, would leave wide slits in the wall for slashing wind and wet. But even a nigger had to have a suit of overalls once in a while? Not at all: put him in guano-sacking and meal-bagging instead. And as for shoes — why, the damn rascal had a pair year before last; if he was fool enough to wear them every day, let him go without.

Add that, under the prevailing system, the landowner commonly had all sales of the product, all settlements, the entire financing and bookkeeping of the unit, entirely in his hands; that he had usually to deal only with the most abject ignorance in his dependents; that his power was inevitably such that he could easily cow or crush any recalcitrant into submission — and the picture is finished.

Few peoples can ever have been confronted with a crueler dilemma than were these planters and labor-employing yeomen of the South. And for none, surely, has the pressure against the maintenance of honor and *noblesse oblige* — the temptation to let go of aristocratic values and fall back to more primitive and brutal standards — been more tremendous.

4

But let us take care to see the result here in perspective. I must not seem to suggest universal and headlong retreat, any uniform and sudden emptying out of the stuff of aristocracy from the South.

So far as that great body of men on whom the complex had never been able to stamp itself save superficially and secondarily — those men in whom it had always been impotent against the old horse-trading instinct and the hard core of the *nouveau* — so far as these were concerned, the process, indeed, tended to be comparatively rapid and simple. Faced with the logic of circumstances, they did not tarry long in coming to terms with it, in making themselves as hard as their individual situations ordained. And some of the worst of them even began before long (without in the least mitigating their assertion of and their belief in their gentility, and often without even putting aside the old naïve habit of noble profession) to find positive delight in the exercise, positive pride in the reputation, of their hardness.

But elsewhere: To begin with, there were those long-realized aristocrats whom I have called the Virginians — a group which, though it does not entirely fit within the frame I have set up here, may, for practical purposes, be treated just as though it did. Typically, they neither could nor would meet the demands of the times. There were men within the fold, certainly, who could and did meet them in their entirety and at their worst. There were, again, individuals of unusual latent energy, who, while holding more or less fast to the better part of their heritage, managed to ride triumphantly through by sheer force. And to this it must be added also that there was in evidence from an early time some normal human tendency (which we shall see emerging more sharply later on) on the part of the young and more malleable to move toward adaptation: some tendency toward immediate and direct decay.

But typically, as I say, they were too firmly bound within their pattern, were at once too soft and too fine. Decay, as it came to them, came rather obliquely than directly; came, for long at least, and ironically, not so much through any even partial surrender to the demands made upon them as through the inevitable consequences of their failure and their refusal thus to surrender. Many of them fell into bankruptcy and found themselves reduced, like their forerunners for whom the cotton frontier of old had been too much, to keeping school or inn. And if the majority survived, they commonly survived to a steadily declining estate.

And flowing with and out of this came terror, defeatism, apathy, the will to escape. A growing inclination to withdraw themselves altogether from the struggle, from a world grown too dangerous; to shut away the present and abandon the future; here to flee to the inglorious asylum of a political sinecure, as likely as not created expressly for the case; there to retreat behind their own barred gates and hold commerce with none save the members of their own caste. A growing tendency to dissociate their standards wholly from reality, and convert them from living principles of action into mere eidolons.

But it is not only the Virginians with whom we have to do. Of the *noveaux* of the Old South, not a few were so far gone in the dawdling habit, so far removed from the nimble diligence of their sires, that they also could not encounter the requirements of the hour and went much the same way taken by their models.

And beyond these were hundreds of others: the flower of those planters and yeomen in whom the notions of aristocracy had fallen on the immensely receptive ground of the old native integrity and decency; hundreds of others who, able and consenting (however reluctantly) to put away languor and ease, to accommodate themselves to the reigning exigencies in every humane and honorable respect, yet, to their everlasting glory, set their faces against them on the inhumane and dishonorable side.

Some of them simply refused to compromise at all: not only would not stint and cheat their dependents, but even clung to the better part of magnanimity; managed somehow to reconcile the assiduous practice of thrift with the maintenance of the old liberal-handed spirit toward the available means; and, in a word, declined to make themselves stingy or mean or petty in any fashion whatever. They wore their patches, they carried lean jowls, they denied themselves and their families, and, if must be, they paid the penalty of economic ruin or decay (and, for all their superior energy, it was so in many a case) with high pride, unflinching and undismayed.

And if, under the law of averages for human nature, the majority of even the better sort did inevitably compromise, then they compromised by iotas and jots — fell back by inches. They compromised no more than was required if they were to avoid extinction. And they did it with reluctance and with genuine grief. They fought valiantly to hold on to the essence of the heritage and strove earnestly to keep alive and potent in their increasingly restless sons a notion of honor distinctly bearing the aristocratic impress, and not altogether without success.

Yet, when all this is said — by token of it, in truth — the central fact stands fast: slowly here, rapidly there, more superficially in the one case, more fundamentally in another, directly or indirectly, the South was slipping back from the gains it had made: was receding avoidlessly and forever from the aristocratic goal of the *ancien régime*. And the old primary, simple, back-country heritage of the vast body of Southerners was swinging continuously up from the obscurity which had sometime engulfed it, toward the mastery of the field again.

On the more superficial side, the change wrote itself unmistakably in the final extinction, along in the early 1890's (at a time, that is, when general violence and, in certain ways at least, the romantic spirit were rolling up to new heights), of the formal duel; the universal enactment of laws against it.

And on the more important side, it wrote itself just as decisively in a gathering tendency toward a more ruthless enunciation, even by good men, of the old brutal individualistic doctrine — which

yet was never felt as conflicting with humane profession and notions of paternalistic right and duty.— that every man was, in
economics at any rate, absolutely responsible for himself, and that
whatever he got in this world was exactly what he deserved.

5

Such was a principal effect of the economic situation on the ruling classes of the South. But there was another effect which we
ought to glance at before proceeding to consider the case of the
poorer whites: that all this increasing difficulty and frustration and
poverty set off a growing restlessness and alarm in these classes.

The matter wore a double aspect. On the one hand, there was
the natural anxiety of every individual for the fate of himself and
his sons; the normal foreboding and terror of his heart when he
looked ahead into a future which became steadily darker and more
menacing from a personal standpoint. And on the other hand, in
such close association with this as to form a single indissoluble
sentiment, there was a not less, and perhaps even more, pressing
social apprehensiveness — a despairing sense that the South as such
was not making the headway which had been hoped for along the
line it was following, was not achieving the economic position held
to be essential to its survival.

And out of this began to emerge the feeling, nebulous at first
but waxing always clearer, that another line must be found, that
somehow some way must be hit upon, at once vastly to widen
the chance for the individual to achieve security and success, and
to bring the necessary wealth and power and strength to the
South in general.

Passing on now to the consideration of the poorer whites, we
find that their fate under the cotton regime was even worse than
that of their superiors. For upon the crackers and smaller yeomen
who turned themselves and their holdings to the production of

the staple, the summons to return to the old frontier heritage, to exhibit the qualities of energy, thrift, and pushing hardness, bore with greatest force of all. For them, indeed, the choice was posed with naked and brutal simplicity. Planted on the lands which returned the leanest rewards, and having no great holdings to be consumed piecemeal while they considered the problem, they had to measure up immediately and completely if they were to keep their heads above water.

Yet, as follows from what we know, they were in general perhaps the least fitted of all groups of Southerners to meet such a demand. Descending from those who in the beginning had had the smallest portion of industry and thrift and acquisitive will — and stripped progressively, through all the intervening years, of these qualities by the passage out and on of those who had been fortunate enough to be born with them; they had been so shaped by long absence of economic and social focus, so habituated to indolence and easy, improvident, undriven living, that they were no more capable of successfully encountering the situation than the softest and most squeamish of their countrymen at the other end of the scale.

Nor, having once succumbed to the lure of cotton-growing, could they ever thereafter fall back to their old way. For the end of the first year or two almost invariably found them heavily in debt to the supply merchant, who drove them with the club of his mortgage to continue in the production of the only crop which meant cash for his hand.

The upshot was that, in mounting numbers, they crashed into disaster. Every year saw thousands of them fail, to be sold out and cut adrift in the world.

Thus, out of the wholesale expropriation of the cracker and the small farmer; and out also, let me be sure to notice, of the extinction of appreciable numbers of the larger farmers and even of people who had been properly called planters, there arose in the South the white tenant and the white cropper, the head and front of the poor-white class from that day to this: a mighty and always multiplying horde of the landless, who, in order to eat, must turn to laboring for their more fortunate neighbors on whatever terms the latter offered.

6

It was a capital development, of course. For here was an end for these people of the independence and self-sufficiency, the freedom from direct exploitation and servitude, which had been so primary for the preservation and growth of the old frontier individualism, for the suppression of class feeling, and the binding of the South into its extraordinary unity of purpose and outlook. The relation of master and man, patron and client, was pouring over into the taboo confines of white men. And the old essentially voluntary and emotional grouping about captains was moving now toward becoming a genuine paternalism — acquiring a basis in force for the exercise of compulsion, and the turning of traditional right and duty into true prescription.

And this, you may think, at first glance, might naturally have been expected to act to overturn and reverse the effect of all that I have been saying previously: to swing these unfortunate ones, and with them the whole body of those common whites who stood in peril of sharing the same fate, back to a clear economic and social focus and to generate in them a sharp class awareness.

Yet, in reality, it was not to be. There was some current set up in that direction, certainly. All through the eighties and the early nineties the common whites may be said, I think, to have been groping in some dim, obscure, and less than conscious fashion toward perception of their position in the Southern world and to have been gathering anger against it. That was one of the elements in the growth of the Farmers' Alliance movement, and the great Populist outbreak of the nineties in which the movement culminated: in the emergence upon the scene of the Southern demagogue as a type, with Ben Tillman of South Carolina as the first great exponent of the role.

But to take it as the decisive element — to make these phenomena testify to the emergence of this groping to the even momentary realization of class awareness in any full sense — to do this, as some of the chief historians for the period have done of late, seems to me to go far beyond the fact. This movement which ended in Populism was essentially only a part of the national agrarian movement; it represented an outburst of the farmer interest against the great cities of the East rather than a class movement within the South itself. The forces behind it here, like the forces behind it in the Middle West, were blind and diffuse rather than clear and pointed: the rage and frustration of men intolerably oppressed by conditions which they did not understand and which they could not control, the most vivid conviction that something was wrong without any comprehensive view of what it might be.

Its attack was directed primarily, not against the planters, and, for all the opposition to the lien laws, not even very definitely against the supply merchants, but against the railroads and two Yankee creations called the Money Power and the Cotton Exchange; its prevailing objective was the seizing of the national government for putting down these monsters. In the beginning it had no extensive local program, and such local program as it afterward developed, though including some desirable minor reforms, like the popular election of United States senators, never really struck into the heart of the internal social problems of the South.

I am not suggesting that there was not something of reality in the notions and objectives of the agrarians. There was. Even the Old South had been pretty much in the position of a European colony set down in a nation side by side with, and forced by the tariff to buy everything it needed from, an economy with a much higher and continually mounting standard of living. For more than half its cotton was sold in the European market, and the price of all of it was fixed, not in New Orleans or Charleston or

Savannah and not even in New York or Boston, but in Liverpool; and so not on the basis of the living standards of the North, but on those of Lancashire and Flanders.

But after the Civil War this position had been made greatly worse. Because of the falling price of cotton, for one thing, of course. Because, for another thing, living standards in Yankeedom were genuinely rising to a striking extent. But also, and perhaps above all, because the tariff gang had now got a completely free hand. The South in the nineties, having to sell its product for the lowest prices in history, was having to buy its wants at prices held to the very highest level that even the Yankee standard of living would bear — by far the highest level in the world. Which is in effect to say that a very great part of even such poor wealth as it could manage to create was being drained off to fatten the pockets of the masters of the North.

And for all this the popular fee-faw-fum of the Money Power — or, as the phrase went and goes, Wall Street — answered with a considerable degree of accuracy. The great banking interests of New York were an integral, and in the last analysis probably the most essential, part of the tariff gang. And, for that matter, these banking interests were guilty of exploiting the South in other ways on their own private account, the whole system of cotton financing I have described here being in large part simply a reflection of the terms imposed by them on Southern bankers and merchants or those persons in Yankeedom who supplied Southern bankers and merchants.

Nevertheless, the fact remains that, so far from proceeding fundamentally from internal division in the South or representing a revolt of the commoners against the ruling orders, the movement with which we deal here distinctly began as a union movement of all the agricultural classes — with planters and yeomen in the van and such poor whites as participated trailing along with more or less of listlessness. " To organize the cotton belt of America so that the whole world of cotton raisers might be united for self-protection " — such, precisely, was the watchword of Macune, the great moving spirit in the growth of the Farmers' Alliance. And Ben Tillman himself was no poor white but a considerable land-owner, who got into politics, according to his own account of the matter, because he was tired of falling in and out of bankruptcy and of seeing his neighbors, both great and small, performing in the same manner, and wanted to see if something couldn't be done about it. Nor was his dominant theme ever the plight of the tenants and the croppers as such, but that of the cotton-grower in general.

And if this movement did eventually bring on division in the South? It brought it on only when the national issue of Free Silver was injected into the case. Moreover, the division which took place along the line of this issue was very far from being clearly a division according to class. True, the majority of the planters and of the old chieftains of the Democratic Party — good con-servatives, like the holders of great property and power in every time and place — fled aghast, and henceforth labored arduously to destroy the whole agrarian movement. True, the majority of the yeoman farmers promptly got their backs up on the other side, bitterly denounced the " gold-bugs " as enemies of the poor and friends of the Yankee harpies, and set themselves fiercely to turning the " Bourbons " and the " brigadiers " out of power at home. But even here the break was by no means coterminous with class. Not a few planters and even some of the old party captains went with the Populists, and a considerable wing of the yeoman class cast its lot with " sound money " and the " Bourbons."

And the tenants and the croppers — the poor whites in the strict-est sense? Here is the conclusive test. The majority of them never departed in the least from their ancient allegiance, held fast to the side of their old captains. And of those who did go in for Popu-lism, the greater number continued always to exhibit that lack of intense enthusiasm I have already noted.

No, we cannot take the movement here as proceeding from, or as testifying to the appearance of, an overt and realized class aware-ness in the South. None the less, it did have in it, as I have said, that element of groping. It did testify, in some secondary but real manner, to the festering of that irritation and resentment which had existed in the depths of the common white even in the Old South — to the advance of at least a great many of these common whites along the way. It did represent to a ponderable degree the flaring forth of an impulse to return to active concern with their economic and social status, and to make use of the political means to the end of its ratification.

Well, but if that is so, I land myself in contradiction? For surely, if the impulse was here, if it was growing, it would inevitably go on? The very bitterness of this Populist struggle, the wounds inflicted, would lend it a vast new impetus, so that hereafter we shall have to reckon with it as a force, swelling slowly in the absolute, perhaps, but nevertheless swelling certainly, and without a break, rising every year more distinctly into view, and every year steadfastly sapping the cohesive power of the Southern complex?

Not so, however. Having swung up to the point of this Populist outbreak, it was in fact to fall back — dead? Not altogether dead, but reduced to essential quiescence for a long while to come.

7

Nor is there any mystery about this, cryptic though it may sound in the bald statement. For when we take into account the whole array of factors involved in the Southern scene in the period, it is plain enough that, however mighty were the forces tending to project these common whites into class awareness and revolt, the forces tending to hold them back were mightier yet.

At the start we need to recall how simple these people were — that they had no training in, and no power of, analysis, no notion of social forces as affecting their lives. We need to remember that they approached the situation I have set forth from within the frame of a pattern accepted as in the nature of things. And that really to suppose them breaking out of it, we have first to suppose them acquiring a whole new habitus of thought and a new complexity of mind.

With that before us, we go on to observe that there was much here, even within the limits of what we have already seen, which lent itself to the maintenance of this approach, which corroborated the habitual viewpoint — much which obscured the situation with which we deal, and kept it from presenting itself to the eyes of the common whites in clarity. Thus, if on the one side the pursuit of cotton was driving the South deeper into general ruin and crowding the mass of commoners down to mortgage-bondage or the estate of the tenant and the cropper, yet there was another face to the matter. It was also, and by virtue of exactly this general ruin and the financial system which made for that ruin, once more flinging open opportunity to certain selected individuals, and more widely than had been the case with the plantation break-up immediately following the Civil War.

Land in these years of plummeting cotton prices and forced sales got to be almost as cheap as it had been on the original frontier; in most places it could be had as low as two or three dollars an acre. Hence whoever was sufficiently industrious and thrifty, sufficiently alive to the main chance, and, let us not forget, sufficiently lucky — whoever could master the trick of somehow extracting a profit from growing the staple, whoever by any manner of horse-trading, of honest enterprise or chicanery, could come by a few dollars for his own — could readily build a small holding into a great one.

But the opportunity on the land was as nothing to that afforded by the career of supply merchant. There was little room here for those not made of the sternest stuff, for those whose will was apt to be deflected by fits of sympathetic imagination. Thousands would attempt it and fail; hundreds of others would barely hang on. But let a man have a firm eye for the till; let him have it in him to remember always that the price of sentimental weakness was disaster, to return a quiet no to the client who was hopelessly involved, not to flinch from the ultimate necessity to which he must often come: the necessity of stripping a father of ten children of his last ear of corn — and his prospects of growing rich were bright.

It is not to be imagined, of course, that all the people who made capital of these opportunities were common whites. The majority probably came from the ranks of the planters and the greater sort of yeomen — or, rather, were more often the sons of men who belonged to these groups. Nor was the planter contingent drawn entirely from the lesser or even the coarser sort of family. We can trace the decay of the aristocratic values here, not alone in the fact that such opportunities inevitably accelerated the retreat from these values of people who had never participated in them very seriously anyhow, but also in the fact that the scions of houses which had gone far into them were drawn off in increasing numbers.

Nevertheless, if the majority were not strictly common whites, a great many were, and some of them were perhaps poor whites in the full meaning of that term. Many times was repeated the story of the farm boy who began his career as a hired hand and crowned it with the mastery of a township — the story of the other boy, born in a cabin, who got a job in a country store at the age of twelve, slaved for years at two dollars a week, sleeping on the counter; opened his own establishment with a dozen cases of groceries at twenty; and swept on to the ownership of an unlimited number of mortgages before he was fifty.

Throughout all the years from the withdrawal of the Army down, men from below were making their way up through these channels and willy-nilly establishing themselves in the ranks of the ruling class. The process went on at such a rate, indeed, that before 1890, and for all the balancing tendency of the many failures, it was distinctly expanding the numbers of the ruling class beyond the old limit.

For our purposes here, this means two things: First, the Southern masses were once more being drained of those energetic and sharp-eyed elements which, had they been doomed to share the general fate, might have been expected to stir up and set off social dissatisfaction. And secondly, the spectacle of the constant elevation of these brothers, cousins, friends, confirmed and kept bright in the masses that ancient illusion of free and open opportunity — led each man among them to acquiesce in whatever happened to him, on the economic side at least, as merely a piece of personal bad luck.

8.

Another obscuring factor we must note is that if the common whites were being deprived of their former liberty and, in large numbers, brought within the scope of direct exploitation, it was rather through the impersonal working out of social and economic forces than through any will or purpose to that end on the part of anybody. So far as the planters were concerned, in truth, they had almost as little actual need for the labor of the common whites now as in the Old South. If there were not Negroes enough in the land — and Negroes easily made available — to furnish the entire required quota of tenants and croppers, then there were nearly enough. As witness the fact that from the time of the appearance of the white tenant and cropper, we find growing up in the South a body of Negroes at loose ends, without any definite place in the economic order or any settled means of support. Moreover, many of the landlords undoubtedly preferred black labor, as being more docile.

Some there were, to be sure, who felt the other way about it. There were local shortages of blacks, too. And like employers everywhere, practically the whole lot of the landowners looked on the creation of a reasonable surplus of labor as a very fine thing in itself. But this wholesale falling down of the masses into availability — this was anything on earth but their desire.

In large measure, and in literal fact, they came to the use of white tenants only through the operation of race loyalty and the old paternalism. They felt, mind you, not the slightest responsibility for what had happened to the dispossessed. They despised them now, as a rule, with an even greater doctrinal contempt than they had felt for them in the old days when they could not achieve rich lands and Negroes. Yet . . . here they were, willy-nilly. Under our planter eyes. Men we have known all our days, laughed with, hunted with, and, in many a case, fought side by side with. Human. White. With white women and white children. And having to find employment — or starve.

And if we feel no responsibility for their having landed in this condition, yet it is the law of our personally humane tradition, you will recall, that none must be allowed to starve — certainly not under our eyes — certainly no white man; an essential part of our high profession, of the profoundest conviction in many of us, that it is our duty to look after these weaker brethren, to the extent at least of seeing that they have some such living as they have been accustomed to.

Give them special advantages? We shall do nothing of the kind. We shall give them the same terms we give the Negro. We shall carry over into our dealing with them very much of the attitude toward labor fixed by slavery. We shall curse them roundly for no-'count, trifling incompetents who richly deserve to starve — always in our peculiar manner, which draws the sting of what we say. But look after them we must and will.

More — the finest and best among us, while holding fast to those same legal terms originally set for the black man, not only will discharge those terms to the letter, but will soften the bargain by spontaneous gifts from our own larders: by the perpetuation and even the extension of that personal care and interest we exhibited toward our poorer neighbors in the Old South. And of course many of us will make precious little profit out of these whites, as out of the blacks. They are going to live hard, but so in this lean world and these lean times are we.

The issue of this is manifest, I take it. Coming to the use of these whites as men conferring a favor, the landlords of the South naturally did not see themselves as any wicked oppressors out of a

Marxist legend but as public benefactors; they swelled with pride
in it, had their ancient complacency and self-approval increased,
their confidence in their paternalistic prerogative as necessary to
the happiness of everybody concerned bolstered. And the common
whites saw it and responded to it in cognate fashion. Instead of
anger and resentment, the dominant emotion of the white cropper
or tenant toward the more fortunate neighbor on whose land he
found himself planted, under whose mastery he found himself
lodged, was likely to be gratefulness.

Even the case of the supply merchant was obscure. For one thing,
few of his customers had any notion of what charges they were
being subjected to. For another, he himself was likely to approach
his calling from within the universal Southern habit of high profession; however cynical his deeds may seem, he almost invariably
thought of himself as a great public patron and came to his clients
with the manner and the conviction of conferring inestimable benefits. And, in fact, hadn't he made it possible for you to grow cotton?
Didn't he enable you to keep on in that pursuit year after year?
And if in the end he sold you out, would you, stout individualist,
have done otherwise in his place? Wasn't he kind about it? Didn't
he often see to it that you got a good place as tenant, either on his
own expanding acres or elsewhere? Grumble at him, hate him
spasmodically — you would, of course. But you would never get up
tenacious resentment enough even to keep alive the co-operative
stores the Alliance was setting up against him.

9

But there was in operation here something more potent than any
of this. We have to observe explicitly that the loss of economic independence, the passing of that old freedom from exploitation
which had been so primary for the Southern pattern, took place at
a time when the long-waging battle of Reconstruction had already
done its work — when patriotism to the South had been raised to

the ultimate pitch, when the determination to maintain this South
in its essential integrity burned at white heat in every proper Southern breast, and when, as the heart of it all, the ancient fixation on
Negro, always perhaps the single most primary thing, had been
drawn to consuming monomania: when the white man's pride and
will, and particularly the common white man's, had concentrated
on the maintenance of superiority to that black man as the paramount thing in life.

For, coming to the matter from this position, the common white
inevitably had his attention taken, not so much by the fact that he
had now to submit himself to the will of another, to take orders from
a boss, to work when he would not himself have chosen to work —
bitter though this might be. What fixed his gaze to the eclipse of
everything else was the spectacle of himself being reduced to working side by side, and on the same place, with the black man; his
Proto-Dorian rank, his one incontestable superiority, threatening to
plunge finally and irretrievably down to extinction. What every
white tenant and cropper, every white man in peril of becoming
such, was crying out for first of all in these years was to have this
threat somehow stayed.

In other words, the old scale of values, so far from being over-
turned by the new conditions, would be once more strengthened
and confirmed. Economic and social considerations remained, as
ever, subordinate to those of race — and country. And such being
the case, why, now, as always in the past, it was ultimately quite
impossible for the common white to do anything effective about his
economic and social plight; and so, of course, quite useless for
him to develop class awareness.

Some more than subconscious perception of that block undoubtedly operated in him throughout. And with his progress to Populism it was to be made manifest to him.

To get on to even such amorphic class sentiment as was really
involved in that outbreak; to the use of the political means for the
realization of even such class purpose as he may be said to have had
there; indeed, for the accomplishment of any purpose whatever

against which the ruling orders of his country uncompromisingly set their faces, he would find himself unavoidably and in the inherent nature of the case splitting the Democratic Party — carrying it into being in effect two opposed and bitterly inimical parties. And in North Carolina, where he carried the fight farthest, he would discover himself drawn by iron logic into breaking out of this Democratic Party altogether, first into alliance, and then into fusion with the Republicans. And as the final term of the matter into co-operation with the Negro voter.

But that, as the event was speedily to convince him, at any rate, was fatally to breach the great bulwark of White Supremacy, white unanimity; to strike down the political mastery so long struggled for, so painfully won; to join with the Yankees and with his own hands destroy the whole canon of his first values and his accumulated loyalties; to bring fully upon himself the thing he most feared.

In Craven County, North Carolina, as the peak and crown of it all, sixty-two Negroes got back into office. In more than fifty of the Tar Heel counties black magistrates sat again in judgment on white men — and, as the orators did not fail to note, white women. Black inspectors passed into white schools and gave orders to white teachers, most of them women. Black laughter rolled in flood through Tar Heel legislative halls once more. Black Congressmen sat at Capitol Hill desks and cast the suffrage of Carolina and Dixie in the councils of the nation. And throughout the Southern land, wherever Populism was sweeping on its way, other black men were gratefully hearing the glad news and surging up in emulation — under the leadership of their white manipulators, confidently preparing to return to power.

In North Carolina the Red Shirts were riding, a maskless resurrection of the Ku-Klux Klan. The conservative Democratic forces were restoring to wholesale intimidation of the black voter and practicing wholesale fraud; were stealing votes by thousands in the confidence, fixed by Reconstruction, that it was entirely justified by the end; in the cool conviction even, I think it may safely be said, that it was no mere necessary immorality but the very shape and substance of morality itself. And everywhere violence was flaring; in the Populist year of 1892, 162 Negros were lynched in the South, the greatest number on record for any year. And in the North — Henry Cabot Lodge and company were joyously capitalizing on all this to furbish up the Force Bill once more; were gleefully preparing to send down the Army again.

And when our common white, our Populist of whatever sort, had come to this: The eyes of his old captains were ominous and accusing upon him. From hustings and from pulpits thousands of voices proclaimed him traitor and nigger-loving scoundrel; renegade to Southern Womanhood, the Confederate dead, and the God of his fathers; champion of the transformation of the white race into a mongrel breed. And in his own heart, as he gazed upon the evidence, it was, in ninety-nine cases out of the hundred at least, echoed and confirmed — fearfully adjudged true.

There could be but one outcome. When he had come to this, he fled, as he might have fled had he discovered himself somehow and unbelievably ranged on the side of the legions of the pit; flung himself back fully into the Democratic frame and made the walls of Dixie solid again.

Is that to say that he abandoned his demagogic political captains altogether and went fully back to the old — that the Tillmans vanished from the scene? Of course, as everybody knows, it isn't. Not when they were as canny as Pitchfork Ben himself, at any rate; not when they were quick to read the handwriting on the wall, decisively to abandon agrarian cause and to come to tacit terms with the conservative powers of the Democratic Party. On the contrary, such men were henceforth to flourish with growing luxuriance. And on the other side of the case, the agrarian fight distinctly marks the end of the careers of the Confederate officers, such as Wade Hampton of South Carolina, and the all but final elimination of the strictly aristocratic type of man from Southern politics.

But that is a story which can best be told later on. It is sufficient now to say that no part of it is in contradiction with the conclusion to which my argument here ultimately comes: that, when he had reached the *impasse* we have seen, the common white of the South did in overwhelming tide abandon his advance upon class consciousness and relapse into his ancient focus.

10

Our account, however, is still no more than half complete. Really to understand what went on here, we have to turn back again to notice that if the downgoing of the masses, the emergence of the white tenant and the white sharecropper, had set off some current in the direction of the development of class consciousness, it had also precipitated another movement.

I have told you that the expropriation and collapse of these masses were not the will or the desire of the planters or the ruling classes generally. But that is to phrase it too mildly. In truth, the spectacle inspired them, even in its immediate reality, with the greatest uneasiness. If none of them felt any responsibility for what had happened, or felt they could afford to give the white tenants and croppers better terms than they gave the black, yet some of the best, those in whom the notion of paternalistic duty to the weak was most firmly planted, were indubitably troubled in their hearts by concern for the common white himself, and particularly for the expropriated yeoman; were haunted by the feeling that reduction to servility in competition with the black man inescapably involved degradation for him. And all of them, of whatever kind, felt the general racial and patriotic implications — its meaning for the convention of white superiority and the increasing ruin of the South.

But if the immediate reality inspired them to uneasiness, the manifest prospect filled them with terror. What the lot of them perceived in some implicit fashion, and what the best and most clear-headed saw more or less expressly, was the same thing the common whites were sensing more and more sharply, and which centered *their* terror. I mean that the power of absorbing these expropriated whites had a definite limit — that the South was hurrying fatally, was indeed already distinctly coming into a time when there wouldn't be room enough on the plantation to take care of both the main body of the blacks and this always multiplying army of white candidates — when these whites would be hurled, not only into competition with these blacks but into the most naked and brutal competition — into a struggle to the death for the means of subsistence.

It was a prospect before which the body of the landlords may be said to have distrusted themselves — certainly one before which the best sort may be said to have distrusted the main part of their fellows. It was too clear that the natural operation of individual economic interest, the temptation to take advantage of this competition to beat down the hire of both contestants, would be too strong; that, in the end, perhaps the majority of the common whites of the South would be driven down, not merely to complete economic equality with the Negro, not merely to a far lower standard of living than the old poor standard, but to such a standard as neither white nor black had ever known.

Yet — the prospect of such a result was intolerable. It was intolerable for the best men of the land from the standpoint of *noblesse oblige*. But infinitely more, even for these, and surely for the generality of the ruling order as for other Southerners, was it intolerable from the viewpoint of racial sympathy, racial pride, and love for the South. For who among all these Southerners doubted for a moment that such extensive economic equality, such ruthless dumping of white men into this intimate competition with the Negro, would end in social equality? Who could believe that, once the convention of Proto-Dorian rank was lost to these common white men, it could long survive to any white man? Who did not see, again, that, despairing of their racial status and made frantic by the desperate contest for bare bread, these whites would eventually be swept fully into the bitterest class consciousness; that this slow impulse, which the master class was at least vaguely aware of from the beginning, would develop a power no barrier and no argument could hold back? Who could not see, in a word, that here was chaos? That if it was allowed to run its course, it was very likely to destroy the entire Southern fabric?

The burning concern thus generated in the master class met and married with that other concern which, as we have seen, was generated in them by their own economic difficulties. And marrying thus, it brought to full conviction — explicitly in the most intelligent of the masters, implicitly in nearly all — yes, and in some manner in the whole body of the South — the feeling that somehow another line must be found: that, without ever abandoning cotton-growing of course, the arm of the land must somehow be extended.

So, under the drive of this conviction in themselves and their fellows, there began to grow up in the minds of some of the best of these masters (the old Confederate captains in large part) an idea — a dream. Let us, in this quandary, take a page from the book of Yankeedom. Let us meet the old enemy on his own ground. Let us, in short, turn to Progress.

Let us introduce the factory in force. Let us, in particular, build cotton mills, here in the midst of the cotton fields. Let us build a thousand mills — and more than a thousand mills, and erect the South into a great industrial and commercial empire.

Yes, and there is something else to which we have already been coming obscurely. " In 1876," wrote an old gentleman to a newspaper fifty years after, " I stood in Fayetteville, North Carolina, and saw white youth after white youth turned away from the polls because they could not read and write, while my horse-boy and other Negroes, taught by Northern teachers, were consistently admitted to the ballot. And I swore an oath that so long as my head was hot, I should never cease from fighting for schools until every white child born in the State had at least the surety of a common school education — and a chance to go as much further as he liked." And already a few men of the stamp of J. L. M. Curry, of Alabama, and William Henry Ruffner, of Virginia, had been crying for a decade and longer that mass education was imperatively necessary if the men of the South were successfully to encounter the conditions of their post-bellum world.

Well, let us begin to grasp the idea more firmly now. Let us, at whatever sacrifice, turn to rebuilding the wrecks of our old state universities left us by carpetbag rule, our dead and dying colleges, to establishing dozens of new colleges and academies. Let us have done with our system of occasional old-field schools, kept by the generosity of this or that great man, by neighborhood subscription, by niggardly state aid and sporadic local tax; and fully accept the public school at last.

And while we are about it, why should we not begin even to provide schools for the Negro? There are those among us who are capable of being moved by the argument of a Curry: that we ought to do it, if for no other reason, because we have got him here and owe it to him. There are many more of us who are capable of being moved by the argument of a Henry Grady that it is really to our interest: that the instructed black man can be trusted never to commit rape, and that taught the elementals and perhaps some mechanics (we shall rigidly veto the idea of academic schools for him), he will be distinctly more useful, both to himself and to us. And nearly all of us short of the poor white, with his unreasoning hate and terror, can grasp the logic of a Charles Brantley Aycock of North Carolina that, since it is going to be done anyhow — since the Yankee is plainly determined on it — since Yankee money and Yankee teachers are pouring down — it would be better if we beat him to the draw and did it ourselves.

It will be the perfect defense against the eternal Yankee charge that what we want is to hold him in brutal ignorance in order to keep him in essential slavery. It will soothe our own qualms — the uneasy stirrings of our mortality before our dealing with him; will at once satisfy our need to make the facts square with our humane professions, and that curious sense of duty the best of us indubitably feel toward him. And (as Aycock, who was himself an advocate of Negro education for the Negro's own benefit, but who knew his countrymen, cannily argued) it will enable us to make sure that he acquires no dangerous notions, to control what he is taught, to make sure that he is educated to fit into, and to stay in, his place.

II

The factory and the school, then. With the first of these we shall create a sanctuary for the falling common whites, and place thousands of them in an employment which, by common agreement, shall be closed to the Negro. Largely in fact, completely in some symbolic fashion, we shall rescue them in the respect they most demand to be rescued: shall mightily reaffirm the Proto-Dorian bond and bear up the tradition of unforfeitable white superiority. We shall give them hope — and indeed not only racial hope. We shall give them a distinctly better economic status than that of the cropper and the tenant.

And at the same time when we are fortifying the racial position of these whites — and ourselves — we shall also achieve that widening of opportunity which is felt to be so necessary. Shall achieve it for ourselves (the masters) and our sons, and for every white man who has it in him to grasp it.

With the factory we shall make the South rich. And winning riches, we shall be able fully to develop the school. And with the school, we shall not only set up a potent guarantee that white men shall not sink into equality with the black, we shall also train our sons, and those of the commoners as well, to take advantage of the opportunities afforded by industrial growth and its commercial consequences, and so to make the land richer still.

With the factory and the school, in fine, we shall finally conquer the frontier left us by the Yankee, complete the victory we hold so precariously on the political side, and establish the South on an impregnable base.

Such was the dream which began to form itself in the brain of some of the ablest and most responsible of the Southern leaders.

And such was the program which, once the dream was in them, they set themselves, with the characteristic Southern genius for action, to realize.

It acted upon the South of the time as the sermons of Peter the Hermit acted upon Europe of the eleventh century. It swept out of the minds of the men who had conceived it, to become in the years between 1880 and 1900 the dream of virtually the whole Southern people — a crusade preached with burning zeal from platform and pulpit and editorial cell — a mighty folk movement which already by the turn of the century would have performed the astounding feat (in a land stripped of capital) of calling into existence more than four hundred cotton mills; which already by the turn of the century would be performing the scarcely less striking feat (for this country) of beginning to build a definite public school system, pitifully inadequate, hardly more than embryonic outside the towns and villages as yet, but growing surely and steadily.

Does the reader perhaps suspect the account of the turn to Progress I give here? Is he inclined to think that, in regard to the factory at any rate, the ascription of social and patriotic motives — the assignment to them of such a decisive role in the matter — is gratuitous speculation? Even that the whole notion of a " dream " and a " program," as of a " crusade " and a " folk movement," is probably only a construction of my private fancy — an *ex post facto* rationalization of something which can be satisfactorily explained on no more complex grounds than the operation of the profit motive upon obvious considerations of abundant cheap labor and proximity to raw material — the operation of the profit motive in the individual?

Then let him look into a celebrated monograph, *The Rise of Cotton Mills in the South,* issued from the Johns Hopkins Press in 1921, and authored by Dr. Broadus Mitchell, of the faculty of political economy in the Johns Hopkins University — and he will find comprehensive and carefully documented proof that the facts were essentially as I have said.

Reading these pages, we hear repeatedly, often from the lips of actual participants or eyewitnesses, that the dominant motive was " essentially one of employment," the recognition that " the mill life is the only avenue open to our poor whites," the only avenue " to provide an escape from competition with the blacks." We find the movement specifically described as the Cotton Mill Campaign; its beginnings expressly assigned, in large measure, to the old Confederate captains; its passage through the South likened to the passage of the great Methodist revivals of the early nineteenth century.

We see the newspapers, led by the *Charlotte Observer* and the Charleston *News and Courier,* swiftly taking fire, falling rapidly into line, until in the end they are a virtually solid phalanx, pouring out a continuous propaganda for the vision. The orators hasten to take their cue from Henry Grady. At Salisbury, North Carolina, one Mr. Pearson, holding a revival meeting in an improvised tabernacle, preaches " powerfully " on the plight of the poor whites, declares that " the establishment of a cotton mill would be the most Christian act his hearers could perform " — and next evening at a great mass meeting the village's first mill is actually organized, with another minister at its head. At Clinton, South Carolina, very much the same thing happens under the leadership of a preacher named Jacobs.

The impulse leaps from community to community, as an electric current leaps across a series of galvanic poles — sweeping the citizens into mass assembly, stirring up the old local patriotism so characteristic of the South and setting these communities to striving to outdo one another in furthering the cause, proceeding on a wave of enthusiasm so intense and so general that in many places where poverty is most rampant, where it seems almost impossible to raise sufficient money to launch a mill, it actually sets yeoman farmers, too poor as individuals to provide even so much as a single share of capital, to combining in groups of a dozen for the purpose; sets laborers to forming pools into which each man pays as little as twenty-five cents a week. And an enthusiasm, moreover, so naïve, so headlong, so uncalculating and uncautious as to be almost beyond belief.

" The student of the origin of textile manufacturing in the South," says Gerald W. Johnson, speaking from the Mitchell record and his own unsurpassed knowledge of the country, " is usually dumfounded by the blithe disregard of rudimentary business principles displayed by the early *entrepreneurs.* Aspiring hamlets built cotton mills without any sort of investigation into the advantages of the locality for textile manufacturing. Only in rare instances was the enterprise headed by a man of any experience in business. . . . The usual plan was to select that man in the community who possessed the people's confidence in the highest degree and draft him into service regardless of his previous training. Thus the new mills were headed by doctors, lawyers, teachers, planters, and even clergymen. . . .

" This procedure is as inexplicable as the ravings of the wildest Bedlamite until one remembers the spirit in which the whole venture was conceived, but then it becomes understandable, if not logical. This was not a business, but a social enterprise. Any profit that might accrue to the originators of the mill was but incidental; the main thing was the salvation of the decaying community, and especially the poor whites, who were in danger of being submerged altogether. The record of those days is filled with a moral fervor that is astounding. People were urged to take stock in the mills for the town's sake, for the poor people's sake, for the South's sake, literally for God's sake. . . .

" There was talk of profit in connection with the founding of the mills, but in these early years it never became the dominant motif. Always it was the prospect of civic and social salvation that was stressed. All the money return looked for was expected to accrue to the poor whites and to drag them back from the edge of the abyss obviously opening to swallow them. . . ."

12

But now, of course, the things we have just been seeing set us down squarely into the question of that great revolution which is supposed to have taken place. It is with and in the birth of this dream of Progress that the South is so commonly said to have " suffered a change of heart," to have acquired " a complete new viewpoint," and, deliberately casting loose from the body of its past, to have embarked with conscious purpose upon the way of Yankeedom and modernity. And it is with and in the widening adoption of this dream, the growth of this program in the years between 1880 and 1900, that the revolution is thought to have been substantially accomplished, and a New South called into existence to stand henceforth in fundamental contrast with the Old.

But that there was no revolution in basic ideology and no intention of relinquishing the central Southern positions and surrendering bodily to Yankee civilization involved in the genesis of dream and program, or in their acceptance by the South at large, is pretty plain, I trust, from the story as I have already told it. So far from representing a deliberate break with the past, the turn to Progress clearly flowed straight out of that past and constituted in a real sense an emanation from the will to maintain the South in its essential integrity.

Let us understand this accurately, however. In actuality, there was enormous innovation here, of course; and not only physical innovation. In its inherent implications it was truly revolutionary from several possible viewpoints. And what is more yet, it quite definitely carried in its womb the potentiality — the logical necessity, even — of eventual revolution from our own special viewpoint.

For to accept this Progress at all was manifestly to abandon the purely agricultural basis from which the Southern world, and ultimately the Southern mind, had been reared. To bring in the factory, to turn to the creation of industrial empire, would be to bring in the town — to turn to the expanding of hundreds of crossroads hamlets into bustling hives, the calling into being of hundreds of altogether new hives. And to bring in the machine and the town, again, would naturally be to bring in the laws of the machine and the town.

To bring in the factory and the town — and, let us not forget, to turn to the magnification of the school — would be, in other words, to set in motion almost incalculably great forces for the complication of the social scene, and the multiplication and intensification of conditions in the Southern world working at cross-purposes with the old Southern mind. Almost incalculably great forces to operate for the notable modification of that mind in detail, and often for its modification in the general direction of Yankeedom and modernity; and in the long run to make for manifest impasse with that mind in fundamentals.

But we must not confuse what, from the vantage point of our own times, we can easily see to have been the inherent content of Progress with what was present to the minds of the men who fashioned dream and program, and to the South in general in embracing them. These men saw — the South saw — that they were breaking with the physical order of the past, certainly; they were very well aware that they were giving up the old purely agricultural way of life. They habitually viewed and spoke of the turn as an epochal change — as a revolution, indeed. More: well before 1900, and though they usually began by indignantly repudiating the term, they were speaking habitually and pridefully of the New South.

Few things are more certain, however, than that in none of this was there any realization that the abandonment of the purely agricultural way and the fetching in of the machine would call for the remolding of the old purely agricultural mind — any thought that it meant the reshaping of the ruling Southern ideal after the Yankee model or any other.

So far as the laws of the machine go, we have to recall that nobody in the world at the time, save only a handful of advanced

investigators who were commonly set down for crackbrains, had
any clear notion that they existed, or that the laws of agriculture
were not entirely applicable in the premises. And surely these
Southerners were as innocent of the existence of such laws as the
Trojans were of the Argives crouching in the belly of the wooden
horse on the day they drew it within the gates of Ilium.

And to measure the real importance in Southern eyes of the surrender of the purely agricultural economy, we must understand
that agrarian sentiment, in the sense of a considered conviction that
the soil offers " the only really human way of life," had never, the
facile assumptions of Allen Tate and the Southern Agrarians to the
contrary notwithstanding, got to be a fundamental constituent of
the Southern mind.

The Old South, as I long ago suggested, had originally adopted
its economy, not out of any conscious choice, but simply in obedience to the obvious mandate of the circumstances. Afterward, to
be sure, conflict with the Yankee had had its effect here, too. Glorification of the purely agrarian scheme of things and scorn for the
factory as a part of the scorn for everything that smacked of the
Yankee had in some degree become an integral part of that elaborate proslavery argument which was growing up in the last decades
before Sumter. And in some quarters this had gone so far under
Reconstruction as to give rise now to a definite anti-Progress party
— a small group of bellicose Southern patriots who would loudly
vociferate that to turn to industrialism was, as Charles Colcock
Jones, Jr., of Georgia, put it, to insult the graves of the Confederate
dead and to abandon true civilization in favor of barbarism.

By and large, however, such intense agrarianism was foreign to
the Southern leaders and the body of the South. Nearly every one
of these Southerners had in him, indeed, the great love of outdoor
life natural to those bred for generations as countrymen. He had,
too, a great hunger for possessing the soil — the outcome of what is
perhaps a native impulse of man, of long habit, and of the great
social value which had attached to the ownership of wide acres in

the Old South. But of conscious loyalty to the agrarian way as a primary pole of his patriotism and pride, of loyalty that could contend with his obvious interest, he had little or nothing.

13

When we pass to the question of how far it was intended to imitate the Yankee, and of the content of the New South as the term was used in Dixie, we find much the same sort of thing. If on the one extreme there was to be an anti-Progress party, on the other it is possible to make out a Yankeeizing party: a little group of leaders who insisted that the best thing the South could do would be to set itself outright to imitate the Yankee civilization. We shall have occasion to observe this party gathering strength hereafter. But they exercised little practical influence on the body of their countrymen in the period with which we are dealing. Moreover, almost to a man, they were fuzzy-witted fellows, without any clear understanding of what it was they were proposing. The aspects of Yankee civilization upon which they poured out their admiration were purely the superficial ones; and their professions of boundless liking for the Northern pattern were accompanied by reservations which in fact vitiated them.

Besides these outright Yankee-izers there was also a much larger number of leaders who felt that Progress necessarily called for certain shifts in the prevailing attitude toward the North — men who before long were taking their cue from the Henry Gradys and the Lucius Lamars, and saying that " The South's fight must be made within the framework of the nation " — that the old belligerence must be softened as incompatible with the growth of the new industrial economy.

Nor was this without some reflection in the South as a whole. We have to recognize, what there has been no occasion to recognize before, that the Old South had always had some sentiment of the nation right on down to the Civil War. And once the Army was gone from Southern soil, that sentiment had begun to assert itself again. Slowly, over refusal to display the national banner on public buildings or on occasions of ceremony, over the example and doctrine of men of great rank and prestige who had sworn never again to clasp a Yankee hand, slowly through the eighties, and then more rapidly, loyalty to the Republic was returning. By the mid-nineties the South, as the test of the Spanish-American War was shortly to prove, was once more one with the North so far as standing shoulder to shoulder with it against any outside foe was concerned. And that the preachings of the exponents of Progress had considerable to do with this seems likely.

It must not be supposed, however, that this implies the utter giving over of antagonism within the nation itself; and much less that it means the growth of a willingness to surrender essential Southern autonomy. In so far as they seem to propose a total forgiving and forgetting, the utterances of the leaders themselves had better be taken with a good deal of salt. We have to remember the Southern capacity for high profession, and to take account of the fact that these same leaders were prone to declaim in quite another key than that of conciliation when the theme was, say, the Yankee and the Negro in Dixie. And as for the body of the South, Walter Hines Page came down from the North in the last years before the Spanish engagement, with the purpose of writing a series of articles which should prove that the Civil War and Reconstruction were forgotten, and that the South, completely absorbed in new ideas and new goals, was rapidly becoming another Yankeedom. But having traveled through the region, he abandoned his project as incompatible with reality.

Ultimately, in sum, the revolution which was present to the mind of the South was in large part merely a revolution in tactics. The surrender contemplated was only such a surrender as a general in the field makes when he gives up untenable terrain in order to bring his forces into position to strike more effectively for victory. The

New South meant and boasted of was mainly a South which would be new in this: that it would be so rich and powerful that it might rest serene in its ancient positions, forever impregnable.

That the final objective did not change is written plain in the quotation I have already set down, that " The South's *fight* must be made within the framework of the nation," and in many another possible quotation:

" The South should . . . make money, build up its waste places, and thus *force from the North that recognition* of our worth and dignity of character to which that people will always be blind unless they can see it through the medium of material . . . strength," said the *News and Observer* of Raleigh, North Carolina, in 1880.

" These," cried the *Columbus Enquirer,* of Georgia, speaking of the multiplying spindles — " These are the *weapons* peace gave us, and right trusty ones they are! "

" We shall see," declaimed Henry Grady in a celebrated address, " how the people of this section, reduced to poverty by war . . . met new and adverse conditions with unquailing courage . . . with what patience they bore misfortune, and endured wrongs put upon them. . . . How at last, controlling with their own hands their local affairs, they began, *in ragged and torn battalions, that march* of restoration and development that has challenged universal admiration." (The italics in these passages are mine.)

The language and the figures, you will observe, are basically the language and figures of the Civil War; and the feeling, I am sure, is the feeling of that war also. In the feeling of the South, Progress stood quite accurately for a sort of new charge at Gettysburg, which should finally and incontestably win for it the right to be itself for which, in the last analysis, it had always fought.

Perhaps, however, the reader is thinking that the question of the South's intention does not really matter much. Granted that the making over of the fundamental pattern was the antithesis of the Southern purpose in the turn to Progress, those inherent revolutionary factors I have referred to would nevertheless still be present? In proportion to the speed with which industry and commerce were brought in, they would be steadily working themselves out during the last two decades of the nineteenth century, regardless of whether the South knew it or not? Gradually but certainly subverting the ancient social order in its deepest foundations? By insensible degrees, but continuously and cumulatively, acting upon and remolding the Southern mind in its basic categories, so that in the end, for all the conscious loyalty and intransigence, the South we actually find as we come into the twentieth century will be one which, if it has not yet fully emerged from the old frame into a new, is at least well into the process — hurrying along the route in mounting tempo?

But, as a matter of fact, the practical outcome was rather the other way about.

BOOK THREE

The Mind of the South
ITS SURVIVAL, ITS MODIFICA-
TIONS, AND ITS OPERATION
IN OUR TIME

CHAPTER I

OF EASING TENSIONS — AND CERTAIN QUIET YEARS

THE SOUTH we encounter as we pass over into the 1900's, so far from being one that sweeps into essential revolution, is really one which has reached a sort of temporary equilibrium upon its ancient foundation. Acting with various other more or less related factors, Progress has not only not brought the primary pattern into decisive metamorphosis, but has for the time being greatly reduced the sum of tensions making for such a metamorphosis, and positively reconfirmed the primary pattern in many respects.

That is not to suggest that the complication of the scene which I have announced was not already in the making, and that social and ideological change was not to be descried. On the contrary.

Thus, one thing to be observed was the rapidly accelerating passage of the planter class into the towns. I say the rapidly accelerating passage because it had really begun so long before as the early days after the Civil War. In truth, there had been some tendency in parts of the Old South itself for the great landowners, unhappy in too close quarters with slavery, and anxious to escape the loneliness which life in the isolated plantation house imposed on even the most hospitable for much of the time, to hand over the management of their estates to hired overseers and move away from the land into congregation. Not a few of the townlets of the Old South had almost no other reason for existence than these purely social ones.

And once the war had destroyed slavery, the tendency naturally grew and spread.

With the advent of Progress, however, this comparatively slow and indecisive movement turned into a veritable exodus. Hundreds of the planters poured into the rising towns to take advantage, in their own persons, of the promised opportunities of industrialism and commerce; and the sons of the planters came in even greater numbers. The draining away of these, again, left life in the country more lonely than ever; moreover, the example was catching; so that presently even those who had no wish to participate personally in Progress were moving in also. By the early 1900's the migration had gone so far that in many districts of the South the larger number of the "big houses" had become merely the shabby dens of overseers or tenants, sometimes black tenants, or, standing empty and abandoned, were falling into staring-eyed ruin under the procession of the equinoxes — that throughout the plantation country, and often in areas that did not strictly belong to the plantation country, *absentee landlordism* was on its way to becoming the rule.

All of which, as we shall see in due time, was significant for our story. But there was something else in process here which belongs more immediately to that story. I mean that the decay of the content of the aristocratic ideal, which we have seen as proceeding apace under the conditions of post-bellum agriculture, was gathering new impetus from Progress.

There is a considerable irony involved in this. For, as I have indicated, Progress was in some sense and in some measure the outgrowth of that ideal. At least, the men who conceived and launched it were, by and large, such men as had best preserved in themselves the stuff of that ideal — men whose motives were, to a considerable extent, genuinely disinterested.

It had to be so, in truth, because, for all the enthusiasm which developed for Progress once it was set going, it had in reality to encounter a decided skepticism in the earliest beginning. In 1880 there was even a positive conviction in the South generally, and especially in such capitalists as it could muster — a conviction based on a few unfortunate experiments in the past — that industry could never be made to succeed here. And there were many so-called experts, such as Edgar Atkinson of Boston, to play on this conviction with facts and figures designed to prove that the cotton mill was a natural monopoly of New England's. Moreover, the record shows plainly that, despite the bold confidence with which they put their dream forward, many of the leaders themselves were privately far from sure the general conviction was not right. For, curious though it may seem, few men appear to have realized the enormous advantage the unparalleled abundance and cheapness of labor would give the South. On the contrary, it was exactly this labor, with its shiftlessness and ineptitude, that was most often urged as a conclusive reason for thinking the scheme was bound to fail.

2

But if the logic of circumstances thus plainly required that the pioneers should be men willing, in their determination somehow to find a way out for the South, to risk a desperate personal gamble, yet, once these had shown the way, once they had demonstrated the practicability of industry in Dixie, it immediately reversed itself and decreed that just there, and precisely because of their qualities, their role as captains of industry should come to an end.

It was not that they would fail to make money. As matters turned out, in fact, the advantage afforded by cheap labor was so massive that it was almost impossible not to make money. The total number of bankruptcies among the early cotton mills of the South can literally be reckoned on the fingers of one hand.

Rather, it was in part that it is the general law of industry and commerce that leadership passes, not merely to those who can make money but to those who can make the most money. And above all it was the very nature of the social objective that these early exponents of Progress had themselves laid down.

That objective, you will remember, was not the building of a dozen mills or even a hundred mills, but more than a thousand mills. And this not slowly, but swiftly, now, as rapidly as the human will could achieve it. A staggering task, when you think about it. A staggering task in any purely agricultural land, however prosperous; since it is axiomatic of agriculture that it nowhere yields any great margin of profit, over and above what is required for immediate consumption, which can be turned to use as capital for the launching of new enterprise. But in the South doubly staggering.

In reality, there was only one way in which it might be accomplished. And that was to make the mills, as it were, multiply themselves. To make such factories as could somehow be got going yield, not only profits, but such fat profits as (being matched with occasional Yankee loans) would in a few years provide capital for the building of more factories.

And for the carrying through of this — the matter is manifest, of course. If the objective was to be reached, what was plainly demanded in the command was not magnanimity, but a single-hearted devotion to the cash-box.

In other words, the logic of circumstances was here once more operating to direct the South irresistibly back upon the ancient simple backcountry heritage at its commoner level, and away from standards of the Virginians. As pointedly as had ever been the case in Reconstruction agriculture, it was marking out adherence to these standards as a handicap for the individual and society alike, and nominating the hard, pushing, horse-trading type of man for the high rewards and the chief roles — even, with Puckish humor, specifying his basically unsocial qualities as of supreme social worth in this crucial hour in Southern history.

From the late 1880's forward, we find the change definitely in progress — men of a generally coarser kind coming steadily to the front — men of the finer pioneer type gradually losing control. There was nothing absolute about it, to be sure. What we have here, strictly, is a tendency rather than a rigid set of facts. The pioneers were not kicked bodily out and did not utterly disappear from the scene. In point of fact, it was so easy to succeed with a Southern cotton mill in these years, that many of them managed to hold on to active power in their enterprises. And perhaps the majority was able to hold on to the semblance of power.

Nevertheless, other and harder hands did often seize the reality of power even in the earlier mills. And what is much more, it was these other hands that largely built and controlled most of the mills established after the primary proving stage was past.

Nor, of course, was the essential process I describe — the selection and elevation of the more selfish type of man — confined merely to the mills. The commercial growth which followed on the rise of industrialism operated broadly to similar purposes, for obvious if not completely identical reasons.

3

Nevertheless, what I have said continues to be fundamentally true. Despite all the changes which might be made out as taking place at the opening of the new century, the sum of tensions making toward revolution had not been increased, but for the time decreased; and, broadly speaking, the prevailing pattern was not being subverted but reaffirmed.

Aside from the hastening of the decay of the aristocratic ideal, none of the new tensions to which Progress was ultimately to give rise had yet made themselves overtly manifest; merely, the ground was being prepared for them, their coming adumbrated. And on the other hand, the old tensions . . .

We have to note pointedly what already appears implicitly herein: that, whatever it might be fashioning in the shadows, this Progress was immediately and obviously doing just the things its sponsors had hoped it might do: with headlong power it was driving back that baffling frontier the Yankee had made, and resolving the quandary in which the pursuit of cotton had some time ended. Specifically, it was completely reversing the economic trend of the South as such. The land, taken as an entity, was no longer plunging year by year into deeper and deeper poverty, but on the contrary was growing — rich? Not that, surely. Both in the absolute and in comparison with the North it was still an abysmally poor land. None the less, those four hundred mills were smoking upon its hills and in its plains now; sleepy villages were growing, in the smell of new pine and the flare of red brick, into towns, indistinct hamlets into villages; and new villages and towns were rising out of the earth beside the flow of rivers and in the midst of the fields.

Planted black and ugly upon her mountains of iron, Birmingham was reddening the night with multiplying sullen fires — born but yesterday, but already a mighty forge. Atlanta, remembering her ashes, was proudly piling mythology upon mythology and boasting herself a phœnix city. In North Carolina grimy, tobacco-stinking Winston was reaching out to swallow up the quiet old center of Moravian piety, Salem; obscure Durham was lifting up its head and pouring its name around the world with the smoke of the cigarette; Gastonia was raising its medieval towers. And far down on the Gulf the ancient beldam, New Orleans, was rubbing the dream of her old-time glory from out her eyes and turning proudly to her new role as mistress to a swelling host of stout, black, rusty, prosaic ships panting upon the Spanish Main or breasting the Atlantic.

Moreover, it must be added to this that with the beginning of the new century we find the direction of Southern agriculture itself reversing also. Or at any rate we find the descent into disaster slackening. Having fallen to less than five cents in 1898, the price of cotton suddenly spurted up the next year to nearly eight cents, and in 1900 to more than nine. Falling slightly again in 1901 and 1902, it rose to more than twelve in 1903; and thenceforward until 1914, when the confusion incident upon the outbreak of the Great War caused it to slump temporarily, it was to average nearly eleven cents — dipping just below nine twice and soaring above fourteen in 1910.

In sum, if nobody could yet call the South rich, it was still unmistakably and swiftly gathering substance.

And by the same token, so also, of course, were many individual Southerners. If the South was not yet rich, there were rich men in it nevertheless. There were men, like Buck Duke and R. J. Reynolds, the new-sprung tobacco magnates of North Carolina, and like the Candlers, the soft-drink magnates of Atlanta, who were already rich by any standard save those of the richest Yankees. There were already textile barons like the Cannons of Concord, North Carolina (predestined towel kings), only comparatively less rich than the masters of nicotine. There were hundreds of textile magnates scaling down from these; hundreds of merchants and bankers and traders of one kind or another — some of them rich even by a Yankee yardstick, and all of them rich by the standards the South had used since the Civil War.

What was integral with this, too, of course, was that economic and social opportunity was being flung wider and wider open to the individual. Such are the curious uses to which words may be bent, indeed, that we can say of Progress, not only that it was beating back that old unhappy, Yankee-made frontier whose essence had resided in the fact that the Southern environment incorrigibly eluded the Southern will, but also that it was at the same time definitely creating a third frontier — a frontier whose essence resided precisely in this opening of opportunity. It was not a perfect frontier in this respect — a great way from it, as we shall find. But it was a real one, for all that.

It was true, wasn't it, that, barefoot in winter, the boy Buck Duke had some time peddled tobacco through the countryside with his father, old Washington Duke, to gain precarious bread? That Reynolds had come to his destined fief, Winston, in true Dick Whittington style, perched atop a tobacco wagon, and barefoot in his turn — that he had not learned to read and write until he was already a rich man? And that, of the emergent masters of

Gastonia, one had begun his career as a peddler, another as an itinerant tinker, and two had been born into the world as penniless bastards?

But there was more here, beyond even the opening of this third frontier. Progress was also achieving that result which had been its paramount and central social objective: that is, it was decisively providing sanctuary for the common whites. I do not mean, manifestly, that it was rescuing the great body of the white tenants and sharecroppers from their estate as such — or even that it was relieving them of having to work side by side, and on practically the same terms, with the black man. Still, by the early 1900's the cotton mills and industry generally had absorbed as many as a quarter of a million of them, or of people who had stood in immediate danger of falling to their ranks; and other industries and the towns had absorbed many more — as well as large bodies of Negroes. Moreover, the number of those who were being thus provided for was increasing with each passing year.

This was not enough — would not be enough — to abolish the surplus of available labor in the land. But, taken with the fact that the advancing price of cotton was cutting down the number of farm bankruptcies, and so of new candidates for employment as tenants and croppers, it was enough to have abolished the threat of that intolerable surfeit of available labor which had once so perilously impended.

Still another thing to be observed in this connection is that, with the arrival of the new century, the Yankee was finally giving over his long struggle actively to coerce the South. In part this was due, no doubt, to simple ennui with an endlessly protracting task. In part, too, it was due to the enthusiastic participation of the South in the Spanish-American War. But perhaps it was due above all to Progress. For if the adoption of the latter did not in reality mean that the South had decided to yield its ancient identity and become merely another Yankeedom, the Yankee nevertheless from the first assumed that it did.

I infer no arrival of any millennium. There were still plenty of hate and spite toward the South left in the North. Yet if the Yankee journalists still came down in hordes, they came now less often to damn. If many Yankee editors still muttered maledictions upon Dixie, the great New York journals, including those which had once been most bitter, had been for twenty years speaking ever more softly. And the chief magazines of the land — the *Atlantic, Scribner's,* even the once rabid *Harper's Weekly* — were waxing almost maudlin in their sympathy.

After 1900, and though just at this time the South, with Populism safely dead, was making bold finally to nullify the Fourteenth Amendment and formally disfranchise the Negro, Henry Cabot Lodge would shrill practically alone on the floor of the Senate regarding the pressing need of sending down bayonets upon the land again — and to galleries that only grinned. And in 1903 the reigning hit upon Broadway would be *The Leopard's Spots,* by Thomas Dixon, Jr., of North Carolina: a picture of Reconstruction from the most rabid Southern viewpoint, and a bitter attack on the Negro.

4

There was another side to the picture, certainly. In the nature of the case as I have stated it, the economic benefits of the new industrialism were far from distributing themselves equitably down the social scale. Whatever the intent of the original founders of Progress, the plain truth is that everything here rested finally upon one fact alone: cheap labor. All the other hypothetical advantages some time urged as belonging to the South quickly turned out in practice to be unreal. Proximity to raw material was balanced out by the differential in freight rates saddled upon the South. Climate, save in its bearing on the cheapness of labor, proved to be a positive disadvantage, for the atmosphere is ordinarily so electric as to make it impossible to handle brittle cotton yarns without expensive artificial humidification. And moreover it set a decided handicap upon the possible efficiency of the Southern workman. Ellsworth

Huntington, in his studies of the relation of climate to civilization, places virtually the whole of the Southern cotton-mill belt within the zone where human energy is necessarily lowest for the United States.

Cheapness of labor, then — such was the South's main advantage. The wages paid in the Southern cotton mills seem almost unbelievable today. To be explicit, what they commonly included was the right to live in some sort of house owned by the mill, either free of charge or for a rent of a dollar or so a week — this, and a money payment ranging from twenty cents a day for bobbin boys, through forty to sixty cents a day for spinners, up to seventy cents to a dollar for weavers, the aristocrats of the cotton mills. Such are the figures set down for 1900 by the United States Bureau of Labor Statistics in its bulletin *History of Wages in the United States from Colonial Times to 1928.*

About these wages there are several things which deserve to be noted. In the first place, and according to the figures of the bulletin I have just quoted, the money payment came to somewhat more than half the wage paid in the mills of New England. And when allowance has been made for the Southerner's advantage in rent, and for the fact that food, fuel, and clothing all cost less in the South at this date — when the question is brought down to one of real wages — it is still to be doubted that the Southern wage at its best was more than two-thirds that of the Yankee workman.

Again, these wages were inevitably such as we mean by the term "family wage." That is, they were on the average just about adequate to the support of a single individual — such wages as required that every member of a family moving from the land into Factorytown, who was not incapacitated by disease or age or infancy, should go into the mills in order that he too might eat. They were such wages as required the labor of the wife and the mother and the woman who was about to become a mother. And — they were such wages as required child labor. In grim truth, one might almost say baby labor. Query any dotard or crone you encounter in a Southern mill town today, and you are likely to hear a tale of their having gone into the mills so young that they had to carry about boxes on which to climb in order to reach the spindles they tended. At six, at seven, at eight years, by ten at the latest, the little boys and girls of the mill families went regularly to work.

Yet further, these wages in the mills of the South were such as were predicated upon the old poor-white standard of living — such wages as involved the carrying over and forward of the debased diet standards we already know.

But it was not only that Southern wages were bad; the hours which had to be worked for them were bitterly long. Sixty-eight to seventy-two hours each week, as compared with fifty-six to fifty-eight in New England — these are the official statistics for 1900. " I have known mills," wrote Edgar Gardner Murphy of Alabama in 1904, " in which for ten or twelve days at a time the factory hands — children and all — were called to work before sunrise and dismissed from work only after sunset, laboring from dark to dark. I have repeatedly seen them at labor for twelve, thirteen, and even fourteen hours per day. In the period of the holidays or at other ' rush times ' I have seen children eight and nine years of age leaving the factory as late as 9:30 o'clock at night, and finding their way with their own little lanterns through the unlighted streets of the mill village, to their squalid homes."

And to top the measure, many of the women who worked such hours had also, of course, to serve their families as cooks and house-keepers!

What this meant for one thing, naturally, was that here was a complete end for these people of that old wide leisure which the common male, at least, had customarily enjoyed in the South. But it meant also a complete end to the old constant contact with sunlight and vital air which had always to some extent balanced out the effect of bad diet and bad living conditions in general. And to this it must be added that working conditions in the Southern cotton mills were extremely unfavorable. Men and women and children were cooped up for most of their waking lives in the gray light of glazed windows, and in rooms which were never effectively ventilated, since cotton yarns will break in the slightest draft — in rooms which, because of the use of artificial humidification, were hardly less than perpetual steam baths.

The harvest was soon at hand. By 1900 the cotton-mill worker was a pretty distinct physical type in the South; a type in some respects perhaps inferior to even that of the old poor white, which in general had been his to begin with. A dead-white skin, a sunken chest, and stooping shoulders were the earmarks of the breed. Chinless faces, microcephalic foreheads, rabbit teeth, goggling dead-fish eyes, rickety limbs, and stunted bodies abounded — over and beyond the limit of their prevalence in the countryside. The women were characteristically stringy-haired and limp of breast at twenty, and shrunken hags at thirty or forty. And the incidence of tuberculosis, of insanity and epilepsy, and, above all, of pellagra, the curious vitamin-deficiency disease which is nearly peculiar to the South, was increasing.

5

We are still not done with the defects of Progress, however.

One curious consideration we need to bring into the reckoning is that Progress was being accomplished so completely within the framework of the past that the *plantation* remained the single great basic social and economic pattern of the South — as much in industry as on the land. For when we sound the matter, that is exactly what the Southern factory almost invariably was: a plantation, essentially indistinguishable in organization from the familiar plantation of the cotton fields.

I have represented the rise of the mills as setting off great town growth. But we must understand that, in the already established towns, the mills nearly always took up their stand, not within the municipal walls and the municipal jurisdiction, but just outside them; and that many of the new towns were not regularly organized municipal corporations at all, but merely the fiefs of the mills.

On their own private property, that is, the mills, typically speaking, built their own private villages. They not only provided houses for the workers, just as the plantation had always provided them for slave and tenant, but like the plantation they provided, and owned, the streets on which these houses stood. They provided commissaries where the workman might get advances of food and clothing against his future earnings, exactly as on the plantation. In large measure—in even larger measure than had been the case with the plantation save in regard to the Negro slave—they provided the churches and schools for the villages and paid the hire of parson and pedagogue. And in even larger measure than the plantation they provided whatever policing there was.

The institution, in short, had literally been brought bodily over. The only considerable difference was that now authority over the unit was, in theory, vested in a number of stockholders in a corporation rather than in an individual. But in practice the difference came to little, for the active head of the mill usually had practical control of the corporation itself.

Manifestly, this is of the first significance for our general argument here. But in the connection immediately in hand, what it means, of course, is that the dependence which had been fastened upon the poor whites by post-bellum cotton-growing was being carried over into industry, and even extended if that were possible. Even more definitely than the tenant and the cropper, the cotton-mill worker of the South would be stripped of the ancient autonomy and placed in every department of his life under the control of his employer. More signally in the case of the masters of the mills than in even that of the masters of the land, the old paternalistic prerogative would be fortified by force and turned into true prescriptive right.

Still another debit which has to be placed to the account of Progress is that the industrial worker had, from the beginning, come in for a ponderably greater portion of social contempt than had been his in any of his roles of the past. Various factors go to explain this, no doubt. In part it was simply the old Southern scorn for anybody who had to work with his hands at the command of another, and especially for anybody who had to work in a gang — coupled with some vague share of the feeling, normal to a purely agricultural tradition, that industrial labor is somehow inherently inferior. But in perhaps greater measure it was a reflection from the fact that the mill village stood so completely apart; that its people formed not only a separate community but a community distinguished by more or less definite physical stigmata — yes, and a community which exhibited to Southern eyes a much more concentrated and obvious picture of unrelieved shabbiness and squalor and ugliness than the countryside, with its wide dispersion of population and its fields and woods and long blue reaches, its inevitable tendency to soften even the horrible into the merely picturesque, had ever done.

Anyhow, it existed. In such epithets as " the factory hill " and " cotton-mill trash " and " lint-heads " and " cotton-tails " and " factory rats," Southerners of the higher and middle classes — and there was definitely beginning to be a middle class now — in 1900 were concentrating an even greater portion of snobbish disdain than was meted out to the sharecropper himself.

But if it was plainly no Utopia into which Progress was ushering the industrial worker, neither was it one into which the rising price of cotton was bringing the common white on the land. If farm bankruptcies were diminishing, they were far from having disappeared. If it was possible now to make a legitimate profit out of growing the staple, yet, what with the charges of the supply merchant as high as ever, it was at best a small one — and one for the achievement of which diligence, shrewdness, and, in the case of the employer of others, not too much sympathetic imagination were only relatively less necessary than before. Among even the yeoman farmers, pinched faces and ragged behinds were still the prevailing rule. And in general the diet and housing of tenant and sharecropper were pegged fast to the standards of yesterday.

6

Finally, to round out the record of the defects of Progress as it subsisted in 1900, we should also look a little more closely at the limitations of the opportunities of the third frontier which I have suggested in passing. What merits specification to begin with is that now perhaps even more than in the past these opportunities, so far as the common whites were concerned, were strictly for the exceptional individual. For manifestly the fact that Progress depended upon the cheapness of labor was a new and powerful block upon any possible advance *en masse* for the lower classes in the South. And nothing could be plainer than that the commonplace individual in these classes had little chance of meeting the stern demands of the time and place.

Nor did the limitations end there. For even the common white with unusual capacity and the requisite energy and hardness, opportunity was still a long way from being perfectly wide open. This will bear stressing, for it is on the assumption that it *was* wide open to him, and in truth, and because of the emphasis upon the qualities of the horse-trader and the peasant, peculiarly and almost exclusively open to him at his lowest and worst — it is on this assumption, and on the evidence of such salient cases as those of the Dukes, the Reynoldses, and the bastard barons of Gastonia, that there has been erected one of the most curious versions of the supposed revolution in Dixie. I mean the version which has it that this revolution was essentially a class revolution; that with the coming of Progress and the opening of the third frontier poor-white trash began to come up in such numbers, and the old master class to go down in such numbers, that by the early 1900's the parvenus had become the real ruling class.

In reality, however, this version of the matter is merely another reflection from the persistent legend of the Old South. Behind all its other assumptions lies the assumption that the old ruling class was a fully realized aristocracy — such a completely realized one that the decay of the aristocratic ideal and the general appearance of the horse-trading type of man at the helm can only be explained by supposing its elimination and replacement by the lower orders. But of course the old ruling class had never been a fully realized aristocracy. And, as I have sought to show all along, the decay of the aristocratic ideal, while proceeding in part from both the rise of men from below and the loss of wealth and power to those who clung most stoutly to its standards, had always proceeded in large part from the increasing tendency of the majority of the members of this old ruling class to yield, in varying measure, to the prevailing exigencies and fall back into the more primitive pattern which was their original inheritance.

Far from enjoying any near-monopoly of the opportunities of the third frontier, the common white who attempted to grasp them had to encounter the competition of men from higher levels, who, in addition to being willing and able to meet the prescribed conditions, were often armed with considerable capital, or at least the means of securing credit. And in every case he had also — until he had definitely emerged — to deal with a certain distinct clannishness in the upper circles. Given fairly equal general claims, it would be much easier for the scion of a plantation to get a loan from a banker who was also the scion of a plantation than for the common sort.

Of all the army of the enterprising and the hard who were seizing command of the mills, the great majority were such men as — the woods-colt barons of Gastonia? Not so, I think. Often they were such men as had already enjoyed some measure of wealth or power; one of the largest contingents having come from the ranks of the supply merchants who for so long had been piling up capital, as it were in preparation for this hour. Mainly, indeed, they were such men as belonged more or less distinctly within the broader limits of the old ruling class, the progeny of the plantation. Or they sprang from the ranks of the yeoman farmers of the piedmont country which fringed the plantation belt proper, which had never had any considerable number of great estates, and which, because of waterfall, was exactly the area in which Southern industry tended to develop most rapidly — from those yeoman farmers who had always definitely associated themselves with the ruling class, and who, in their primitive local communities, had often actually made it up in large part.

We must take care to preserve perspective here. The widening of opportunity was indubitable. The Dukes and the Reynoldses and the Cannons were real. Many men who had not clearly belonged to the ruling class before were coming up into it; and that ruling class was being expanded as it had not been expanded since the days of the first cotton frontier. Moreover, it was being greatly shaken up and rearranged. The men of the piedmont were coming in for a rapidly increasing share of the totality of power. And many of the names that had once been mightiest in council were, as we know, little heard of any more, and some of them were utterly gone from the record; while other names that had been unknown or obscure were towering toward the first dignity. By the same token, the general tone of the ruling class was growing cruder. Yet when all this is said, I think it can be safely said, too, that the same great circle of people who had participated, in one degree or another, in power in the Old South still continued to supply the majority of the members of the ruling class, and perhaps, in the aggregate, still held predominant sway. And I am not at all sure that the statement is not true to this very day.

In any case, it was so little true that the poor white enjoyed peculiar access to the new opportunities or that there had been any poor-white revolution that the majority of the men who clearly had come up from under derived rather from the lesser yeoman farmers who stood next above the poor whites than from the latter proper. Such was the case with the Dukes and the Reynoldses. And there is evidence that such was the case even with the bastard barons of Gastonia.

There were numerous men in the South in 1900 of whom it could be said truthfully that, though they were plainly climbing into the ruling class now, they had begun as sweeper boys in the mills.

There were numerous such men of whom it could be said that their fathers had been tenant farmers. But there were precious few of whom it could be said truthfully that their sires had been share-croppers.

And when we inquire a little closely into the case of the sweeper boy, we are immensely likely to find that he was in reality the son of a neighboring farmer who enjoyed the favor of the master of the mill, and that he had been brought into the factory for the express purpose of learning the business from the ground up. Or that his family was one of those (there were many such) which had been only temporarily reduced to the mills, and that the superintendent had taken a great liking to him. Or that his parent had been the boss machinist, or the village barber, or even the village parson. Or that if it was actually true that the father had been a tenant or an ordinary mill worker, yet he had originally been a stout enough yeoman.

7

But when the whole of this debit score of Progress is taken into account, we still inevitably come back to the fact that its total effect was as I have said.

In general this surely calls for no laboring. Here, obviously, was hope for the South, as such, in the points where it most required hope. Here was hope for every Southerner in that sentiment of the South which stood at the center of his being. And here, con-trariwise, was an end to that despair, that terror, that haunting vision of ineluctable defeat ahead, which in the black days of Re-construction had crawled behind the most determined Southern assertion. Here, in a word, was triumph for the Southern will; and so here, finally and naturally, was an enormous renewal of con-fidence in the general Southern way.

Nor does the special case of the upper classes, and of all those who were coming into these classes from below, call for much laboring, either. Apart from a dwindling few who still clung to nostalgia and barred shutters, they were naturally full of cheer, both for the South and for themselves. They were naturally full, too, of a rising gratefulness toward Progress and its makers. And, of course, they were being greatly fortified in that ancient individualism which had always been the bedrock of the Southern pattern and the Southern character.

The case of the common white, however, requires somewhat more extended attention.

Thus, one fact to be noted is that if Progress was failing to yield him an equitable share in its economic benefits, it had none the less brought him certain distinct gains even here — had conferred upon him benefits which were properly economic, or which under his psychology passed for such. The mill worker had a job now and was relieved from the terror of starvation which had been a part of the threatened surfeit of available labor.

And if this house they gave him to live in was almost invariably a poor one, perched on stilts along some godforsaken ravine or red hillside, it was nevertheless not only such a house as was entirely acceptable under his historical standard, but a very definite improvement on anything he had ever known. It was actually a better house than most of those of the yeoman farmers, to say nothing of the huts of tenant and cropper. For it was by ordinary tight against the rain if not against the wind, and usually it had been painted — both rarities in the rural South.

As for his pay, he had cash in his pocket. The head of a family, collecting wages for a wife and half a dozen children, had more cash in his pocket at the end of a fortnight than he had commonly seen on the land in a year. He and his might revel in the unaccustomed sensation of ringing the stuff down on a counter — by skimping their diet yet a little more, might enjoy such coveted luxuries as " store-bought " tobacco and snuff and calico and Chicago-tailored shoddy — could eat candy or drink soda pop. In their simple eyes, therefore, the wages did not seem bad; they almost constituted affluence.

The tenant and the cropper had their gains, too. If the surplus of available labor was not destroyed, if they were not completely secured in making such a living as they were used to, yet it was comparatively so. And if their diet and housing had not improved, it was still not quite true that the landlords were taking all the increased increment from cotton. Some slight portion of it was indubitably trickling down the scale, as witness the fact that even the blacks were no longer usually garbed in gunny-sacks.

Again, it has to be remembered that the other evils and defects in Progress which I have recited here as belonging to the case of the common white figured in his consciousness as such only cloudily or not at all.

If the opportunities of the third frontier were not perfectly wide open to him, they were none the less sufficiently so to have relieved pressure within his ranks and to have refurbished the ancient illusion in his breast. Given the spectacle of men springing up all about him, given his tradition, it was inevitable that the ambitious commoner should be full of hope and belief — inevitable that the ordinary unambitious jack-in-the-mass should be once more set in the old comfortable conviction that if only he chose, he might get on with the best of them.

The " family wage," the labor of women and children, long hours — every one of these was already, and immemorially, in the mores of the industrial worker. All of them were simply the standards of agriculture fetched over into industry, and not only of Southern agriculture. And so, like the industrial worker in New England and Lancashire seventy-five and a hundred years before, he accepted them as in the nature of things.

There was the fact, to be sure, that if he had worked fourteen hours a day on the land, he had done so only in the harvesting and growing seasons. But the Southern mills ran only when orders and profits were to be had. There were many holiday periods, without pay but usually not without a limited credit at the " company store." Moreover, he had from the first demanded a regular half-holiday on Saturdays, and by 1900 it was beginning generally to be granted. And if this were not enough, if he awoke some morning full of nostalgia for a seat on a fence and the smell of the pinewoods, it was the simplest thing imaginable to swap places with some tenant or cropper eager for cash in his pocket. From the beginning, in truth, there was a constant and pretty extensive flow backward and forward between the land and the mills — a fact which was not without its significance.

If his wife came down with a misery in her chest and took to spitting blood? If there were pains in his back and a ringing in his ears? If the baby born next door was a queer, still brat which would plainly never be right in the head? These were evils, certainly. But, ungiven to even the most elementary analysis, he scarcely referred them to the mills in the least. Quite literally, and in the most unquestioning faith, he thought of them — as his preachers thought of them, and as Southern people at large thought of them — as direct visitations from the hand of God, inexplicable, or explicable only on the hypothesis of sin, and to be borne without complaint.

8

If the bringing over of the plantation into industry meant that he was at the command and mercy of the masters of the mills, the fact was lost upon him. The plantation was the only pattern of large-scale organization he knew. More, it was in essentials the only possible one in the premises. He had to have a house to live in, and as obviously could not find it ready-built in the Southern towns or provide it for himself. And if the masters of the fiefs were largely paying for church and school, for preachers and schoolmasters and policemen, they were doing it — out of scoundrelly calculation?

Nothing of the kind. At least, if there was any part of that here, it was almost wholly subconscious. In the main, they were doing it simply because these things, like houses, had to be provided from somewhere and because the burden was plainly too great for the worker himself. Because, the worst labor-sweaters included, they

were themselves nearly always pious men. Because they were full
of the ancient Southern love for the splendid gesture. Because they
shared in the rising enthusiasm for education — genuinely felt that
a degree of schooling would be an excellent thing for the children
of the masses, provided of course it did not interfere with their duty
to work. Because it was an essential part of the Southern paternalistic tradition that it was the duty of the upper classes to look after
the moral welfare of these people and get them safely into heaven
at last — because that tradition had been introduced and firmly established in the mills by the founders of Progress — because it was
so ingrained in Southern thought and expectation that it would
scarcely occur to anybody to defy it — because it was so bound up
with the Southern notions of the *good man,* of leadership, and of
aristocracy, with all that the man coming up in the scale naturally
aspired to represent and body forth, that it gloriously flattered his
vanity.

The whole, in short, was largely meant and entirely conceived
by the mill-owners as a benefaction. It genuinely did contain much
of benefaction. The village parson and schoolmaster naturally and
continually and in the best of faith represented it as pure and unal-
loyed benefaction. The upper classes, looking on from the viewpoint of Progress, of course saw it in the same fashion, and did not
fail to say so. When the workman went into a store in the town,
he was certain to hear — when the doctor came down into the mill
village, he was sure to remind him — how great was his debt to
the good people who were making these benefactions possible. The
Southern newspapers, headed by the Atlanta *Constitution* and the
Charlotte Observer, the orators at political rallies and picnics,
the pulpit at large, nearly every organ of publicity or captain to the
South — all these were constantly — had been for twenty years increasingly — dinning it into the worker's ears that here was benefaction practically without parallel in human annals.

And to top the measure, the baron rarely used his power beyond
the limit traditional on the plantation and was not often too arrogant in its exercise. Men were discharged arbitrarily; but there

was perhaps less of that here than has been common elsewhere. And there was not enough of it to arouse any general resentment, or even any general feeling of insecurity. When election time came around pressure was brought to bear on the voting workman, of course. But always it was brought in the shape of a hand on the shoulder and friendly advice; from within the pattern of the old-fashioned paternalism, and in the light of the unstudied knowledge that it was far easier to cajole these people, to flatter and suggest, than to command and threaten.

Thus it fell out that the common white in the mills accepted the plantation system in industry, not only without question, but as being as great a benefaction as he was assured it was.

But he was increasingly despised? That, at any rate, would not be utterly lost upon him? Not entirely, no. As Harriet Herring, of the University of North Carolina, has pointed out, the cotton-mill worker of the South tended from the beginning to exhibit a greater class-awareness in the narrow sense than had ever been the case with any other common white — a certain suspiciousness and self-conscious sullenness. He would be a man apart, indeed, partly out of his own choice. He would have separate churches and schools even where the mill was built within the limits of a town which already had fairly adequate church and school facilities, partly because the upper classes snobbishly objected to associating with him, but perhaps more because he himself was uneasy and embarrassed in such company.

But we must not suppose that there was anything raging and flaming about this. We must not picture him as subjected to open snubs and taunts — as intolerably wounded in the ancient pride of his kind, and so as brooding bitterly and continually, as consumed with an ever more implacable resentment. As a matter of fact, his perception of the case was occasional and intuitive rather than constant and conscious. For the old law of the South still held in these years quite as certainly as ever. If he was more greatly despised, yet, as always, it was mainly behind the arras — and that not so much by way of any hypocrisy or calculation as because the despisers were genuinely reluctant to offend whomever they did not suspect of the will to offend themselves, because their own scorn was itself largely confined to the narrow social sphere, because, when they stood face to face with a man, they were always sharply aware of him, as a member of a class, yes, but first and foremost as a human individuality. The boys of the town and the boys of the mill might carry on an interminable war of gibes and stones, precisely as Thomas De Quincey has described them as carrying it on in Manchester a hundred years before. But for the rest . . .

9

The master of the mill stood to his workmen as the immediate representative of the upper classes, of course. And it was an inherent part of his paternalistic approach, a natural corollary of the bringing over of the plantation system, that, as I have before suggested, the old easy personal relations should have been brought over too. The baron knew these workmen familiarly as Bill and Sam and George and Dick, or as Lil and Sal and Jane and Lucy. More, he knew their pedigrees and their histories. More still, with that innocent love of personal detail native to Southerners, he kept himself posted as to their lives as they were lived under his wing; knew their little adventures and scandals and hopes and loves and griefs and joys. Day by day he moved among them full of the small teasing jests and allusions to kinsfolk so dear to the Southern heart, of ready and benign counsel, of sympathetic interest and concern for Granny Meg's rheumatism or the treasured cow that had died — a concern which in even the most hard-bitten wage-shaver was somehow and characteristically real at the core.

Did he want hunting and fishing companions? He was often likely to take them from the mill. Sometimes, in truth, when there was holiday, he might pick up the whole crew, man, woman, and chit, and carry them off to a barbecue or picnic, where, as likely as not, his women might appear, a little cool and remote it might be, but sweetly gracious after the tradition of the South.

And when the workman went into the town, there was still much the same personal atmosphere that had always existed. As in the old days, there was nearly always some more or less exalted person to invite him into the closet for a drink. And as of old, there was the inevitable great lawyer, towering, leonine, long of coat and mane, the breathing epitome of the Confederacy, to drop a familiar hand upon his shoulder and warm his heart with confidential chat about the Proto-Dorian bond of the Democratic Party.

Another factor which must not be lost sight of in estimating the reaction of the industrial worker to his wages, hours, and general condition is that, granted the Southern objectives, it was all quite necessary. Did he himself see that? I believe there can be no doubt that he at least felt it — that in some biological and less than conscious fashion he apprehended the case with considerable clarity. And consciously he was surely quite as much aware of it as he was aware of the evils in his situation.

Yet another consideration which deserves to be brought into the equation is the enormous escape from loneliness which was involved in the shift to village and town life — the expansion afforded to the naturally intense gregariousness and conviviality of these people.

Nor should we overlook, in the particular connection of the individualistic pattern, the influence among the industrial workers of a character we have had little occasion to notice before: the Southern mountaineer. The forgotten man of the land, he was not at all the intended beneficiary of Progress. But in the closing decades of the nineteenth century the revenue officers of the United States were pressing ever more closely upon his major source of livelihood, the production of illicit corn whisky — and the wages paid in the mills seemed to him nothing less than fabulous. So by 1900 many thousands of him had issued from his crags and coves to take up life in the mill villages.

In effect, it was almost exactly as though so many pioneer back-woodsmen had been miraculously introduced into the scene. Mured up in his Appalachian fastness, with no roads to the outside world save giddy red gullies, untouched by the railroad until the twentieth century was already in the offing, this mountaineer had almost literally stood still for more than a hundred years. He no longer wore the coonskin cap and the moccasins of his fathers. And, though there had been few slaves in the mountains, he had acquired a hatred and contempt for the Negro even more viru-lent than that of the common white of the lowlands; a dislike so rabid that it was worth a black man's life to venture into many mountain sections. But, for the rest, he might have fitted easily and naturally into that company of gaunt and hungry men who took the western way with Boone in 1775. No other such individualist was left in America — or on earth. Moreover, having arrived in the mill village, his native approach would be little modified. For, un-like the majority of the lowlanders, he would often continue to own his farm in the hills, and so would remain a genuinely free agent.

The presence of a large body of such men would have had marked effect on the psychology of the Southern mill worker in any case. But what made that effect still more signal was that, never having been subjected to the continual loss of the most able indi-viduals, which had been the case with the common whites else-where, this mountain stock averaged unusually high; and mountain men came to leadership out of all proportion to their numbers — in such numbers, indeed, that many Yankee observers were led to report, quite incorrectly, that the majority of all Southern cotton-mill workers was of alpine extraction.

And at last — there was in the case of the common white, of every common white, the factor which lies plain on the surface of what I have already said: that Progress had snatched his supreme value, his racial status, back from the brink of peril and made it secure once more. The men in the mills had been entirely removed from all direct competition with the Negro; and the fact of indirect competition, if not altogether lost upon them, was perceived only through an immensely shadowy intuition. As for those on the land, if the tenant and sharecropper had not escaped competition with him, if they had still to work side by side with him and on much the same terms, they had nevertheless, like the South in general, escaped the haunting terror of that too-intense competition with him, that fight to the finish for the means of subsistence. They could at least feel sure now that the existing distance between themselves and this black would not be further lessened.

10

With all this before us, the case of the common white under Progress is now as clear, I hope, as that of other Southerners. From the beginning the total effect was, of course, toward a mighty confirmation and revivification of the individualistic outlook — a revivification quite as great as that in the upper classes. And more — toward the development of gratefulness on the part of the masses: a wide, diffuse gratefulness pouring out upon the cotton-mill baron; upon the old captains, upon all the captains and preachers of Progress; upon the ruling class as a whole for having embraced the doctrine and brought these things about; upon Progress *per se*, as the instrument of salvation both for the South as such and for themselves.

We come at length into position to understand a connection I suggested long ago. Appearing concurrently with Populism, Progress undoubtedly played a considerable part from the first in restraining and attenuating whatever impulse to class consciousness entered into that movement. And coming to growth at the same time, or hard upon the same time, when Populism was fetching up short in an *impasse,* it combined with and completed the work of that *impasse.* In the late nineties the common white was not only drawing away from every thought of revolt; he was drawing away with cheerfulness. The ranks of the South were closing, not merely because of the Negro; the impulse toward class awareness and class action was dying down, not only because it had been signally demonstrated that the way to its development was hopelessly blocked, but also because the tensions and irritations that had given rise to it in the first place were being removed — precisely because the new wave of individualism and the gratefulness born of Progress were everywhere sweeping up in the breast of the common white and choking off the thing at its source.

Draw this whole account of Progress into focus, then, and we palpably have that equilibrium of which I spoke in the beginning. Distinctly, the South had, in the immediately manifest facts, overwhelming good reason to be feeling what it inevitably was feeling at the opening of the twentieth century, that all its troubles were solved or being solved, that mastery was achieved or being achieved. That it had succeeded or swiftly was succeeding in creating a world which, if it was not made altogether in the image of that old world, half-remembered and half-dreamed, shimmering there forever behind the fateful smoke of Sumter's guns, was yet sufficiently of a piece with it in essentials to be acceptable, a world which by and large would serve as a reasonably proper garment for its mind. And that it had now only to go forward upon the way in which its feet were set, through ever more pleasing prospects, to the realization of its native and most high destiny.

And its story down until the outbreak of the World War is, in its predominant aspect, almost entirely the story of its increasing absorption, as a unit, in this conviction and the pursuit of Progress — the story of a broad calm on all fronts — a calm broken now and then, to be sure, but broken only as the surface of a great pool is broken by vagrant raindrops from a distant summer cloud.

The cotton mills multiplied enormously. From having four and a half million spindles, 23 per cent of the nation's total, in 1900, the South had come in 1910 to have more than eleven million, 39 per cent of the national total, and more than the whole country had had in 1880. And from consuming 40 per cent of all the cotton consumed in the United States, it had come to consuming 53 per cent. But it was not only the cotton mill. There was an ever increasing tendency for industry and enterprise to pour over into other channels. We have already sufficiently seen, indeed, that almost from the beginning the cotton mill had been paralleled by the tobacco mill and the iron mill, to which we may add the mining of coal and iron. But now, under the touch of Buck Duke's millions, hydro-electric power sprang into being, and by 1910 the energy of a million horses was pulsing in the wires of Dixie. And literally a hundred lesser industries made their appearance. By 1914, and apart from the cotton mills, there were at least 15,000 manufacturing establishments of one sort or another in the South; and though most of them were exceedingly small, yet in the aggregate the value of their product far exceeded that of the cotton mills themselves.

And side by side with this went a tremendous growth and multiplication of towns. By scores, dozing market villages came fully into the current of Progress in these years, built themselves a factory, routed the cows and pigs from grazing in their streets, began to lay down pavements and car tracks and to dream megalomaniac dreams. The so-called skyscraper — a building from eight to twenty stories in height — came on the scene. So did the department store proper. And so did the Chamber of Commerce.

From having less than 40,000 people in 1900, Birmingham was pressing upon 150,000 in 1910. Atlanta, doubling its population, had more than the latter figure. New Orleans, adding a hundred thousand people, was towering into the rank of the second port of America. North Carolina's Durham and Mississippi's Jackson tripled their numbers in the decade. And Jacksonville and Tampa in Florida; Macon in Georgia; Charlotte in North Carolina; Vicksburg, Hattiesburg, and Meridian in Mississippi; Spartanburg in South Carolina; Roanoke in Virginia — all these, and many more, doubled, nearly doubled, or more than doubled their populations. Even Richmond gained fifty thousand souls, Memphis thirty thousand. And the count of towns with more than ten thousand people rose from seventy-five to a hundred and fifty; while the count of towns with about five thousand people quadrupled.

And what went with this, again, was a lush flowering of the old local patriotism and particularism native to the South, which we have already seen as figuring in Progress from the beginning. State frantically sought to outdo state, town to outdo town, at once to further the great common enterprise and to get the lion's share of the new industry and commerce for themselves — by increasingly extravagant provisions for tax-exemption over long periods, for free lands for the new mills and their villages, and for subsidies from the public purse.

It is the story, this one of these years, of an always mounting hymn of thanksgiving for Progress, of the appearance of Rotary and a great outburst of boasting, a vast upsurge of vociferous pride in " the biggest towel mill on earth," in " the biggest cotton mill under one roof in the world," in car loadings and bank clearings and millions of this and millions of that.

And, finally, it is the story of a mighty development of the passion for education. By 1914 every state had some sort of uniform school system, virtually every rural community had its schoolhouse, and all together there were nearly eight million pupils in the public schools of the South — almost as many in proportion to population as the rest of the nation could show. The standard, to be sure, was still pathetically low. The rural school was ordinarily a one-room shack and ran only three to five months in the year. And the teachers, grotesquely ill paid, were literate only by the most elementary measure. Nevertheless, the South, spending a hundred million dollars in this year of 1914, had plainly come a great way, and was preparing to go farther still.

Higher education was prospering, too. Legislative appropriations for state universities and colleges more than tripled in the years from 1900 to 1914, and so did the expenditures of the religious sects upon their schools. Everywhere plants and faculties were expanding. And throughout the South, farmers, with the vision of Progress before their eyes, were sweating and slaving — sometimes literally half-starving themselves — in order that their sons might go to college and come back " to be somebody " in the county town.

II

But now, there was of course change involved in all this growth and absorption in empire-building. It rises up and becomes manifest in the very telling of the story. And yet — as regards the Southern mind, which is our theme, how essentially superficial and unrevolutionary remain the obvious changes; how certainly do these obvious changes take place within the ancient framework, and even sometimes contribute to the positive strengthening of the ancient pattern!

Look close at this scene as it stands in 1914. There is an atmosphere here, an air, shining from every word and deed. And the key to this atmosphere, if I do not altogether miss the fact, is that familiar word without which it would be impossible to tell the story of the Old South, that familiar word " extravagant." Probably it would mean nothing if I said that the skyscrapers which were going up were going up in towns which, characteristically, had no call for them — in towns where available room was still plentiful, and land prices were still relatively low — for it would merely be said that the Middle West was doing something of the same silly sort. But if I told you that they were often going up in towns (like Tar Heel Charlotte and Winston and Greensboro, or South Carolina's Columbia and Greenville and Spartanburg) which had little more use for them than a hog has for a morning coat — in towns where there was no immediate prospect of their being filled, unless by tenants willing to forgo a meal now and then in order to participate in such grandeur?

Softly, do you not hear behind that the gallop of Jeb Stuart's cavalrymen? Do you not recognize it for the native gesture of an incurably romantic people, enamoured before all else of the magnificent and the spectacular? A people at least as greatly moved by the histrionic urge to perform in splendor, and by the patriotic will to testify to faith in their land and to vindicate it before the world's opinion, as by the hope of gain and the belief that tomorrow's growth will bring forth tenants in profusion?

But I generalize too easily, I am a little fanciful and maybe a little dubious, and of course I ought not to be so. Well, but listen now to that boasting — to that great outburst of pride I have alluded to. There are strange notes — Yankee notes — in all this talk about the biggest factory, about bank clearings and car loadings and millions. But does anybody fail to detect the authentic Southern pitch and tone? Does anybody fail to hear once more the native accent of William L. Yancey and Barnwell Rhett, to glimpse again the waving plume of, say, Wade Hampton, that trooper whose perpetual gasconade so irritated William Tecumseh Sherman?

Or, again, does anybody imagine that these new boasts have eliminated the old? Then let him listen to the orators, as I myself listened to them as a boy in North Carolina in 1914. Let him observe how certainly such a boast as " First at Bethel, farthest at Gettysburg, and last at Appomattox " precedes these new ones; how certainly the latter are felt merely as the crown upon the former; how the cheers spring up for the one as for the other; how surely the adjective " Southern " sounds through the whole.

Nevertheless, there is Rotary, the sign-manual of the Yankee spirit, the distillate, as it were, of the Yankee mind; and not the most fanciful man will venture to suggest that its appearance in Dixie is not witness to a most profound and searching change in Southern psychology? But I am not so sure.

If one took the Southern extravagance and brag, if one took the old Southern gregariousness, the unaffected delight of every proper Southerner in the company of his fellows; if one added to these the Southern love for high and noble and somewhat nebulous profession, and the Southern joy in the sense of participating in tremendous though indefinite enterprise and in mysterious bonds; if, again, one added to all these the old horse-trading instinct, and the continual growth of that instinct under the conditions which had reigned since the Civil War, I think we should hardly have to suppose more than an unfortunate decline in the dignity of the Southern manner — the grafting of Yankee backslapping upon the normal Southern geniality — to arrive at a startlingly accurate portrait of Rotary, exactly as it was to flourish in this country. I am myself, indeed, perpetually astonished to recall that Rotary was not invented in the South.

And when we turn from Rotary as an institution to the men who made it up, when we go on to examine the heroes and captains of Progress as they stood in 1914, and the forces in the South which they bodied forth, we find much the same story continually unfolding. These men, as I suggest, distinctly had the stamp of George F. Babbitt upon them; and their example was combining with the whole flow of the times to set the stamp of Babbittry ever more closely upon those about them, and especially upon the young men who were boiling out of the Southern colleges.

The element of calculation was by now an immeasurable great force in the lives and characters of these men — was becoming an immeasurable great force in the life and character of the South at large. There was a word — " smart " — which was increasingly upon Southern lips in these days, a word serving as the touchstone and accolade of success under Progress. And what was epitomized in this word was, first of all, of course, a constantly mounting acquisitiveness, the fact that the mere making of money was everywhere getting to be the ultimate test of a man, a growing obsession in the upper classes, in all the ambitious elements of society, greater in the towns, but great enough even in the countryside. This, and a rapidly rising pride in and admiration for cleverness in acquisition. And more still — a rising pride in and admiration for cleverness in acquisition that was in fact no more than cunning, an increasing carelessness as to the scrupulousness of the means employed.

12

Nor was this the sum of the matter. By 1914 we can begin distinctly to discern that calculation was also seeping more and more into the great fabric of the Southern loyalties of the captains of industry and commerce, and indeed of the ambitious classes as a whole, though not, to be sure, of every individual in these classes. The matter was most obvious in the case of the religious pattern. On every hand men of business position and aspiration were showing a continually more rigorous zeal for going to church and having everybody else go to church; for passing the collection plate, teaching Sunday school, and leading and multiplying prayer meetings. Terms like " salvation " and " grace " and " soul-winning " occupied their grave lips on Sundays and Wednesday nights as absolutely as talk of making money occupied them for the rest of the week. Furthermore, they were growing remarkably more liberal with their purses. No few of them were ostentatiously adopting the Hebraic law and dedicating the tithe of all their income to the service of heaven, and were engaging in campaigns to dragoon everybody else into doing the same. Out of their pockets missionaries to the heathen of China and Europe were multiplying. And so were new churches. In fact, new churches were building in Dixie almost as fast as factories, the old simple chapels giving place in all the towns to ornate piles in early Dayton Romanesque or a kind of Gothic it was easy to believe the Goths had actually invented.

And nobody who looked closely into all this could have escaped the unpleasant feeling that one very potent element in it was the sense that it paid, materially and immediately — that interest was figuring here more definitely than it had in the past. Nor was it only the laymen who were being infected. The old-fashioned Southern minister was gradually giving ground to men who had the stamp of Babbitt upon them as clearly as any of their parishioners — brisk, unctuous, and greatly given to grandiose schemes for the creation of an always more elaborate "organization" and ever larger "plants"—men as obsessed with the passion for large figures as any factory-builder, and as full, too, of the competitive spirit, noisily anxious to have a greater church and a greater enrollment than the parson on the next street or in the next town.

And interest was all too obviously beginning to play strange tricks with the judgment of such parsons. Let a parishioner only have sufficient money and a willingness to gratify their passion for building and outdoing, and let him only be sufficiently unbending in his public declarations of adherence to the moral code laid down by the evangelical sects, and he was increasingly likely to find himself a steward or a deacon or a presbyter, in spite of the fact that it was notorious that he was a pirate in commerce and that he passed his free evenings in making most unholily merry.

But if the growth of the spirit of calculation was most evident in the religious field, it was surely not confined to it. Nearly all these men of business belonged now, of course, to that Yankee-izing party which we have seen as appearing before 1900; professed loudly to being militant apostles of change. But in reality the changes they were talking about were only such relatively minor ones as would plainly serve to further their chances of making money. When it came to a question of the fundamentals of the Southern pattern, they were in fact growing distinctly more conservative, if that were possible—precisely because of the gathering knowledge within themselves that the Southern *status quo* presented a nearly perfect stage for the working out of their personal ambitions—precisely because of the gathering perception that the Southern mind was a mighty bulwark for its preservation.

We can see what I speak of here beginning to peep through quite clearly if we look at one of the earliest instances of open challenge to the Southern scheme of things. I have reference to the case of Dr. Alexander J. McKelway, Southern secretary for the National Child Labor Committee, who from 1903 onward waged a constant battle for the enactment of child-labor laws in the South, and particularly in North Carolina.

McKelway was a Presbyterian clergyman of Charlotte. And the organization which he represented had been founded at the instance of a Southerner, that Edgar Gardner Murphy whose writings I have already noted. Moreover, it had the nominal backing, at least, of a dozen famous Southern names, including those of such men as Ben Tillman of South Carolina and Hoke Smith of Georgia. Nevertheless, the embattled mill masters and their allies pitched their battle straight along the line of an appeal to Southern patriotism; raising the old magic rallying-cry of "Yankee interference" and "Yankee invasion," they charged — without any evidence save only that the New England mills had already long since begun to suffer grievously from Southern competition — that the latter were the real moving force behind the committee, that they had created it for the express purpose of destroying Southern industry, that they were furnishing all the money for the campaign, and that McKelway very well knew it.

In the hands of some of the principal newspapers and such journals as the *Textile Bulletin,* published by David Clark of Charlotte, McKelway indeed became just another scalawag out of Reconstruction — the target for such a flood of abuse, pitched in the characteristic personal vein of the South, that to this day he is remembered in North Carolina, by most people who remember him at all, with angry contempt.

Nor was the appeal directed only to general patriotism. In the newspapers and particularly in a pamphlet by an official of the North Carolina Manufacturers' Association, it was argued broadly that McKelway's program was un-Christian, because it represented "class legislation" and so set brother against brother, because it violated the Biblical right of the parent to absolute command of the child, and because it was an effort to do by "coercive action" what had better be left to be worked out in God's own good time through the instrumentality of the mill-owners themselves; and that it represented unconscionable "meddling" with the individual's sacred right to do what he pleased with his own — "a cruel indignity" to both the mill master and his workman, an "oppression " which would quickly spread from the mills to the farm, the beginning of the end of all individual liberty, and an opening wedge for Socialism, a Godless European invention which, as everyone knew, was already engulfing Yankeedom.

Moreover, the appeal succeeded perfectly, for practical purposes. The mill interests had the backing in these years of virtually the whole body of their workers and the whole body of farmers and landowners.

It is interesting to note, however, that this does not mean that no child-labor laws were adopted. From the moment they were once proposed, indeed, nothing could have been more sure than that the South would adopt some sort of child-labor laws. Not to have done so would have been to fly in the face of its humane convictions, its love of high profession and noble gestures. Hardly a soul was ever found in Dixie to contend that child labor was in itself a good thing. Simply, it was said that it was better than having the children running wild in the streets, better than starving families, better than ruining Southern industry and halting Progress. Still, it was generally agreed, something would have to be done; not only for the reasons I have suggested, but also because the South's old defensiveness was turning more and more, as Progress advanced, toward conciliating the frown of the world, in so far as that did not involve surrender.

Furthermore, the industrial and commercial forces themselves generally, though not entirely, acquiesced in this position. It would have been better if they had been left entirely alone, but if laws were wanted they didn't mind so long as they were " reasonable " laws. And so, before 1914, all the principal Southern states had laws barring child labor under the age of twelve.

But these laws were so filled with " exceptions," with tender regard for widows, for aged parents, for any parents at all who would state that they needed the earnings of their offspring, that they would have been useless in any case. And they either neglected to specify penalties of any sort or specified such vague and inconsequential penalties as could alarm no one. Furthermore, not a single

Southern state made any serious provision for enforcement; not one set up more than the shadow of an inspection service.

13

But, of course, simply to recite this story is to bring out clearly the proposition I have already laid down: that Progress was in many respects once more actually strengthening rather than weakening the hold of the Southern pattern. And if still further proof is wanted, it can be found in the fact that it was just in these years, when calculation was slipping into the religious pattern after the manner I have described, that we discover the Southern ministers rising swiftly toward the zenith of their power.

It was in these years, that is, that they were able at last to extend their sway over public affairs to the point of writing their Puritanical code definitely into the law of the Southern states. All these states but two adopted statutes wholly or partially prohibiting the manufacture and sale of liquor during the period, and even Virginia would succumb in 1916. And prohibition may serve to sum up a host of similar cases — the suppression of red-light districts (with the ironical result that the majority of Southern hotels immediately turned into brothels), the extension of the laws against gambling, the revivification of ancient blue laws, and so on.

I am not suggesting, naturally, that all this happened suddenly and without relation to what was happening in the rest of the nation. There had been a prohibition movement in the South for fifty years, a movement which was of course continuous with the national movement. But it had hitherto made such little progress that attempts in the late nineties to enact such laws by popular vote were everywhere overwhelmingly defeated.

I suggest nothing so untenable, either, as that the rising element of calculation in religion and morality was the sole explanation of the swiftness and completeness with which change came about after 1900. Any number of considerations clearly entered into the case. One was the perfectly sincere conviction on the part of thousands of good, simple souls — especially among the yeoman farmers — that prohibition would actually wipe out or at least greatly decrease the consumption of alcohol. Another was the will to completer mastery of the Negro. Cuffey, when primed with a few drinks of whisky, was, and yet is, lamentably inclined to let his ego a little out of its chains and to relapse into the dangerous manners learned in carpetbag days — to pour into the towns on Saturday afternoon and swagger along the street in guffawing gangs which somehow managed to take up the whole breadth of the sidewalk, often to flash razors and pistols when anybody ventured to object. And it seems genuinely to have been believed that to forbid the sale of legal liquor, and so presumably to force up the price of the bootleg product, would be to deprive him of alcohol altogether and so make it easier to keep him in his place. Certainly the argument was much used in winning over the hard-drinking poor whites.

But when these things and all else that can be adduced is brought into account, I think there can still be no doubt that the waxing eagerness of parsons and business men to please each other was a decisive element in the matter. On no other hypothesis can we quite explain the fact that almost nobody of any business importance or ambition opposed the scheme; that dozens of men who had formerly made no bones about their disbelief that temperance could be achieved by sumptuary law now lent prohibition their significant influence or at least silently acquiesced in it.

What was also contained in this was the further widening of the old split in the Southern psyche between Puritanism and hedonism. For if the land was growing officially more sternly moral, it is not to be supposed that the old love of pleasure, and particularly *verboten* pleasure, was lessening. Already perhaps the hardest-drinking section of the American nation, the South would go on making its claim to that distinction stronger and stronger.

Almost nobody who wanted a drink felt bound to do without it merely for having voted for prohibition. And, of course, nobody had to do without.

Merely, on the one hand, the sense of the clandestine became always more distinctly a necessary ingredient of the highest enjoyment; and on the other, the sense of sin and the need for absolution in more or less orgiastic religion always more pressing. It is not by chance, I believe, that it is in this time that we find the traveling evangelist, as typified in such men as Mordecai Ham of Kentucky, and "Cyclone Mack" (Baxter McLendon) of South Carolina, multiplying in Dixie with a rapidity unexampled since the early nineteenth-century revivals, and tent revivals everywhere drawing hysterical throngs, not only from among the degraded poor whites but also from the highest levels of society.

14

Perhaps, however, the reader is thinking that in the case I have just been describing, and in truth in the whole development of calculation in the South, the men of industry and commerce, and probably the entire Southern people to some extent, must have finally passed over the line into true hypocrisy, so that, in the end, there was revolutionary change of a sort here.

But to suppose it would be, I think, to miss the truth. If the stamp of Babbitt was upon the new order of business men, upon the new order of ministers, the ultimate fact remains that it is not in terms of Babbitt or the Rev. Elmer Gantry that they are finally to be understood, but only in terms of the long-developing pattern of the past.

Tartarin, not Tartufe, is still the true key figure. These men are simpler, more naïve, less analytical than their compatriots in Babbittry at the North; they continue to be better described by that passage from Henry Adam's *Education* which I have quoted than by anything else. And their secret is at last the secret of that simplicity and that pervasive unreality which has always been associated with their simplicity, rather than any genuine Pecksniffery.

If they are more given to calculation than before, there is nevertheless little of downright cynicism in it. In such journals as the *Textile Bulletin,* in such parsons as Ham and McLendon, perhaps, but even here we must not be too sure. And for the majority, no, there is almost nothing of it. Even in their commercial chicane there is a kind of curious innocence when set against that of a Yankee captain of finance. They go about the making of money in dubious ways as boys go about stealing apples — not only without having ever once looked into or perceived but without even guessing the social implications of the case — in the high-hearted sense of being embarked upon capital sport, in the conviction that at most they are breaking the senseless rules of fusty schoolmasters.

Of the claims of society upon them they have as restricted a notion as any of their fathers in the Old South. In many ways a more restricted one, indeed; for between there lies the long story of the decay of the aristocratic ideal, a story in which this whole account of the growth of calculation in them is of course only another chapter. Morality as it is generally understood in the South in 1914 — as it is commonly understood and preached by the ministers themselves — is the obligation not to break into one's neighbor's strong-box, the obligation not to commit adultery, to refrain from gambling and swearing and strong drink — the obligation, precisely, always to stand militantly for these standards, however much one may fall from them in one's personal conduct, and humbly to seek atonement for these falls. This and nothing more? Not quite.

All that I have been saying about the growth of calculation adds up, as I say, to merely another chapter in the history of the decay of the aristocratic notion of honor. Nevertheless, we should do very wrong to suppose that this notion had entirely expired. That so much is true in some fashion goes, indeed, without saying. There were many men in the South, in all classes from the scions of the old Virginians down to the small yeoman farmers, many men in in-

dustry and commerce, in whom the thing yet lived, and would go
on living, a bright and vital flame, many men whose essential integrity had been but little or not at all corroded by the spirit of
calculation. But, apart from these, it was possible to discover it
still working strangely and deviously and intermittently in the
lives and minds of exactly the men who were distinctly under the
sway of the kind of calculation I have described.

Here, for example, was the master of a cotton mill, born on a
great South Carolina plantation, who notoriously bilked minority
stockholders in his enterprise, by using his ownership of the majority of the stock to vote himself and his sons exorbitant salaries
which consumed the body of the profits — and yet might be
trusted, as certainly as his father and grandfather, to repay a loan
secured by nothing but his oral promise, though it cost him bankruptcy. Or here was another, infamous even in the South for his
labor-sweating, a man who, having contracted his goods to Yankee
merchants at a price, habitually employed cunning lawyers to break
the bargain when a better price offered elsewhere — and yet a man
who fiercely disowned his son for seducing a factory girl, not because there was scandal — there wasn't — not even purely because
it violated his understanding of the Seventh Commandment, but
also because, as he himself put it, it was the act of a cad thus to
make a plaything of another human creature!

In sum, the morality which reigned in the South in 1914 was
at once exceedingly narrow and fantastic. But within its limits
these men were in all sincerity quite usually the sternest of
moralists.

If the case is clear even in the field of commercial chicane, it is
clearer yet elsewhere.

If these men were waxing always more ostentatiously religious
because of the perception that it paid, it is not to be imagined that
this perception was, characteristically speaking, a conscious one, or
that they were not as genuinely and honestly pious as before. What
they were really doing more than anything else was unconsciously

contriving a bargain with Heaven, in which their assiduous performance of duties held to be pleasing to it, their ready response to
the suggestion of the ministers, their raising of new and magnificent temples, should ensure its favor and both their continuance in
positions they liked or their advance to positions they coveted, and
their final entry into bliss.

But that very bargain itself testified to their vast removal from
even the beginning of crass atheism or agnosticism — to the depth
of their sincere and unstudied belief in the old Southern concept
of God as the master of an earth in which every man occupied his
place because He had set him there, and in the perhaps logically
incompatible but always associated Southern conception that He
could be dealt with, that indeed He demanded to be dealt with,
on the basis of a *quid* for a *quo*. For nothing is more obvious than
that men infected with any degree of doubt or cynicism concerning
their faith do not either believe in or contrive such bargains.

And if, in truth, the perception of these Southerners went forward to grasp the immediate social advantages which would naturally accrue to the constant and devoted practitioner of religion in
an intensely religious country — the business opportunities, the in-
vitations to the right houses, the chances for good marriages — yet
these were felt and accepted naïvely as merely the further natural,
just, and entirely deserved rewards which Heaven vouchsafed to
those who pleased it by " living right " and furnishing an exem-
plary model to others.

Similarly with their rising perception that the Southern *status
quo* was admirably adapted to serve as a stage for their personal
purposes. By 1914 it was an absolute axiom in the South that whoever built a factory or organized a business was *ipso facto* a social
benefactor and a patriot of the first order. Indeed, such was the influence of the memory of the genesis of the movement, and such
was the drive of the desire to further Progress, that the newspapers
and other agencies of public opinion had erected a sort of tacit convention, in which they seemed to believe implicitly and which the

public at large seemed to accept in the same manner, whereunder social benefaction and patriotism were the sole motives for building factories and organizing businesses!

Given that, then, and given the Southerner's native tendency to render all his impulses in terms of the highest purposes, it is easy to understand that these men would inevitably see themselves as they were represented, and translate their calculation into quite other terms — have no consciousness that it existed. Their will to maintain the *status quo,* as it was represented in their own feeling about it, would be simply and exactly their will to see the South go along on the road to Progress.

Nor must it be forgotten that their feeling here was itself full of reality. Almost to the last man, they were as patriotic and loyal to the South as they were pious. It was precisely these Babbitts, of course, who were building those skyscrapers in cities which had only the most dubious use for them. And who were risking their money on industrial ventures which, however calculated to bring to the towns the kind of glory they wanted, were often exceedingly questionable from the standpoint of practical business.

To say of them, as I have, that they translated their calculations into terms of patriotism is, indeed, almost to libel them. The truth is rather that calculation and patriotism, as they understood it, here moved so fully in the same direction that the latter completely absorbed and overlaid the former, to the point that it is impossible to say where the one begins and the other ends.

If they appealed to the Southern pattern, yet they appealed as men who were entirely bound within that pattern rather than as men standing without it and coolly estimating its uses. If they cried: "Yankee invasion!" against the McKelways, if they invoked Southern religion, loyalty, and individualism, yet they invoked them as one brother invokes another to hold the common bond dear. They were genuinely concerned lest the march of Progress be slowed or halted, genuinely concerned for the preservation of the pattern to which they had been born and reared.

Speaking by and large, shifty-eyed hypocrisy was the last thing to be discovered in them. They looked at you with level and proud gaze. The hallmark of their breed was identical with that of the masters of the Old South — a tremendous complacency. They walked about the Southern land with the consciousness of goodness and integrity written large upon them, as men who have served God and their country well, as the Twelve Great Champions of Christendom must some time have ridden about the land of Charles, King of the Franks.

15

And so it went all along the line in these years. On all sides there was change, but everywhere it was taking place within the lines laid down in the past.

One thing that I ought to chronicle in connection with the theme to which I have just been paying attention — the decay of the aristocratic ideal under the impact of Progress — was that the very Virginians themselves (the old genuinely realized aristocrats), never wholly immune to the thing, were now succumbing, and would henceforth succumb, to the lure of commerce and industry in growing numbers. Even in Charleston the scions of the great families were at last setting up for bankers or brokers.

The significance of this for our purpose is manifest. Such men did not, of course, turn at once into horse-traders. Most of them carried their inherited standards over into the new occupations as far as they could, and that perhaps had some effect in softening the characteristics of the cruder sort. But in the nature of commerce they inevitably lost ground and came more and more to be merely the commonplace business man and less and less the aristocrat.

Well, and if the content of the aristocratic ideal was continually dwindling in so many ways, was the claim to aristocracy — the old concern with coats of arms and pedigree and the mythology of the plantation — at last beginning to wane too? Do not suppose it. Progress, indeed, had brought in a mythology of its own, whereunder it had become fashionable in some quarters to lay claim to having been "born in a log cabin" and to have begun life as a plow-boy or a sweeper in a cotton mill — to pass as the man of great energy and intelligence who had made himself rich and powerful by his own unaided efforts. I use the term "mythology" advisedly; for the claim was by no means strictly confined to those of whom it was quite literally true, but, in the upcountry at least, was also made by men who had been born well up in the social scale. That is not to say that they lied outright. There were precious few men of whatever rank born in the Southern country-side before 1900 who had not some time served as plow-boys. And in many of the small towns of the upcountry it was the custom for the young sons of business and professional people, including the executives of the mills, to do a summer's turn in the factories. But the implication here was clearly false, the measure of reality such as belongs to myth and legend.

For all this, however, the notion of aristocracy continued — and, as I may as well say at once, continues to the present — to dominate social relations and aspirations in the narrow sense. Money, to be sure, was almost a *sine qua non* of social position now — more even than property had been in the old days. Money, in fact, was as certainly the final arbiter of rank in the South now as in Detroit or San Francisco. Without it, it would take a very great name indeed to hold on to its quondam place in the sun.

Every Southern town had its quota of families, impoverished and playing obscure roles in the economic life of the community, making their livings as clerks, or even sometimes as mechanics, but clinging to the belief that grandfather's local prominence, real or imagined, somehow made them the salt of the earth. And some of these went on being invited to the "right houses," though, as years went on, they would tend to be forgotten.

Yet if money was necessary to social position, pride in its possession almost invariably translated itself into terms fixed by the aristocratic complex as it had been brought forward from the Old South. And so much was true even of those people who went in for the new mythology of Progress. It would perhaps be unbelievable in any country less habituated to unreality in these matters, in any men less accustomed and less eager to romance about themselves in every available vein. But I have heard them boast within the limits of a day both of having been born "in a log cabin," and of being the scions of the Great Red Kings of Ireland — of having sometime been a cotton-mill hand, with the implication that they were entirely self-made, and of having had the first gentlemen of the county for their (quite legitimate) fathers!

16

The situation was curious in other respects. Here, on the one hand, were those people who had some authentic claim to descent from slave-owning planters, and who had enough money conclusively to pass the pale and be reckoned as in society. And on the other, the newcomers, often with much more money than the older set, as naïvely sure as any parvenu planter of the 1830's that the achievement of wealth had automatically transformed them into gentry, and bent on being recognized for such. What that meant, for one thing, was that behind the arras society (in the narrow sense, of course) was more or less divided into two not always entirely friendly camps. The older group, full of possessiveness for their ancient distinctions and often jealous of the greater wealth of the *arrivistes,* snubbed the latter at every safe opportunity. And these retaliated in the only way they knew, by making a more splendid show than their tormentors could match.

But whatever went on behind the tapestry, it must not be inferred that the *nouveaux* were not accepted publicly. Everybody might know that George Washington Groundling's father had been a drunken old farmer whose forty acres were perpetually under mortgage, and who bore upon his head the shame of having hid out in the woods to avoid being drafted into the Confederate Army. Still, George W. was president of the First National Bank, and master of five cotton mills. George W. was said to be worth half a million dollars, and indubitably had the making and breaking of most of the families of the county — including, probably, your own. And so, and though he was known secretly to vote the national Republican ticket and the thing was bitter in your throat, what you said in effect was: " Oh, Mr. Groundling, we think it just too wonderful that all by yourself you have got up to be one of us, and won't you come to dinner Sunday and bring dear Mrs. Groundling? "

On occasions you had to go further still. George W.'s son, Oscar, was going to marry Lucy Lamar? It was a fine match for Lucy, everybody agreed, for now Lucy's father could pay his grocery bill. But it clearly would never do to have it that a Lamar was marrying with common clay. Hence it would be necessary for you to play your part in a sort of general conspiracy whereunder George W.'s line would be metamorphosed into what the local newspaper called " an old Southern family." To do quite right by Lucy and to satisfy your own sense of the fitness of things, it probably would even be necessary for you to aid and abet Mrs. Groundling and the Groundling girls in calling in a genealogist; in demonstrating that Groundling was only a corruption of the Old French *Grauntligne,* and that a certain Viscount Fulk de Grauntligne, who was questionless the ancestor of George W. and the explanation of his masterful qualities, had certainly gone to England with William in 1066.

Closely associated with this, naturally, is the proposition that the legend of the Old South was being still further rounded out in these years. It is just now in fact that Southerners themselves fully got around to adorning every knoll in the Old South with a great white manor-house, and to populating the land with more black slaves than China has Chinese. It had to be so, you see, if the great company of people who either were altogether new or had come far up from their original position on the fringes of the upper classes were to be given backgrounds felt to be adequate under the Southern convention. Moreover, it was now exceedingly easy. Hitherto the presence of large numbers of persons (some of them crochety)

who had actually lived in the Old South had always acted to restrain too large pretensions on the part of the newcomers. But the
majority of these inconvenient carry-overs were gone now, fewer
people were any longer really able to say whether a claim were true
or not, and so fiction would henceforth have a clearer field.

What went along with these things also was the further decline
of the Southern manner. Manners in the land remained better —
remain better still — than in any other part of the nation. None the
less, the overshadowing of the greatest of the old families by new
wealth, the clinging of the old families reduced to poverty, the
climbing of the new — all this was increasing, and has continued to
increase, the general feeling of insecurity in rank over and above
what had been general in the Old South, with the natural result
that the old heavy condescension toward whoever was suspected of
failing to be sufficiently impressed became more prevalent than
ever, though I am far from implying that it has ever become universal. The genuine Southern lady often remains to this day what
she undoubtedly was in the past, one of the kindest souls alive.
Nevertheless —

There is a story told by Howard Mumford Jones of his first
evening at a boarding-house in Chapel Hill which admirably illustrates how the unfortunate thing was beginning to infect even very
high levels. The woman who kept the house was no ordinary
boarding-house mistress, but a member of a family which is one of
the oldest and best in the Tar Heel country. Yet on this evening
she fixed her new embarrassed guest with an accusing eye and proceeded to recite him the harrowing tale of how the Yankees had
stolen the silver of her family during the Civil War and so left
them practically ruined — the implication somehow being, as poor
Jones felt, that these Yankees included all Yankees, especially himself.

Such a failure of consideration on the part of such a woman
is partly explained, I have no doubt, by the personal approach
natural to the Southerner — by the fact that, accustomed to identifying herself completely with the South and its story, she ingenuously

tended to reverse the process and to see in every Yankee a genuine representative of Yankee misdeeds. But it is ultimately explicable, I suspect, only on the hypothesis of her own inner uncertainty, and the unhappy fear that a mere Yankee might fail to comprehend her actual claims to rank.

CHAPTER II

OF RETURNING TENSIONS — AND THE YEARS THE CUCKOO CLAIMED

So, in part and predominantly, things stood in 1914. But already the proper laws of industrialism were beginning to assert themselves, counterflow was setting up beneath the surface, and forces were so definitely moving toward the revival of tension in the social and mental pattern of the South as to make what I have said about the great calm after 1900 a little untrue.

Thus, by token of the industrial growth of the years, it was no longer so inexorably necessary that the wages of the factory worker should remain so low as they had been. If the thousand and more mills were built, the dream now, certainly, was of many thousands more of mills, and of towns that should rival those of Yankeedom. And if that was going to be realized, the dreamers plainly needed — or rather thought they plainly needed — to preserve some advantage over the Yankee in the matter of wages.

Nevertheless, by 1910 the barons and the stockholders of the mills were exhibiting a tendency to turn a smaller proportion of the total profits back to the building of more mills or the expansion of industry and business in general, and to take more for their own personal purposes. The barons, like the bankers and chief merchants, were now building large white and columned houses which represented the notions of slightly Neanderthalish architects as to what the old plantation house had been like. Huge automobiles, in red and brass, stood in front of their doors. The wives of the *nouveaux* were climbing into the country club, which had made its appearance, the U.D.C. and the D.A.R., turning longing eyes toward the Colonial Dames, and even dreaming of building a grander house yet in the subdivisions which were gradually appearing in the pinewoods and farmlands about the towns. Their daughters were going away to swank schools in Virginia or on the Hudson, to return with a gelid stare, even to go abroad with Mr. Cook.

And all along the line the lesser beneficiaries of the new order were turning themselves to following up and imitating these great ones as well as they might.

That is to say, the profits of Progress — which were primarily the profits of cheap labor, let it not be forgotten — were going now to create an accelerating material and physical contrast in Southern towns, and to widen the social gulf between the upper classes and Factorytown in proportion. Inevitably, the big showy new houses made the drab cottages of the mill villages look drabber still. And in the nature of humanity, the people who sat in the big houses and the big automobiles began to be more remote from the people in the mill village, to look down upon them from a greater height and more coldly. And of course that gave tone to the feeling of all those who sought to imitate them.

The mill worker, coming downtown in 1914, would encounter — not outright coolness yet. Not generally, anyhow. Nevertheless, the general atmosphere was several shades less cordial and personal than in the past. And moreover the very baron himself was beginning to reflect the same thing. He still almost invariably knew his workers by their first names, but absorbed more and more in his new house, in fascinating motor trips, in Rotary, he had less and less time to maintain his old intimate touch with their affairs.

But it was not only the profits of Progress that were making for the widening of the social gulf. The program of education, which was the other half of Progress, was pointing the same way. That is not necessarily to say that the *whole* effect of the program was in that direction. Perhaps it wasn't. I think the democratizing effect of the grammar and high schools has been exaggerated, but such mingling of the two sides of the railroad tracks as actually took place may have had some general tendency of the sort.

However, it was not of this that I was speaking, but of a special case under the head of education. One of the earliest manifestations of the passion for extending the Southern schools had been the establishment of " agricultural and mechanical colleges " under the land-grant laws of the United States. In the South, as elsewhere, these schools had been intended originally to be farm-life schools where poor young men might acquire the rudiments of agriculture and some mechanical craft. But in the South, as in the rest of the nation, they speedily grew into technical schools of professional pretensions if not rank, with fees not much if at all lower than other Southern colleges. And, above all, they grew into schools of what is called textile engineering.

The young men who attended them were often poor; but they were not poor within the meaning of the term as the original sponsors of such schools had used it. And many times they were not poor at all. For during the first decade of the century, the cotton-mill chiefs and powerful stockholders in the mills began more and more to send their sons to them for training as textile experts — perhaps adding two or three years at such Yankee schools as the Massachusetts Institute of Technology and the Wharton School of Finance to round off the process.

Which adds up to something significant, seeing that these young men were increasingly coming home to fill up the hierarchy of the cotton mills, which had been the greatest single field of opportunity Progress had opened up to the underdog, and through which many men who, if they had not generally been strictly the progeny of the more ordinary sort of mill worker, had certainly been both poor and badly educated, had in fact made their way up. Given a baron with several sons, one of them would now go in training to succeed his father. Another would be likely to take over the superintendency — a fat job, after the achievement of which anything had been possible to the man from below. And others, with a view to an ultimate superintendency or to turning cotton-mill entrepreneur on their own account, might take jobs as overseers — even sometimes as straw bosses. Or, lacking the baron's sons, there would be, of course, the stockholder's. Or, lacking even these, there would still be a growing crew of school-trained young men eager for jobs.

It was far from universal yet. None the less the third frontier, so far as the mills themselves went, was definitely receding, and the way up was beginning to close on the common white in the mills much more fully than had been the case.

2

But I have perhaps given the impression in passing that the worker's pay had not risen at all, whereas in fact it had. The average hourly rate paid spinners in 1914 ranged from eight to nine cents. But this was still from thirty to forty per cent lower than the prevailing rate in New England. And in terms of real wages, it is doubtful that there had been any increase; for after the panic of 1907 living costs had been climbing rapidly in the South, as in all America.

In hours the gain was more genuine, but slight. The 72-hour week was gone, but 60 to 63 hours was still the rule even for women and children. And despite the nominal child-labor laws, many thousands of children from nine to twelve still worked in the mills, though before 1920 compulsory school laws would tend to raise the limit to twelve and fourteen.

All together, then, the Southern mill worker had pretty fair cause for complaint. Here were conditions beginning to shape up so that, logically, he might have been expected to begin to pick up where Populism had left off and move back toward class consciousness.

Nor was he entirely without response to this logic. Looking casually at the scene, you might easily have concluded, indeed, that he was responding to it directly, vigorously, and with clear eyes. For in 1913 a big strike would break out in Atlanta, and from there spread to other places in Georgia, South Carolina, and Tennessee. But it is necessary not to read more into this than it contained.

There had been strikes in Dixie long before this, for that matter. In the late 1880's, at the same time the Farmers' Alliance was springing up, the Knights of Labor had attempted to organize the Southern workers and had actually succeeded in calling a few walkouts. And from 1898 to 1902 the American Federation of Labor's newly organized National United Textile Workers' Union had entered the South. In truth, it had been formed, in part, for the specific purpose of entering the South; for the competition of cheap Southern labor had pretty well stagnated the wages of the New England cotton-mill workers. And at Atlanta, Augusta, and other places it also had signed up workers and called strikes. At one time in those years it had 235 nominal Southern locals. More, a Southern man, Prince Green, of Columbus, Georgia, was actually president of the organization from 1898 to 1900.

But all this had been mere foam before passing gusts, as, in fact, the attempt of 1913 was also to be. Every one of the strikes failed. And such strength as the unions had seemed to muster faded overnight. The Knights of Labor were gone from Dixie even before Homestead; the NUTW retired in despair after 1902, not to return until 1913; and though it kept its walking delegates on the scene after its defeat at Atlanta in that year, its active strength among Southern workers was nil.

The fact about the Southern mill worker was plain. He was willing enough to join the union as a novelty, and to strike. It was a part of his simple childlike psychology and curious romantic-hedonistic heritage, in fact, that he was willing to join any new thing in sight, from a passing circus or the Holy Rollers up — or down. Those tinpot fraternal orders which afford an opportunity to strut in uniform or costume or to posture as the champion of heroic causes have nowhere flourished more than in Southern cotton-mill towns and villages.

And as for going on strike, it afforded a magnificent prospect of taking forbidden holiday, thumbing his nose at authority, maybe of an extended spree, and certainly of an uproar and a fight; in sum, a glorious chance to be the hell of a fellow, and to satisfy both his gregarious love of the sense of standing shoulder to shoulder with his fellows and his individual egotism. Nothing could have been more strictly in his vein.

In addition, it gave him an opportunity to work off in dramatic fashion whatever grievance he might feel about his work. These people were entirely capable of walking spontaneously out of a mill when their pay had been cut below the common level, when the boss attempted to impose new conditions upon them, or when they were denied some particularly cherished boon, like a holiday at Christmas. Because of the very intensity of their individualism, they were perhaps even more capable of it than workers elsewhere. And in fact most of the strikes were inspired by such grievances and had the character of unstudied mass action rather than of unionism. In most cases the union not only collapsed once the strike was lost but numbered no more than a negligible fraction of the workers in the mill until the strike had actually begun.

But when it came to fixing a grievance continuously in view and methodically preparing for a strike by regularly paying union dues, they were quite incapable of it. And as for winning a strike — they hadn't a chance. So much follows from what I have just said, from the lack of coherent organization and the absence of a war chest. It followed, too, from the very carelessness of their psychology — from their willingness, once they had discharged their irritations, had their lark, and begun to get hungry, to drift cheerfully back to work, regardless of the fact that even their immediate aims had not been accomplished. But it followed for far vaster causes — which, however, we can more conveniently examine later on. It is enough here not only that unionism had no hold in the South in 1914 but that there was as yet no soil in which it could really take root — that the worker's irritation at his estate was still far too nebulous and discontinuous.

Nevertheless, I think what I have said is true — that in some dim manner the cotton-mill worker of the South was beginning perceptibly to respond to the logic of the circumstances, and that some degree of irritation was here. And 'for better and more decisive proof than the sporadic strikes, we may turn to politics — that characteristic field of Southern focus — and, specifically, the election of Cole L. Blease as Governor of South Carolina in 1912. For Blease was the first of the Southern demagogues to appeal directly and consistently to the cotton-mill workers as their peculiar candidate and champion. Back in the nineties Tom Watson of Georgia had, indeed, tried it for a moment, but had hastily dropped it; and thereafter nobody had taken it up again until Blease now employed it with success.

Blease was not in truth, however, a protagonist of the actual interests of the mill people. And his rise did not at all testify to the entry of economic realism into Southern politics. On the contrary. He had no program for the benefit of the factory workers. And once he had come into power, his single accomplishment in their behalf would be to fling open the gates of the South Carolina penitentiary through the pardoning power — a deed which was very gratifying to them as to other common South Carolinians, because of the conviction (not without ground) that the pardoning power in the state had hitherto been used with gross favoritism, but which, for all that, obviously had little to do with their true needs.

Indeed, Blease could not have functioned as the active advocate of the cotton-mill workers had he wanted to — and there is no evidence that he ever did want to. For there before him was the fateful lesson of Populism. To attempt to carry through a tangible program in their behalf would inevitably be to raise class conflict, and to raise class conflict would inevitably be to split the Democratic Party into irreconcilable factions. And that, again, would be to threaten the Proto-Dorian front and lay the way open to the return of the Negro in politics. Which, in its turn, would be perfectly sure to alienate a great part of the mill people themselves.

And even if this last had not been so, it would still have been virtually impossible for Blease to win as the active champion of the mill people, just as it would have been virtually impossible for Tillman to win in the 1890's as the active champion of the tenants and share-croppers, had he in fact been such. For every state in the South, save only North Carolina, at that time made the payment of poll taxes for the two or three years prior to an election a prerequisite to the exercise of the ballot, and in Alabama the voter could — and to this day can — be required to show receipts for every year after his majority! Moreover, to cap it all, South Carolina and Alabama imposed property qualifications — in the former the possession of three hundred dollars' worth of real and personal property.

It is equivalent to saying, of course, that the voter was often disfranchised — or that he sold his vote to whoever would pay his poll tax or arrange the case for him and add a drink into the bargain. Two to six dollars or more was a sum not lightly to be paid out by mill-hand or sharecropper. And it is probable that less than half of either group in South Carolina and Alabama could meet the property requirements.

Strictly speaking, the restrictions applied only to general elections and not to the Democratic Party primaries — would operate with total effect only in case of a complete showdown with a new party arising to contest the absolute Democratic sway. Actually, however, among an ignorant electorate the distinction was not always clearly drawn. And many thousands of the poorer whites failed to participate even in the primaries, on the stubborn assumption that they could not vote at all without the tax receipts.

3

In other words, the politics of the South in 1914 was fully barred away from — as devoid of — social and economic focus as it had ever been in the past. And really to grasp a Blease we have thoroughly to understand the pattern to which he belonged — of course, that of the demagogues from Ben Tillman down. And to understand that pattern, in turn, we had better begin by realizing that, in its dominant aspect at least, it was simply a natural enough

term at the end of a long series of terms. In some very genuine
sense the whole story of politics from Andrew Jackson down —
through the Yanceys and Rhetts and the fire-eaters of Klan and
Red Shirt days — had been one of constant progress in demagoguery. In the sense, that is, that, as we have seen, it was the
story of a continual progress in the personal and the extravagant
— a continual contest on the part of every man to outdo all others,
both in time past and in the contemporary scene, in whipping up
the tastes and passions of the Demos with ever more personal and
extravagant representations of the South in full gallop against
the Yankee and, even more, the Negro.

I think the demagogues would have appeared if Populism and
economic and social irritations had never been heard of. A people
long fed on strong meat infallibly grows to demand stronger and
stronger meat still. And in the South it was unavoidable that a
time should come when the best efforts even of the captains of
Reconstruction and their direct heirs would no longer seem wholly
adequate. For these captains were generally in some ponderable
degree under the influence of the aristocratic notion. And in their
most extravagant appeals to sectional or Negro hate there was generally something of that uneasiness of conscience over the possible
consequences which had all along belonged to the better sort of
Southerner, and so some element of restraint. But restraint would
come more and more to be the last thing that the masses of Southerners, including many men who belonged in point of wealth and
power to the upper orders, and untroubled by scruples or fears for
the outcome of unbridled hate, wanted.

Hence the Tillmans. Pitchfork Ben himself owed his success
from the beginning primarily to his great skill in using high histrionic gifts to body forth the whole bold, dashing, hell-of-a-fellow
complex precisely in terms of the generality themselves. And,
above all, to the fact that he brought his nigger-baiting straight
down to the levels of the more brutal sort. And after him virtually
the whole host of the demagogues, in their turn, would owe their
success to their capacity to carry the thing farther yet. Here was

the ineffable Jeff Davis larruping the specter of the black man up and down the hills of Arkansas. Here were Tom Watson and Hoke Smith riding hard upon him in Georgia. Here was W. K. Vardaman roaring to his delighted Mississippians: " The way to control the nigger is to whip him when he does not obey without it, and another is never to pay him more wages than is actually necessary to buy food and clothing." And here finally was Blease, as the capstone of it all.

The day he stood up at the famous old rallying-ground at Filbert and, with his audience screaming hysterical approval, defended lynching by bellowing: "Whenever the Constitution [of the United States] comes between me and the virtue of the white women of the South, I say to hell with the Constitution!" the whole tradition of extravagance, of sectionalism and Negrophobia in Southern politics had come to its ordained flower, and descended at last fully to the level of the most brutal viewpoint in Dixie. And it was that day, too, more than any other in his career, that he bound the cotton-mill people conclusively to his cart, and not only the cotton-mill people but the majority of the commons of every kind, not to say many people of more or less great pretensions. For that heroic voicing and gorgeous inflaming of their own sentiment and passion, they took him to their hearts and made him their great champion with a fullness beside which any considerations of economic irritation became at best only incidental.

But Blease and all such fellows from Tillman forward were nevertheless in some fashion *rebels* — the center of a bitter conflict? Of course. But rebels, not against the social and economic set-up as such, but simply against the job-holding hierarchy of the established Democratic organization. In every state such a hierarchy existed, sometimes taking on the form of a rigid machine, sometimes that of a looser aggregation of cliques. Originally composed of the Confederate captains and their wealthy planter allies, they came more and more to be made up of a cruder sort after the passing of Populism and the advent of Progress. As I have said elsewhere, not only the Confederate captains (who would have been eliminated by age, anyhow) but also the strictly aristocratic type of man tended to vanish from Southern politics after the nineties. In all instances, however, the hierarchies remained solidly conservative; were dominated by and devoted entirely to the interests of the planters and, with increasing emphasis as the years went on, the new industrial and commercial magnates.

And these hierarchies maintained a strict and closed order of succession. The men who were to succeed to the high offices were carefully handpicked years in advance, sometimes even before they had reached their majority. Usually they were from families which already had strong connections within the hierarchy; preferably they had some claim to Confederate tradition; and in every case they were such men as conformed rigidly to the conservative type cherished by the hierarchy. They prepared for their honors by long years of service to the party, which is to say the hierarchy, on the stump and in local organizing activities; and came up through the successive grades only as men ahead made way for them and they received the nod from the high command. In any given election year never more than two or three men, and many times only one, would be eligible under the convention of the order for such a job as that of governor or senator. And whoever did not have the stamp of eligibility upon him was bound to stand aside under pain of losing such honors as he already enjoyed, or of being altogether cast out of the hierarchy.

It was just against this closed succession that the demagogues were primarily rebels. All of them were ambitious and daring mavericks, who either had been unable to get a foothold within the hierarchy or had not got on as fast as they felt their capacities justified. Ben Tillman himself was such a man, and those who came up after Populism were even more clearly and decisively such.

But it was a desperate and dangerous game these men played, of course — seeing that the hierarchy held the whole election machinery in its hands. They needed every vote they could garner; if the masses were disfranchised in part, they were not wholly so;

and nothing I have said is to imply that the rigid conservatism of the regular party organizations, the fact that they served no interests save those of the upper classes, was utterly lost on the instinct of the masses, with their narrow class feeling and their old vague pique and envy. Moreover, the people, having got used to the highly colored monsters conjured up by Populism, went right on demanding them after the fight had been abandoned.

Thus, as much after Populism as during it, attacks on Wall Street, the Cotton Exchange, and that indefinite but exceedingly villainous race called " the rich " — all identified with the regular party organization and particularly the hierarchical candidates of that organization against whom they were immediately arrayed for the prize of office — tremolo references to their own origins among " the common people," and sighs for " the horny hands of toil " and " the poor, hard-working, God-fearing farmer " formed a part of the stock in trade of all the demagogues second only to nigger-baiting. In addition to flattering and delighting the common man with fiery representations of himself masterfully hazing the black man, these demagogues would also flatter and delight him with equally fiery visions of himself, in the persons of these his champions, elbowing the always a little resented lordly ones out of the seats of power, or at least sitting side by side with them.

4

Naturally enough, these men were hated and bitterly fought by both the party hierarchies and the classes the latter represented. The class division, as I have indicated, was never complete. Both Tillman and Blease always had some planter following. But by and large the upper crust was militantly against them. The party organizations everywhere used their control of the election machinery, not merely to disfranchise as many of the demagogues' followers as possible but often to steal votes outright, in the high conviction, fixed by Reconstruction, that, since they had no doubt their cause was righteous, it was wholly justifiable. And planter, banker, factory-owner, professional man, and editor foamed against the Tillmans and Bleases for " arraying class against class," with all the old intensely personal blackguardism native to the region. In South Carolina the fight over Tillman waxed so hot as to eventuate in the killing of N. G. Gonzales, editor of the Columbia *State*. And fist-fights and cutting-scrapes revolving about the name of Blease were numerous.

It was easy to see the scene as one torn by the most genuine sort of class struggle in politics. But that appearance was mainly illusory. The upper classes were naturally made uneasy and angry over the appeals of the demagogues to the masses' awareness of themselves as " the poor." And of course the better sort of Southerner despised their ruffian appeals to race hatred. But the extent and depth of all this can fairly be gauged by the fact that the hierarchies' own candidates often adopted the methods of the demagogues in one measure or another. For instance, Cotton Ed Smith, who was elected to the United States Senate from Blease's own state in 1908, there to remain to this day. The candidate of the South Carolina Democratic hierarchy, Smith was peculiarly the representative of the rich planters and the industrial and commercial interests, and throughout his career he has served them faithfully and exclusively. But he got elected by dressing up in a farm hat and riding about the state on a farm wagon loaded with cotton, quavering over " the poor, hard-working, God-fearing farmer," and inveighing against Wall Street and the Cotton Exchange, precisely as Tillman had done, in heroic and highly picturesque profanity — by these things, and by nigger-baiting as blatant and as barbarous as Blease's own.

What mainly explained the smoke and heat about the Tillmans and Bleases was something quite simple and obvious: the astonishment and outrage of the hierarchies and the classes they represented that anybody should dare to challenge their traditional exclusive privilege of naming the succession to office and appeal over their heads to the masses, whose historical role it was merely to follow where they were led and to vote for one of the men offered them; the will of these hierarchies and classes to hold on to that privilege *in toto*. Such was the true extent of genuine class struggle here.

And when these demagogues had won the Democratic nomination anyhow: We return to the fact that, bound within the lesson of Populism, they not only never had any concrete program to offer the commons but never tried to do anything real for them once they were in office — that politics in the South went right on serving only the interests of the upper orders quite as though the demagogues had never been elected at all. And to that must be added the fact that they rarely made any systematic and determined effort to destroy the subsisting hierarchies. They built up their own machines, surely, but these machines were devoted to their perpetuation in office rather than to raising up a whole new succession. The people, for that matter, went right on voting for the candidates of the hierarchies most of the time, entirely content with having only an occasional Blease for their own.

Hence the hierarchies could and did accept these demagogues. Not that they ever took them to their bosom. Far from it. But they did find it entirely possible to tolerate them as members of the Democratic Party and the Proto-Dorian front with themselves; and might even, when the occasion required it, and in return for support for their own candidates, lend such a nominee grudging support at the polls.

Do I make it sound coldly cynical and calculated? I do not think it was greatly so. We have to remember that all these men, including the demagogues, were simple, unanalytical men, operating within a pattern they had been born to. If it were not always strictly true that the demagogues were the progeny of the poorest sort, as they claimed, it was certainly true that all of them had been familiar with the lot of the poorer farmer from childhood up, and that they were the heirs at once of the forces that had produced Populism, of the tradition of that movement itself, and of the most fanatic Negrophobia in Dixie. It was probably the great secret of their success, indeed, that they profoundly and perfectly summed up in their proper emotions and their own proper minds the things the masses felt.

It is just because of this, however, that Blease's explicit appeal to the cotton-mill workers — which is what we were originally concerned with — seems to me conclusive evidence that these workers were beginning to respond to the logic of the circumstances I have noted, and to become remotely aware of themselves as an estate whose interests were not always identical with those of their masters. The man was a sort of *antenna,* as it were, fit to vibrate in perfect unison with their exact sentiment — in his every word and deed precisely to render what, given all the forces at play upon them, they most secretly wanted: the making vocal and manifest of their slowly gathering melancholy for and resentment against their economic and social lot, without ever losing sight of the paramount question of race.

5

But now in 1914 there was thunder on the Somme and the Marne. And for the next five or six years events would operate with great force once more to reverse the process, to turn back the Southern mill worker's irritation, and to reduce tension. After 1916 so much would follow naturally from the fact that his energies would be absorbed, like those of other Americans, in the common national excitement and in the common national purpose of winning the war. But the case was more direct than that.

For, after a pause in the fall of 1914, the cotton mills of the South (and the cotton mills, of course, may stand for all industrial establishments) were to come in for an enormous increase in business. With the mills of Lancashire, northern France, and Germany bottled up by the war, America was to capture most of the world's trade in cotton goods. And once the American flag was raised in

France, domestic orders would swell rapidly. Thus before long every Southern mill would be running night and day. And before long, again, there would begin a vast expansion of equipment, a swift and unparalleled surge of Progress, the headlong throwing up of new mills — until by 1920 there would be nearly twenty million spindles whirring in the region.

Even before the entry of the United States into the war, this had already had dramatic effect on the case of the workman. Now, for the first time since the Civil War, the surplus of labor in the South was absorbed. And with 1917 and the universal draft, that surplus was to turn into a shortage — with the result that wages shot upward. In 1920 the spinner would be making several times as much as he had made in 1914, in from 55 to 57 hours a week — about $16 to about $24. And weavers would be making as high as $30 or even more.

It was no magnificent wage when set against the really fabulous profits the mills were making — from 30 or 40 per cent up, in some cases, to 350 per cent! And in New England the scale still averaged nearly a third more. But it outran the dizzy rate at which living costs were mounting, and to people conditioned as these were it looked like El Dorado. Given the system under which a whole family worked, a single household might command an income of a hundred dollars a week or more!

And that meant all sorts of splendid things. That the mill worker could have an automobile now, that toy and symbol of modernity which more than anything else, probably, had fixed his envy for those above him. And he could buy brilliantly striped silk shirts at ten and twelve dollars each, and suits and hats and narrow-toed cordovan shoes from behind the awesome plate-glass windows in the towns.

So much, and more still. Dresses for his women that made them look like something besides bags of meal tied in the middle. Pretty hats and shoes, and rouge and perfumes and geegaws. Pianos and phonographs. Ten-cent cigars, with the bands proudly left on. And far from being least, it would no longer be necessary to wait im-

patiently for Saturday night to plod to the "airdome" (marvel-
ously metamorphosed now into multiplying Imperials and Bijous)
and achieve catharsis for all melancholies and frustrations and
irritations in the horse-opera, the vicarious kisses of Mary
Miles Minter, Mary Pickford, Marguerite Clark, or Francis X.
Bushman, the antics of John Bunny, Fatty Arbuckle, or the eternal
Chaplin.

And, of course, it meant that his more basic living standards,
and particularly his diet, would be rapidly improving, too? Even
that he would be beginning to acquire a bank account, to make
himself more secure and independent in the future than he had
been in the past? In general, however, it was not so. Typically, he
spent his money with a childlike simplicity of improvidence and
abandon, which was the perfectly natural issue of his long training
in irresponsibility and his romantic-hedonistic tradition — almost
entirely for things such as I have suggested, which tickled his love
of pleasure and of show. Sometimes he might feast on fancy foods,
and he showed some tendency to add steak, pork chops, and fish
to his diet. But he continued to regard these things as mere luxuries,
to be dispensed with in favor of anything else he might want.
Nor did the upper classes in the South fail to note these facts and
put them down, with the old smug, unexamining assurance, as
simply more proof that he was quite incapable of any really better
way of living.

In one respect, however — that of housing — his basic living
standard was often improving, not because of any effort or demand on his part but because of the huge profits the mills were
making, and the will of the mill-owners to avoid paying out any
part of such profits in the heavy corporate surtaxes the Federal
government was claiming for war purposes. These taxes could be
escaped only if the profits were turned back to the capital structure of the corporation — a fact which was an important element
in the great rush to expand equipment and build new mills. Also,
it explained something else which was very common in these times:
the issuance by the mills of large stock dividends. One mill at

Greenville, South Carolina, actually issued such a dividend for three hundred per cent of its capitalization!

But neither building new mills nor stock dividends could absorb the profits to the point of altogether balking the publicans. Hence the mill-owners bethought themselves of their paternalism and began to expend part of the bonanza upon their villages, which also were capital, of course. Barrels of good money went for huge Y.M.C.A.'s, community houses, and other do-good institutions pleasing to the vanity of Lord Bountiful, which the canny mill worker usually avoided sedulously. But much went more sensibly, to give the workman and his family better quarters. In nearly all the new villages the old shack and tenement standards were abandoned. The houses built were cheap little coops, but they were not all cut to the same monotonous and ugly pattern; they were clean and snug and painted and cheerful; and most of them were equipped with electricity, running water, and plumbing, in place of the kerosene lamp, the communal pump or open well, the tin laundry tub, and the outdoor privy. Even in some of the older villages, especially about the larger towns, such installations were made.

What went to ease tension further was that the third frontier, which had been closing in 1914, was now again expanding — certainly to the point of refurbishing the old belief in free and open opportunity which had always been so important for the preservation of the common Southerner's individualism.

As much follows, for that matter, from the increase in wages. If the workers characteristically spent their money as I have said, of course the more ambitious and shrewd among them — the exceptional individuals — did not, but often took advantage of the case to build up a small capital for themselves or their children. In the period many of them would emerge from the mills to enter small businesses of one kind or another, often to fail, but often to succeed, too. And in the years immediately after the war an occasional one among them would have bank balance enough to send his son to college or technical school.

Again, the rapid multiplication of the mills far outran the production of technically trained men by the schools in these years, and particularly after 1917, when the war began to claim the great body of college men. Once more, as in 1900, there were, for the time being, jobs all along the line from straw boss up to, though perhaps rarely including, superintendent, open to whoever could fill them, regardless of background. What went to bolster the illusion of unlimited opportunity, also, was the general spectacle of the ease with which a mill could be organized and built — the rise of many superintendents and understrappers to be mill-owners on their own account.

6

With the coming of the 1920's, however, the current would shift again, all this itself would begin to be turned about, and many circumstances would once more come into play to make for increasing tension on the industrial front, and to bear with growing pressure on the Southern pattern and mind.

Already by 1919 the European cotton mills were back in the field, and Japan, hitherto of no importance, was on her way to becoming a serious competitor. This meant simply that American mill-owners now found themselves with productive equipment too great for the markets they could hold permanently. And what added to the troubles of the Southern mills was that, as a result of those extravagant stock dividends issued in the war years, many of them now turned out to be over-capitalized for the new conditions.

The immediate result was a war of price-slashing and dumping, eventuating in a wave of bankruptcies. But it did not end with that. What was plainly called for here was some kind of rational agreement among the mill-owners themselves for the retirement of the least efficient equipment and for a system of production quotas. In fact, some vague effort in that direction would eventually be made with the establishment of the Cotton Textile Institute. But in the main such agreement was quite impossible to the traditional outlook which belonged to the Southern barons. As unanalytical as ever, most of them seemed to have no understanding of their troubles, and laid them to the inexplicable operations of chance or the stock market. Hereafter, in truth, most of them would proceed on the theory that the fantastic profits of the war years represented a normal standard. And with that in their heads, they would follow a course of complete individualism, every man driving his equipment as hard as he could.

The upshot was that henceforth the Southern cotton-mill industry was to be a more or less sick one. Its whole history from 1920 onward is that of a series of dizzy surges and plunges. First, over-production, a flooded market, and dumping at any price; then a depleted market, with rising prices and frenzied night-and-day production; and then over-production, with its concomitants and consequences, all over again — this was the story which repeated itself with monotonous regularity.

And for that it was the workers who inevitably paid the main part of the price. For the end of the war and demobilization had naturally restored the old surplus of labor to the South. Wage cuts began almost immediately. From 1920 to 1925 the level fell almost by half, until in the end the scale ranged from about $11 a week to about $19. That, you will observe, was still in the neighborhood of twice as great, in money terms, as had been the case in 1914. But it is doubtful that the gain was much more than merely apparent, since the 1920's were a period of living costs but a little less high than those of the war years. What has to be taken into consideration also is that the policy pursued by the mills resulted in many periods of curtailment or stoppage. In a majority of the mills the worker would not average employment over three-quarters of the time, and in some of them not half the time. So if his weekly wage, as measured in money, was perhaps twice as much as it had been in 1914, his annual wage was not.

At all odds, there the fact of a great drop from the scale of the war years was obviously calculated to operate upon his mind as wage considerations had never operated upon it before. Here was the loss of something he had possessed and become accustomed to, a real standard to be looked back upon and not merely an imaginary one to be dreamed of and hoped for.

Fully to appreciate the case, moreover, we need to set it against the whole background of the 1920's, and not merely against the high living costs which prevailed.

The general character of the time is too familiar to call for any extended exposition on my part. Everyone knows that for all America it was an era of inflation unparalleled in the nation's annals, because of the unparalleled expenditures of the World War; an era of easy money and consequent megalomania, both private and public; an era in which Arthur Brisbane each morning informed a gratified populace that deflations and panics had been abolished, and warned: "Don't Sell America Short!" and in which Presidents of the United States, apparently in good faith, could encourage a stock market, plainly gone insane, to go on pyramiding manifestly fictitious values; an era obsessed with bigger and bigger building, wilder and wilder speculation, and the confident faith that the future held only "two chickens in every pot" and "two cars in every garage."

And into this the South, natively more extravagant than the rest of the country, more simple and less analytical, entered with the most complete abandon. If these years were years of increasing sickness for the old all-important cotton-mill industry, they were nevertheless to be the heyday of the dream and program of Progress.

Every town and hamlet had its Chamber of Commerce now, backed by Rotarians, Kiwanians, Lions, and what-have-you, and engaged with a passion that outdid even that of the past in trying to overpass every other town or hamlet in securing new industries and commercial enterprises.

For that matter, they would keep on multiplying even the cotton mills themselves. Southern capital would not often go into them after the middle years of the decade. But there were the New England mills, increasingly unhappy under the competition of Southern labor — as the Chambers of Commerce were not slow to see. And so, before long, advertisements were appearing in the Eastern newspapers and the trade journals eagerly inviting them to come South and take advantage of the " cheap and contented, 99 per cent pure, Anglo-Saxon labor " and fantastic inducements in the shape of free sites and tax-exemptions. Nor did the Yankee mills delay in beginning to respond. By 1930 the South, which had 43 per cent of all the productive spindles in the nation in 1920, would have 58 per cent of them. And a good part of that gain represented a corresponding loss to New England.

There was irony in this, and menace to the national economy. The South, which had so often had its own economy and social order dislocated by the intervention of the North, with the New England Yankee at its head; the South, which was the most backward section of the United States by all the indices commonly used to measure civilization, in some part precisely because of the Yankee's long strafing and exploitation of it, was now using the combination of that backwardness and the notion of Progress taken over from Yankeedom to begin gravely to upset the economy of the most advanced section of the country! To throw thousands of men out of employment in New England, to half-paralyze commerce there, to injure all the vast network of commerce throughout the East which was inextricably bound up with New England commerce, and to begin to undermine the sources of revenue for those governmental activities upon which New England's claim to lead the march of American civilization mainly rested!

And for the South itself it meant something just as grim: that now the absentee landlordism which we have already glanced at as growing up in agriculture was being introduced into the industrial scene, and in far more menacing form. Practically none of the men who removed their mills to the South would themselves remove there or develop any interest in the region save as a source of profits.

Through its own connivance and at its own desire, Dixie was now being worse exploited than ever the tariff gang had dreamed of. What with free sites and the waiving of taxes, about all it was getting out of the removal of the New England mills was the stingy sums paid in wages, and by them paid out to the merchants — this and the patriotic exaltation of the conviction that it was somehow making the land rich and great. All the rest, including of course the difference between the wages actually paid the workers and the general standard of the nation, was being drained off to the North, to benefit nothing but the pocketbooks of a few individuals. The increased employment, in a land where population kept right on outrunning the available jobs, was a boon of a sort, perhaps. But a boon purchased at the appalling price of virtually giving away the inherent resources of the section, physical and human.

In these absentee-owned mills, moreover, the highly personalized humanity of the old paternalistic pattern practically vanished. Sometimes, indeed, the Yankee barons abolished the pattern altogether, save perhaps for maintaining their own villages, and sent in cold-faced Northern slave-masters to run the mills on strictly business-is-business lines. More often they hired Southern men as bosses, though not without saddling them with spies and " efficiency experts "; and, finding out as well as they might what was expected of them under the convention of the South, had it done after some mechanical and often grudging fashion. But nearly always it was obviously done with a sole view to keeping the worker docile and so to making more profits. To the mill-owner sitting comfortably in Boston or Providence, the mill worker in his Southern factory was not much more a concrete human personality than if he had been a peon or a coolie on some Cuban or East Indian plantation.

7

The continued multiplication of the cotton mills, however, was only a small part of the building fever that raged in the South in this decade. Industry in general so developed that in 1930 nearly two million people would be employed in manufacturing establishments. And the towns grew by great bounds. Over the whole land hung the incessant machine-gun rattle of riveting hammers; in many places the streets were like those of a rebuilding war area, with the yawning walls of old buildings coming down and of new buildings going up; for solid miles through Dixie the old fashionable residential districts of the years from 1880 to 1920 were being riddled by office buildings, store fronts, filling stations, and the like; and about the periphery of all these growing places a ring was thrusting swiftly outward, composed in part of a maze of warehouses and spur tracks, and in part of new, sometimes modest, more often lordly, and sometimes genuinely beautiful residential suburbs.

Atlanta rose up to have a quarter of a million people. So did Memphis and Birmingham. Houston, more than quadrupling its 1910 population, soared to 300,000. New Orleans gained another 100,000 people, Richmond 60,000. Chattanooga, Knoxville, and Dallas tripled their 1910 figures — the last to pass beyond the quarter of a million mark. Norfolk, Fort Worth, Charlotte, Columbia, Greenville, Montgomery, Jackson, all doubled over 1910. And literally a hundred lesser towns doubled or tripled. Strictly in the decade from 1920 to 1930 the total urban population of the South increased nearly twenty-five per cent.

But if the passion for actual building assumed tremendous proportions, the passion for dream building and for speculating upon that dream building, as it developed in the extravagant, romantic, and Progress-haunted South, was Gargantuan. For every real new factory, for every real new skyscraper plastered with mortgages, ten imaginary ones immediately leaped up in the mind of the secretary of the Chamber of Commerce and his Rotarian followers. For every ten thousand of new population, fifty thousand was envisaged.

Were there lots under water in the swamps of the Everglades, or in the not too inviting and inaccessible peaks in the Blue Ridge? They became at once "The Playground of the Nation." Was Blanksburg, for all the fact that it was genuinely growing, still in reality only a straggling market town where farmers came to spit tobacco juice on the courthouse floor? It was destined. Already the real web of new concrete roads was reaching out to make it the center of five counties, and dream roads were weaving upon all the maps of the future. Already you could see the great sweep of its towers and spires lifting up — the sweep of a thousand like it over the mighty vista of the imperial Dixie to come — golden in the purple morning.

Such visions, once conceived, were accepted by both their sponsors and the public — in this country so long trained to believing what it wanted to believe — as being practically as good as realized actuality; with a result that is comparable to nothing but the speculative boom of the 1830's at which we have before glanced, or the Mississippi and South Sea Bubbles. Every man who fancied himself as a trader (and there were few men in the South who would not come to fancy themselves as traders in these years) and who could command the easy credit of the time rushed to get in on the ground floor and lay hands on something, anything, that might be of value in the megalopolises of tomorrow; maybe to hold on to it, but more likely to sell it to another eager entrepreneur of the future, and hurry on to something fancied to be more pregnant with coming riches still.

The consequence was that realty and business values shot up at an incredible rate. Business lots that had been worth $2,000 in 1910 came to be worth $50,000 or $100,000. Lots remote from any existing business district often got to be reckoned as business lots and to be priced accordingly. And residential property hastened to follow the lead of commercial values. Even farmlands, far out in the country, which yesterday had sold for $50 or $100 an acre, often turned into " subdivisions " through the magic of a few stakes and markers, to be held for $10,000 an acre in the certainty that " in just a few years this will be practically downtown." Stocks in local corporations many times got to fetch twice or even three times their normal value; stocks in enterprises that had no existence save on paper went for fat premiums; and the very cotton-mill stocks themselves regularly sold for fancy prices, though people were already sagely saying that they were good stocks not to have.

8

And in all this, manifestly, there was much that was significant for the story of the social and mental pattern of the South.

Thus, for one thing, the third frontier was being expanded again. Broadly speaking, indeed, these were the years of the greatest opportunity for the acquisition of easy riches, or rather the seeming of easy riches, that the South had ever seen. And that, in its turn, naturally meant that the ruling class was once more enlarging. But not so greatly as you might expect, and, as I have already suggested, perhaps not greatly enough to change much the conclusions as to the make-up of this class which I drew in the last chapter. For if the third frontier was expanding, yet, as the inevitable result of the vast increase in values and that growth in the large-scale organization of industry and business which, in the South as elsewhere, was characteristic of the 1920's, its *threshold* was also rising.

To get into almost any sort of business now, a man had to have, both absolutely and relatively, many times as much capital as formerly. Would he turn merchant, for instance? He would have to encounter the competition, not only of large local establishments but also of chain stores. And so it went in most fields. Which is to say, of course, that the odds were now more heavily weighted against the rank and file of underdogs than even in the past.

That is far from saying that they were decisively weighted against all underdogs. Credit, as we know, was easy. Moreover, the predominantly speculative character of the times operated to throw emphasis back upon the horse-trading heritage with even sharper definition than ever before. As in the 1830's, the scene was ideally set for the boomer and the shark. And whoever had any notable capacity for shrewd bargaining and for capitalizing upon the overheated imaginations of his fellows, and could manage to demonstrate as much to a banker, would have little difficulty in securing backing. Many thousands of talented traders and promoters were in fact making their way up from below during the period.

But in the end only a relatively small number of them would come *all* the way up to the top. For that top itself was rising rapidly. That is to say, the men who had already belonged to the ruling class before 1920 were themselves growing rapidly more rich and powerful, and at a tempo which it was extremely difficult for any newcomer to match, at least when these members of the ruling class possessed the necessary capacity for bargaining and inciting the imagination of the public with visions of the dream cities of the future. For they not only already had capital to begin with, but also they naturally could command the easy credit more readily. In many towns in the South, indeed, a sort of closed clique, composed of the bankers and their selected cronies and understrappers, all but monopolized the available credit (often in blithe disregard of banking laws) and, in consequence, the really good opportunities.

It might almost be argued, as a matter of fact, that the ruling class was narrowing rather than broadening. Or at any rate that a new super-group was being imposed on top of the general body. The class would remain a whole in the broad sense, but, particularly in the states where Progress was making the greatest gains, a small group of industrial and commercial barons who had far outstripped the rest at making money — bankers, the larger manufacturers, utility magnates — would wield an increasingly great share of the actual power. And not only of economic and general social power, but of political power as well. More and more these groups would dominate the regular state organizations of the Democratic Party, and their office-holding hierarchies. And more and more, laws would be made or left unmade at the instance of the lobbies they maintained in the state capitals.

On the other hand, the South was now conclusively coming to have a middle class. In some sense it had perhaps had a middle class all along — in the yeoman farmers. But the sense had been a very vague one. And it was not until the rise of industry and commerce and the towns that a really definite middle group had begun to grow up. Now in the 1920's, however, it was, as I say, clearly marked out, against the growing wealth of the ruling class — a numerous army, ranging from small property-owners, small traders and small speculators, and run-of-the-mine professional men, down through clerks, bookkeepers, schoolteachers, and white-collar people of every sort.

Its emergence was perhaps potentially a little ominous for the social and intellectual solidity of the South in a distant and as yet entirely indiscernible future. Even immediately, as we shall see in a moment, it was in some fashion significant for such a division. But by and large it was significant of anything else on earth, for the present, rather than division between these people and the classes above them. Caught, almost to the last man and woman, in the vision of Progress and the mighty South which was coming, they remained among the best romantics and individualists in Dixie. If they chafed a little sometimes under the thought that they weren't good enough to be invited to the big houses in the fashionable suburbs, yet they associated themselves to the people in those houses with the loyalty of those who not only are convinced that their interests are identical with those of the ruling class but also confidently expect presently to join it on their own account. Every trader, every clerk, every bookkeeper, committed to the illusion of free and unlimited opportunity, was engrossed in dreams or schemes whereunder, he felt, he would surely achieve position and wealth for himself out of the rosy whirl about him.

But here we pass from the field of purely social phenomena to that of ideology. And when we come to that, there is more which deserves to be said, though most of it is only a development of what we have already seen growing up, and so can be said briefly.

One obvious thing was that these Southerners of the 1920's were passing more and more into the mold of Babbitt — that the passion for money-making, pride in and admiration for acquisitiveness, carelessness as to the means employed to the end, and the spirit of calculation in general were all feverishly increasing. " Makin' any money? " Such would become the almost universal greeting among the more ambitious orders in the towns in these years. And the same moral obtuseness which would leave the nation virtually indifferent to the Teapot Dome scandals would show itself in the South, too; and not only in regard to that case, but also in local cases.

As it was used now, there was in that word " smart " some portion of the same implications contained in the words " *onore* " and " *virtù*," as, according to John Addington Symonds, they were used by the men of the Renaissance. That is, there was in this South of the 1920's, far from universally, but widely and increasingly, something of positive delight, infecting both actor and spectator, in the vision of a man pushing straight to his goal of material success in contemptuous scorn for the squeamish fears that stopped weaker men, and never doubting that his own ego was its own sufficient justification.

9

With these things before us, we are ready to return to the case of the cotton-mill worker.

What it all added up to was that, at the very time when his pay was being cut to about half what he had come to count on in war times, the physical and social gulf which we have seen as already opening appreciably by 1914, was now widening again, and more signally and rapidly. If the houses in the multiplying new suburbs were still not often really grand by Yankee standards, they were a good deal grander than the South had ever known on any extensive scale before, and far more numerous. Lifting proud faces, freshly white and red and yellow, from a semi-forest of cool green foliage and over wide lawns, trim hedges, and spacious, winding avenues, they pointed the contrast with the parched dinginess of the mill villages much more decisively than the pre-war town houses had done. And in the streets and upon the new concrete highways, ever more sleek and splendid automobiles were thronging, to inflame the mill worker's envy.

True, as I have said, his own housing had sometimes improved. And in many cases, particularly if his family were large, he would be able to hold on to an automobile of sorts, and even, toward the end of the period, to buy a radio — that latest plaything of modernity. But the improvement in housing had never begun in the majority of the mill villages, and nearly everywhere it would stop abruptly with the post-war collapse. The factory housing of Gastonia, for instance, remained, and to this day remains, very largely a slum — though, because of the relatively wide spacing, not perhaps so repulsive a slum as can be found in some of the mill towns of Pennsylvania and New England. And the automobile our mill-hand held on to would commonly be a limping old jaloppy, fit to incite titters downtown.

But if the physical gulf was growing wider, the social gulf was opening even more broadly. As the towns expanded, the big-house people in the larger places no longer knew even the lesser burghers or anybody at all save their own immediate business and social associates. In such a place, the mill worker might wander the streets all day now without ever receiving a nod or a smile from anybody, or any recognition of his existence other than a scornful glance from a shop-girl.

In the smaller towns the ubiquitous great lawyer was still around with his familiar hand and warm greeting, but even he was not always certain these days to remember your name. And for the rest, the people in the small-town big houses were naturally doing their best to imitate the people in the big-town big houses, including the cultivation, so far as they might, of the remoteness which was creeping naturally into the manner of the latter; and the business men downtown in these smaller burgs, increasingly absorbed in manipulating intangible values and in their pursuit of wealth and the dream of Southern empire, inevitably had less and less time to take account of such matters as the personality of a mere workman.

In both great and small towns, moreover, the emergent middle class, as it became more and more aware of itself as such, was not only imitating the ruling orders but also outdoing those orders in the toploftiness with which they looked down upon the cotton-mill people. That, of course, on the principle, which we have already had much occasion to note, that those who stand closest to the line on which a distinction is drawn are those who insist upon it most hotly. It is what I meant when I said awhile ago that the full appearance of this class was in some fashion immediately significant for division in the South. If it signified no breach between these people and the upper classes, it did mean that the mill people were now more completely set apart than ever.

In the mills themselves the gulf was growing, also. Most of the old barons were dead or dying, and when they weren't, were usually so engrossed in golf at the country club or in the mania for speculating in land values or stocks that they had no time left for the practice of their ancient amiable habits. In the main, their shoes were filled now by their sons or successors. Many of these had been trained in the tradition of the old close personal relationship between master and man and, particularly in the smaller mills, often sought to continue it; but they were commonly quite as much absorbed in the country club and speculation as their elders, and so in their turn had little time really to cultivate it. Too, the generally greater spread in their education and background made it more difficult for them to get close to the worker than it had been for their fathers.

Still another thing that sometimes cut straight across the tradition was the Yankee cult of the Great Executive. Seducing the vanity especially of the young men who had been educated in the Northern business schools, and their imitators, it led them to surround themselves with flunkies and mahogany and frosted glass, with the result that the worker who had been accustomed to walking into the Old Man's office without ceremony could no longer get to them save at the cost of an effort and a servility which were foreign to his temper and tradition.

These men of the new generation would by ordinary go on contributing to and supporting the mill churches and schools, might in many instances make a great show of knowing their workers by their names and occasionally forgathering with them over the soda-pop box in the company store; but they did it, in part perhaps because of growing calculation, but more for the same reason that they wore a dinner jacket in the evening: because it was something one was supposed to do in the circumstances — habitually and mechanically, but, typically speaking, without the direct interest and zeal which had belonged to the older men.

That is to say, the feeling which had lain at the heart of the old notion of paternalistic duty was fast dwindling, leaving only the shell — at the same time that the notion of paternalistic *privilege* was remaining as strongly entrenched as ever, and even perhaps being expanded. The new barons, to a man, held tightly to the conviction of their right to tell the worker what to do — as, for instance, how to vote in an election — though now they often told him through understrappers rather than directly. And some of the more hard-bitten among them were beginning to resort to overt use of that power to coerce which had been the baron's all along, and to emphasize their advice by firing whoever was discovered to have flouted it.

10

But I have been speaking throughout this chapter just as though the cotton-mill workers were the only Southerners who were coming out at the little end of the horn of Progress, and of course it was not so. I have dwelt on their case simply because, as the oldest and most numerous single group of Southern industrial workers (they numbered about 400,000 in 1930, or approximately a fifth of the total of Southern factory workers), they were obviously the spearhead of the common whites in relation to Progress — the group for which the laws of the new mechanical order would naturally be expected to begin to work themselves out most immediately and manifestly.

In point of fact, the cotton-mill worker was often better off in some respects than other types of industrial laborers; perhaps even than most of them, aside from such relatively small groups as the full-fashioned hoisery workers, the rayon workers, and the cabinet-makers in the furniture factories, who, having to have a high degree of skill, were paid from twenty to thirty-five dollars a week or more. And at his best he was sometimes not much, if at all, worse off than such artisans as masons, carpenters, and painters, despite the greater wages these latter were paid at the period. This for the slightly ironic reason that it was only for the cotton-mill worker that the old plantation scheme of housing held. For him alone did the industrial masters of the South provide lodging along with his job. All the rest — industrial and craft labor alike — as they crowded into the towns must find their own lodgings.

And it was characteristic of the Southern towns that they failed signally to build adequate and decent low-cost housing to accommodate this swelling working population; and especially after 1925. So much follows naturally from the fictitious rise in real-estate values — itself largely based, so far as it was based on anything tangible, on this very growth in population for which the influx of labor was mainly responsible — and the wide general disparity between these values and the wages paid. But, as regards white labor, it followed from something else also: that it was a good deal more profitable to build houses for Negroes — a case I shall discuss more fully later on.

There were a good many small and flimsy houses built in Southern towns during the 1920's, to be sure; usually in scrubby little suburbs located unpleasantly close to the garbage dump, the gas works, or railroad yards. But they were held at such figures as to be quite out of the question for the great body of industrial labor. And the craftsmen, mechanics, and so on who did rent or buy them on the installment plan (the word "buy" is a misnomer in the premises) paid at a rate that was out of all proportion to their earnings.

The upshot was a constantly increasing tendency toward overcrowding. Into the old cottages of the poor, designed for only one family and often having no other facilities than an open well and an open privy, two and sometimes even three families began to wedge themselves. And from that center the overflow spread outward. Sometimes into quarters that had originally been built for Negroes. Sometimes into new shacks built by the standard that prevailed for the Negro — quarters for which the sanitary facilities might sometimes consist only of a water spigot for every half-dozen shacks and an open privy for every two or three. Sometimes into huge ramshackle shells thrown together for the purpose and misnamed "apartment houses" — miserable wind and fire traps, often with only one bathroom for three or four families. And always and everywhere into the old large town houses of the more prosperous, vacated by the exodus to the suburbs.

It was in the last, in truth, that overcrowding perhaps came to its worst. Islanded among the new stores and garages, or still ranged in relatively unbroken rows along their streets, these houses were held as immensely valuable property. Not many single families that would agree to live in them would be likely to have the money to pay the rents which were asked. And so, while some of them were made into respectable boarding- and rooming-houses and the like, into many of them the poor came crowding, four, six, or even eight families to the house. Or sometimes these houses became proletarian rooming-houses: swarming warrens, with four or five persons herded into each room.

The conditions were appalling almost from the first. For it was quite impossible to heat such huge, drafty old places with the scant means at the disposal of the poor. None of them had any sanitary facilities save the sketchy ones that were considered adequate for one family under pre-war standards — many times only a single bath for a whole house. And the owners, holding them purely with an eye to selling the lots on which they stood for a fabulous price, generally refused, not only to improve them, but even to keep them in repair; with the result that they decayed rapidly and sank more and more into being mere filthy dens.

By 1930, in sum, a large part of Southern labor, particularly in the greater and more rapidly developing towns, was living under slum or semi-slum conditions, which were considerably worse than those that, by and large, prevailed in the cotton-mill villages.

Meantime, the common whites on the land — the small farmers, the tenants, and the sharecroppers, still outnumbering all industrial labor more than two to one in 1930 — had been coming in for their share of trouble, too. Economically, indeed, they were perhaps faring worse under Progress than any other Southern group.

To be sure, cotton was to fetch a pretty fair price throughout the whole period from 1915 onward until the arrival of the great depression, and sometimes it was to fetch amazing prices. After the temporary slump in 1914, the war demand caused the market to rise rapidly and continuously, until in 1919 it shot up to thirty-five cents, the highest price quoted since the Civil War. Next year it slumped as precipitately as the cotton mills, falling to sixteen cents. But about that time the boll weevil crossed the Mississippi on its march from Mexico, devastating whole cotton counties in the deep South and penetrating right up to the northernmost limit of cotton-growing, in North Carolina — with the result that by 1924 the staple had climbed back to twenty-three cents.

Thereafter came another great expansion of cotton acreage (itself immediately explained by the rising price), particularly in the Staked Plains of Texas. And something else: a definitely increasing foreign competition for the cotton market of the world — in its turn springing in great measure from the high tariffs (those ancient oppressors of the Southern cotton farmer) imposed by the Harding and Coolidge administrations and the mounting inflation in the United States, both of which operated to make it harder and harder for cotton processors abroad to lay hand on dollars with which to pay for the Southern staple, and so caused them to begin to think of finding a supply elsewhere. In India, in China, in South America, and in the Soviet Union, the production of the staple was expanding. And in the same period the competition of the new synthetic fiber, rayon, began to make itself felt. Hence once more the price began to shelve steeply off, dropping to ten cents in 1926, only to move back to eighteen the next year.

Nor was it only cotton (or tobacco, the price of which roughly paralleled that of cotton) that contributed to the income of the Southern farmers in these years, but also prohibition. State prohibition had had the effect of turning some of the tenants and lesser landowners to moonshining even before the war. But with the adoption of national prohibition and the cutting off of all legal supplies of liquor, the price of the illicit product, easily made from corn, began to rise with great speed. Before 1920 it was selling as high as five dollars a pint, and such prices were to continue until after 1925. Under that lure many thousands, not only of tenants but also of farmer-proprietors, would abandon their fears and scruples and take to its manufacture.

But for all the relatively high price of the staples and the new source of income, the Southern farmers were nevertheless far from being in clover — on the whole, indeed, were losing way rather than gaining it.

II

Like the cotton-mill workers, they would have their halcyon period of unprecedented prosperity during the war years. And would use it, to a great extent, just as the cotton-mill workers had used it: after the romantic-hedonistic pattern fixed in the past. Considerable numbers of the more aspiring yeomen, to be sure, would turn it to the purpose of extending their land-holdings, and sometimes a tenant or occasionally even a sharecropper would take advantage of it to climb into the landowning class. But for the run — "Whiskey, gambling, indulgence in sexual pleasures, purchase of useless articles of luxury, and excursions to distant towns, absorb their profits . . ." wrote Professor R. P. Brooks from first-hand observation of the tenants of the Black Belt in Georgia, and pretty well summed up the case, not only of the generality of tenants but also, with more or less modification, of great numbers of the farmer-proprietors.

And with the 1920's and the increasing depredations of the boll weevil, the farmers were to suffer a fate almost identical with that of the mill workers. Those who stood most directly in the weevil's path were to suffer a much worse fate. Many thousands of landowners in the deep South saw their fields turned into wasteland and themselves reduced to bankruptcy; and many more thousands of tenants and sharecroppers were driven to emigrate *en masse,* either to other sections where the ravages of the weevil were not so extreme, or to the cities. Everywhere they went to glut the labor market and further debase the living standard.

But even the farmers who escaped catastrophe were to have their earnings cut about half from what they had come to know. To be exact, the average annual return per acre for all the cotton farms in Dixie during the period 1920–27 was a little more than $29, whereas the average return per acre in 1919 had been more than $60, and the average annual return for the period 1915–19 had been nearly $50. Set against the less than $11 average for 1898, this still looks pretty fat, of course; and even against the $21 annual average for the eight-year period immediately preceding 1914 it looks hopeful. But, as in the case of the mill worker's wages, the gain here was more apparent than real, being mainly balanced out by the rise in living costs. Nor must it be overlooked that these living costs were almost as real to the Southern farmer as to the industrial laborer, since the cotton farms, as well as the tobacco farms, almost universally had to import food for both man and beast.

But the farmer, after all, could escape that? There was nothing in the world to keep him from growing his own food? You might have thought as much, for about this time he was beginning to be deluged with sage advice from governors and editors and almost everybody else who set up as authority, with the slogan: " Live at Home." But in fact the thing was generally impossible, as his advisers might have known from a little elementary analysis. For essentially the same financial system which I described long ago was still hung around his neck — as it is to this day. The banker had commonly come into the equation now; sometimes to take over from the time merchant the whole financing of local farms; more often, perhaps, merely to enable the merchant to extend the scope of his operations. But the total effect of that was simply to make it more likely than ever that a man would have to pay the maximum charges to secure the credit he needed.

Saddled with such burdens, the majority of Southern farmers, whether sharecroppers or tenants or landowners, would remain in debt year in and year out, never getting far enough ahead to finance next year's operations for themselves. And in consequence they had to yield to the demand which the ultimate creditors of them all, the bankers and the time merchants, laid down as the prime condition of credit: that every available inch be planted in the one crop which was most readily convertible into cash: cotton — or tobacco.

But these were only a portion of the difficulties the white man on the land was encountering.

I have said that, in the conditions which prevailed after the Civil War, the ante-bellum plantation had begun to break up, and the ownership of the better lands to be somewhat more widely distributed. And so far as the break-up of the plantation — of all larger land-holdings — goes, it was a process which was to continue on into the twentieth century. So much followed from that flight of the greater landowners into the towns which I have already indicated and which went steadily on throughout the years, until by 1920 there were great areas in which it was next to impossible to find a plantation house still occupied by its old masters. But it followed much more fully from something else — that after the Civil War the population of the South had been constantly increasing, at a far greater rate than that of any other part of the nation. As late as 1920, according to the figures of Howard Odum's *Southern Regions,* the average number of children under five years of age per thousand white mothers in the eleven former Confederate States east of the Mississippi was 724, as against 428 for New England and 538 for the nation. And even in 1930 the number was still 551, as compared with the national average of 479 and the Far Western average of 375!

This great growth of population is of wide general importance for the story of the South, of course. It was the pressure generated by it that in the last analysis mainly built the towns. With the presence of the Negro, whose birthrate was even higher than that of the whites, it explains the perpetuation of the reservoir of surplus labor, which kept industrial wages low. And also it accounts for the fact that always since the Civil War there had been a steady stream of emigration away from Dixie to the North and West (in 1920 nearly three million persons born in the South were living outside its borders), which had had the effect of robbing the region of some of its most energetic and intelligent elements.

But the effect that concerns us here is the obvious one: that it meant that the holdings of the fathers of one generation had had continually to be divided among multiple heirs in the next — that a plantation of, say, a thousand acres, a farm of two hundred, was likely to be split up among a half-dozen, even a dozen or more, children or other claimants.

In the single decade between 1900 and 1910, according to the United States census, the number of Southern farms containing less than a hundred acres increased by nearly 350,000. And by 1930 almost eighty per cent of *all* Southern farms contained less than a hundred acres, while less than one per cent contained more than 500!

But the corollary you might naturally expect — that a constantly increasing proportion of the whites on the land would be becoming owner-operators, and that opportunity for achieving ownership would be always waxing — does not follow.

We come back upon that final difficulty which I have announced. Briefly, it was this: that the price of land had gone up greatly in these years. In part, this was a natural enough reflection of the growth in population, which of course increased the competition for the soil, and of the generally higher price brought by cotton from 1900 forward. The rise of Progress and the growth of the towns, inevitably involving a general and authentic lift in values, had some normal effect for the purpose also. And so did the old native hunger of Southerners for possession of the soil, and even perhaps the notion that gentility inhered in the possession of large portions of it. For these had their bearing in the development of a tendency, visible all along from the 1890's, for business and professional men who made money in the towns to turn a considerable portion of their new wealth to buying up farms.

But perhaps the greatest factor of all was that impulse to fevered speculation which was to be so great a part of Progress in the war era and the twenties. There was nothing absolutely new here. The South always had vented its horse-trading instincts by speculating in land, its single greatest possession, even during the blackest years after the Civil War. Even in those years, as I have said elsewhere, it never quite lost its capacity to believe the thing it was most anxious to believe: that, come next year, cotton at last would begin to fetch always more handsome prices. And once prices had actually begun to improve a little, that romantic faith took fire anew.

12

With the arrival of the war era, however, it really came into its own. Here at length was the old dream apparently coming true: here was cotton sweeping toward a price of forty cents with such celerity that the soberest and most cautious traders began to talk of fifty cents, and the more excitable sort of a dollar. And so throughout the South, in the towns, in the countryside, men — virtually all men who had money, who could borrow money, or who could get credit — began to engage in a scramble to buy land; to buy it for all sorts of reasons, but above all because they confidently expected to sell it again tomorrow for a thumping profit.

At the peak, in 1919 and 1920, I myself saw lands that had sold for two dollars an acre in the first years of the century fetch three hundred dollars.

Afterward the general slump and the fall in the price of cotton slowed up the process a good deal. Through the whole of the twenties, indeed, speculation in land would not again reach the level of the war period. None the less, the romantic belief that the price levels of the war somehow represented normal levels was as common in respect to cotton as it was in regard to the cotton mills. And that, plus the general tendency of the time, served to keep land speculation still going at a more or less frenetic rate. Moreover, during this decade increasing numbers of tenants, of the sons of land-owning farmers who found their portion of the family heritage too small, and of farmers generally — most of them under the influence of the notion that war prices were the prices to which cotton would presently return — eagerly availed themselves of the easy credit facilities and set out to buy farms or extend their holdings. By 1930, banks in the cotton and tobacco country would often hold mortgages on half the land in their counties!

Thus, although the price came down from the war heights, it nevertheless remained greatly inflated. As much does not appear, indeed, on the basis of the average figures, for in 1930 the average value of Southern farms was less than half that of those in the Middle West. But what has to be taken into account is that the South was full of land, reckoned as farms or parts of farms, which was nearly or entirely worthless, either because of the boll weevil's depredations, because cotton and tobacco had worn them out, or because of erosion. In 1930 the region had well over half the nation's total of 150,000,000 eroded acres. And, in fact, land of any degree of fertility generally sold in most parts of the South in this decade at from fifty to two hundred dollars an acre.

But such prices were all out of proportion, obviously, to the actual earning value of the land when planted in cotton. If the price of the staple was relatively high, yet the farmer was saddled not only with the burdens already mentioned, higher living costs and the same finance charges that had always been his Old Man of the Mountain, but also something else — even the better land, long devoured by ravenous cotton (and tobacco was even more rapacious), was coming to require ever larger and larger quantities of commercial fertilizers. The South's annual bill for such fertilizers was now about twice that of all the rest of the nation. Add these burdens up, and it becomes manifest that even the farmers who owned their land in fee simple were not much better off than their fathers had been in the nineties. About as much as the overwhelming body of them could hope for was to earn meager wages for their labor. And thousands of them on the poorer lands were, as always, even unable to do that.

But when to these burdens was added, in the case of the tenant striving to escape from his status, or the heir to a few acres seeking to extend his holdings to a size that would support a family, the inflated value of the land — the necessity of making large annual payments plus an interest reckoned on the basis of general farm financing charges in the land — why, the odds became next to impossible. Numbers of men did, in fact, somehow make the grade;

almost any local community could show you some of them, share-croppers included. But, for myself, I can never cease marveling at the wonderful combination of peasant frugality, back-breaking toil, shrewdness, and luck which was involved.

And for every one who thus succeeded, many more, including not a few who had begun as owners of adequate acreage, failed. I have said already that, despite the continual breaking-up of the larger land-holdings into smaller units, the proportion of owner-operators did not increase. The *numbers* of such operators did increase, to be sure, until 1920, after which they began actually to decrease. But when it came to proportion, it was always not the owner-operators but the tenants and sharecroppers who were increasing. In 1900 about 36 per cent of all white farmers in Dixie belonged to these classes. In 1930 the proportion had gone up, in face of the growth of the rural population, to about 45 per cent. And the fact was writ-ten even more grimly and dramatically in other statistics which revealed that the proportion of tenants over thirty-five years of age was constantly increasing — a thing which indicated, of course, that larger and larger numbers of those who had begun in that estate or were reduced to it were now unable to escape from it.

Nor was even this all. The same *pinch* that made it so difficult for a tenant to escape his status, for many landowning farmers to hold to their possessions, also operated upon the landlord of the tenant and the sharecropper. Only relatively less than in the lean years of the preceding century, he was hard put to it now to ex tract any reasonable income from his holdings. And so he was inevitably subject to the same temptation to grind or cheat his de-pendents which had beset his father. More than that, the infection of the general spirit of the times — the spreading from the towns of the lust to make money without too tender regard for the method — was apt to make him more susceptible to that temptation than his fathers had been. The earnings of the cropper sometimes fell to quite incredible levels — as low as ten cents a day per member of his family. And it was a rare tenant of any sort who found himself with anything left when accounts were settled at the end of the

year. Great numbers of them, in fact, remained in debt to the
landlord year after year, just as they had always done.

There is more still to be noted specifically — that, as tenancy was
increasing and the lot of the common man on the land was growing worse, absentee landlordism was also multiplying. That will
be manifest, I take it from what I have already said, as being inherent in the continued flow of the old planter families and larger
landowners into the towns, in the fact that so many town-dwellers
had long been buying and trading in farms, in the whole pattern
of speculation, which often substituted for local ownership the
ownership of somebody, or even a corporation, located counties
or states away. But what also contributed was that thousands and
thousands of small landowning farmers were moving into town to
become industrial or white-collar workers, and that in many cases
they preferred to hold on to their bits of the soil and rent them to
tenants and sharecroppers rather than sell.

Such, then, was the economic plight of the common white on
the land in the post-war period.

The issue of it all in purely psychological terms requires little
going into, I think, for it is plain that, if the necessary changes are
made, the case is paralleled by that of the cotton-mill worker which
I have already set forth. Obviously, the same great gulf that was
opening between the wealthier beneficiaries of Progress and the
industrial worker in the towns was also opening as against these
common whites in the countryside. Obviously, the growth of absentee landlordism often meant that the tenant saw his landlord
now only occasionally; often, he saw him not at all, but dealt with
him only through an agent. And obviously all this heads up to
mean that the old intimate easy relationship which had once obtained was dwindling and attenuating, and that the common white
on the land, like the mill worker, was more and more losing social
value and being increasingly despised.

And let it be observed, as we leave the theme, that I speak of
the rural common white in general and not merely of the tenant
and sharecropper. From the first, the people of the towns had

tended to develop a kind of supercilious contempt for all country-men, including the yeoman himself, after the fashion of townsmen in all times and places. And the steady passage of the gentry away from the land and the growth of wealth and sophistication in the town caused it to grow and spread, until it infected practically the whole urban population down to mere market villages. In some of the lowland areas of the South the terms " farmer " and " country jake " had got to be nearly equivalent to " white-trash," and fully surrogate for " boor " and " clown " — words not present in the ordinary Southern vocabulary. And if the attitude was not as highly developed in the upcountry, it was still distinctly present.

The Southern tradition of good manners and personal kindliness would generally tend to keep it from breaking out openly in the face of the victim. Nevertheless, there it was, a very real fact with which the yeoman had to reckon in every important social situation — as, for instance, when he came to the problem of finding acceptable husbands for his daughters.

13

The meaning of this extended exposition of conditions in the South in the 1920's is clear enough, I hope. It adds up to this: that in the cotton mills, in the towns generally, on the land, the common white had increasing cause in the decade to feel irritation — that there were here powerful forces to move him toward the development of class consciousness all along the line, and to prompt him at last to begin anew where Populism had ended thirty years before.

And as he had not been wholly immune to the logic of his situation in the years about 1914, so he was not wholly immune to it now. As one who lived in the South at the time, I am convinced that the decade was a period of slow subterranean ferment, of the sluggish, almost imperceptible, but real movement of vague currents beneath the surface.

Oddly enough, however, the best proof of that is not to be found, as one would expect, in the more heavily industrialized states, but in one predominantly rural. After a brief flurry in the post-war slump, there were no strikes of any importance until the end of the period and the arrival of Gastonia. On the political side, the common whites of South Carolina clung to Cole Blease, indeed, but they kept him in the United States Senate, where his single service to them was to keep before the startled gaze of the nation the vision of their eternal assault upon the black man. And for the rest, North Carolina, the chief industrial state of them all, had not a single candidate to challenge the succession of the established and highly Bourbon party hierarchy; Georgia and Tennessee were in the same boat; and Alabama had only Tom Heflin, who, though he posed as a commoner of sorts, was anything else than an active economic and social champion of that estate.

But in Louisiana there was Huey Long. An amazing fellow if ever there was one, he belonged essentially to the traditional pattern of the Southern demagogue as I have exhibited it. He was full of the swaggering, hell-for-leather bluster that the South demanded in its heroes and champions; and in addition he had a kind of quizzical, broad, clowning humor, and a capacity for taking on the common touch, that had characteristically been the stock-in-trade not only of the more successful demagogues but even of many of the best of the older leaders, notably Zebulon Baird Vance of North Carolina. But if Long belonged essentially to the traditional pattern, he definitely carried it forward another great step from the point it had reached with Blease, and greatly modified it in many respects.

He was, I believe, the first Southern politician to stand really apart from his people and coolly and accurately to measure the political potentialities afforded by the condition of the underdog. I do not imply by that, however, that he is to be counted entirely for a cynical scoundrel. On the contrary, his utterances give me the quite distinct feeling that, though he was no son of poverty himself, he had in his heart some genuine sympathy for the " wool

hat " boys of his state, and in his brain a dim but grandiose vision
of himself some day, somehow, leading them into a new promised
land. Certainly at the least he was wholly Southern in his capacity
to represent all his deeds to himself as proceeding from the most
splendid motives. In his jesting humor, in his dealings with the
skeptical tribe of reporters, he often delighted, indeed, to represent
himself as simply a brazen master-manipulator of the calculus of
demagoguery. And he never let his sentiment and his vision get
in his way when any question of practical politics or boodle was at
stake. Nevertheless, if you look into his serious deliverances, it is
hard to avoid the sense that there was in him an almost wistful
conviction that he was the destined liberator of the people who
shouted after his car.

In any case, he was the first Southern demagogue largely to leave
aside nigger-baiting and address himself mainly to the irritations
bred in the common white by his economic and social status. A
completely normal Southerner toward the Negro, he knew very
well how to give a completely convincing and satisfying representation of White Supremacy rampant. But his rise to the Governor-
ship in 1928 was but little due to that factor.

Withal, he managed with wily care to see that he never fetched
up in the *impasse* where Populism had come to grief. And what
makes that a little wonderful is that he was also the first Southern
demagogue — the only one to date — successfully to set himself, not
to bring the established state machine and hierarchy to terms
but to overwhelm it altogether and largely replace it with one of
his own. For that was an enterprise manifestly big with the possibility of splitting the Democratic Party in Louisiana wide open,
to the point of again raising the Negro issue.

The wonder recedes, though, when we observe that in the end
he remained — such was his wiliness — always well within the
pattern of the Southern demagogue as we already know it. That is,
if he overran the old hierarchy, he was perfectly willing to do business with any politician, regardless of his antecedents, provided
only he was willing to acknowledge his own supreme overlordship.

And he made that easy for most of them by simply never carrying his deeds in behalf of the commoner so far that the issue was fairly and squarely joined between himself and the ruling classes of Louisiana at large.

Here again he carried the pattern a good deal forward, to be sure. Whereas the Bleases had done virtually nothing for their following beyond inciting and discharging their emotions, he did a number of concrete things that the common people of his state greatly wanted done. For one, he built good roads into the swamp and hill areas, long ignored by the old order — thereby opening to thousands an opportunity to better their lot by such enterprises as truck farming. For another, he forced the Legislature to provide free school-books — no mean boon for sharecroppers, tenants, small farmers, and town workmen, with the large families usual in the section. And he sailed tremendously into the corporations, which, entrenched in the old hierarchical machine, had been avoiding the payment of a fair share of the taxes of the state, and into the city machine of New Orleans, one of the most prehensile in the nation.

But he did little considering the enormous revenues he collected from taxes and the contributions of his followers all down the line, most of which went for boodle purposes. And what he did was mainly done at the expense of those who were unable to make trouble. In a predominantly rural state, the corporations and the New Orleans machine were too weak to hope to overthrow him unless they could get the bitter-end support of the planters and the rural ruling orders in general. And that support these, though they commonly hated him for having usurped the command of the party, were generally not willing to give; partly because they often sympathized with him about the corporations, partly just because of the perception within themselves of the danger of raising the racial issue again, but above all because none of his deeds seriously injured them — many of them, in fact, such as the new roads and the transfer of a greater portion of the tax burden to the corporations, actually tending to benefit them.

That was the crux of the case. In this predominantly rural state, he never once confronted the really significant problems of the common man in the country, such as tenancy and sharecropping. Such program as he had for the amelioration of their condition was at best a patchwork of half-measures — until he invented his national "Share-the-Wealth" program in the 1930's, itself, of course, not a rational program at all, but simply a descent into the last paranoid depths of demagoguery. And in the ultimate analysis, it is only in degree less true of him than of his predecessors and contemporaries in demagoguery that his chief accomplishment for his clientele was to delight and give outlet to their emotions, in the vision of themselves, made one flesh with him, swarming over the battlements of Wall Street as embodied in the corporations, and driving out of power its minions, the haughty gentlemen of New Orleans and Baton Rouge.

Yet, when all this is set down, the central fact on which I have insisted holds, I think. Huey Long did represent a long step in the development of the Southern demagogue, a definite passage toward increasing attention to and emphasis upon the economic and social case of the common man. And his appearance, his swift rise, and the worshipful enthusiasm of the crowd for him, all stand as evidence that there was a ground swell in Dixie in these years. . . .

14

But, as I have said, that swell was sluggish and vague for the most part. At the end of the period the masses of the South were still infinitely far from having returned to even such irritation and agitation as they had displayed at the beginning of Populism.

Nor is it too difficult to understand why. For if there were great forces here to drive hard upon the inertia of tradition and move the commons toward the development of more than rudimentary class consciousness, there were also, as always before, other even more tremendous forces which operated to hold them in their ancient pattern.

Some of these, of course, lie plain on the surface of the story as
we have already seen it. If the odds were rising against the run-of-
the-mine in this speculative era, yet it always has to be remembered
that now, as in all times past, these constantly had before them the
spectacle of men making their way up the scale. Men could and
did sometimes surmount the odds against tenants and sharecroppers, escape from the spindle and the loom, and make their way
from the bottom to riches, or to such competence and position as
was satisfactory to the less vaulting ambition. And so once more
the fact was obscured, once more the illusion of free opportunity
for all was accepted without definite question, with no more at
most than sullen bewilderment on the part of individuals among
the younger generation, than sad puzzlement on the part of some
oldster gazing back on long years of effort rewarded with little
more than meat and bread.

What contributed to the same effect was the infection of the general spirit of the times. With the patriotic faith in Progress already
drilled into them for forty years, with every platform and newspaper full of Prosperity and the dream of the greater South to
come, all the ambitious sort, in industry and on the land alike,
entered into the prevailing romantic belief and feverish expectancy
almost as completely as the higher classes. And even the indolent,
unaspiring ruck felt cheerfully if vaguely that very fine things for
everybody were probably just around the corner.

Not to be overlooked, either, is the increasingly dazzling power
of the town — its great and growing entertainment value, and its
role in diverting and discharging emotion. With its towers, its
bright shop windows, its glittering signs, its blaze of white light
at night, its theaters and bands and parades, its crowds, it in effect
made permanent for a simple country-bred people the old once-a-
year circus or traveling carnival. For the workman who dwelt
within its bounds or purlieus, every evening might be a sort of
fete night, upon which he need spend nothing if he did not choose.
For the sharecropper, tenant, farmer, it stood on the horizon as a
fascinating haven, full of the promise of delights, when his estate

should be no longer bearable. And for the country fellow and the
worker of the remoter and more lonely cotton-mill villages alike
— for male and female — :

To go into the town on Saturday afternoon and night, to stroll
with the throng, to gape at the well-dressed and the big automobiles, to bathe in the holiday cacophony; in the case of the women,
to crowd happily along counters and finger the goods they could
not buy; in the case of the males, maybe only to stand with the
courthouse habitués and talk and spit tobacco juice, or in the press
about a radio loud-speaker blaring a baseball or football game
from the front of a store and let off steam with the old hunting
yell; maybe to have a drink, maybe to get drunk, to laugh with
passing girls, to pick them up if you had a car, or to go swaggering
or hesitating into the hotels with their corridors saturated with the
smell of bichloride of mercury, or the secret, steamy bawdy houses;
maybe to have a fight, maybe with knives or guns, maybe against
the cops; maybe to end whooping and singing, maybe bloody and
goddamning, in the jailhouse — it was more and more in the dream
and reality of such excursions that the old romantic-hedonistic impulses found egress, and that men and women were gratefully
emptied of their irritations and repressions, and left to return to
their daily tasks stolid, unlonely, and tame again.

Still another factor which belongs to the case is the growth of
orgiastic religion. It is just in this decade of the most rapid expansion of Southern industrialism, of speculation, and of the rapid
widening of the physical and social gulf between the classes that
we find such sects as the Holy Rollers and the Church of God (an
unorthodox Baptist congregation organized in Tennessee, and
sometimes also called Holy Rollers on their own account) establishing themselves widely and solidly in the South — in the mill
villages, in the poorest sections of the towns, and even in the countryside. And it is just at this time also that the traveling, feverish
evangelists — the Hams, the Cyclone Macks, the Gypsy Smiths,
and the Billy Sundays — reach their heyday.

That the two sets of phenomena were closely related is manifest on the most casual investigation. Thus the preachers of the frenetic sects themselves officially ascribe their great success, next after the workings of the Holy Ghost, to the rising demand of the people for a place where they might worship without feeling ashamed of their clothes and manners, and a religion that would stress and give outlet to emotion. And all the evangelists insisted even more than the politicians on their own lowly origins, and discoursed continually on the theme of the superior virtue and piety of the poor as against the stiff-necked rich, and the certainty that in heaven it would be the former who would sit at the head of the table.

Evidence of the same sort is to be found, too, in the quite typical case of the very name of the Church of God, and in its official hymn — a curious song, entitled "The Great Speckled Bird of God" and sung quaintly to the tune of "Blue Eyes," wherein the sect is represented as a kind of ugly duckling among peacocks: The One True Church among a host of Byzantine pretenders given over to the worship of idols; poor, humble, despised now, but destined in the end to emerge to dazzling glory while the old haughty ones are cast into outer darkness, presumably to burn in the pit as the faithful look pleasantly on from oriels in the skies.

Beset with difficulties beyond his control and comprehension, increasingly taken in his vanity, puzzled, angered, frightened, the common white tended, like his fathers before him in the early days of the nineteenth century and in the Reconstruction time, to retreat into other-worldliness and, in the solace and the hope he found there, to resign himself to his lot in this world as of no more moment than a passing shadow cast on the sun by a cloud. And at the same time he retreated also toward the primitivism which had accompanied other-worldliness in his fathers. The general hysteria of the rising sects, manifesting itself in such beliefs as complete sanctification and such practices as speaking in tongues and holy rolling, plainly represented a direct revival of the hysteria — the fits, jerks, barks, and rolling frenzies — of the great Methodist and Baptist camp-meeting days; a hysteria that had never at any time wholly died out. Merely, the thing had now been vulgarized

by the thin jazziness which seems to be the necessary concomitant
of industrialism everywhere, and had also been infected by the example of the Negro's voodooism; as witness the fact that these
congregations sometimes went all the way with the black man and
adopted such notions as a belief in the magic powers of a handker-
chief which had been blessed by some holy man with unusual
capacity for stirring up emotion.

Nor is it to be supposed that the tendency I describe here was
confined only to those who succumbed to the fanatic sects. The
charge made by the latter that the old orthodox evangelical churches
had become " intellectualized " was an absurdity. But there was a
kind of truth in the companion charge of " coldness and formality."
That is, these churches had naturally been for long growing more
and more circumspect in their exhibitions of emotion. And, moreover, this was the great age of Babbitt and his influence in the
church. So far as the usual downtown church went, it was now
almost as impossible as in the North to distinguish the minister
from any other business executive bent on pleasing his board of directors and hanging up a record as a go-getter and a builder, or to
distinguish the institution itself from another factory or Rotary
club.

At the same time, however, there was also in progress in these
evangelical churches during this decade a powerful and constantly
growing movement back upon other-worldliness and primitivism.
It extended through all the social levels, for that matter (we shall
look at some of the reasons for that shortly), and issued in such
phenomena as wild revivals, conducted by Billy Sunday or some
other such evangelist, in many of the South's most fashionable
churches — revivals which often lasted for many weeks, filled the
front pages of the newspapers, and obsessed whole towns and
sections. But it was most notable in the congregations of the mill
villages, the shabby sections of the towns, and the country.

Among all these the ministers insisted only less warmly and constantly than the tent evangelists and the preachers of the unorthodox groups on the view that earthly life is a mere bauble. Just as

warmly and constantly they held forth, too, on the superior virtue and piety of the poor, and the corollary that these would outtop the " rich and worldly " in paradise, though they carefully skirted any explicit identification of the latter with their own immediate overlords. Revivals tended to increase in frequency, duration, and intensity. Hymns in use changed with great rapidity, and each new lot was more jazzily febrile than the last. Sermons everywhere ran to ominous and highly colored pictures of the present and future condition of the world, based on the obscurities of the Prophets and the Apocalypse.

15

As yet, however, we hardly do more than touch the circumference of the case. At the heart of it stood a great plexus of fears and hates, which, moving beneath the surface of the reigning optimism and faith in Progress, operated enormously to engage the attention and energies of the common whites, as they operated to engage the attention and energies of nearly all ranks of Southerners — to counteract the drive toward class division on economic and social questions by a more powerful drive toward cohesion and the tightening anew of the old solidity: the fears and hates which were to issue in such phenomena as the Ku Klux Klan and the anti-evolution campaign which headed up in the trial of John T. Scopes at Dayton, Tennessee.

In part these fears and hates were continuous with the vast mass neurosis which afflicted the whole of the United States, and even more the Western world in general, in the decade. Like Yankee soldiers and the soldiers of Europe, Southern soldiers had served for long months on the carrion fields of France — had stamped upon their shaken nerves for as long as they should live the macabre memory of interminable passage through a world of maggoted flesh, lice, mud, bedlam, and the waiting expectancy of sudden death. That, and the grim knowledge of how easy it had been to kill, how easy it would be to kill again.

And what was directly true for the men who had seen action was vicariously true for all the men of the armies and the civilian population as well. In uniform or in mufti, all alike had lived these months with the same vision before them, brought immensely closer to them by the new and expanded means of communication than had ever been the case in the past; all had lived absorbed in war as peoples had never been absorbed before — in a war which violated all subsisting ideas of military glory, which particularly violated the Southern notion of military glory as fixed by the *beaux sabreurs* of the Civil War, but which they must still somehow make glorious and dress up as a crusade for civilization.

With startled, horrified, and yet strangely eager gaze, that is, they had seen the men of all the evening lands, themselves included, flinging away the established standards of their daily living and returning upon a savagery that was more savage than any savage had ever dreamed, because it used all the accumulated knowledge of civilization for its ferocious purpose — the ape-man shouting triumphantly through the earth — the old wild, terrible brute inheritance from the caves of the Dordogne and the hills behind Babylon; the inheritance which, labeled the Natural Depravity of Man and Original Sin, had immemorially haunted their fears: breaking the bonds so painfully and so slowly and so imperfectly imposed upon it, and shambling forth, with little red eyes, free and proud.

And now, as the years went on, it would be increasingly clear that the " peace " made at Versailles had not really succeeded in chaining it up again — that the world in which they lived was not and would not be again the old fixed, certain, familiar, and easy world they had known before 1914. Strange new ideas and faiths and systems were sweeping through the Western lands, and all the old ideas and faiths and systems were under attack, in danger, crumbling or even vanishing in places. Everywhere were doubt and change and chaos and flux and violence. In Russia there was godless and propertyless and coldly murderous revolution. In Italy a whole nation had gone back to the mores of the Mongol hordes and turned itself into a permanent army camp, worshipping the war-god of old Rome, and dedicated to the dream of restoring a pagan Roman Empire by bloodshed and rapine. The German Siegfried stirred restlessly and ominously in his shackles. England and France were plainly sick, decaying, unable to make up their minds either really to play the ruthless role they had assigned themselves at Versailles or to try to live up to their pious professions in the League of Nations.

The world, in a word, clearly stood poised above disaster. Nobody might be sure that tomorrow the dark prophecies of a Spengler might not come dreadfully true — that civilization might not completely collapse into the chaos of recrudescent and blood-drinking barbarism.

And so they were afraid, these Southerners, like all Americans and like all Western men. Afraid cloudily and, as always, without analysis, even subconsciously and blindly, but none the less really for all that. Afraid of all that stood without them, and perhaps even afraid of themselves. And because of their fears, desperately determined to hold fast, even in spite of themselves, to their own old certainties — somehow to island themselves impregnably from the threatening flood. In the South as in the North, the very feverish insistence upon and concern with Progress in these years was perhaps in some sense a projection from that will: an assertion of a passionate desire to keep on believing, willy-nilly, in the great master faith of the nineteenth century, that man was necessarily destined to continual advance through always more signal achievements to always more splendid goals.

But above all, because of their fears and their will, they were filled with hate for whatever differed from themselves and their ancient pattern. For hate, of course, is always and everywhere the correlative of fear: the mechanism through which men most often fortify themselves against their terrors. And these men were superlatively ripe for hating. The organized propaganda of the war had drilled them in the habit of hate with a thoroughness and an intensity entirely without parallel in prior human history. And, moreover, the very contacts of the soldiers of the expeditionary forces with their allies had probably contributed to the same end.

Contact with other peoples is often represented as making inevitably for tolerance. But that is true only for those who have already been greatly educated to tolerance. The simple man everywhere is apt to see whatever differs from himself as an affront, a challenge, and a menace. And though the soldier might sometimes find something in his allies to admire and even to like, not to say a great deal more to jeer at with more or less good-natured contempt, yet what he was most likely to bring back from contact with Catholic, unpuritanical Gallic civilization, and with the perversely upside-down Englander — what he was most likely to bring back for diffusion among the general population was not tolerance but a heightened sense of the rightness and superiority of his own way, and a heightened fear and dislike of all difference. And by so much as his pattern was more simple and unvaried, as he was more trained to suspicion and distrust of difference, as he was less accustomed to contact with alien persons and ideas, this was probably more true of the Southerner than of other American soldiers.

As in the North, so also in the South all this hate and fear issued, in part, in fear for the nation as such, and in hate for whatever was felt or imagined to threaten it. What I have just said about contact with the allies certainly held true here, too, *mutatis mutandis*. That is, the contact of the Southern soldier with the Yankee soldier, of the Southern population at large with the Yankee soldiers in the Southern cantonments, had renewed their awareness of the old line of cleavage. At the same time, however, their feeling of the common bond with the Yankee as against all outsiders, the sense of the nation and mystical loyalty to it, had been tremendously enhanced. And so the militant and intolerant "Americanism" propaganda by such national confraternities (themselves of course the product and embodiment of the common national fears and hatreds) as the American Legion and the Patriotic Order of Sons of America, with their "Red perils" and "alien menaces," nowhere found more receptive soil than in Dixie.

But in the South it did not stop with generalized concern for the nation. Characteristically, the stream of fears and hates generated by the war and conditions in the Western world poured back within the frame of the South itself, fixed upon Southern themes and translated itself into Southern terms, met and merged with certain rising fears and hates native to the old Southern pattern, and so contributed to the renewal of a concern like that which had reigned in the years before 1900 — a concern which fixed itself precisely on the line of the old Southern patriotism and the will to the preservation of the ancient pattern.

16

The very passion for " Americanism " in the South was at least in great part the passion that the South should remain fundamentally unchanged. " Red perils " and " alien menaces " sound absurd enough in connection with the region — seeing that it did not have and never had had even the most minuscule radical or alien problem of its own. But then, the North had no real Red problem either, and no alien problem that called for any great excitement. Almost the sole content of immediate actuality in these phantasmagoric terrors was, as is well known, just the peril of the labor movement, to the interests, real or imagined, of the ruling classes, and particularly the possibility of a labor movement that should stand to the left of the highly conservative American Federation of Labor as shaped by Samuel Gompers, William Green, and Matthew Woll.

And when that is clear, the case of the South becomes more explicable. If the Yankee manufacturer, long accustomed to labor unions, could be so wrought upon by fears that he could without conscious hyprocrisy, though of course not without the unconscious cunning of interest, see even the lumbering AFL as at least dangerously close to being Red, then it is readily comprehensible how the Southern cotton-mill baron, remembering unhappily its occasional forays into his territory, should get to see it as the flaming archangel of Moscow itself — why the organs of the Southern trade, such as the *Textile Bulletin* and the *Manufacturers' Record,* promptly set up the formula: labor organizer equals Communist organizer.

Furthermore, when one recalls how central for Southern patriotism was the idea of Progress, and how much that Progress — the continuing industrial and commercial development of the country — was felt at least to be dependent upon the preservation of the advantage of cheap labor, it is easy to understand how the general Southern sentiment would attach itself to the same formula. And not merely among the classes which stood or thought they stood to benefit by it.

There was in the South in these years a curious, widespread, and active antagonism among the working men themselves to the idea of unionization. In great measure that is explained, no doubt, by their old intense individualism, plus the memory of the unfortunate experiments with the idea in the past. But it also indubitably had in it a glowering suspicion that maybe, even probably, unionism was Com-*mune*-ist, and so a menace to their Southern heritage. That itself was largely the result of the preachments or inferences of the newspapers, politicians, and other masters of the public psychology, most of whom had explicitly or implicitly adopted a formula very like that of the trade journals as their basic premise in the case. But I suspect it was in some part the result, too, of the old vague but real participation of the people in the spirit of Progress — the dim but genuine sense that it was somehow incompatible with the high prosperity of the community which was sure to come.

The case of the fear and hatred of the alien menace in this country so little used to aliens is even more manifest. One factor was that the common people wholly, and even upper-rank Southerners largely, lumped all aliens indiscriminately together as carriers of the Communist seed. Another was that the presence of the Negro and the long defensive fight against alien-infested Yankeedom had vastly intensified in Southerners generally a feeling, common in some degree to most peoples, that they represented a uniquely pure and superior race, not only as against the Negro but as against all other communities of white men as well. " Ninety-nine per cent pure Anglo-Saxon " was not merely a part of the advertisements of cheap labor designed to lure Yankee capital South but also one of the proudest boasts for home consumption. Naturally, therefore, they were extraordinarily solicitous for its preservation, extraordinarily on the alert to ward off the possibility that at some future date it might be contaminated by the introduction of other blood-streams than those of the old original stocks.

And over and beyond this, what could be more natural than that a people with the population problem of the South, a people always unable to find enough jobs to go round, should have felt violent instinctive alarm and anger over the merest suggestion of hordes of aliens (imagined to have far lower standards than the South's own) pouring in to make the competition for subsistence more bitter than ever?

True enough, there was not in reality the least immediate prospect of any such thing happening — little discernible prospect of its ever happening, in view of the fact that immigration to the United States was constantly declining — unless we are to suppose the alien workers of New England and Pennsylvania beginning to follow their mills South, a thing they showed no inclination for. But, as we know, fantasy was easy for Dixie. Moreover, the restaurants of Greeks and the stores of Jews — who were usually thought of as aliens even when their fathers had fought in the Confederate armies — did multiply rapidly in the country in these years of town growth, and now and then a wandering alien from the North would turn up to take a job in the mills, promptly to be made so uncomfortable that he usually fled. And this was quite enough measure of fact for the people here to build upon.

Certainly, the connection existed. Throughout the decade the mill workers were periodically exercised by sudden rumors — which kept on recurring though none of them ever proved true —

that some Yankee absentee landlord was going to discharge his Southerners and replace them with aliens imported from his establishments in the North.

And with that I shall for the present leave the theme of the intertwining of the hates and fears bred by conditions outside the South with conditions inside. We shall presently see more of it, but we can best do that in connection with those fears and hates native to the Southern pattern which, as I have said, the new world fears and hates met and merged with and which deserve examination in their own right.

17

Of these, the first were resurgent fear and hate of the Negro. I call them resurgent, not, of course, because they had ever fallen into quiescence, but because, as a result of the increasing feeling of mastery and of the definite establishment of White Supremacy, plus the increasing absorption in Progress which followed the collapse of Populism, they had begun almost at once to fall back from their old peak intensity and would go on falling slowly back throughout the quiet years prior to the World War.

So much is written quite clearly in the signal drop in lynching. In the ten years from the opening of 1890 to the close of 1899, a total of 1,111 Negroes were lynched in the United States. But in the next ten years the number fell to 791, and in the five years after that to 288 — the last figure representing nearly a fifty-per-cent decrease from the maximum incidence of the crime. And if these figures are not strictly confined to the South, they are for comparative purposes quite as good as if they were. For of the grand total of 3,397 Negroes lynched in the nation from the beginning of 1882 until the close of 1938, only 366 were lynched outside the former Confederate States, and of these 185 were lynched in the border states of Maryland, Kentucky, West Virginia, and Missouri, themselves more than half Southern.

Here again, however, we come upon one of those cases where

it is necessary to measure the facts accurately and to draw nice distinctions. If you followed through the single line of the evidence of lynching, you might readily conclude that I have proved too much — that in reality the whole curve of racial fear and hatred moves continuously downward not only in the pre-war years but also in the 1920's. For, once set going down the incline, the lynching rate would go on falling fairly steadily. It showed little drop during the five years after 1914, indeed — the national figure being 275 as against the 288 of the preceding five years — but these, of course, were the war years, years of great tensions and violent passions, ready and eager to find an outlet in any kind of violent action. And in the next decade it almost exactly halved itself over the preceding one, the number of victims in the nation coming down to 281, of which the last year of the period, 1929, accounted for only seven — the lowest number on record for any year down to the present save 1938, when the score was six, and 1939, when it was three.

What was even more striking was that one state, North Carolina, had no lynchings at all for the eight years 1922–9 inclusive; that Virginia had only four in the same period; and that even Alabama had none in the four years 1926–9. More striking still, after 1914 the number of *prevented* lynchings rose rapidly: after 1921 it was always larger than the number of completed lynchings, and in some years was triple and quadruple the latter. And, perhaps most striking of all, after 1914 lynchings in all Southern towns of more than 10,000 people, regardless of their location by states, became so rare as practically to be nonexistent — and, moreover, the territory immediately surrounding such towns in considerable degree reflected the same change.

From this and from other collateral evidence, some of which we shall glance at in other connections, not a few observers, both Yankees and Southerners, did hasten to draw some such conclusion as that I indicate. Articles in the chief magazines hopefully announcing that the South was beginning to generate a wholly new attitude toward the Negro, were common even before 1910; commoner in the 1920's, despite an occasional doubting voice in the professionally skeptical *American Mercury*. And in 1929 so astute a social critic as Oswald Garrison Villard, writing in *Harper's,* could actually see the whole color line in the South as in process of fairly rapid disintegration!

But such conclusions were much too facile. Not that there wasn't a measure of truth in them. I think there is no doubt that in addition to the decrease in the activity of racial hate and fear in the period between the end of Populism and the World War, there had taken place in the South a very considerable diminution of the *potential* of these emotions. Feeling now that the black was mastered, the best men of the upper classes had time to begin to recover perspective. And among these the convention that no white man of any self-respect would participate in a lynching or indulge in nigger-hazing of any sort was propagated with increasing energy from the opening of the century; it went on gathering impetus even in the twenties. Nor is it necessary to suppose that this was without some effect all down the line. Never afterward, neither in the 1920's nor since, would the general level of fear and hate for the Negro begin to approach the old heights which had existed in the three closing decades of the nineteenth century.

Nevertheless, we need to be careful not to exaggerate the extent of the drop, and not to assume that the lynching record proves that the process was always continuous and cumulative. So far as the body of the people is concerned, the evidence for the vast survival of these emotions is plain in the very existence of the Vardamans, the Cole Bleases, the Cotton Ed Smiths, as well as in the fact that the number of attempted lynchings still ran very high. But it is plain enough, too, for the other end of the scale from the masses that not even the old proper aristocrats or their descendants were as a group by any means ever entirely restored to calm in the matter. The presence of larger numbers of these people in Virginia than in the other states quite probably went far to explain that state's increasingly good lynching record. But, as Virginius Dabney has pointed out, it was John Temple Graves, an aristocrat by birth, who was largely responsible for the great Atlanta race riot in 1907 —

who asserted that, in order to protect Southern Womanhood, the South was justified in lynching any number of innocent Negroes to make the race find out and reveal the identity of the man guilty of a purported crime! And if John Sharp Williams, in some respects one of the most notable men the South has produced since the Civil War and an aristocrat to his fingertips, won election to the Senate partly by decrying Vardaman's nigger-baiting, yet he disgraced himself in his last days by openly defending lynching in that assembly, quite as though he were Cotton Ed Smith all over again.

As for the ruling class in general, the evidence is equally conclusive, so far as these regions where lynching was still common were concerned. I mean the evidence that, far from attempting to prevent lynchings, the police in such areas almost invariably connived at them and very often actively participated in them, sometimes serving as masters of ceremonies in the application of gasoline and torch or in adjusting the rope to the victim's neck; and (significant for the whole spirit of the South, for that matter) that customarily when a lynching took place, neither local nor state officials made any honest effort to apprehend and punish the criminals. The police either didn't investigate at all or reported, tongue in cheek, that they were unable to identify anybody, though who the guilty parties were was commonly neighborhood knowledge. Judges, attorney-generals, and governors almost never made any attempt to spur them into the active performance of their duty. When, for a wonder, they did, they got no co-operation or support from the body of " best citizens " in the local community or the state; on the contrary, the ranks closed now as always, and all investigators got was grim warnings to mind their own business under penalty of tar and feathers.

In his *Lynching and the Law* Chadbourn lists only eight cases, involving 54 persons, of conviction of Southern lynchers for the whole period from 1900 until the end of 1929, and he need not have stopped with that year. In one of these cases — in Alabama in 1920 — the criminals got off with penalties ranging from fines of a hundred dollars to three months in jail. In another — in Texas in 1920

— jail terms of two years were suspended. And in none of them was the punishment at all commensurate with the offense of murder.

But what has all this to do with the ruling class? The answer is obvious. The policeman everywhere is a simple soul primarily interested in keeping his job and studying how to do the things which he cannily observes his masters — the ruling classes, of course — really want, to that end. And since, as we have repeatedly seen, the ruling classes of the South, operating within the old paternalistic frame, had extraordinary powers over the whole social body and over government — still stood to the people almost as military captains — this was in the nature of the case particularly true of the Southern policeman. The case of judges, governors, and so on is just as plain. Arising from the ruling classes everywhere, and everywhere being politicians, they are everywhere in large part primarily the organ, as it were, of those classes and reflect in themselves the precise temper of those classes. And that also was especially true in the case of the South, where the whole hierarchy of the Democratic Party and its office-holders took its measures almost solely with regard to the ruling orders and their wishes.

The usefulness to politicians of nigger-baiting and of allowing lynching as a means of pleasing and holding the masses must be taken into account, to be sure. But I do not think it much changes the final conclusion. Contrary to widespread popular belief, which the South itself has fostered, the persistence of lynching in the region down to the present has not been due simply and wholly to the white-trash classes. Rather, the major share of the responsibility in all those areas where the practice has remained common rests squarely on the shoulders of the master classes. The common whites have usually done the actual execution, of course, though even that is not an invariable rule (I have myself known university-bred men who confessed proudly to having helped roast a Negro). But they have kept on doing it, in the last analysis, only because their betters either consented quietly or, more often, definitely approved.

18

Still, the fact does remain that, as I have said, the practice had
virtually disappeared in North Carolina and Virginia, in all the
greater towns, and in many rural areas adjacent to those towns.
In all these places, which in fact embraced the major portion of the
Southern population, lynching was, when still attempted, being
regularly prevented. And by virtue of what I have just been arguing, that does prove that here at least fear and hate of the Negro
were becoming an increasingly negligible element in the psychology
of the ruling classes?

It does not follow. The example and the precept of the best
sort certainly had their effect here on all their fellows of the ruling
orders, both through direct infection and also through a kind of
shamefacedness before their great moral authority, even among
those who still secretly hated what was felt as increasing softness.
The first is clearly reflected in the rise and extensive growth of such
useful groups as the Commission for Interracial Cooperation and
the Southern Association of Women Against Lynching, the latter
of which has addressed itself particularly to destroying the idea that
lynching serves for the protection of Southern Womanhood. And
both factors played their part in the fact that after 1900 most of the
newspapers began to be at least nominally against lynching (sometimes they still apologized for it in the concrete case), and that in
the 1920's an increasing number of them, with the *Enquirer-Sun,*
of Columbus, Georgia, at their head, began to be very actively
against it.

Yet the dominant fact in the case was much less that fear and
hate of the Negro had ever tended to become a negligible part of
the thinking of the great portion of the ruling class in any part of
the South than that the falling back of hate and fear into relative
inactivity in the quiet years after 1900 had furnished a frame in
which various other powerful forces, themselves having nothing to
do with fear and hate, had been enabled to begin to operate to di-

vorce the subsisting fear and hate from their old easy, virtually automatic egress into mob violence.

These forces were of various sorts. One comparatively late comer, for instance, was that an effect of the war, the general labor shortage, and offer of high wages by labor agents from the North, who poured down into Dixie almost as numerously as the carpetbaggers had once done, would be to set off a mass emigration of Negroes to Yankeedom, which did not end until after the beginning of the great depression of the 1930's. The result was in some ways disadvantageous for the blacks left in the South, for the planters and labor-employing farmers set themselves ruthlessly to stem the tide by the traditional Southern methods of violence and coercion. The pattern of essential peonage which had generally persisted ever since the Civil War was reaffirmed and tightened; extra-legal patrols and sheriffs' posses engaged in a campaign of terrorization and forceful restraint; and the whip came back into more general use than in a long while. But when the planters and their supporters attempted, as in the early days they sometimes did, to clinch their hold on the Negroes, to terrorize them *en masse,* by lynching one too obstreperously bent on escape, it quickly became apparent that they were overreaching themselves. Any such lynching, any lynching of any sort, so far from resulting in the final servile submission of the blacks, was likely to sweep them into mass hysteria; with a precipitate resolution that not even shotguns could stop, to empty a whole locality of them overnight.

At long last, that is to say, the economic self-interest of the planters and their associates, which had always generally been assumed to run parallel to Negrophobia and to be actively served by lynching, had begun more or less clearly to run the other way about — in some sections, especially in the deep South, so clearly as to override reluctance on the score of personal fear and hate and to make many of the landowners view any lynching within their purview with bitter anger; to set them to using all their power to drive the police to put down the crime.

For the most, however, it was Progress that was the father of the forces of which I speak. This appears almost overtly from the fact I have already noted that it was largely in the new and growing towns and in the areas in which they stood that lynching tended to fall off most rapidly. Everywhere, indeed, the degree of decline in mob violence of a given locality could be closely correlated to the degree of that locality's advance in Progress. Virginia was something of an exception to the general rule, since it had not and has not yet become one of the leading industrial states of the South, but its case is perhaps sufficiently explained by the large number of the descendants of the old Southern gentry and by the fact that its Negro population was relatively smaller than that of any other Southern state. North Carolina had a relatively small Negro population, too; but the correlation between the fact that it was the only Southern state almost completely to have abandoned lynching and the fact that it was by far the most fully commercialized and industrialized of them all is still remarkably striking. And just as remarkable, on the other hand, is the correlation between the fact that Mississippi remained the most rural state and the fact that it continued to have the highest lynching rate — even when it is remembered that it had also the highest relative Negro population.

So it went everywhere. The South had become, as it were, a country divided into a crazy-quilt of zones. Given a zone in which the town and factory and commerce had grown to be predominant, you found invariably that lynching was either disappearing or declining rapidly. Given one which remained dominantly rural, and you found that in close proportion lynching continued to flourish.

Such a result followed in part from the fact that Progress tended continually to give increasing impetus in its votaries to the old impulse to apologize before the frown of the world and to attempt to conciliate it, which had always existed side by side with the impulse to defy and flout it. But it followed more importantly from the inherent nature of the town. It is a part of the general law of the town everywhere that its inhabitants rarely lynch; that the tradition of direct action by mobs natural to the frontier and the

open, little-policed countryside tends more and more to die out.
For restraint and complexity, as I have noted before, are the very
essence of the town: the policeman is everlastingly at one's elbow,
and all the processes of the common life are carried out, not as on
the frontier or in the country, where every man does pretty much
everything for himself, but by indirection and surrogate. And this
is particularly true of the industrial and commercial town, dedicated, as it is, to the ends of maximum production, maximum sales,
and maximum profits.

19

The masters of these Southern towns, in so far as they were concentrated on industry and commerce, had had their economic self-
interest divorced from the lynching pattern even more notably than
the planters in the case at which we have looked. As I have said,
Negroes were never used in the cotton mills save in incidental capacities. And though there were factories of some sorts, such as the
tobacco mills, where they were employed in considerable numbers,
such was the exception and not the rule. And much the same kind
of thing holds for commerce. Hence the industrialists and commercialists would not, as such, have any economic motive left for the
terrorization of the blacks.

There was a less negative aspect to the matter, however. The
economic interest of the masters of the towns was not only being
divorced from the lynching pattern but also, like that of many of
the planters, increasingly set in active opposition to it. That proceeded, plainly enough, from the very fact that they were growing
always richer; for men everywhere as they grow more rich grow
also more cautious and distrustful of disorder — or rather of all
disorder which they do not conceive to be directly useful to their
own self-interest. And especially men in towns, where property
grows so much faster than on the land, where it takes forms easily
seized or destroyed — as money and houses and the mills them-

selves — and where it is no longer possible to *palpate* what the people are thinking, where, because of the gulf between the social levels, it is possible to imagine all sorts of dread ideas and purposes brewing in the brains of the close-faced men who dwell in the mean streets and the alleys.

Moreover, the processes of commerce are essentially orderly and deliberate; they follow a fixed procedure and, beyond a certain limit, cannot be hurried or dislocated. As for industry, the machine, of course, is the very image of order, the embodiment of a fixed, rigidly conventionalized procedure through time, and the antithesis of the headlong impatience of a lynching mob. Is it unlikely that all this had its effect on the mental pattern of men who dealt with it day by day and fixed all their hopes on it, whether as worker or master?

But there was a more immediate and certain cause for the swinging of the self-interest of the masters of the town in direct opposition to lynching, so far as they were interested in industry, and all of them were, in the ultimate analysis. I refer to the fact that the machine is a jealous and exacting taskmaster. The plow-boy may dream the whole day through as he walks behind his beast and still get his field broken. The old-fashioned artisan, beset by a fancy or an emotion, could dawdle for hours and days over his task with no other damage than a slowing of its progress. But the modern high-speed machine demands from its human helpers the most alert concentration on the task in hand, else in short order the huge quantities of ruined material and the dislocation in the schedule of deliveries have eaten up the master's margin of profit and are hurrying him to bankruptcy. For that reason above all, therefore, the masters everywhere are against all excitements and disorders — against whatever operates to fix the attention and emotions of the workman powerfully enough to hinder him from falling swiftly into his robot groove when the whistle blows.

The very romantic-hedonistic pattern of Saturday activity which I have sketched was frowned on by the cotton-mill heads of the South for exactly that reason. From the beginning they have always fumed and stormed against the violent and heroic tendencies of their workmen. And in so far as calculation figures in the case, the will to discourage those tendencies has been an important constituent in their support of churches for the workers. Yet even religion itself is exciting also and can be a tremendously disturbing force for the efficiency of the worker, as the barons well know. They would never dare oppose it publicly, or even refuse to lend it support in every case, but I have myself heard them grumbling in private against the effect on their workmen of a too prolonged and too intense revival.

As for lynching, it is clear enough without further pursuit of the theme, I trust, why, quite apart from the question of personal fear and hate for the Negro on general racial grounds, even when such fear and hate were strongly present, the masters of the towns were often inclined to frown on lynching, and in large numbers to exert themselves to see that the police put it down in their boroughs and in the country that surrounded them.

To the point here also is the fact that the ground was increasingly better prepared for their success in weaning those below away from it. The general considerations I have set forth in regard to the town applied to the underdog too, but there were special factors in his case as well. Thus, since no Negroes lived in the cotton-mill villages and few even passed in and out of them, the whites there lived almost completely removed and insulated from the black man, save as they encountered him briefly in the streets on their Saturday excursions.

But that, you might reasonably think, suggests a great fall in the substance of their fear and hate rather than mere divorce between these emotions and the lynching pattern. So, logically, it does — on first thought, at any rate. But my own observations bear out the conclusion reached by nearly all those who have observed the matter closely, that in fact the cotton-mill worker was likely to fear and hate the Negro even more than the poor white on the land.

It may be that their very isolation had something to do with that. Contact between the Negro and the rural poor white had always been and remained peculiarly intimate after a fashion. Though they scorned him in their way, yet white croppers and tenants at least would not infrequently sit on the black man's steps and even in the kitchen with his family, talk with him of the hazards of the seasons and the elements which they faced in common, laugh at his cunningly humble little jokes, and expand their egos in the comfortable sense of sitting among inferiors, who were yet not unpleasant, as a friendly dog is not unpleasant. The cotton-mill worker, on the other hand, was left to nurse his inherited tradition of fear and hate, so to speak, almost in a vacuum, viewing the black man for most of the time at a distance which stripped him of all personal and even human characteristics.

Furthermore, his occasional closer contacts with the blacks were likely to be of a sort perfectly calculated to stir up the fires of fear and hatred. For the Negro, with his quick perception in such cases, had promptly grasped the peculiar attitude of contempt with which upper-class white men regarded the mill worker, and had taken it over on his own account — made his scorn for " po' cotton-mill trash " as manifest as he dared on every available occasion.

Nevertheless, if the isolation of the mill people did not diminish their fear and hate but instead increased these emotions, it still did operate very largely to remove them from the stream of circumstances which gave rise to lynching. And something of the same kind was probably true of the common sort in the towns generally, for they, too, usually lived in some degree more remote from the Negro than was the case in the country. At least, they were in less active economic competition with him. Hordes of blacks had poured into all the towns from the first, and in many cases they made up from a third to more than half the total urban population. But most of them had gone into domestic service or other menial callings despised by the whites. Only relatively small numbers of them even attempted to enter the mechanic trades. And when competition in a trade did develop, as when white men began to move into the barber shops, once almost exclusively manned by Negroes, the latter were routed so quickly and thoroughly that there was no time for trouble to develop. Occasional angry conflicts did occur, naturally, but on the whole they were too inconsiderable and too infrequent to give rise to widespread feeling.

20

But now in the years after the war, as I have said, fear and hate of the black man, having diminished greatly in activity and even to a considerable extent in potential, was beginning to swell again — never to rise even close to its old Reconstruction and Populism levels, and never to be potent enough to reverse or halt the downward trend in lynching, but still powerful enough to demand more active outlet.

For here in abundance were circumstances to make the South's feeling that the black man had been mastered, never completely secure, less and less certain.

A salient and obvious thing was that the Negroes who had served in the army had tasted strange experience which fitted ill with their established role in Dixie. They had seen Negro officers, and the spectacle of Southern white soldiers, cursing bitterly under their breath, perforce saluting them. In fact, a few of the Southern Negroes had themselves been officers, to the vast joy and pride of all their kin and acquaintance — of the whole people, for that matter. And in France they had seen stranger things still. In that topsyturvy land the Negro soldier had encountered a white people who, if they were not wholly without prejudice against him, were only mildly touched with it. So far as the prostitutes were concerned at least, he had even found himself allowed to approach and enjoy the white women of this people — had sometimes actually found himself preferred by them.

Inevitably, therefore, these blacks came back home now with a bolder lift to their heads, a firmer, more rolling step, and a new light in their eyes, which, lying half hidden most of the time, was yet calculated periodically to flash out into open insolence or provocation on the slightest pretext or sometimes none at all.

Something of the same sort was true, too, of the Negroes who came back to live in the South after a period of life in the Northern cities (many of them moved back and forth between the sections as Northern employment fluctuated up and down) or even only to visit and show off for a few days or weeks. As they were quickly to discover, the Yankee, confronted with the presence and the competition of large numbers of them, would not react very differently in essentials from the Southerner. The race riots in St. Louis and Chicago in the early post-war years were the worst the country has known. And restrictions and discriminations of all sorts would, in practice, continually increase. None the less, these Negroes had experienced at least nominal and legal equality. Their children generally went to the same schools with the white children; Negroes could and did crowd into the front of street cars and busses, sit with white people in trains and theaters and in many restaurants — in fine, were free of the irksome network of Jim Crow laws that had held them since the time of their birth in Dixie: a thing immensely and even disproportionately warming to the heart of a simple and wistful people greatly susceptible to and enamoured of the outward appearance of things. Furthermore, those who had lived in such districts as Harlem had often acquired the over-sleek dress and chatter, the jazziness and naïve " sophistication " affected there, and, in their simplicity, returned to the land of their origin with only half-veiled scorn, not only for their stay-at-home black cousins but also for the generality of the white people, and particularly the rural white people.

And of course the example of these and the returning soldiers did not fail of effect, varying in measure but often quite evident, on the body of the Southern Negro population, one of the most suggestible on earth.

Within the South itself something similar was breeding also, something arising, ironically enough, out of the background of the official Puritanism of the region — out of prohibition and the suppression of the red-light districts. With the passage of the trade in alcohol wholly into the hands of bootleggers, white men, of course, virtually monopolized the wholesale manufacturing part of the business; but the actual peddling of the stuff, or at least its delivery, more often than not fell to the Negro, especially in the hotels, where the black bellboys enjoyed an almost complete monopoly of the business — keeping out competitors from outside by threats of betraying them to the police. And once the suppression of red-light houses and the streetwalker had turned most Southern hotels into public stews, these bellboys had also acquired a virtual monopoly of the trade of pander and pimp, and demanded and secured from the white prostitutes they served all the traditional prerogatives of the pimp, including not only a large share of their earnings but also and above all the right of sexual intercourse — often enforced against the most reluctant of the women, again under threat of betrayal to the police.

The result was the rise of a horde of raffish blacks, full of secret, contemptuous knowledge of the split in the psyche of the shamefaced Southern whites, the gulf between their Puritanical professions and their hedonistic practices — scarcely troubling to hide their grinning contempt for their clients under the thinnest veil of subservient politeness and, in the case of the bellboys, hugging to themselves with cackling joy their knowledge of the white man's women. And this also drifted out to infect large numbers of other Negroes.

Even more significant developments were taking place on higher levels, however; in large measure the product of Progress, particularly as the latter was connected with the notion of education for the Negro.

As I have pointed out, perhaps the most powerful single consideration in the South's adoption of the idea of public education for him had been the will to take control of his instruction away from the Yankees who were swarming in to start schools, and to fit him to stay in the place intended for him. And undoubtedly the same motive had been very powerful in the founding of the numerous church and private schools also established for him.

From the first, however, it had not worked out wholly as planned. The Yankee schools, far from retiring from the field, had held on and even extended their efforts. And as the years had gone on, it had become more and more difficult to hold even the Southern-supported-and-dominated schools to the purpose.

To teach him to read and write and cipher and then, if he must have some sort of "higher" education, to teach him to plow a straight furrow and milk a cow (most of the "colleges" began as farm-life schools) and perhaps ground him in some mechanic trade such as blacksmithing — this had been the original program, a sort of weak reflection from the Booker T. Washington idea as developed at Tuskegee. But since almost no Southern white would agree to teach in Negro schools, they had perforce to be staffed in the beginning largely with Yankees, who, handpicked though they might be, rarely had any sympathy with the Southern idea and did their best to sabotage it. Moreover, the white mechanics of the South were always bitterly hostile to the idea of training Negroes to be their competitors. And, finally, the Negroes themselves, fired both by the teachings of their instructors and by the example of members of their race who were going away to the great white man's colleges and universities in the North to become lawyers and doctors and professors, were immensely eager for academic learning and generally apathetic toward the Southern program.

Thus, and though the South dealt with them most niggardly — always spending at least five dollars, often ten or fifteen, for the education of each white in the schools for every one spent for each Negro — the Negro school system began slowly to add grammar and high school units, and the "colleges" and "academies" to grow into something more or less deserving the name. By the end of the war period thousands of blacks were acquiring therein — often at the price of incredible effort and sacrifice — at least some of the rudiments of a fair education; and with that, naturally, something of the feelings and attitudes — the rising pride, the wondering, and the questioning — which belong to the educated man, especially the educated man who finds himself in a position of established inferiority.

More — Negro teachers had long been multiplying in the higher institutions, and now a new type of man was increasingly moving into them, in spite of efforts to keep him out: men trained at Howard or Hampton or the Yankee universities, and exposed to the ideas of such Negro leaders as W. E. B. DuBois, James Weldon Johnson, and even the belligerent and cynical George S. Schuyler. With the exception of an occasional youthful instructor with more passion than discretion, they usually went about their tasks gingerly and sought to inculcate in their students the idea that the white man, after all, had to be lived with, and that nothing was to be gained by hot-headedness. But they nevertheless did pass on their ideas and by both teaching and example serve to build up and reinforce in these students a pride which was at bottom quite incompatible with the established Southern view of the destiny and behavior proper to the black man.

21

All this, in its turn, had its repercussions among the Southern Negroes at large. Indeed, it was beginning quite definitely, if slowly, to change their whole leadership. After the war the old-fashioned Negro preacher and schoolmaster, at once both pompous and fawning, who had formerly served almost exclusively as the bellwethers of their race, became steadily less and less common, giving place to men who, whatever they lacked in the absolute, were at least more or less trained for their jobs and who had acquired something of the new attitude growing up in the schools.

Finally, to complete the tale, many Negroes had been coming up the economic ladder. By 1930 about twenty-one per cent of the colored farmers of the South owned their own farms — a small enough proportion, surely, but still representing a notable increase since Reconstruction days, when Negro ownership had first got established. And in many places Negroes were making headway as business men, even bankers, among their own people. In Durham, North Carolina, they had actually succeeded in building up a large and flourishing insurance company. And in all the principal towns of the South there were Negroes prosperous enough to ride in large and expensive automobiles and to live in large and expensive houses — to the snarling disgust of many whites.

Most of these Negro Babbitts were a good deal more interested in exploiting their race than in attempting to improve its general condition. But a few of them were lining themselves up with the new leadership. And all of them were important as fixing the attention of the whites and for their influence on the Negro masses, who eagerly identified themselves with them and saw in their success a sort of triumph for the whole race.

Throughout Dixie, in short, the Negro was slowly lifting his head and beginning to grow perceptibly more assertive. And everywhere there was in evidence a subtle but quite real change in attitude — a rising sullenness before brutality and indignity, a growing tendency to fierce outburst when pressed too hard, a mounting reluctance, especially in the more northerly parts of the section, toward acting out the role of Jim Crow or Uncle Tom. And sometimes, as I have suggested, brash cockiness and bumptiousness.

So far did the new assertiveness go that in some places — as Richmond, Charlotte, Raleigh, Greensboro, Atlanta, and Memphis — the Negroes would be reaching out cautiously to claim the ballot. Southern legal mastery in this regard had been temporarily destroyed when in 1915 the Supreme Court ruled that the Grandfather Clause was in conflict with the Fourteenth Amendment, only to be restored in some of the states by the adoption of a lily-white rule for Democratic Party primaries. Nevertheless, the Negroes in the places named and in others like them slowly began to attain the vote. In every case the primary breach was made in municipal elections — because a dominant faction or a political boss, like

Crump, of Memphis, desired and needed some extra votes for one reason or another. But in 1928 they got their hand in at national elections, because the Democratic leaders were in a panic over the prospect of their states breaking out of the historic form and voting for Herbert Hoover against Al Smith.

For all these reasons, therefore, the South was afraid for the precarious mastery it had with such great difficulty established. And the fear and hate conjured up by these things poured out to meet the world currents of fear and hate (nowhere else did the two streams more signally fuse) to conjure up yet another reason for fear and hate — the bogy of the Negro turning Communist and staging Red revolution in the South.

There was in fact little sound basis for any such fear. The Negro was at once too docile — and he remained essentially so despite the rising sullenness — and too realistic; on the one hand he was very far from having developed sufficient resentment against his masters to be amenable to the notion of revolution, and on the other he knew sardonically well just how little chance of success such a revolution would have, how certainly he would merely bring ruthless terrorism down upon himself if he attempted it alone, and just how fatuous was the dream, entertained by foolish Communists in the North, that white men of the lower orders could be persuaded to join with him against their ruling kin. Nor did the Marxian vision of a dull and unvarying proletarian order, created by solemn German and Russian brains, at all fit with his vast humorousness, his restless casualness, his supreme hedonism and love of the spectacular and dramatic, and his individualism — which, alike from his own impulses and the example of his white masters, was an intense as that of anybody in the South. And the atheism of Communism was calculated to offend and frighten his intense religiousness even more than it offended and frightened that of the Southern whites.

Nevertheless, he was obviously the worst exploited and oppressed of Americans. Communism, as the South had been quick to discover, advocated " social equality " for him. And if the Bolshies made little extended effort actually to proselyte him until after the beginning of the great depression, their newspapers and magazines, which were passed from hand to hand in the South as fearful exhibits, were full of lamentation over his plight and confident announcements that he was ripe for their gospel.

Moveover, there were those segregated black slums which honeycombed every Southern town. From the beginning the houses which made them up had been built with an eye to returning the white owners not less than twenty per cent annual profit — often much more. And the municipal authorities, proceeding on the absurd and cynical theory that Negroes paid no taxes, had everywhere consistently ignored them and their claim to the ordinary municipal services. Thus they had quickly got to be the worst slums in America — long rows of crazy shacks or shambling rookeries, packed as close as might be along fetid brooks and creeks, railroad tracks, alleys, or unpaved red gullies which answered for roads, or abutting directly on swarming sidewalks, with from three to a dozen Negroes per room, all but universally letting in the wind and rain, lighted by oil lamps or a smoking fire (when there was a fire), often without sanitary facilities, almost never with more than a stingy privy here and there. And the whole area generally without street lights.

And though the segregation of these slum areas served in some part to reduce friction between the races, yet in other ways it served to feed the white man's fears. There they stood, behind the white man's houses, half-hidden in the daytime, dark, mysterious, and ominous in the nighttime. Out of them the jungle beat of drums; the wild chanting gibberish of nameless congregations packed in unlighted halls; the rhythmic swell of jazz and stomping feet in "piccolo houses" (a name applied to dance halls equipped with nickel-in-the-slot phonographs); high, floating laughter; sudden screams, rising swiftly from the void and falling abruptly back into it again — all these sometimes rolled up to the white man's ears as he sat with his family in the evening, or snapped him to nightmarish awakening as he slept in the ghostly hours.

What was going on there? That was the question his everlasting uneasiness of conscience before the black problem must inevitably set crawling in the back of even the most unanalytical of minds. Lust, violence — everyone knew that. But these men and women who came out of those places in the morning and into the white man's houses and streets — yes, the white South delighted to say and believe that it knew the black man through and through. And yet even the most unreflecting must sometimes feel suddenly, in dealing with him, that they were looking at a blank wall, that behind that grinning face a veil was drawn which no white man might certainly know he had penetrated. What was back there, hidden? What whispering, stealthy, fateful thing might they be framing out there in the palpitant darkness?

So the South was afraid on the score of the Negro and Communism. It was a silent fear for the most part, only rarely getting into the newspapers, not often quite openly proclaimed by the orators. But there it was, real enough for all that, constantly adding fuel to hate and fanning the feeling of the need for more active expression of that hate.

22

Another great group of Southern fears and hates fixed itself on the line of what I have called the savage ideal — the patriotic will to hold rigidly to the ancient pattern, to repudiate innovation and novelty in thought and behavior, whatever came from outside and was felt as belonging to Yankeedom or alien parts. And here, perhaps even more signally than in the cases we have already observed, it was the passion for Education, which was the other half of Progress, that played the prime part.

As we have seen, the leading motives in that passion, as it had sprung up in the last decades of the nineteenth century, had been two: the will to train the South's sons to take advantage of the opportunities afforded by industrialism and commercialization, and precisely the purpose of maintaining the savage ideal intact — of thoroughly stamping the traditional pattern upon the rising generations, especially in the colleges and universities, which ultimately determined what would be done in the lower schools.

But cunning Odysseus had ineluctably been fetched within the gates with the Trojan horse and could not be forever kept shut up. From the first, indeed, Southern pride itself had operated as a force, making (usually unconsciously) against the repudiation of the modern mind. The men in charge of the Southern colleges, those who patronized them, those who felt interest in them, warmly desired that they should be recognized not only at home but in Yankeedom and abroad. And that necessarily meant giving them not only more money but also other things. The grudging but gradual enlargement of curricula, for one. And even more important, the employment of men of high attainments and distinction as teachers, some of whom would necessarily have to be Yankees. And once that had begun — well, hedge such men about with restrictions as you would, make their lives miserable with perpetual spying and admonitions, dismiss them if you heard it whispered that they had uttered the mildest heresy, drive many of them into voluntary flight, and still something of their knowledge, the force of their spirit, the independent power of their minds, would remain to leave a lasting impression.

Working toward the same goal was the fact — itself in considerable measure a reflection of the defensive pride of the South — that from the inception of the Progress era increasingly large numbers of Southerners, having finished their undergraduate work, poured into the North or even went abroad to study in the great universities. Many of these European- and Northern-trained men never came home again, preferring the greater comfort and security of a post in a Northern school. The South was being drained of its strength and brains, not only through the operation of population pressure but also through that of the savage ideal and its great intolerance. Nevertheless, hundreds of them did come back; and though they tended, perhaps, to be the lesser sort, by no means all of them were, not a few having deliberately elected to return out of a sense of duty to the South.

Slowly, slowly, almost imperceptibly until after the opening of the century, and then more rapidly, the frame was beginning to loosen.

In the early 1900's William Louis Poteat, returning from study at Wood's Hole and the great biological laboratory of the University of Berlin to his alma mater, the Baptist Wake Forest College in North Carolina, had begun to teach biology without equivocation, to set forth the theory of evolution frankly and fully, as having, as he said, more evidence behind it than the Copernican theory — certainly the first wholly honest and competent instruction of the sort in a Southern evangelical school, and the first in Southern schools of any sort save such exceptional ones as I have before noted.

What is more wonderful, he survived, though a storm swirled about his head all the years of his life, and though he needed all his quite unusual gifts as a diplomat and an orator to accomplish it — and not only survived but in a few years was made president of his college.

Seeing that, others plucked up heart; from this beginning such instruction spread slowly over Dixie until by 1920, though there were plenty of schools left in which the old attitude still lingered, it was no longer true of any of the more important ones. And with the teaching of biology growing intelligent and candid, the teaching of the other sciences of course followed suit. All through the years after 1900 laboratories were being built on every Southern campus of the slightest rank and were coming to occupy a larger and larger place in the scheme of instruction.

In the social sciences, the strait-jacket had been stretching and rending also. Powerfully held in the traditional feeling that their proper role was to propagate the old sentimental-romantic legend, to defend the South and brace its self-esteem, the professors of history progressed toward a more rational method slowly enough. Nevertheless, by 1910 there were a number of historians in the schools of the South who had definitely moved beyond what had been customary in their craft — notably John Garrott Brown (destined to an early death) and the men trained by W. A. Dunning at Columbia University, such as W. L. Fleming of Alabama, J. W. Garner of Mississippi, and J. G. de Roulhac Hamilton of North Carolina.

Some of these men were still prone to collapse, on occasion, into sentimentality and chauvinism. Fleming, for example, went to a great deal of trouble to argue that the Black Code enacted by the Southern legislatures immediately after the Civil War was not designed to restore essential slavery, though a simple reading of these laws is sufficient to confute him — unless we are to suppose that to have no real control over the disposal of one's labor and one's personal movements does not constitute essential slavery. But it was not always so. And they had all acquired a respect and even a passion for facts which ordinarily would triumph over their prejudices. Moreover, what they had begun would be carried further by their students and the younger men who followed them.

In economics the advance was even slower. Adam Smith still was generally presented as having the same absolute validity as Isaac Newton. And the teaching of the branch was mainly in the hands of dull men who carefully avoided examining the current scene in the South itself.

But in sociology a very notable beginning had been made. For as early as 1911 Howard W. Odum had come back from Columbia, where he had written his notable monograph on the social and mental traits of the Negro, to begin to teach in his native Georgia. And a few years later he removed to the University of North Carolina, to enter upon the work there which has made him famous.

23

But the mention of Odum suggests something else which ought to be made explicitly clear here. If I say that the economics faculty, for instance, avoided the current Southern scene, it must not be thought that such was the invariable rule for all the faculties. On the contrary, there was in evidence, from the late 1890's on, a growing tendency on the part of a growing handful of men to turn directly to examining and criticizing the South. And still further, there was also a growing tendency for the majority of the faculty in many schools to back them up in it, or at least to maintain their right to their heresies.

In 1902, for instance, Dr. Andrew Sledd, a professor at Emory College in Georgia, published an article in the *Atlantic Monthly* in which he not only scourged lynching but also attacked Jim Crow laws as incompatible with fundamental human rights. For that Emory immediately dismissed him, and his colleagues on the faculty, perhaps intimidated by the uproar of the press against him as a " Boston equality citizen " (he was, in fact, a Virginian), silently acquiesced. But Florida University promptly gave him a job, and a few years later made him its president — though it afterward discharged him for the ironical reason that he couldn't increase the number of students fast enough. Shortly after that, however, Emory was removed from its village of the same name to Atlanta and reorganized as Emory University; and Sledd was invited to return to its faculty, where he remained until his death.

Again, the very next year after Sledd's article, John Spencer Bassett, then serving as professor of history in Trinity College, a Methodist institution at Durham, North Carolina, which has since become Duke University, published an article in the *South Atlantic Quarterly,* issuing from Trinity and edited by himself, wherein he carried iconoclasm to the point of asserting that, after General Lee, Booker T. Washington, the Negro, was the greatest man born in the South in a century. The demand for his dismissal was so great and strident that even Josephus Daniels, in general one of the most liberal and intelligent editors the South has had, was swept into the current and regularly printed the professor's name as " bASSett." But the president of the college told the trustees that he would resign if Bassett were sacrificed, and the whole faculty secretly went on record to the same effect. Faced with that ultimatum, the trustees, after a stormy debate, voted to retain him.

It is unnecessary to exaggerate the meaning of this. There were many factors at play in these decisions — the threat of the standardizing authorities to strike Trinity off the accredited list, for instance, and the concern of many of the professors for their own professional status. It is perhaps not without significance that Bassett, though a native North Carolinian, did not tarry long before retiring to the North. And there would yet be other instances of the triumph of intolerance in the schools. Enoch M. Banks, a native Georgian, was dismissed from the University of Florida faculty in 1911 merely for saying in the *Independent* that in the Civil War " the North was relatively in the right, while the South was relatively in the wrong." Nevertheless, the slow development of criticism and tolerance for it within the academic circle was indubitable.

With the coming of the 1920's, however, what had gone on growing desultorily through the years was to receive enormous new impetus, to take on form and cohesion and direction. One important factor for this result was Progress itself, for along with the feverish rise in the urge to build and speculate in industry and commerce went a surge in the passion for Education — taking the characteristic form of pouring out money more and more lavishly on it. The great part of these new funds went to the public school systems, with the result that the old-fashioned country schoolhouse almost disappeared from most sections of the Southern landscape, to give place to the consolidated rural school, with large buildings and many teachers. But the colleges and universities, public and private, almost universally came in for greatly expanded income also. And for these, this meant not only more buildings and laboratories and libraries, better facilities for teaching and research, and the employment of many more instructors, but also the ability to pay such salaries as would attract more brilliant and distinguished ones. There was a veritable influx of such men from the North, both native Southerners and Yankees, in the years between 1920 and 1927.

The old-fashioned type of history professor was still plentifully in evidence, but in the better schools the younger men were all likely now to smile when a chauvinistic student protested a plain statement of facts. In the economics department the young men were beginning to tweak Adam Smith's nose, and occasionally one of them would even be quoting Karl Marx under the rose. Freud, Adler, Jung, Watson, Dewey, Veblen, Nietzsche, Spengler, names like these were the stock-in-trade in increasingly large numbers of classrooms. Already when Mr. Mencken's celebrated essay " The Sahara of the Bozart " appeared, there were a few men in Southern English departments to suggest that while it all might be very wicked, it still had an uncomfortable lot of truth in it. And before the decade was out, all of them with any claim of dignity of intelligence would be confessing as much; and some of them were neglecting Thomas Nelson Page in favor of Ellen Glasgow or James Joyce — or perhaps Irving Babbitt and T. S. Eliot.

At the University of North Carolina, Odum and his associates, such as Rupert Vance, were carrying out, with the aid of Rockefeller funds, the monumental series of studies which was to culminate in the publication of *Southern Regions in the United States* in 1936. The cases of the Negro, his psychology as well as his sociology; of the cotton-mill worker; of the tenant and sharecropper, of the cotton farmer in general; of cotton altogether; of the wasted resources of the South — all these and many more were coming in for the most exhaustive investigation and analysis. And elsewhere much of the same sort of work was going on — as at Emory University, which having started out so badly had ended by becoming one of the most enlightened centers of social and economic and racial inquiry in the South.

And out of Chapel Hill and all the lesser centers which followed Odum's lead, numbers of young men and women were going out through the schools of the South to hand on and expand the new attitude in ever widening circles. By the end of the decade even the high schools were beginning remotely to feel the influence, both of the new knowledge and of the new inquiry.

In the nature of this book, I cannot do proper justice to all the men and institutions who played their part here. There are literally a hundred names — like that of E. C. Branson, whose work in rural socio-economics at the University of North Carolina was second only to Odum's — which belong to the story in its entirety. And an account of what was going on at all the institutions involved would fill up many pages.

On the other hand, it is not to be assumed that I imply any universal renaissance in the Southern schools in the period. As a matter of fact, a great many of them remained little affected by the new forces. In perhaps the majority of them, indeed — as, for instance, the University of Alabama — the tendency to inquiry into the South's social structure made only desultory headway, and change was to be measured much less in the increase of knowledge and thoughtfulness and tolerance than in the reduction of the academic department to the status of an appanage of fraternity row and a hired football team. So late as 1931 Dr. Carl Taylor was dismissed from his post as dean at the North Carolina State College of Agriculture and Engineering mainly because his activities in behalf of free speech and civil liberty had antagonized the cotton-mill magnates who dominated it. And three years later still, poor Clarence Cason, who taught journalism at Alabama, felt compelled to commit suicide, in part at least because of his fear of the fiercely hostile attitude which he knew that both the school authorities and his fellow faculty members would take toward his criticisms of the South in his *90° in the Shade,* published by the University of North Carolina Press a few days after his death.

None the less, what I have said sufficiently indicates, I trust, the important thing for our purposes: that a decisive breach had been made in the savage ideal, in the historical solidity and rigidly exacted uniformity of the South — that the modern mind had been established within the gates, and that here at long last there was springing up in the South a growing body of men — small enough

when set against the mass of the South but vastly large when set
against anything of the kind which had ever existed in Dixie before — who had broken fully or largely out of that pattern described by Henry Adams in the case of Rooney Lee and fixed by
Reconstruction; men who deliberately chose to know and think
rather than merely to *feel* in terms fixed finally by Southern patriotism and the prejudices associated with it; men capable of detachment and actively engaged in analysis and criticism of the
South itself.

Were all such men, then, confined strictly to the schools? Obviously not. Merely, the new spirit had its chief citadel and center
of propagation there. There were in fact men scattered here and
there in the active life of the section, some of them in important
places, who were in one measure or another of the same sort —
editors, professional men, writers, even occasionally business men
or ministers. We shall see more of some of them as we proceed.

24

And, of course, the spectacle of this phenomenon rising more
and more clearly into view inspired fear and hate in the majority
of Southerners of every class who were still committed to the old
beliefs and ways and the conviction that absolute conformity to
them was necessary to the safety of the South.

Here were many thousands of fathers aghast at the spectacle of
sons, sometimes daughters, for whom, often, they had sacrificed
painfully — serious young men and women who profoundly believed what they said, or perhaps more often who spoke in part at
least out of the mere ebullient defiance of youth — returning home
from school to say that they thought Mr. Darwin was right; echoing
fearful ideas from that man Freud, who sounded as though he were
in the pay of the Kremlin; quoting Henry Mencken and George
Jean Nathan, and mocking the ministers; speaking disrespectfully
of old Mr. Frumpit, the banker, and old Mr. Peter Hamilton Stackhouse, of the Stackhouse Cotton Mills, Inc., quite as though every-

body, including the Frumpits and the Stackhouses, didn't know they were the saviors of the community in the past and its hope for the future; using words like " exploitation," and talking of something called " society," just as if it were not true that every man was in his place because the combination of his own qualities and the will of Heaven had set him there; perhaps, in their first naïve delight in rebellion, expounding Karl Marx and admiring Russia.

And not only the fathers. The young man returning to his native place, particularly if he lived in the larger towns, might now and then find a few people tolerant enough by education or native temperament to listen to him amiably and quietly and perhaps to encourage him in some of his notions. But the general effect on the community, in all classes, was to produce terror and anger in one degree or another.

This terror and anger arose in part from that always growing calculation at which we have looked. Industrialist and commercialist saw a direct and potent threat to their immediate and future interests in such social studies as those at Chapel Hill, and in the infectious sympathy of occasional instructors for labor unions. The landowner and planter saw it in the growing conviction in the schools that a Negro was more than a mere work animal, in the inquiries into the status of the tenant and the cropper; the politician of the established Democratic hierarchy in the challenge to his axiom that the end justifies the means, in the new concepts of what constitutes good government; and the demagogue in the increasingly devastating analysis of his main stock-in-trade, Negrophobia; the minister in the rise of the old enemies of his power, science and rationalism, the new psychology. And all these, and almost every man at all who profited under Progress or who hoped to have himself or his sons profit under it, saw it in the development of free inquiry and analysis altogether, as inevitably tending to upset the *status quo*.

The very commonest white, indeed, saw it as a menace to his interests, or at least to his ego, once it had been called to his atten-

tion by his masters; he felt within himself that it all constituted
a danger to his conventional status as the superior of every Negro
whatever. Perhaps he also resented the new learning and the new
freedom of ideas as tending to widen the gulf between himself
and those who went in for them.

As in every time past, however, the element of calculation here
flowed over, through the medium of the old easy capacity for unreality and the old habit of high and noble affirmation, to consoli-
date with, and to emerge wholly in the form of, terror and anger
for high religion and high patriotism to the South, for the preservation of the way handed down by the fathers, tested by experience,
and hallowed by the blood of the Confederate dead. Yes, and of
terror and anger as against the Red Peril. For with that the new
developments in the schools were promptly and very explicitly
linked.

This modern mind was that same Faustian hell-compact which
had so long been betraying Yankeedom into " infidelity," wasn't
it? And before that it had originally come out of Europe, which,
as everyone knew, was simply a hotbed of materialism and decadence and corruption. And was not Karl Marx himself indubitably
a direct product of its everlasting corrosive action, its will to inquire into all things and submit them to the test of rationality, to
recognize nothing as sacrosanct and taboo? And since that was
so, why, plainly it didn't matter where you began, whether with
Darwin or Nietzsche or Freud or John Watson. All of them were
common exponents, in the last analysis, of a common movement
for which the logical culmination everywhere was atheistic Communism.

So the reasoning, so far as there was reasoning, ran. Already the
thing had seduced over half the Western world far along the road
toward that goal. Already, as you could see conclusively in the
New York *Herald Tribune,* the Chicago *Tribune,* and all of Mr.
Hearst's Orphic journals, Yankeedom was being hurried the same
way. And here it was, putting down dangerous roots in the South
itself, which had so long and successfully quarantined it at the

Potomac. Let it grow, and the South, too, would collapse into paganism and Communism, into moral and physical ruin. Was it not manifest that even now many of the young men and women who were coming out of the schools no longer went to church? That some brashly proclaimed themselves agnostics or even announced their adherence to atheism — the very hallmark of Red Russia itself? Even doubted property? As for the moral effect of it all, there was evidence to hand, ready made.

For the South, in large segments of its younger people at least, had not escaped the general Western collapse into barnyard morality which followed the war. Nor can it well be denied that there was some ground for associating this with the rapid extension of the ideas of the modern mind. The prime source of it was unquestionably the natural backlash from the war and the mood of fear and disillusionment which we have seen already. Prohibition played its part, too. When that is said, however, the fact remains that the general dissemination of the modern ideology — often by piecemeal and at third hand, of course — with its predominant emphasis on biology and mechanistic philosophy and its skepticism about everything which has not been rigidly established, certainly had its effect on the case also. The more animal sort eagerly read into it *carte blanche* for the free exercise of their appetites. And on even the best the immediate effect of almost sudden contact with it was apt to be the collapse of old standards without the creation of adequate new ones — the development of a feeling that, since man was apparently no more than a frail mote of protoplasm suspended for a fleeting second in a gleam of light in the midst of impenetrable and immeasurable darkness, it was pretty silly to make such a pother about his deeds and standards.

The breakdown was in evidence everywhere in the South, as in the rest of America and the West. But it was in the colleges and universities, precisely where the modern mind most flourished, that it reached its greatest development, or at least that it was most plainly on view. Swinish drunkenness, eternal and blatant concern with the theme of sex, and promiscuity in one degree or another flourished — not so extravagantly as rumor had it, surely, but still to such an extent that it was impossible to be blind to it. For every young man or woman profoundly impressed with the giants of the modern mind, there were a hundred who were impressed with the people of Aldous Huxley, Michael Arlen, and, above all, Warner Fabian, and who took them as their own models of smart and sophisticated conduct.

The matter had a double aspect. On the one hand, this bawdy outburst struck straight against Southern Puritanism and senti-mentality — particularly the cult of Southern Womanhood — and so served to add to the sum total of fears on its own account. And not only among those who were themselves untouched by it. What I have said with regard to the South being in some fashion afraid of itself is particularly applicable here. For in the bottom of the minds of even the most flauntingly " emancipated " of these youths, the old sentimentality and Puritanism bred in their bones from birth still lurked, and often started up to torture the young woman with longing for the old role of vestal virgin, the young man with longing for the old gesturing worship of a more than mortal crea-ture — to make them continually restless with the subconscious will to escape into being more nearly whole again. And one result of this was that they usually kept right on giving lip service to the ancient tradition and forms.

There is a passage in Carl Carmer's *Stars Fell on Alabama* which admirably illustrates the point:

" One of the rituals of the university [of Alabama] dances is that of a fraternity of young blades entitled the Key-Ice. During an intermission the lights are turned out and these young men march in carrying flaming brands. At the end of the procession four acolytes attend a long cake of ice. . . . Then the leader, mounted on a table in the center of the big gymnasium, lifts a glass cup of water and begins a toast that runs: ' To Woman, lovely woman of the Southland, as pure and chaste as this sparkling water, as cold as this gleaming ice, we lift this cup, and we pledge our hearts and our lives to the protection of her virtue and chastity.'

" Frequently the young man is slightly inebriated and the probability is that he and his cohorts are among the better known seducers of the campus, but no one sees any incongruity in this."

But if the new looseness served to engender fear on its own account and to further widen the old curious split between profession and practice, it also served, as I have said, as an immensely valuable exhibit for the opponents of the modern mind in Dixie — an exhibit admirably calculated, because of its coincidence with that mind in the colleges and universities, to convince simple minds that the whole natural fruit of that mind was decay and madness and ruin and would eventually be Communism.

In the name of religion, of morality, of patriotism, of the purity of Southern Womanhood, and of the will to avert the Red Peril, then, the accepted leaders of the South proclaimed their fear and hatred of the new spirit which had wormed its way in — in their name called up the fear and hatred of the masses against it. And now, as in all times past, it was quite impossible to say where calculation ended and genuine religious conviction, sentimentality, moral notions, and patriotism began. You could say with fair confidence that calculation was greater than at any time before. You could be reasonably convinced that calculation played the major role in the hot zeal of such journals as the *Textile Bulletin* for returning the schools to the status of pure stamping mills for the old pattern. But beyond that —

25

Thus ends this sketch of the complex of fears and hates which greatly absorbed the energies of the Southern people, high and low, in these years. As I have said, that absorption goes far to explain why the masses in the mills and on the land developed economic and social focus so slowly, despite the swiftly widening gulf opened up between the classes by Progress and speculation. But these fears and hates also serve, in one degree or another, to explain many of the most striking phenomena of the South in the period.

Thus the whole complex was certainly the primary factor in that swing back to primitivism in religion which I have noted in another connection — in the sweep of the so-called Fundamentalism through the region, until even men of great dignity in the community could be brought to grovel and weep at the mourners' bench of Mr. Sunday. The whole movement was finally just such a movement as we have looked at in the Reconstruction period — an attempt to retreat upon the past and make sure of the support of the heavenly powers by way of escaping from dangers felt to be too great to be faced without such assistance — to achieve the feeling of security against those dangers. And of course the thousand and one "drives" of one sort or another, such as North Carolina's Tatum Committee, which sought to remove the works of every distinguished man who has lived since 1850 from the university library at Chapel Hill, or Florida's Bible Crusaders of America, which waged a systematic campaign to eliminate every form of intelligence from the schools of that and other states — all these were simply a part of the same thing: the active expression of the hate portion of the equation.

It is to these fears, also, that we must look for the explanation of what went along with the retreat to primitivism and indeed constituted an essential part of it: the resurgence of a bitterly narrow spirit of Protestantism, and, as the reverse of that, the outburst of anti-Semitic and anti-Catholic feeling. The South had relatively few Jews — certainly not enough to constitute a Jewish Problem under any rational view of the case — and few Catholics, save in Louisiana. But fears and hates often clothe themselves in old forms. And the Jew, of course, was a butt and a scapegoat as old as Christianity. All the protests of scholars have been quite unavailing to erase from the popular mind, in the South as elsewhere, the notion that it was the Jew who crucified Jesus. And in addition there was the consideration I have already suggested: the Jew, with his universal refusal to be assimilated, is everywhere the eternal Alien; and in the South, where any difference had always stood out with great vividness, he was especially so. Hence it was perfectly natural that, in the general withdrawal upon the old heritage, the rising insistence on conformity to it, he should come in for renewed denunciations; should, as he passed in the street, stand in the eyes of the people as a sort of evil harbinger and incarnation of all the menaces they feared and hated — external and internal, real and imaginary.

And as for anti-Catholicism, militant Protestantism, as we know, had always stood at the heart and center of the South — had here, perhaps, survived in its pristine vigor of feeling more fully than anywhere else on earth. And militant Protestantism, it is general knowledge, is synonymous with anti-Catholicism, as it has been from the beginning. For the Protestant all through the centuries, the Catholic even more than the Jew has stood as the intolerable Alien, as the bearer of Jesuit plots to rob them of their religion by force and of schemes for new and larger St. Bartholomew's. In the South, and especially the rural South, moreover, that feeling has probably always been fed and kept alive by the relative infrequency of contact with Catholics — on the same principle which I have indicated in the case of the cotton-mill workers and the Negro. Certainly anti-Catholic feeling has always been extraordinarily strong in Dixie; it had often flared out before now — would be perfectly certain to blaze out as fear rose and the need of scapegoats increased. And when to that was added the Presidential candidacy of Catholic Al Smith throughout the 1920's — the case is manifest. Here was final proof to millions of Protestants in the South, as in the rest of America for that matter, that the Pope was plotting to seize the White House.

Again, it is these fears and hate, plus this attempt to withdraw into the past and revive an exaggerated simplicity of religious belief and dogma, that does a great deal to explain something else. I mean that it was in exactly this time that the ministers of the evangelical sects finally towered up to their greatest power, until

almost literally nobody in the South dared criticize their pronouncements or oppose the political programs they laid out — until Bishop
James Cannon could actually sweep five of the former Confederate
States out of the Democratic Party and into voting the hated Republican ticket.

And all that, taken together, helps to explain why the South was
notoriously the backbone of national Prohibition — why, though
sensible Southerners who had any contact with the facts were well
aware of its effect for corruption and swinishness, no organized
opposition to it developed anywhere in the region.

So I might go on at length, setting out the various Southern
phenomena and their relation to the reigning fears and hates. But
it is only necessary, I think, to glance more closely at the Ku Klux
Klan and the anti-evolution drive which headed up in the trial of
John T. Scopes at Dayton.

I am aware, to be sure, that it has been maintained that the Klan
was a mere accident — just another tin-pot fraternal order, created
by the half-cracked brain of a starveling Methodist parson, which
would have died quickly if the New York *World* and other Northern newspapers had not seized upon it and made it an excuse for
indulging the old habit of strafing the South, and so at once adver-
tised it and got the South's dander up in favor of it. But this is
merely an example of clever journalism, scarcely meant to be believed. And that conclusion is not changed by the claim that the
name of the organization was suggested by accident, and Ward
Greene's amusing story that the persons who posed for the first
photograph of " Klansmen in full regalia " were in fact Atlanta
Negroes hired for a quarter apiece.

In its essence the thing was an authentic folk movement — at
least as fully such as the Nazi movement in Germany, to which it
was not without kinship. And its name was no accident, save as the
movement of the planets among the stars may be an accident, but a
significant projection from the past into the present, a meaningful
witness of the continuity of Southern sentiment.

Its body was made up of the common whites, industrial and

rural. But its blood, if I may continue the figure, came from the upper orders. And its bony framework and nervous system, the people who held it together and co-ordinated and directed it, were very near to being coextensive with the established leadership of the South. People of great prominence in industry and business, indeed, were often, though not always, chary about actually belonging to it, but they usually maintained liaison with it through their underlings and the politicians. And its ranks swarmed with little business men. Except in North Carolina and Virginia, the rural clergy belonged to it or had traffic with it almost *en masse,* and even in those two states the same thing was true in many districts. It was true, too, in many towns throughout the South, and everywhere the great body of the ministers either smiled benignly on it or carefully kept their mouths shut about it. Planters joined it by the wholesale, and more often than not worked with it when they did not join it. So did the landowning farmers generally; indeed, in proportion to their numbers, these perhaps went into it or sympathized with it more generally than even the unpropertied commons.

And as for the politicians, whether maverick demagogue or hierarch, it was the exception who did not either go into it or, more usually, bid for its support by playing along with it in one degree or another. It was a little comic in 1936 to hear one conservative Southern politician after another solemnly denouncing Hugo Black as unfit for the Supreme Court because he had had some connection with the Klan back in the middle twenties. For if the rule that to have had traffic of any sort with the Klan constituted a bar to high office, had been adopted and enforced, most of them would have had to resign their own posts and ambitions.

Moreover, the Klan summed up within itself, with precise completeness and exactness, the whole body of the fears and hates of the time, including, of course, those which were shared with the rest of America and the Western world. That is why, somewhat modified for the purpose (particularly in leaving out the anti-Yankee bias which was quite plainly present in its Southern form), it eventually spread far beyond the borders of Dixie. It was, as is well known, at once anti-Negro, anti-Alien, anti-Red, anti-Catholic, anti-Jew, anti-Darwin, anti-Modern, anti-Liberal, Fundamentalist, vastly Moral, militantly Protestant. And, summing up these fears, it brought them into focus with the tradition of the past, and above all with the ancient Southern pattern of high romantic histrionics, violence, and mass coercion of the scapegoat and the heretic.

Here in ghostly rides through the moonlit, aromatic evening to whip a Negro or a prostitute or some poor white given to violating the Seventh Commandment or drinking up his scant earnings instead of clothing his children, or merely given to staying away from church; to tar and feather a labor organizer or a schoolmaster who had talked his new ideas too much — in slow, swaying noonday parades through the burning silence of towns where every Negro was gone from the streets, and the Jews and the Catholics and the aliens had their houses and shops shuttered — here was surcease for the personal frustrations and itches of the Klansman, of course. But also the old coveted, splendid sense of being a heroic blade, a crusader sweeping up mystical slopes for White Supremacy, religion, morality, and all that had made up the faith of the Fathers: of being the direct heir in continuous line of the Confederate soldiers at Gettysburg and of those old Klansmen who had once driven out the carpetbagger and tamed the scalawag; of participating in ritualistic assertion of the South's continuing identity, its will to remain unchanged and defy the ways of the Yankee and the world in favor of that one which had so long been its own.

26

An authentic folk movement, beyond a doubt: such was the Klan. And such also, in only comparatively less complete measure, was the anti-evolution movement. For it cannot be dismissed as the aberration of a relatively small, highly organized pressure group made up of ignorant, silly, and fanatical people, as some writers have attempted to do. Having observed it at close range, I have no doubt at all that it had the active support and sympathy of the overwhelming majority of the Southern people. And not only among the masses. In 1926 the Southern Baptist Convention, made up wholly of the leading ministers and laymen of the most numerous sect in the region, and representing a very fair cross-section of Southern leadership, formally adopted a statement that: " This convention . . . rejects every theory, evolutionary or other, which teaches that man originated or came by way of lower animal ancestry." And the Education Board of the Church adopted the same statement shortly afterward.

What stood at Dayton and demanded the conviction of Scopes under the Tennessee law forbidding the teaching of evolution in the state-supported schools — what sat down before the legislatures of all the Southern states and demanded similar or even more stringent laws — was far more than any band of hillbillies. And what actuated it and what it demanded were more than appears on the surface. The Darwinian doctrine was indeed no more than the focal point of an attack for a program, explicit or implicit, that went far beyond evolution laws: a program proceeding not only from Fundamentalist religious fears but from the whole body of the fears we have seen, and having as its objective the stamping out of all the new heresies and questioning in the schools and elsewhere — the restoration of that absolute conformity to the ancient pattern under the pains and penalties of the most rigid intolerance: the maintenance of the savage ideal, to the end of vindicating the old Southern will to cling fast to its historical way.

Clarence Cason has suggested something of the kind before me. And I do not believe that anybody who looks into the matter carefully and candidly can avoid the conclusion that it is fundamentally true. The anti-evolution organizations were everywhere closely associated with those others which quite explicitly were engaged in attempting to wipe out all the new knowledge in the schools, to clear all modern books out of the libraries. " Yankee infidelity " and " European depravity " and " alien ideas " were their standard rallying-cries. They warned constantly and definitely that evolution was certain to breed Communism. Just as clearly and as constantly, they warned that it was breaking down Southern morals — destroying the ideal of Southern Womanhood. One of the most stressed notions which went around was that evolution made a Negro as good as a white man — that is, threatened White Supremacy. And always, as what I already say indicates, they came back to the idea of saving the South, appealed to and spoke in the name of exactly the old potent patriotism of the region.

Before I leave the theme, however, there are several other things which need to be said, by way both of setting the case of the Klan and the Fundamentalist anti-evolution movement in better perspective, and also of calling attention to the fact that these two movements seem to have carried in themselves the seed of decay and defeat.

One of them is that as time went on, opposition to them steadily gathered head in the South. There had been opposition from the first, of course, and outside the schools, where it naturally flourished vigorously. Many thousands of the older men bred in the best tradition of the South (and regardless of whether they belonged to the old aristocratic or semi-aristocratic orders or were plain people), remembering the abuses and outrages which had disgraced the early Klan in its later days, distrusting the use of the state's power for allegedly religious ends, or thinking sagely that the schools themselves were the best judges of what they should teach, refused to have anything to do with either movement or in any way to lend them approval. So did thousands of the younger men, either because of their tradition or because they had — often quite unconsciously — come to some extent under the influence of the new tolerance centering in the schools. And some of them were courageous enough to speak out their convictions: editorial writers like Gerald W. Johnson and Nell Battle Lewis in North Carolina; Douglas Freeman, Virginius Dabney, and Louis Jaffé in Virginia; Julian Harris in Georgia; and Grover Hall in Alabama; ministers like Baptist Edwin McNeill Poteat of South Carolina; politicians like Carter Glass of Virginia. Indeed, such men had such complete control in Virginia that neither movement ever got thoroughly established there.

But with the passage of time more and more men of serious intelligence began to heed the warnings of these, to examine into the movements, and to realize their implications for the South. In Alabama, Grover Hall, whose long series of editorials against both in the *Montgomery Advertiser* was to bring him the Pulitzer prize in journalism, won increasing support not only from the Birmingham *Age-Herald* and *News* but eventually, so far as the Klan went, from most of the dailies in the state. In Georgia, Julian Harris, who had long waged his fight against both the Klan and the whole Fundamentalist position single-handed, was joined by the *Macon Telegraph* and other papers in the battle on the Klan. In Tennessee, the Memphis *Commercial-Appeal* at length took up the cudgels against the Klan, but it continued to give its blessings to the anti-evolutionists. In Alabama, Senator Oscar Underwood unloosed scathing rebukes on the Klan, though he knew probably it meant the end of his Presidential ambitions. In Georgia, Governor Thomas W. Hardwick ordered the Klan to unmask, knowing certainly that it would close his political career. And so it went.

And seeing these take their stand, still others began to pluck up heart, to venture opposition in private at least. More, many of the leaders of all sorts who had joined the Klan or trafficked with it, began to get out of it or back away from it, and something of the same sort began to happen among those who had gone in for Fundamentalism and its politics — in part because they were disgusted with the crimes of the Klan, and ashamed before the amazed laughter of the civilized world at the " monkey laws " and the Scopes trial, in part because of canny doubts about what the eventual outcome might be for themselves. And after 1925 a rapidly growing exodus of all the more decent elements from the rank and file of the Klan would begin.

In the very hour when they seemed to have it in their power to do what they had plainly set out to do, the people themselves showed a curious hesitancy and revulsion — a strange unreadiness to go through with it. The same disgust for the Klan's crimes and the same proud shrinking from the thought that the South was being treated as a comic land because of the anti-evolution laws and attacks on intelligence, which assuredly moved some of the leaders, probably had something to do with that in the more informed levels in general. The old respect for Education, reasserting itself continually, entered into the equation, too. After all, men of native good sense and decency everywhere felt themselves bound to respect such men as Poteat of Wake Forest, and Harry Woodburn Chase and Frank Porter Graham of Chapel Hill, however much they were opposed to them — felt dimly in the depths of their minds, when they saw them come boldly out in defense of academic freedom, that they might know better what they were about than had been supposed. And beyond even that, it is not improbable, I believe, that the modern mind itself, the spirit of the world in the time in which they lived, had in some imponderable measure touched even the simple also, had all unconsciously entered into them to plant the tiny germ of inward doubt. Perhaps the very Klan and Fundamentalism themselves testify in the end to the beginning of the subtle decay of the old rigid standards and values, the ancient pattern; perhaps they proceeded from that distrust of themselves which I have before noted in Southerners, and represented an ultimately unsuccessful attempt to draw themselves back upon the ancient pattern to escape the feeling that, against their wills, the seeping in of change might claim them also. Perhaps they stood at last, these people, bemused before their own minds, condemned to inactivity by the sweep of current and counter-current through them.

At any rate, there the hesitancy, the drawing back, was. After the Scopes trial, for all the indubitable majority opposition to Darwinism, only two states went on to pass anti-evolution laws, and those two were the two which by all standards were the most benighted, Mississippi and Arkansas. And if other movements against intelligence in the schools continued occasionally to flare up, they invariably died of inanition. As for the Klan, though it blazed up brilliantly in the Al Smith campaign of 1928, I think there is no doubt that thereafter it was doomed simply by increasingly swift internal causes.

But the demise of these movements was to be greatly accelerated by new forces. For now at hand were circumstances to swing first the masses and after them the masters of the South back to sharper and more intense economic and social concern than they had known in decades — than they had ever known, in fact.

CHAPTER III

OF THE GREAT BLIGHT — AND
NEW QUANDARIES

It is fairly common knowledge now that the great depression began in the United States a good deal sooner than the stock-market
crash of October 1929 — that creeping slowly up in Europe in the
post-war years, it reached this country as early as 1927. That year
the figures for car loadings and sales began clearly to testify to an
ominous slowing down in the pace of industry and commerce.
And if afterward the pendulum swung back again, it was largely
due to the increasing hysteria of speculation and to high-pressure
methods of installment selling.

And in the South it was naturally the textile mills which first
began to suffer from it, on the industrial and commercial front at
least. Perhaps they were not actually greatly depressed even in the
spring of 1929. But orders had fallen off considerably, were falling
off more rapidly. And what was worse from the standpoint of the
owners, it was no longer possible to make profits which were considered adequate. Part of that was due to the phenomenally bad
organization I have already referred to. Even more of it was due
to the fact that, during the war and after, the mills, the majority
of which were controlled by a single family or a " ring " of two or
three directors, had taken to paying exorbitant salaries to the officials
— all members of these families or " rings," of course. Salary totals
from twenty-five to fifty thousand dollars a year, for men who often
rendered little more service than to act as go-betweens for the
production superintendent and the so-called " commission houses "

which served as selling agents in the North, were quite common in small mills capitalized at no more than a half-million dollars or even less.

But the immediate precipitating factor in the case was that the mills of New England, which had remained depressed throughout the period since the war because of their inability to meet the competition of low wages in the South, had at length hit upon a device which for the moment enabled them to compete again and so inevitably to drive down prices. I mean the use of the so-called stretch-out system, under which, by forcing him to spend every working moment at the peak of nervous concentration, an operative is made to care for several times as many machines as was formerly considered a fair assignment — sometimes with a nominal increase in total pay, usually without it, and sometimes even with an actual reduction.

Faced with that, the masters of the Southern mills responded in characteristic fashion — in the only fashion, indeed, that they ever had known — by proceeding to take the difference out of their employees in one way or another. Wage cuts became fairly common by the spring of 1929. And shut-downs grew more frequent as the management waxed increasingly nervous about the huge stocks of goods which were piling up in their warehouses.

And — the stretch-out was introduced into Dixie, to become the match to the powder of the slow irritation and restlessness which I have predicated as slowly growing up beneath the surface in the whole period after the close of the war. The wage cuts were bitterly resented, coming as they did at a time when prices showed no indication of ever following suit, and so serving to renew and accentuate the old soreness — never lost — inspired by the contrast between their estate in the war time and afterward. The shut-downs contributed to the same purpose, and in addition stirred up fear for the future. But what served to inflame anger far beyond any of this was the stretch-out itself.

For many families its immediate effect was a sharp and tragic reduction in income; since hundreds of workmen, for the most part highly skilled heads of families, were thrown out of employment because they were unable to adjust themselves to the new demands upon them. What was perhaps more important was that it violated the whole tradition of this people — of the South, indeed. To be wrenched out of the old, easy-going way so long native to the country, to be required to exhibit more energy than the climate allowed for — that was in itself bad enough. But to be deprived of one's dignity as an individual and made into a sort of automaton; to be stood over by a taskmaster with a stop-watch in his hand (a taskmaster who himself would have an " efficiency expert," usually a Yankee, at his elbow), and checked on at each visit to the water-cooler or toilet; to be everlastingly hazed on to greater exertion by curt commands and sneers, and to have to stand periodically and take a dressing down with a white face, just as though one were a nigger, under the ever present threat of being summarily dismissed — for this people so immensely proud in its curious way, bred to the ancient Southern notion that each was a white man like any other, that each in some fundamental fashion was as good as any white man who walked the earth and entitled to be treated with respect and consideration; bred, too, to the heritage of knowing the masters of the mills on the old casually intimate terms — for such a people, that was well-nigh or wholly intolerable.

The result was the first genuinely serious labor revolt the South had ever known; the first that represented a more than casual and passing break with their masters. In March and April of 1929, strikes broke out in four widely scattered quarters — at Greenville, South Carolina; at Elizabethtown, Tennessee; at Marion, North Carolina; and — at Gastonia. Two things about them are worth noting. The first is that, in Gastonia and Elizabethtown, they broke out in mills owned by absentee Yankee landlords; and the second, that all of them began in the characteristic Southern form of spontaneous, unorganized, almost unpremeditated walk-outs. The United Textile Workers of America had, in the usual American Federation of Labor fashion of the time, been sleeping through its opportunities and did not even have an organizer present at any of the places where the strikes arose. It was this more than anything else which gave Communists Fred Beal and George Pershing and their National Textile Workers' Union a chance to crowd into the scene at Gastonia and take charge.

But if I call these strikes the first genuinely serious labor revolt the South had had, it is also to be said that they were inevitably and necessarily doomed to defeat from the beginning.

For the quite simple reason, so far as that goes, of the presence of the old Southern reservoir of surplus labor. And not merely untrained labor. There were those thousands who had been in the mills at one time or another, and who were often glad to grasp a chance to escape from the status of sharecropper or even tenant and get back to the mills by serving as strikebreakers — people who, in their naïve individualism, were innocent of the notion implied in the word " scab."

For the reason, also, that militant interest was arrayed against these strikes. The masters of the mills were naturally terrified for their profits, both present and future, which as we have before seen, they felt to be dependent upon the maintenance of cheap labor and the *status quo*. But these were only the beginning. Every stockholder in the mills — and they numbered hundreds of thousands — was likely to feel the same way, and was already in a humor to be an easy victim to fear and rage, for the reason that his dividends, eaten up by the bad management and the fat salaries of the mill officials, had already long been dwindling. And beyond these, the officials and stockholders of almost every industrial establishment of any sort.

2

Indeed, the whole business community of the region, devoted as strongly as the mill masters to the notion that the maintenance of cheap labor and the *status quo* was essential to their well-being, participated in the feeling that the strike represented a direct and intolerable threat to their personal interests; as did all those swarm-

All the states have redoubled their efforts to attract industries from the North or to persuade local capital to build factories by holding out extravagant and often questionable inducements. North Carolina, for example, justifies a particularly atrocious sales tax, which falls most heavily upon the people least able to pay it, the Negroes and poor whites, on the ground that further taxes on industry will keep the state from acquiring new factories. Shortly before the enactment of the Federal Wage and Hour Law, South Carolina repealed a wage and hour law for the textile industry in the state on the recommendation of Governor Maybank, who argued that it was keeping factories out. And in the deep South several of the states have turned to more or less modified versions of the so-called Mississippi Plan.

This scheme, originally devised by Governor Hugh White, of Mississippi, and enacted into law by the Legislature of that state, authorizes counties and municipalities to issue bonds for the building of factory plants, which are handed over without cost to manufacturers who will provide machinery and operating capital. The law also provides for the complete suspension of taxes on such manufacturers for long periods. And what is not provided by the law but is an essential part of the scheme is that every effort is to be used to keep labor costs extremely low.

Many towns and counties in Mississippi have eagerly taken advantage of the plan. And the wages paid in these community-built but privately owned factories have often fallen below the levels fixed by the Wage and Hour Act, which has been very laxly enforced throughout the South.

It is unnecessary to be too suspicious of the motives behind the scheme. Characteristically, it undoubtedly has in it much of patriotism, for Mississippi is the Southern state which has had the least industrial development, and one of those which have been most beset by unemployment as a result of the collapse of cotton.

But it really solves nothing — in fact, operates to make ultimate conditions worse. It gives away the wealth of the South on a scale hitherto unprecedented in a region which has always too eagerly given away its wealth. And it exacts no adequate advantage, even by immediate standards, in return. The people who mainly gain from it are the merchants and bankers. And that gain is purchased at the price of the virtual enslavement, the constant degradation, of masses of the common whites. Carried through in an extensive fashion, the plan might well result in the creation of a true and permanent proletariat in the South — something it has so far escaped, however closely it may have skirted it — with all the evil consequences that this involves. The South desperately needs new industries, as desperately as it needs a rational agriculture, but not at this price.

It is far easier, I know, to criticize the failure of the South to face and solve its problems than it is to solve them. Solution is difficult and, for all I know, may be impossible in some cases. But it is clear at least that there is no chance of solving them until there is a leadership which is willing to face them fully and in all their implications, to arouse the people to them, and to try to evolve a comprehensive and adequate means for coping with them. It is the absence of that leadership, and ultimately the failure of any mood of realism, the preference for easy complacency, that I have sought to emphasize here.

24

This analysis might be carried much farther. But the book is already too long, and so I think I shall leave it at this. The basic picture of the South is here, I believe. And it was that I started out to set down.

Proud, brave, honorable by its lights, courteous, personally generous, loyal, swift to act, often too swift, but signally effective, sometimes terrible, in its action — such was the South at its best. And such at its best it remains today, despite the great falling away in some of its virtues. Violence, intolerance, aversion and suspicion toward new ideas, an incapacity for analysis, an inclination to act ing thousands who hoped to profit under Progress, on the side of either legitimate business or speculation; and all the eager hosts of young men who had been training in the colleges with an eye solely to grasping the commercial and industrial opportunities afforded by the prevailing order — and of course nothing I have said about the development of the new spirit in the schools is to be taken as suggesting that these had not remained the majority of the entire student body. Sometimes, indeed, these would be the most rabid of all in their anger against the strikers; would outdo even the mill masters themselves in their readiness to cry with burning eyes: "Shoot 'em down." All these, and all those who hoped even that their sons would be able to grasp gain and position from Progress. In sum, and even more saliently than we have seen in another connection, nearly the total of the ambitious classes, including the straw bosses in the mills, quite often even the more aspiring sort of mill worker himself, and the mass of landowning farmers.

For that matter, the rural property-owners, from the great planter to the farmer who hired labor only in cotton-picking season, would feel that their interests were even more directly menaced than this indicates. For if the unionism and the strikes succeeded in industry, would they not in time be likely to reach out into the countryside also? Would not their spirit at least come eventually to infect not only the tenants and croppers, all white farm labor, but perhaps the very Negroes?

But there was vastly more involved than the mere combination of the presence of an easily available surplus of labor with the feeling of so many people that their interests were endangered. For here again the sentiments aroused on the score of interest passed over to join forces with those which belonged to the traditional Southern pattern, and as usual to emerge almost wholly in the form of concern for the values involved in that pattern.

One of the important constituent elements of the emotion of the heads of the mills themselves was an astonished, highly self-righteous indignation, proceeding from the fact that they had so long been accustomed to looking upon themselves as the saviors of the South and the conferrers of benefactions upon both their workmen and the public at large. And this feeling was quite generally shared by the whole people, and especially by those of the upper orders.

From what we have seen of the steady dwindling of the spirit which had once belonged to the pioneers in the business, and of the old amiable relationship between master and man — even from the very introduction of the stretch-out itself — it is manifest that there wasn't much logic in such a reaction. But logic, as we know, scarcely was the forte of anybody here. However much they might have grown away from the old tradition so far as their obligations under it went, the men in control of the mills clung stoutly to the notion that merely by operating them on any terms they entitled themselves to the complete gratefulness of workman and public, and to be regarded as leading patriots of the South. And the people long accustomed to that viewpoint accepted it so absolutely that the prevailing attitude toward the strikers was that they were grossly disloyal, first to the mill, and then — if you listened closely, you could sometimes hear it come out quite explicitly — to the South as such.

What contributed to that last even more than this, however — what aroused the most militant feeling of patriotic resentment against the strikes — was the universal assumption in the business community and the people in general that the preservation of cheap labor was imperatively necessary to Progress, and that the safety of the South itself was bound up with Progress. If this thing succeeded, then the land might find itself plunged back again into economic disaster, its people deprived not only of individual opportunity but also of their pride in its ever mounting growth to greatness and power in the nation and as against Yankeedom — might even find itself thrown back into the fearful prospect of bitter-end competition between white and black for the mere means of subsistence, with all that this meant for the racial values of the region. Hence it must be put down at all costs.

But the strikes came into conflict with the Southern pattern even more profoundly than this — struck back far beyond the things that had grown up from the ancient fundamentals since the beginning of industrialism, to collide head on with these fundamentals themselves. With the old frontier tradition of individualism, for instance, which we have seen as being preserved and even in some respects strengthened by the flow of historical circumstance. The body of the Southern people, including both mill masters and business men in general, were in this year of 1929 as innocent of the implications inherent in modern industrialism — of the notion that when men are brought together in large numbers and made absolutely dependent on capital for the right to earn their daily bread, they can no longer be dealt with by the standards of property and right which prevail in an agricultural or handiwork community — as they had been in the days when Progress was just adopted. They had little more conception of it than their ancestors in their log cabins in the early American backcountry.

As they saw it, the question was plain and simple. The mills were their owners' to do with wholly as they pleased, without regard to anything but their own will, just as a thirty-acre farm was the farmer's or a house was the householder's. The master of the mill had the right to set wages and hours at whatever figure he chose. And if the workman didn't like them — this was a free country, and it was his right to reject them or to quit. And if that in practice meant his right to starvation for himself and his wife and children? Let him take what he could get, save his money, and he wouldn't have to put up with it long. A lot of rich men had started poor, hadn't they? Anyhow, this world was no bed of roses for anyone, and it behooved every man to make the best of things. It was nonsense to say that an unmarried man couldn't get out of the mills if he wanted to — look how many had. And a man with a family ought rightly to think about his family first — learn to hold in his dislikes instead of flying off the handle and making trouble for them. Rich men had to put up with a lot of things they didn't like, too.

But if the workman did choose to quit, then he plainly ought to get off the premises and go on somewhere else to look for a job, and not gang up with others of his sorry sort to deprive more honest men of the right to take the vacated jobs, even to deprive the mill of its right to run when and as it pleased. No, sir! If you let them get away with that, there would be no more safety for the property and personal rights of anybody. Next thing they'd be telling the factory-owners exactly who could work in the mills and who couldn't, what they could make and what they couldn't, to whom they could or could not sell. Next thing they'd be taking post with shotguns to tell the farmer he had to take back the farm labor he had fired, and what he had to plant — even coming into your house and telling your wife how to run it — taking charge of everything.

And so the masters of the mills, business men in general, planters, the farmers in their fields, faced it with hot-eyed anger and determination to have none of it in Dixie. And, for that matter, not only the upper and middle classes. The very common whites of the rural areas, the tenant farmers and sharecroppers, whom — apart from those who hoped to get jobs in the mills at least — you might reasonably expect to have been on the side of the strikers, generally showed a rabid dislike for them and their cause. Save for mild sympathy from a few minor groups like the by now fairly well-unionized printers, they encountered apathy or hostility from even the body of industrial labor in other fields — precisely on this ground of individualistic feeling.

3

Only relatively less clear-cut was the conflict of the strikers' cause with the established religious sentiment of the South. I indulge in no mere cleverness when I say that, under the essential Calvinism of outlook which had been fixed by slavery before the Civil War even in the non-Calvinist sects and riveted home by the conditions of Reconstruction, it was widely felt in all classes that the strikes constituted a sort of defiance of the will of Heaven. Repeatedly I myself heard more or less definitely expressed in North Carolina at the time the conviction that God had called one man to be rich and master, another to be poor and servant, and that men did well to accept what had been given them, instead of trusting to their own strength and stirring up strife. Perhaps there was injustice by weak human standards, but there was a justifying reason at last why all things should be as they were.

Side by side with that, however, went also the old Arminian doctrine which had always paralleled it in the South, and which indeed has always moved along with Calvinism everywhere: that Heaven apportions its reward in exact relationship to the merit and goodness of the recipient — that both the mill-owners and their workmen were already getting what they deserved.

Nearly the whole corps of the evangelical clergy, including the pastors in the mill churches, took their stand on one or the other of these doctrines, or both of them at once; either openly and directly or by the inherent implications of the things they said. A small group of the younger Methodist ministers who either had come under the influence of the new learning and the new spirit in the Southern schools or had been brought into contact with modern sociology at Northern universities and theological seminaries, had indeed begun to show signs of concern about the condition of labor in the South. The Baptists and Presbyterians, too, had a few men of the same stamp. But most of these were too timid to risk challenging the plainly overwhelming Southern sentiment, and I can't say that I much blame them. On the other hand, open denunciation of the strikers from the pulpit, or denunciation by innuendo, was common. Men should live together as brothers — such was the burden of the pronouncements, with the clear implication that it was only the strikers who were to blame for the fact that they did not.

Interest — at least the subconscious interest of men who had often themselves become almost indistinguishable from Babbitt, who associated mainly with him, or who drew the main part of their salaries and the expenses of their churches from his contributions

— naturally entered into this. But I think it would be a grave mistake to suppose that it was in general the dominant element in it — including, especially, the case of the mill pastors. The ministers were, after all, not only the guardians of the old Southern theology but also exponents of the whole Southern pattern, including that militant individualism which itself had an almost religious value.

Still another part of the pattern with which the union idea and the strikes inevitably came to grips was the ancient hierarchic feeling and system of the South. That is, they plainly violated the whole notion, first fixed in the Old South and developed by the military organization of the Confederate Army and the semi-military organization of society in the Reconstruction era, added to and strengthened by the rise of industrialism, and added to, also, by the service of so many men in the armies of the nation during the World War — the notion, originally of the moral right, now of the prescriptive right, of the captains of the upper orders to tell the people what to do and think — the whole notion of society as divided into such captains on the one hand and willing and eager followers on the other.

That was one of the factors in the indignation of the masters of the mills. The revolt of the workers against the stretch-out presented itself to them not only as an act of ingratitude and disloyalty to themselves and the South, but as one of active rebellion against both their own and all other rightful authority — just as it might have presented itself to a Confederate officer at Gettysburg if his command had refused his order to charge. And that feeling was shared by all their associates not only in industry and commerce, but in all fields whatever: by the ministers (I think this unquestionably went far to explain their reaction); by the politicians of the established Democratic hierarchy, who, almost to a man, were extraordinarily insistent in their demands that it be put down; and, very loudly, by the planters. Nor was it generally only the captains, but that vast majority of the people themselves, who had always subscribed and still subscribed to the hierarchic idea and system.

Rebellion — I heard the word in North Carolina at the time from the mouths of all sorts of people, ranging down from the most powerful political personages of the state to farmers and clerks and little grocerymen. And what was plainly contained in it was the idea of rebellion both against the State (in the generic use of the term) and against all social order.

Finally, it is worth observing that the strikers also found themselves and their cause ranged against that old antipathy to the Yankee and all his ways which had always stood at the core of Southern patriotism. It was out of the North, you see, that the whole union idea had come to the South; and it was from there also that practically the whole body of the organizers had come also. It is not to exaggerate much to say that these organizers were generally felt to be a sort of guerrilla shock troops come South again after sixty years to renew the Reconstruction fight.

And when to all this was added the fact that the Communists had succeeded in horning into the situation at Gastonia, of course the strikes were doomed. After that catastrophe had been allowed to happen, the AFL union hastened to come upon the stage, and nowhere else did the strikers have anything to do with the Communists. But that made no difference. Probably it would have made none in any case, in view of the fact that labor unionism was already strongly linked up in much of the popular mind with the idea of Red and alien menaces. But Gastonia did serve to clench the matter, to fix solidly in the minds of the great mass of Southerners the equation: labor unions + strikers = Communists + atheism + social equality with the Negro — and so to join to the formidable list of Southern sentiments already drawn up against the strikers the great central one of racial feeling and purpose; and, in fact, to summons against them much the same great fears and hates we have already seen as giving rise to the Ku Klux Klan.

So far as I know the Ku Klux Klan, already pretty thoroughly moribund, nowhere participated as such in what followed. But the effect was exactly the same as if it had. In the name of patriotism and religion and White Supremacy and all the values dear to the South the people closed ranks and faced the strikers with a fierceness of anger which is quite unimaginable for one who did not witness it — a fierceness of anger greatest in the vicinity of the strike centers, but quite manifest far from the scene. And, as always, this was to issue at its peak in the characteristic fashion of violence and mass coercion.

4

First, civil liberties were generally suspended by the municipal corporations involved, and the police and hired strikebreakers set to harry the strikers. Then the most powerful newspaper in North Carolina published an editorial arguing that, since the Communists wanted to destroy the existing government, they were not entitled to protection under its laws. And immediately afterward overt violence broke out in Gastonia, when a mob of masked men, led, as is now common knowledge in the territory, by business and political figures of the town and neighboring towns, destroyed the hut in which the strikers and their Communist leaders maintained their headquarters.

Against that voices were raised in the schools and elsewhere. President William Louis Poteat, of Wake Forest College, and President Harry Woodburn Chase, of the University of North Carolina, issued a public statement demanding that the strikers' civil liberties be respected, and that steps be taken to punish the instigators of violence. In her column in the Raleigh *News and Observer* Nell Battle Lewis hurled the epithet "barbaric Gastonia," and the editorial columns of that paper and the *Greensboro Daily News* took up the cause of the strikers, somewhat more cautiously. And others of the more liberal editors in the South vigorously protested the violence and high-handed methods, sometimes even maintaining that the strikers had a case.

But it was like the sound of a whistle in the clamor of battle. The sentiment of the community was to be made abundantly clear. At Gastonia Police Chief Aderholt was killed while engaged in an attempt to break up a strikers' meeting — quite probably by a gun in the hand of one of his own officers. At Gastonia a woman striker named Ella Mae Wiggins was killed while *en route* to a meeting, when armed men in a speeding automobile fired into the truck in which she was riding. At Marion twenty-one strikers, fleeing from tear-gas, were shot in the back by sheriff's deputies, and six died.

For the killing of Aderholt, Fred Beal, who was not even present at the scene, and six other strike leaders, some of them natives, were immediately jailed for " conspiracy to murder." It was manifest that there was no credible evidence for the charge, and that the murder of the officer was the last thing Beal could reasonably have wanted; but the trial, held at Charlotte, was little concerned with evidence, being given over instead to a minute inquisition into the views of the defendants on religion, politics, and the Negro, and to florid exercises in rhetoric and appeals to sentiments by some of the most notable adepts in mob psychology in the South. The prosecutor dramatically produced Aderholt's weeping widow, recited the records of her own and her dead husband's family in the Confederate Army and the World War, and in the name of all the Southern traditions demanded that she be revenged. And both he and all his collaborators appealed to the jury, made up of farmers and small tradesmen, on the ground that " the mills belong to the mill-owners to do with as they pleased precisely as your farms and places of business belong to you." So Beal and all the other defendants were convicted and sentenced to prison terms of from five to twenty years.

In contrast to that, the evidence pointed pretty clearly to the identity of the man who had fired the shot which killed the Wiggins woman; and there was no doubt at all as to the identity of the Marion deputies. Nevertheless, it looked as though the culprits would never be brought to trial. And when at last they were, the juries, again composed of farmers and small tradesmen, promptly cleared them, after hearing much the same arguments used in the Beal case.

But the strikes were doomed not only because of the tremendous forces ranged against them in the South generally, but also because of the great forces operating against them within the ranks and the minds of the mill workers themselves.

Given the great surplus of labor in the South, it is obvious that the only real possibility of launching a successful labor movement lay in securing the united support of at least the majority of all the mill workers in the section. But, with relatively unimportant exceptions, the movement here never spread beyond the limits to which it had been confined in the beginning. Themselves still completely individualistic and particularistic in outlook, the workers elsewhere felt little duty or desire to come to the aid of their fellows in Gastonia or Marion or Greenville or Elizabethtown. Even where they themselves were fuming over the same conditions which had precipitated the strikes, they were unimpressed with the need for united action, and thought only in terms of their own immediate locality. And the identification of the movement with Communism often turned mild sympathy or apathy into angry hostility.

Particularism, in fact, went further than this. In the towns where the strikes took place, they were always confined to one or two mills and never grew to include any save those in which they had begun. Most of the workers in the other hundred and more mills in the vicinity of Gastonia took good care to make it perfectly clear that they were not identified with the strikers, and in many cases displayed a marked antipathy toward them. And the same was more or less true in the other places. Nor is that the sum of it. Even in the mills where the strikes took place, there were many dissenting workers who were eager to go on working and who refused to have any part in the walk-out, especially among those people who were drawn from mountain stock. These were usually as anxious to see the strikers defeated as any mill-owner; sometimes they even lent their services to the opposition.

But perhaps the greatest of the forces within the workers' camp which made the success of the strikes impossible were those in the strikers' own minds. For if it was true that they had developed more coherent and fixed resentment than they had ever exhibited in the past, it was still far from true that they had developed enough of it to begin to break down the old common pattern in which they were fixed as completely as any group of Southerners.

And when, in addition, they found themselves set down for Communists, for atheists and " Negro equality citizens," it became simply intolerable. Under the cold and dangerous glance of their old captains, economic and political, under the stern and accusing glance of their ministers, they wilted much as the Populists had once wilted, turned shamefaced, shuffled, and, as the first joy in battle and in expressing their will to defiance died down, felt despairingly that they probably would be read out of the Democratic Party in this world and of paradise in the next.

So the strikes failed. None the less, they had demonstrated beyond question that the level of dissatisfaction was rising slowly in the mill workers of the South. And though the unions promptly collapsed, just as they always had, yet the struggle left some ponderable effect behind it. Looking back upon it today, it stands out as a sort of — Lexington? Rather as a sort of Boston Massacre — the point at which something which had been essentially unthinkable before suddenly began to be more thinkable. Immeasurably far away was Yorktown as yet, or even Saratoga. Still, hereafter the notion of labor unionism would distinctly be more present to the mind of the Southern workers, as something occasionally to be thought on at least.

5

But in the years which immediately followed, there would be little chance for it to do more than to lie fallow. For now the great blight was sweeping over the South, as over all the American country and the world. By 1931 most of the Southern textile mills were either standing closed or operating only two or three days a week at best; and wages were down to from three to eight dollars for a full week's work in most places. But you did not strike or even think of striking, since it was too clear that the mill-owners, who had been crying wolf for years, were at last telling the truth when they said that they were making no profits. Nearly all of them, in fact, were increasingly and perilously in the red, and many of them, caught with topheavy financial structures and large stocks of goods which they could not dispose of at any price, were falling into bankruptcy, including many of the landmarks of the industry which had once been considered as most solidly established.

Yes, it was true that the great columned house on the hill had been sold from under Old Man Stackhouse, and that the Stackhouses, all eleven of them, were living in a dingy little three-room apartment in an unfashionable neighborhood full of garages and filling stations, and were planning to set up a " tourist home " to make a living if they could get a rental agent and the grocer to extend them credit enough for a beginning. And it was true, too, that though the very rich Groundlings still held to their mills, old Mrs. George W. had herself driven up to the A & P Store in the Packard last night after the doors had closed, and persuaded the manager to open up again and sell her fifteen cents' worth of beefsteak — " yessir, he told me about it out of his own mouth."

And it did not stop, as you could easily see, at the textile front, but extended all along the whole industrial line. There were men like old Ward, the ironmaker (I cite an authentic case), who told his workers that he was sorry he had to cut their wages fifteen per cent, but what with his daughter in school in Switzerland and his wife spending the summer at Asheville, his personal expenses made it necessary — men who cynically took advantage of the prevailing conditions to drive down wages when it was quite unnecessary. But the general condition was indubitable. The tobacco mills in North Carolina and Virginia were still prospering, but the air above Birmingham was growing as clear again as that above the textile towns, and the great seagoing ships lay rusting by companies in the harbor at New Orleans.

And on the commercial front the same grim story was being repeated, as all the follies of the decade of speculation began at last to come home to roost. In those park-like suburbs the weeds were growing on the lawns, and paint was beginning to crack and blister. Thousands of the houses stood empty, their sometime masters dispossessed by mortgages; other thousands were being sold for half what they had cost; and if the majority of those who had " owned " them kept on living in them, it was only because the market for them was long since hopelessly glutted and because the realtors and mortgage companies still hoped to escape having the water squeezed out of their holdings.

Downtown the architects were closing out their offices and looking for jobs as taxi-drivers. Lawyers, doctors, engineers, commercial agents of every sort, sat twiddling their thumbs and gazing despairfully out of their windows into a world increasingly blank of customers. Bankers, faced at last with the consequences of their long recklessness or their long carelessness of the banking laws, were beginning to commit suicide or go to jail, banks to close in ominously increasing tempo. Long rows of stores stood empty; the merchants still in business looked at you with hollow eyes, measured up two and a half yards of gingham when you ordered a pound of lard. Richmond, Greensboro, Charlotte, Atlanta — all the commercial nerve centers stringing southward along the Southern Railway, took on the air of those old dead towns of Belgium and the Hanseatic League. You could hear your heels ring as you walked in their streets, left to go dirty and unkempt.

Florida had turned from El Dorado into a desert set about with curious ruins of gigantic hotels and towns, half-completed. And the same fate had overtaken all the resorts of the Blue Ridge mountain country and elsewhere. Towns and counties were beginning to default on their bonds; Asheville, in North Carolina, was in bankruptcy.

And so, if you were a textile worker, an industrial worker of any sort, any man with a job, the last thing you thought of was striking. Instead, you listened with set jaw as the children cried because supper was all gone and they were still hungry, gazed with straining eyes into the lowering future, went early to work, stayed late when.

the boss asked you (and hang the hour laws), and prayed to heaven
to preserve your job to you against the pinched-faced and desperate
thousands pouring out of the silent and broken mills and endlessly
converging upon those that still limped on, begging for a job, any
job, your job; and preserve it from the still vaster and, if that were
possible, even hungrier crowds pouring in from the countryside.

For if industry and commerce were sick, King Cotton also was
growing continually sicker, and in the end would fall into worse
case than had ever been known in the past, even in the nineties. As
the demand for cotton goods over the earth receded and the mills
all around the globe slowed down, the demand for the staple of
course gradually declined too — at a time when Southern production was hanging near peak levels, and when foreign production
also was growing greater than it had ever been before. In 1929 the
Southern crop totaled nearly fifteen million bales, and the foreign
crop eleven and a half million — with the result that the price
swooped down from twenty to twelve cents. Next year it came on
down to eight.

Then in 1931, a splendid growing season, plus the general failure
of the individualistic Southern farmers to heed the warnings of the
Agricultural Department, fetched in the third greatest Southern
crop to date: over seventeen million bales. That year the foreign
crop mercifully declined by two million bales, but the world carry-
over from the previous year ran to about thirteen million, with the
result that the total available world supply rose to about thirty-nine
million, as against an annual world consumption which had gone
down to twenty-three million. Promptly the quotation on the New
York cotton exchange descended to five cents, and on the local
Southern markets it went even lower than that.

It was the conclusive disaster for the South. Immediate disaster
for farmer, planter, tenant, and sharecropper, manifestly — disaster
precisely like that in the nineties. But it was a disaster which struck
through the whole economic structure of the region, also, and
which, bceause of that, came back to visit more than immediate
disaster upon the agricultural population.

The banks, already tottering, now found themselves with vast stocks of mortgages which were entirely worthless as collateral with the Yankee bankers who, faced with swarming armies of depositors definitely terrified for the safety of their savings, were calling on them for payment. They turned to selling out the land as rapidly as they could, only to find the market so overwhelmingly glutted that it was impossible, and so they began to plunge into bankruptcy at the same pace as the banks in the Middle West.

And this growing collapse of the banking structure meant, of course, a rapid curtailment of credit over and beyond what had already been made necessary by the depression in general. The rate at which business and industrial establishments were closing greatly accelerated. And planters and labor-employing farmers found themselves either unable to secure credit at all or unable to secure sufficient credit to maintain their old scale of operations. The number of acres planted in cotton in 1932 would be eleven million less than in 1929.

Many of the planters abandoned their lands altogether, or turned them over to their tenants to dig a living out of if they could — without seeds or fertilizers, without foodstuffs for the work animals, and, in the case of the cropper at least, without work animals. Numbers of the farmers did much the same sort of thing and hurried into the towns in the, usually, vain hope of finding employment. And the planters and farmers who held on had perforce to make the hardest possible terms for their tenants and sharecroppers. Having always gone essentially hungry for a reasonably good diet, the great body of the sharecroppers, white and black, would begin to go hungry in the full sense of the word after the fall of 1931, and the tenants would not generally fare much better. And hordes of these people who had neither employment, means of subsistence, nor any place to go were wandering along every road from county to county and state to state, or crowding into already overcrowded slums in the towns and cities, in the hope of securing aid from the always totally inadequate, often downright niggardly local relief funds.

6

Such was the general picture of the South in 1932. Everybody was either ruined beyond his wildest previous fears or stood in peril of such ruin. And the general psychological reaction? First a universal bewilderment and terror, which perhaps went beyond that of the nation at large by the measure of the South's lack of training in analysis, and particularly social analysis. Men everywhere walked in a kind of daze. They clustered, at first to assure one another that all would shortly be well; then, with the passage of time, to ask questions in the pleading hope of thus being assured; but in the end they fled before the thought in one another's eyes.

And along with this there went in the case of the masses a slow wondering and questioning, and in the end a gradually developing bitterness of desperation. They had laughed at first, uneasily. But afterward, when they heard from the pulpit that it was a punishment visited upon the people from the hand of God as the penalty of their sins (and they did hear it in almost solid chorus from the ministers), they accepted it in some fashion, and, as always, without demur. Yet beneath that acceptance something else was plainly going on. More completely and helplessly in the grip of social forces than Southerners had ever been before — even more completely and helplessly perhaps than in Reconstruction and Populist times — they blamed the Yankee, in the shape of Wall Street, as their fathers before them had blamed him, muttered curses against the name of Morgan as the epitome of it. But beyond that they puzzled with furrowed brows at a vague shadow looming over them — the shadow of organized society. For the first time in the history of the South they dimly felt the thing was there, and groped to make out its shape and form and nature and to comprehend how it came to have so much power over themselves, as a child gropes to grasp the far-away woods and hills through the pane of his nursery window.

And in the last days before the coming of Roosevelt, some of them, despairing of making sense of it, were falling into the impatient mood natural to simple men when confronted with what defies their understanding and wishing that they might sweep it all aside and start again with a more readily comprehensible world; they were using the word "revolution." Very cloudy was their wishing, very far were they from the will to action, very greatly did they fall short of being the majority as yet, and very unclear was every one of them as to precisely whom and what it was he meant to rebel against. Nevertheless, there the word was, marching about in the open. I myself heard it in the most conservative communities in North Carolina, both rural and urban, and from men of sober and grave mind.

In the classes, moreover, there was something of a correlative mood. With the best of all possible worlds crumpling about their ears, the ruling orders, or at least a surprisingly large number of the people who made them up, were more nearly shocked out of the old smugness than they ever had been. For them also the shadow of organized society had swung close enough to be almost palpable, and in their turn they were fumbling for its meaning, too. Now and then one of them was actually wondering if after all it were true that noses were manifestly made for the bearing of spectacles. And many of them were exhibiting a strange humbleness of spirit — were confessing that it was possible that they, the South, America, the world, had been following false gods all during that long period of speculation in the twenties, were granting even that their leadership had perhaps not been as wise as it might have been, and that reforms were going to have to be made to set things right again. At the summit of the matter, indeed, some of them were actually — not embracing the notion of revolution, certainly, but, at the last, viewing it with the apathetic eyes of men who have looked so long on terror that they no longer feel much of anything. They were talking of it in quiet voices as something which was sure to come soon or late, unless there was a great change, unless there was a great change.

And so it fell out that no section of the country greeted Franklin Roosevelt and the New Deal with more intense and unfeigned enthusiasm than did the South. Probably, indeed, no other section greeted them with nearly so much enthusiasm.

It was obvious enough that the basic Rooseveltian ideas, with their emphasis on the social values as against the individual, and on the necessity of revising all values in the light of the conditions created by the machine and the disappearance of the frontier, ran directly contrary to the basic Southern attitudes. And moreover, the New Deal was in some respects actually to aggravate the bad conditions in the South, or at least to seem responsible for it. Take the case of the agricultural program, for instance.

As I have already indicated, the collapse of credit consequent on the low price brought by the cotton crop of 1931, plus the naturally discouraging effect of that price itself, had resulted in a great reduction of acreage planted to cotton in 1932. But in the first year in which the New Deal curtailment and subsidy schemes came into effect — 1934 — the acreage was to go down to less than twenty-eight million acres, which represented a decline of over thirteen million acres from 1931, more than twenty million from 1926, and more than six million from even 1910! And in 1935 the figure would remain about the same. All of which meant, naturally, that unemployment among tenant farmers and sharecroppers was again enormously increased.

In industry also, first NRA, with its increased wages and shortened hours, and afterward the Wagner Labor Relations Act and the Wage and Hour Law were to have a somewhat comparable effect. For these acted on the owners of the cotton mills and those of nearly all other sorts of factories to move them to seek to dispense with as many employees as possible — in the case of the cotton mills by making the stretch-out virtually universal, and in all cases by turning increasingly to the use of machines wherever they could be made to replace labor — a tendency which has continued right on down to the present.

7

But the South took no cognizance of any of this. Roosevelt was hope and confidence after long despair. And more than that, he was hope and confidence riding under the banner of the Democratic Party, over what appeared then to be the emaciated corpse of the Republican Party, under whose rule catastrophe had arrived. For the South, in truth, it was almost as though the bones of Pickett and his brigade had suddenly sprung alive to go galloping up that slope at Gettysburg again and snatch victory from the Yankee's hand after all. And many and many a man felt in his inmost soul that it was really worth having endured the unfortunate Mr. Hoover for four years to have achieved at last the satisfaction of seeing the old Black Radical enemy and oppressor brought to complete rout and ignominy. I have myself heard the sentiment pointedly expressed.

Nor was it only that Roosevelt was Democracy hopeful and confident. He was also Democracy triumphant — Democracy sweeping dramatically and swiftly toward success. Probably it was in many ways only temporary and inadequate success, bought by doubtful means. But there it was for the time being, indubitably; however much it might be true that the New Deal was at least partly canceling out its own purposes in the South, as in the rest of the United States, the overwhelmingly dominant fact was that it had rescued the section — again, along with the nation at large — from the vicious circle of increasing ruin in which it had been caught from 1929 forward.

First it proceeded to save most of the bankers who were not already wholly liquidated, dead, or in jail. Usually, that was accomplished, indeed, by having the depositors agree to lose a more or less great part of their savings. Nevertheless, it wasn't long until these depositors themselves did begin to recover what was left of their wealth, whereas most of them had once despaired of ever again seeing any part of it; hence everybody was content.

And having saved the bankers and the depositors, this New Deal, with its huge spending, its wide benefit payments, and its various programs, was going on plainly to get the wheels of the whole economic machine to rolling again — with a vast creaking and reluctance, to be sure, but quite perceptibly none the less. If rural unemployment was increasing as a result of the farm programs, that fact was nothing to the majority of the rural population as against the fact that cotton would bring a peak price of nearly twelve cents in 1933, nearly fourteen cents in 1934 and 1935, and that in 1936 it would actually climb up to nearly fifteen cents. And if the devaluation of the currency made those prices somewhat illusory in reality, that fact of course went generally unnoted. When to that was added the relief programs, the very existence of the increase in unemployment was largely obscured, not only for the South in general but even for the unemployed themselves. For WPA wages or direct relief payments did more than barely make their condition tolerable for these dispossessed ones; often, in the case of the least ambitious, it actually made their whole life much more tolerable than it had ever been before.

The Democratic politicians in Washington who managed the practical distribution of relief funds, observing cannily that money spent in a section which was certain to be Democratic anyhow could have no effect for political purposes; observing also that the South had always stoutly maintained that lower wages than those paid elsewhere in the nation were justified here because of alleged lower living costs; and being pressed by the Southerners among their own ranks and by the Southern politicians in general, not to make the payments in the section large enough to " spoil " those on the relief rolls for private employment — these politicians dealt with Dixie with a striking niggardliness. WPA wages ranged from less than thirty dollars per month up to fifty or a little more, according to the state in question and the skill of the worker, but in no case much exceeded half that paid in the East, and in all cases was a great deal less than that paid in any other section of the country.

Scanty as this was, however, it generally exceeded what a sharecropper, black or white, and many tenants, could make even when they had employment and even when their whole families worked — for that matter what many day laborers, servants, and so on in the towns could make, also. For the tenant and sharecropper it had the disadvantage, certainly, that it called for working all the year round instead of less than half the time. But the hours were so short and the labor generally so light that this made little real difference. Hence it was natural enough that among the unambitious and unproud their passage from productive employment to the relief rolls was not felt as an unbearably unpleasant turn of affairs.

Similarly in industry. If the total possibility of employment was being reduced as the employers turned to a greater use of machines, that fact was blotted out of view by the consideration that the mills at last were starting up again, running with more and more regularity, that wages were back to something more like the old levels, and that hours had been reduced beyond the wildest dream ever before harbored by Southern workers. Even the cotton-mill stretch-out, at bottom still bitterly hated and resented, became almost supportable for the moment.

Relief and Social Security played their part here, too: in providing refuge for the workers who remained unemployed, or in easing the fears of those who had jobs as to what would happen if the worst came about and they lost them.

And finally, not only industrialists, landowners, and labor, rural and agricultural, but the whole business community felt hopeful again. Business was increasing only inch by inch perhaps, and had a long way to go before it would be really good. Nevertheless, it was plainly on the upgrade. Even rents were beginning to rise again and the realtors, the very speculators who survived, began eagerly to conjure up visions of saving all the water in their properties yet.

Thus the South, essentially as unanalytical now as it had always been, bothered neither to observe that the New Deal ran counter to its established ideas and values or to weigh it in any wise, but took Mr. Roosevelt and all his purposes to its heart with a great burst of thanksgiving. And in the first glad relief of escape from terror and defeat, even the ruling classes carried, or seemed to carry, that mood of candor and humbleness of spirit which they had begun to show before Roosevelt to greater lengths still.

From every public platform, the politicians of the established Democratic machines, enjoying such patronage as they had never before imagined, unanimously declaimed over again every utterance of Mr. Roosevelt's; announced that the South, like the nation, had plainly been wrong in the 1920's, had too long neglected its duties to the underdog; declared their undying allegiance to every objective of the new order — seemed half to mean it; to anyone who was not acquainted with the Southern habit of making words serve for deeds, would have seemed wholly to mean it.

And the mood found echo in virtually every editorial page, including even such standpatters as the *Charlotte Observer;* in virtually everybody one met in the streets. The very bankers and many of the factory masters echoed it with no more than a few cautious reservations.

8

Looking at the South in those days, indeed, one might readily have concluded that at last the old pattern was on its way to conclusive break-up, that new ideas and a new tolerance were sweeping the field, and that the region as a whole, growing genuinely social-minded and realistic, was setting itself to examine its problems with clear eyes and dispassionate temper — in a word, that the old long lag between the Southern mind and the changing conditions of the Southern world was about to end. And if, having looked once, the observer had gone away and continued from afar to search in the news from the section for evidence to bear out the conclusion, he might have gone on to the present believing it to be entirely sound. For great and real changes were indubitably taking place, and others were in the making.

There was the fact, for instance, that the Southern people in most of the states were throwing off the incubus of prohibition; and in the larger towns at least, even showing a growing tendency to cast off such bonds as the old Sunday blue laws, in the teeth of the bitter-end opposition of the clergy.

What lay behind this immediately was probably the prevailing enthusiasm for Mr. Roosevelt, the desire to carry out all his suggestions to the limit. But what made it possible for even that enthusiasm to override the obstacles in the way was the fact that the great debacle in Hoover's Administration had definitely shaken the undisputed sway over politics which the ministers had formerly exercised. Southern people of all classes, perhaps more generally than the relatively more complex population of the rest of the nation, blamed and resented Mr. Hoover for all their troubles. And blaming him, they inevitably turned to remembering that it was the ministers who had led the South to abandon its historical allegiance to the Democratic Party in 1928, and so, especially in the towns, to doubting that their pronouncements on politics were always and necessarily inspired by Heaven.

Incidentally, it is interesting to note in this connection that no extensive religious revival developed in the South in the years of the depression, though the off-brand hysterical sects capitalized on it greatly to extend their membership and influence. In view of the history and tradition of the section, such revivals might reasonably have been expected to be one of the most certain reactions to the prevailing terror and despair.

But ultimately, perhaps, the new breaking of so-called moral bonds testified to more than the immediate factors I mention. To the fact that, here as everywhere, life in the town was having its cumulative effect and making inevitably for the slow dissociation of traditional concepts which no longer fitted the needs of the environment. To the slow filtering, if only at fourth hand, of the modern ideology through considerable segments of the urban population; and to the fact that in the depression period of wondering and questioning, men had sometimes turned their new doubts on other things than economics. In fine, to a still cloudy but genuine growth toward rationalistic attitudes, a certain weariness with the old feeling that the word atoned for the deed, and a developing sense that candid acceptance of innocent hedonism was a way of life better adapted to town-dwellers at least than covert indulgence behind official Puritanism — a mounting impatience with taboo for mere taboo's sake.

The thirties would also witness a further decline in lynching, though the first half of the decade threatened to prove that the practice was actually on the increase. In 1930 a total of twenty Negroes was lynched, as against seven in 1929. The next year the figure was twelve. In 1932 it dipped abruptly to six, soared to twenty-four in 1933, declined only to fifteen in 1934, mounted again to eighteen in 1935.

What explains this surge it is hard to say. The most obvious guess is that it was a reaction to the prevailing emotions of terror and despair; an attempt on the part of the harried rural white population to reassure itself by performing the old White Supremacy ritual, to achieve both relief from intolerable tensions and the old desperate, pleasurable sense of power associated with the action. But it is difficult to reconcile the assumption with the record for 1932, when these emotions were presumably at their height, or with that for the next three years, when terror and despair were certainly receding. That is, unless we are to suppose that in 1932 apathy, the issue of terror and despair, had gone so far as to benumb any effort at alleviation even by such feverish devices as lynching, and that after Mr. Roosevelt's election returning exuberance gave a fillip to the crime. Perhaps the true key to the matter is that any new reduction in the incidence of the crime was likely to remain precarious for a considerable length of time, and that the record for any one year or even several years would in a great measure depend on the law of chance as it governed the development of local incidents apt to give rise to the crime.

At any rate, such organizations as the Association of Southern Women for the Prevention of Lynching and the Commission on Interracial Cooperation were greatly extending their influence even as the surge was in progress. The former had devised an effective scheme for combating the practice by appointing as observers in every county where it was possible women of high social rank, whose duty it was to find out about threatened lynchings before they happened, telephone the sheriff or police chief and urge him to do his duty by preventing the offense, and then to telephone every other important man of good will in the community and ask him to do the same. And both organizations had carried out elaborate studies of lynching, clearly demonstrating such things as that it did not protect Southern Womanhood but only endangered it. And these studies, in turn, had been picked up and passed on by the more enlightened newspapers.

In 1936, as in 1937, the number of Negroes lynched was eight. The following year saw it reduced to six. And in 1939 it dropped to three, just one fifty-fifth of that for 1892.

In the field of social legislation, again, quite remarkable things were going on, or at least things which seemed remarkable when set against the past. Thus, this period was to see child labor in the mills almost disappear, though not in commerce. Years before, indeed, it had been partly eliminated by the adoption of compulsory school laws by the states. But under the lax child labor statutes its use in the vacation period, often running to six months out of the year and even longer, had still been quite common. Now, however, these laws were generally strengthened, and in some cases, as in North Carolina, the age limit was raised to sixteen years.

All the states were adopting social security and old-age pension laws, to avail themselves of Federal *largesse*. An increasing number of the larger towns were sponsoring slum-clearance projects. And with the destruction of NRA and its labor codes by the Supreme Court, some of the states would enact laws considerably reducing the legal hours of labor for textile mills, other industries, and some branches of trade, though the merchants, often among the worst labor sweaters, universally escaped.

9

In the schools the growth of the modern mind and the new analysis and criticism was going steadily forward. They had been considerably crippled, of course, by the reduction in income consequent upon the depression. In truth, the more reactionary forces in the various states, and this was particularly true in North Carolina, had more or less successfully taken advantage of the prevailing mood of the depression to cut appropriations for the state universities more than was made necessary by the collapse of the general economy, in the hope of starving the new spirit out and rendering its activities impossible. At Chapel Hill there was for a while a veritable exodus of distinguished professors to more lucrative and promising jobs in the North. But the men who were most immediately valuable to the South, as Howard Odum and Frank Graham at North Carolina, generally stayed on.

And the losses of funds and great names were to a large extent counterbalanced by two other considerations. One of these was that now fairly large numbers of the young Southerners who were joining the faculties had been trained in the new attitude and viewpoint. The other was that the students were now more amenable to the thing. This generation of youth was probably the soberest-minded the South had ever known. The colleges still swarmed with those who dreamed hopefully of acquiring riches as Babbitts, of course; but the more intelligent sort were aware that they belonged to a world quite unknown to their fathers and were willing and sometimes eager to lay aside the old sentimentality and unrealism and try to understand the case.

For all their handicaps, the universities and colleges of the South were generally to become more intelligent and more useful in the thirties than they ever had been before.

The period would see the publication by the University of North Carolina Press of a mass of searching material about the South, of which the most considerable items were Howard Odum's great sociological compilation, *Southern Regions,* Rupert Vance's *Human Factors in Cotton Culture* and *Human Geography of the South,* and *These Are Our Lives,* a compilation by the Federal Writers' Project which is one of the most enlightening and moving human documents ever printed. But it is significant that it was not merely North Carolina men who wrote the books and monographs published at Chapel Hill, but men in schools scattered over all the South.

There were still plenty of Southern colleges whose only claim to respect was a football team, but they were becoming fewer as the years hurried on.

In journalism, too, the decade was to see a notable development of intelligence and realism. Under the editorial direction of Virginius Dabney, the Richmond *Times-Dispatch* developed into one of the most liberal newspapers in the nation; one which so far dared to flout the tradition of its milieu that it campaigned against the poll tax in Virginia and in 1938 supported the Wagner-Van Nuys anti-lynching bill, in both cases against the active opposition of Senators Carter Glass and Harry Flood Byrd.

For my own part, I have always been doubtful of schemes for Federal control of lynching, fearing that their net effect on the South would only be to rouse its trigger-quick dander, always so allergic to the fear of Federal coercion, and so tend to increase rather than suppress the practice. But that does not change the fact that the stand of the *Times-Dispatch* was an unusually courageous sort of journalism.

In Raleigh Jonathan Daniels made the *News and Observer* equally liberal, at least on the economic and political side — sometimes waxing almost too uncritical in his eagerness to champion the underdog: surely a curious charge to bring against a Southern editor.

At Charlotte J. E. Dowd, one of the owners of the *Charlotte News,* took over the editorial reins of that once stodgy journal and made of it one of the most lively, intelligent, and enterprising in Dixie. In 1937 this paper, through a member of its staff, Cameron Shipp, carried out the most uncompromising and thorough survey of local slum conditions ever carried out in a Southern town.

The Richmond *News-Leader,* the Norfolk *Virginian-Pilot,* and the *Montgomery Advertiser* — all already distinguished for intelligence — added steadily to their reputation for liberality in the decade. In Birmingham John Temple Graves II and Osborne Zuber made the *Age-Herald* and the *News* consistently tolerant. And in Atlanta the *Constitution* and the *Journal* at least acquired a more open-minded attitude than had formerly been theirs.

Just as important was the fact that many of the smaller newspapers were now getting more liberal and intelligent editing. One of the happy results of the depression, from the standpoint of the welfare of the South, was that it had gone a long way toward halting the old exodus to the North of talented young men with journalistic ambitions. The development of standardized daily journalism helped to that end, also. Unable to secure jobs in the East or Middle West, they were perforce driven into service at home, and carried their brains with them. They were far from free, even where they owned their papers, and had to proceed against the prevailing prejudices with great caution; but in the course of time they gradually enlarged their latitude.

10

Mention of university presses, newspapers, printing, suggests something else that properly ought to be noted in this connection. The South had now begun to have a greatly flourishing literature.

All along from 1900 Ellen Glasgow had of course been exercising her irony on her native land, in a long series of tales which grew constantly more penetrating and impatient of sentimentality. And in 1925 she produced, in *Barren Ground,* what I judge to be the first real novel, as opposed to romances, the South had brought forth;

certainly the first wholly genuine picture of the people who make up and always have made up the body of the South.

In the same period there was also Cabell, playing Olympian Zeus on Monument Avenue, and in both the Poictesme and Lichfield, Sill, cycles holding up a thinly hidden mirror to his fellow countrymen and their notions. That Colonel Rudolph Musgrave is a Virginian and a Southerner anyone can see. But so, I have no doubt, is Jurgen or Florian de Puysange. And the Cabell women are all concocted in very great measure out of the legend of Southern Womanhood, just as Horvendile is unmistakably related to the most celebrated character in the repertoire of the Southern pulpit.

It is true, I am sure, that these are in their essence also timeless shadows, without place save that they dwell upon something which approximates the earth. They stand in some wise for men of every race and age, at least in the Western world; the universal legend of fair women; the hoary myth of evil made splendid flesh and weary and perilous wisdom. And all of them are exhibited to us against the background of their creator's own tenderly mocking perception, are themselves sometimes for a little endowed with it. But in the shape of their personal being, in their own view of themselves and their fellows, in their peculiar tradition, they are none the less decisively Southern.

The very Cabell rhetoric is in some sense an inheritance from the Southern rhetoric of the past. That rhetoric passed through the prism of his mind, tamed to his humor and made seemly, but still wearing ineluctably upon it the stamp of its origin. And if this seems preposterous, then let the reader try to imagine it as having been fashioned by a man of any other country.

But if Miss Glasgow and Cabell had been upon the scene all these years, H. L. Mencken indulged in only rhetorical exaggeration when he wrote " The Sahara of the Bozart." At Nashville there were the Fugitive poets, and in New Orleans there was some stirring of literary activity. But save for these exceptions the literary state of the region was to be accurately measured by Thomas Dixon, Jr., whose many rabid novels, and especially *The Clansman,* which was made into the moving picture *The Birth of a Nation,* probably contributed no little to stirring up racial feeling and to the creation of the Ku Klux Klan.

But the twenties were to see a rapidly accelerating growth, which went along with and in fact constituted a part of the same essential movement toward intellectual freedom which was in evidence in the schools. In Kentucky Elizabeth Maddox Roberts, who properly belongs to the South, produced *The Time of Man.* In South Carolina Julia Peterkin and DuBose Heyward appeared. In New York Laurence Stallings, a Georgian, contributed to *What Price Glory?* the saltiness which made it a dramatic success. In Atlanta there was Frances Newman. At Chapel Hill Paul Green wrote *In Abraham's Bosom,* and Professor Koch's students turned out their Carolina Playmakers productions in profusion, invented a new American folk drama. And besides these there were many more: Conrad Aiken, Emily Clark, with her sharp-tongued *Reviewer,* Gerald W. Johnson, Roark Bradford, Evelyn Scott, W. E. Woodward, Isa Glenn, Maristan Chapman, Clement Wood, and so on and so on.

Behind them came a swelling troop of younger men and women, eagerly following in their footsteps. The end of the decade saw Thomas Wolfe and William Faulkner tower into view almost simultaneously. The thirties opened with Erskine Caldwell's *Tobacco Road.* And thereafter the multiplication of Southern writers would go on at such a pace until in 1939 the South actually produced more books of measurable importance than any other section of the country, until anybody who fired off a gun in the region was practically certain to kill an author.

The makers of this new literature differed widely in their viewpoints and interests, of course. For instance, Mrs. Peterkin and DuBose Heyward, while exhibiting an enormous freshness in their approach to the Negro — they were the first Southern novelists to deal with him in recognizably human terms instead of those of the old convention — still retained considerable vestiges of sentimentality. Both were prone to see only the poetical or ingratiating aspects of the Negro's lot.

On the other hand, not a few of these writers — perhaps even a majority of those who came up in the twenties — showed a marked tendency to react to a new extreme, and as they sloughed off the old imperative to use their writings as a vehicle for glorifying and defending Dixie, to take more or less actively to hating and denouncing the South. Thomas Wolfe made Eugene Gant openly hate the section. And though Faulkner has denied that he has any interest in anything but the individual, there is in his works a kind of fury of portraiture, a concentration on decadence and social horrors, which is to our purpose here. The case of Caldwell is manifest. And readers of the *American Mercury* in H. L. Mencken's time as editor will recall that baiting the South in its pages was one of the favorite sports of young Southerners of literary and intellectual pretensions.

In reality they hated the South a good deal less than they said and thought. Rather, so far as their hatred was not mere vain profession designed to invite attention to their own superior perception, they hated it with the exasperated hate of a lover who cannot persuade the object of his affections to his desire. Or, perhaps more accurately, as Narcissus, growing at length analytical, might have suddenly begun to hate his image reflected in the pool.

All these men remained fundamentally Southern in their basic emotions. Intense belief in and love for the Southern legend had been bred into them as children and could not be bred out again simply by taking thought; lay ineradicably at the bottom of their minds, to set up conflict with their new habit of analysis and their new perceptions. And their hate and anger against the South was both a defense mechanism against the inner uneasiness created by that conflict and a sort of reverse embodiment of the old sentimentality itself. Thomas Wolfe almost explicitly makes Eugene Gant recognize as much.

The continuing power of the Southern heritage upon them is curious to observe. Wolfe's rhetoric, far more obviously than Cabell's, is directly descended from the old Southern line.

But that will scarcely do for Faulkner and Caldwell? These, as everyone knows, had been to school to the Middle Westerners and the Russians and to Joyce.

They had, certainly. And yet it seems to me that when you drain off the extraneous elements, the long flowing grace of Faulkner's best sentences, his loving choice of highly colored words, often plainly stuck in merely for their own sake, is — personal, yes, but also distinctly Southern. And perhaps it is not best to be too sure even about Caldwell's carefully stripped style.

When we turn from the manner of their writing to the question of its content, the matter is clearer. Growing steadily more realistic; in the case of the Caldwells and the Faulkners, sternly rooting out not only sentimentality but even sentiment or, so far as it was possible, emotion of any sort, these new Southern authors remained in some curious fashion *romantics* in their choice of materials — shall we say, romantics of the appalling. Or am I mistaken in thinking that the essence of romanticism is the disposition to deal in the more-than-life-sized, the large and heroic, the picturesque and vivid and extravagant?

Even the dullest critics have observed that Wolfe's people rise straight out of Brobdingnag, that their gestures rock the forests about Asheville. He himself once attempted to explain it on the score of his own great size. And the pedestrian, matter-of-fact realism of Dreiser or Ruth Suckow is poles away from the realism of Faulkner's decadent gentry and savage poor whites, or of Caldwell's Jeeter Lester and Ty Ty Walden and their outrageous broods.

To that it can be retorted, of course, that the South, by my own account of it, is itself an extravagant and vivid and even more-than-life-sized land. Nevertheless, I am convinced that the analysis I put forward retains a great deal of validity. Not even the South is one solid explosion of dynamite, which is about the impression you get from the Southern books of the late 1920's and the earlier thirties. This, indeed, is the chief criticism to be made of these books, at least when we attempt to regard them as a picture of the South, as everybody has done: telling the truth in detail, they fail to tell it in adequate perspective. The effect is much as though a painter had set out to do a portrait by painting only the subject's wens, warts, and chicken-pox scars.

I am inferring nothing so foolish, naturally, as that the Southern heritage was the sole determinant in shaping the writers to whom I refer, or, indeed, that the personal mind and character of the men themselves was not the primary element. Merely, the artist does not live in a vacuum, and like other men is compounded out of all his experience from birth. That Wolfe's great size had a good deal to do with the size of his Gulliverian giants seems to me eminently probable, but so also did the fact that he was a Southerner.

But I have diverged a little. To return now: the main point here is that, however much the new Southern authors might differ in their approach to their material, and regardless of what faults they might still display, nearly all of them had decisively escaped from the old Southern urge to turn the country into Never-Never Land, that nearly all of them stood, intellectually at least, pretty decisively outside the legend; and so were able to contribute to the region its first literature of any bulk and importance. And at the same time, in one measure or another, to cast light on the Southern social scene and direct attention to Southern social problems. The very concentration of the hate-and-horror school upon their chosen materials served the latter purpose admirably, regardless of their own intentions.

To which I should add that, as time passed, the hate reaction and its loud profession in some quarters tended to dwindle. It is not often to be observed in books published in the last two or three years. The calm, good-humored criticism of Jonathan Daniels's *A Southerner Discovers the South* and of the *North Georgia Review,* an able little quarterly published at Clayton, Georgia, by Lillian Smith and Paula Snelling, is now becoming generally characteristic.

II

The proposition that Southern writers of any importance were generally moving toward a more clear-eyed view of the Southern world even has a certain applicability to a group which might seem to stand wholly outside what I have been saying. I refer to the so-called Southern Agrarians, who made their appearance in the late twenties, with the center of their activity at Vanderbilt University in Nashville, and who were led by John Crowe Ransom, Allen Tate, and Donald Davidson.

Primarily this group was one which turned its gaze sentimentally backward. Its appearance just as the South was moving toward the crisis of the depression, just as Progress was apparently sweeping the field, just as the new critics and writers were beginning to swing lustily against the old legend and the old pattern, was significant. In a real fashion these men were mouthpieces of the fundamental, if sometimes only subterranean, will of the South to hold to the old way: the spiritual heirs of Thomas Nelson Page. And their first joint declaration, *I'll Take My Stand,* was, like their earlier prose works in general, essentially a determined reassertion of the validity of the legend of the Old South, an attempt to revive and fully restore the identification of that Old South with Cloud-Cuckoo Town, or at any rate to render it as a Theocritean idyl.

But the attempt was made with enormously intellectualized arguments, which itself is evidence of how far the South had moved on its highest levels, how far the new spirit had invaded even conservative quarters like Vanderbilt. The yearning of these men toward the past had encountered and mingled with all that yearning for the past which, in Europe and America, has moved in an unbroken stream since the early-nineteenth-century revolt against Rousseau. They had read the *Summa Theologica* of St. Thomas Aquinas, were steeped in Spinoza, Hobbes, Kant, all the philosophers; they worshipped at the shrine of Dr. John Donne (the Donne of St. Paul's deanery and the esoteric poems rather

than the author of " To His Mistress Going to Bed," of course);
they had been influenced in varying degree by De Maistre, John
Ruskin, Ferdinand Brunetière, the neo-Catholicism of Hilaire
Belloc and Gilbert Chesterton, the neo-medievalism of Belloc and
Chesterton and T. S. Eliot, by Irving Babbitt and Paul Elmer
Moore and Norman Foerster.

They distrusted science almost as warmly as Bishop Wilber-
force had once distrusted it, felt with conviction that it assumed
much too arrogantly to be on the verge of illuminating the whole
of the vast range of illimitable darkness which is the mysterious
universe, that its total effect on men was to make them too smug
and knowing and brightly hard, to loose the old bonds without re-
placing them with new ones or having the capacity to replace them
with new ones — perhaps not altogether without reason. They distrusted industrialism and its effect on mankind and the South even
more positively, and certainly not without reason. They had more
than a few doubts about democracy. Arrant individualists, they
yet recoiled from the monadism which, swinging up through the
centuries from the Renaissance, was flowering in the chaos of our
times; felt the pressing need for the revival of values, and above
everything a religious faith, which should again bind Western men,
or at least some portion of them, into a unified whole.

Being poets (the old Fugitive group formed the core of the
Agrarian group), they longed for a happy land into which to project their hearts' desire. Being Southerners, and so subject, subconsciously at any rate, to the old powerful drive toward idealiza-
tion of the fatherland, they caught up all their wishing and all
their will to think themselves back into the old certainties and
projected them upon the Old South as the Arcadia in which they
had once been realized, and to which return would have to be made
if salvation were to be achieved.

Yet, as what I say indicates, and despite their strong tendency to
preciosity, there was from the first a good deal more realism in
them than in any of the earlier apologists and idealizers. Theirs
was to be no close repetition of the pro-slavery argument of Harper,

Dew & Company, with every shred of evidence relentlessly twisted to their purpose.

It is not true, as was foolishly charged by the Communists and others who should have known better, that they consciously inclined to Fascism. And it is not true, as Sherwood Anderson and an army of followers clamored, that all that moved them was simply the nostalgic wish to sit on cool and columned verandas, sip mint juleps, and converse exquisitely while the poor whites and the black men toiled for them in the hot, wide fields spread out against the horizon.

It is true that Allen Tate got into near-Fascist company as one of the editors of the *American Review,* though that was the result of sympathies which had nothing directly to do with Fascism. I think he was quite candid when he protested to the *Nation* that he would join the Communists if the only alternative were the Silver Shirts.

It is true also that the majority of the contributors to *I'll Take My Stand* were primarily occupied with the aristocratic notion in their examination of the Old South. And it is true, finally, that they took little account of the case of the underdog proper, the tenants and sharecroppers, industrial labor, and the Negroes as a group.

Nevertheless, they did take much account of the small landowning farmers — the yeomen. A minority of them, with John Donald Wade of Georgia University as the most eminent, was even more concerned with these people than with the planters. And practically every contributor to the book confessed openly or tacitly that the Old South was in the main more simple, plain, and recognizably human in a new country than the legend had ever had it in the past. Furthermore, it may be said that the virtues they assigned to the Old South were essentially the virtues which it indubitably possessed. Save for the fact that they insisted on making it a good bit more contemplative and deeply wise than I think it was, they are much the same virtues I have myself assigned to it at its best: honor, courage, generosity, amiability, courtesy.

Merely, the Agrarians refused to observe the faults of the Old

South and the operation of its system upon the people who lived under it. And, above all, to confess that the diseases which presently afflict the South are not and cannot logically be made to be, as they maintain, solely the fault of the introduction of industrialism and commercialism, but in very great part flow directly out of the pattern laid down in the Old South itself.

As time has gone on, however, they have tended to modify their views in the direction of realism. The tendency to idealize the Old South has gone steadily on, indeed. It is to be observed plainly in such books as Allen Tate's *The Fathers* and Caroline Gordon's *None Shall Look Back*. And above all in Stark Young's *So Red the Rose*. It is more than a little ironic that the last novel was written by a man who prefers to live in New York (an Agrarian by remote control, as it were) and who serves the *New Republic* as drama critic. But the case serves brilliantly to illustrate the power of the South over its sons even when they flee from it, and is perhaps explicable enough on the theory that distance tends to heighten and not lessen romantic nostalgia.

But despite the persistence of this tendency to idealize, the movement toward realism which I mention has gone forward, too. Taxed by most of the critics with having no knowledge of the elements of sociology and economics, at which they were inclined to sneer in *I'll Take My Stand* and their early essays in the *American Review,* the Agrarians were not long in setting out to remedy the lack, and they have gradually exhibited more respect for the facts in these fields. Moreover, they have gathered many new converts, some of whom are well versed in the social sciences and have no patience with precious nonsense about them — converts of whom the most notable is Herbert Agar of the Louisville *Courier-Journal.*

Again, when the critics pointed out their lack of awareness of the underdog in *I'll Take My Stand* and charged that Agrarianism was only a nebulous piece of poetizing about the joys of communion with the soil, without definite form or objective, they tacitly admitted the justice of the indictment by expanding their doctrine into a " program." Ever since they have spent a great deal of ink in deploring the growth of tenantry, sharecropping, absentee land-lordism, and industrial proletarianism; have continually maintained that the South could never be healthy again until the land was widely distributed among small holders. In the hands of such men as Mr. Agar, the argument here has become very extensive and formidable. But it cannot be said that their " program " is yet properly such, for they have never got around to telling us precisely how the redistribution of the land is to be brought about — though that is not to be too much held against them, since the problem is obviously one of staggering difficulties.

These Agrarians have had the bad influence of encouraging smugness and sentimentality in many quarters, and even of giving these vices sanction as a sort of higher wisdom. But it is fair to say that this has probably been well balanced out by their services in puncturing the smugness of Progress, in directing attention to the evils of *laissez-faire* industrialism, in their insistence on the necessity of developing a sensible farm program for the region, and in recalling that the South must not be too much weaned away from its ancient leisureliness — the assumption that the first end of life is living itself — which, as they rightly contend, is surely one of its greatest virtues.

12

But, for all the changes that were going on and being made in Dixie, it would still have been rash to adopt the conclusion which I have assigned to my hypothetical observer: to assume that the vigor had gone out of the old pattern and that it was speedily being relegated to the limbo of things past and done with. If it was breaking down in the most intelligent quarters, and if perhaps more serious fissures than those I have mentioned were slowly developing, its power over the body of the South would remain tremendous, even conclusive, and would exhibit itself with great distinctness.

As fear and despair receded in the ruling classes, smugness came back with hope. Characteristically and generally, the economic masters of the country fell gratefully back into their old simple, unanalytical outlook and their habit of considering only their own interests and those of their class, sloughed off their late dim and painful concern to understand the forces swirling about them, and forgot their vague professions of social awareness. Before long, and while eagerly availing themselves of all opportunities to seize benefits from the government on their own account — loudly demanding more, in fact — they were heartily cursing Mr. Roosevelt for all that they found wrong; and especially for the fact that they could no longer make money as in the good old days of the twenties, to which they now hankered warmly to return. Nothing could ever be right again, they said in chorus, until That Man was got rid of, the spending stopped and the budget balanced, the people on the relief rolls turned off to root or starve, and the foolishness about wages and hours done away with, so that a man could be made to do an honest day's work for what his employer felt he was worth.

In industrial and commercial quarters, rage against Section 7-A of the NRA code was evident from the earliest days, though they were generally pleased with the monopolistic and price-fixing provisions of the law. Also common was " chiseling," sometimes in the form of secret underbidding of competitors to get business; the textile industry, for instance, was already headed toward chaos again before the Supreme Court destroyed NRA. But particularly in wages and hours.

Men who would have scorned to take advantage of their competitors in any illegal or underhanded way, fudged on the wages and hours of their employees in the calm conviction that it was only a way of redressing a wrong against themselves. And the more cynical sort of employer slashed pay and extended hours pretty much as he pleased. I myself knew of cotton and hosiery mills in which the minimum weekly wage scale was as much as three dollars lower than that provided by law, and in which the fifty-five-hour week continued to be worked.

Naturally, the workers were resentful, but, remembering their late experiences and noting that competition for jobs remained fierce, they accepted it for the while in sullen silence.

Nevertheless, the feeling that " Uncle Sam " had somehow become their champion had an enormous influence upon them. That far away and immensely great power, always personalized in their speech and thoughts, had long enjoyed among the factory workers of the South a respect amounting to awe, and particularly after the World War. The minimum wage set by NRA for the first time furnished them with a definite yardstick by which to measure their estate, and so engendered in them a much more solid conviction of just grievance than they had ever possessed before. And the fact that " Uncle Sam " had set his approval upon the idea of collective bargaining by guaranteeing them the right to it sent their opinion of the unions up again, made them lend a much more attentive ear to the organizers.

The AFL union the United Textile Workers of America, coming into the South now, established locals with ease and celerity; though it was often necessary to do it secretly, despite the NRA guarantee, because of the menacing attitude of the mill-owners and the police.

But even where open organization was tolerated, the factory-owners were almost never really reconciled to the union idea. And as quickly as NRA was destroyed, they hastened with one accord to attempt to break up the locals and to do away with all that the code had achieved for the workers. Wages were widely cut, and the old hours were generally restored.

That rapidly brought on the great strike of 1934, a strike which was destined to fail, though Mr. Roosevelt saved it from being a complete rout by stepping in to arrange a settlement at the last moment. Probably, it would have been bound to fail in any case, for the reasons I have before set down. If the Federal government's policy had stiffened the workers' backbones, it had not performed the miracle of making over their minds, not to mention those of other Southerners about them, in a few months.

But the time had been badly chosen; for, as a result of the secret cutthroat competition and the uncertainty which followed the passing of NRA, the mills were more or less in the doldrums again and not much worried about the stopping of production for a period. Furthermore, the strike had been launched precipitately and without any adequate provision for feeding the strikers and their families. I am told, indeed, that Francis Gorman, who, as vice-president of the UTWA, directed the strike, has maintained ever since that he only ordered the strike because it was plain that the Southern locals were taking the bit in their teeth and striking anyhow, authorization or no authorization. Whether that is true I don't know, but such precipitance would have been strictly characteristic.

Far worse was the fact that the union workers, anxious for a united front and resentful of the great army of their fellow workers who, as always, still held fast to absolute individualism and refused to have any part with unionism, resorted to violence and coercion, in the shape of the so-called "flying squadrons." Men crowded automobiles and trucks, swept down, singing, shouting, and jeering, upon unorganized mills, shut off the machines, and more or less peremptorily demanded that the workers there join them at once. For this also Gorman has disclaimed responsibility. And it is quite likely that it was in fact the invention of the native tradition.

In any case, its effect was poisonous. One immediate and inevitable result was to get the back of the non-union workers up and so to widen the breach between the two groups, to make the conversion of the independent party wholly out of the question. At Cliffside, North Carolina, a dyehouse worker in one of the large cotton mills there stationed himself on the tower at the entrance and attempted to pour raw sulphuric acid on the members of a " flying squadron " as they sought to make their way in. And often the non-union workers met the raiding parties with fists or drawn guns. That in turn angered the unionists, who had been generally good-natured to begin with, and so created a definitely dangerous situation.

Observation of that, again, operated upon the more timid, upon

all but the stoutest and most reckless as the first delight in the assertion of power and determination and the old joy in violent action
passed, to revive the old fear of the consequences and the old questions about the rightness of it all. At Grover, North Carolina, a
local publicly announced that it was surrendering its charter, after it
had gained recognition from the mills, on the ground that, after
looking into the matter, it had concluded that unions were incompatible with Christianity.

Just as fatally, the play with violence lent color of fact to the
charge of rebellion which, now as before, the mill-owners and the
community at large had immediately lodged against the strikers,
gave good excuse to call out the militia and for orators to declaim
about " the right to work," and confirmed the anger of the community. At Lawndale, North Carolina, a privately owned, non-
organized mill village, the farmers of the surrounding countryside
poured in with their shotguns to back up the armed workers when
rumor (which fortunately proved untrue) had it that a "flying
squadron " was coming over from the near-by town of Shelby. At
Union, South Carolina, the union organizers were beaten and
hustled out of town by the police. And when, at Belmont, North
Carolina, a militiaman, through either brutality or nervous excitement, killed an unmenacing striker with his bayonet, the Tar Heel
authorities ignored the whole affair for a while and eventually gave
it a perfunctory whitewashing.

13

But if the strike failed, yet it, like Gastonia, left behind its resid-
ual deposits.

For one thing, renewed fear for the power of the mill-owners
which had again been demonstrated. These people settled back
into the long, slow patience which is combined so oddly in them
with their sudden violence when aroused; and their ingrained conservatism, holding them to old ways and ideas and making them

extremely suspicious of innovation, remained the dominant element in the scene. And still, hereafter there would be less and less of the old easy attitude of trust in the mill-owners, especially among the natural leaders. The faces of even the rank and file were increasingly apt to be a little veiled as they stood around the Coca-Cola box at the company store and listened to the boss's story — if and when he still bothered with that custom, which was less and less often.

Nor did it stop with growing aloofness from and distrust of the mill-owners. There was a distinct feeling in many of the workers, which sometimes became explicitly articulate in the leaders, that they had been betrayed and dealt unfairly with by the Southern captains in general — by the lawyer politicians and the business people downtown, whom they had so long trusted and looked upon as their ultimate leaders, the men whom they had turned to for the comforting hand on the shoulder and whom they had followed with proud devotion as the heirs of the great captains of the Civil War and Reconstruction.

We come here, indeed, upon the beginning of a fissure which was potentially important, since it threatened the old solidity which had for so many years been the foundation of all that was Southern. Henceforth the mill people would stand — wholly apart from the Southern body politic? Of course not. But increasing numbers of them, at any rate, would display a suspicious sullenness which definitely went beyond the old chariness with which they had always met the narrow social contempt which the South visited upon them. For politicians of the established Democratic hierarchy whom they had once cheered, many of them had nothing now but words of contempt. And some of them encountered business men, even anybody who by his dress might be taken for a business man, with thinly veiled hostility.

With the passage of the Wagner Act, the Textile Workers Organizing Committee, an affiliate of John L. Lewis's Committee for Industrial Organization, set up shop in Atlanta and began the first systematic attempt to organize the Southern textile workers permanently — to find the task easier so far as interesting the operatives themselves was concerned.

But not so far as the mill-owners or the general business community were concerned. Some few of the more intelligent mill-owners had by now concluded that unionization was perhaps inevitable, and had no great objection to it provided it could be extended to the whole South. Kemp P. Lewis, a leading textile-manufacturer of North Carolina, was such a man. I am told that the Haneses, with their great knitting plants at Winston-Salem, also have long felt the same way. And there are others, as witness the fact that Mr. Lewis could even get together a delegation to journey to a wage-and-hour-bill hearing in Atlanta and argue *for* the measure!

This is not to suggest pure disinterestedness. Fact is, the mills in North Carolina and the other older industrialized states of the South, having long made the lives of Yankee manufacturers a nightmare with cheap-labor competition, are themselves now growing uneasy over the competition of the mills springing up in the deep South, which use only the cheapest labor the law will allow (often cheaper than it is supposed to allow) and which have other advantages. Hence unionization of the whole South might well be a boon for them. And they are adamant in their demand that there must be a good prospect for such unionization before they will consider it for themselves.

None the less, their attitude does represent a great advance in rationality.

In the general business community of some of the towns of the upper South, at least, there are also to be found occasional men who feel that the attempt to head off unionism is to play Mrs. Partington, or who have come to suspect that unionization of the mill workers might not be such a bad thing for their own self-interest. Not a few of the merchants, in particular, have made the grudging discovery that more money in the pockets of the workers means more trade and profit for themselves.

For practical purposes, however, none of this yet amounts to much. The body of both the mill-owners and the business community at large is still almost as determinedly opposed to unionism as in the past.

George L. Googe, spokesman for the AFL textile union which has just moved into the South to oppose the TWOC, tells quite another story, indeed. Early in 1940 Mr. Googe issued a public statement to the effect that a practically miraculous change had come over the masters of the South since his last encounter with them some years ago. They did not turn out with bands and floats to receive him, he said; still, they were ready enough to talk terms with him.

But Mr. Googe's statement seems to have been merely a move in the game of labor politics, designed to convince the mill-owners and business community that his organization would be easier to deal with than the TWOC. And it does not at all fit with the story of Miss Lucy Randolph Mason, publicity director of the TWOC (the lady, it is worth noticing, is a Virginia aristocrat of the same family as the celebrated John Randolph of Roanoke), or with the public record.

Not many mills or towns have acted on the advice of the *Textile Bulletin* and defied the Wagner Act. But there have been instances even of something very like that. In 1937 the police commissioner and police chief at Memphis publicly issued warning that no CIO representatives would be allowed to enter the town. And when they came in anyhow, they were chased out and at least one was seriously beaten, with the authorities tacitly admitting that they were responsible for the proceedings. Warnings similar to those at Memphis were also issued at Macon, Georgia, and other places. And Miss Mason charges, with plenty of evidence to back her up, that the recent revival of Ku Klux Klan activities in Atlanta, Greenville, South Carolina, and other points has as a chief purpose the systematic intimidation of the workers and the union organizers. The Klansmen stage parades through mill villages where the organizers are active, burn fiery crosses in sight of union gatherings, throw ghostly picket lines around union halls, kidnap and whip leaders of the union spirit among the workers on " moral " charges, and so on.

For the most part, however, undercover methods have been preferred.

A young woman organizer was sent by TWOC to M——, Georgia, in response to the request of some of the workers of the town. Arriving in the evening, she retired to a hotel room and was not long in observing that there seemed to be a great many noisy automobiles passing under her window. Looking out, she found that a long string of cars was circling the block, horns going, all eyes directed to her room. Next morning before breakfast she was called on the telephone by the mayor, the county attorney, the sheriff, and the chief of police, who demanded that she stay in her room until they had talked to her. She refused, insisted on meeting them in the hotel dining-room in the presence of a witness.

At the conference they explained sorrowfully that they could not be responsible for her safety if she insisted on staying in town. What? she demanded indignantly; were they telling her, as the responsible authorities of the place, that they could not enforce the law as against a band of hoodlums whose intention they tacitly confessed they knew, whose identity might, therefore, well be suspected to be known to them also? They squirmed. Oh, no, no, no. Only, the county attorney explained gently, a Negro had been lynched in the place a few months before. And of course they had prosecuted — they always could prosecute. But now, really, had the prosecution done the dead Negro a bit of good?

The young woman was a resolute sort, stayed anyhow, scared the officials so thoroughly with her grim promises as to what price they would pay if she were harmed that she was not molested. But not all organizers have been so lucky. Some have been shot at from ambush or have had to dodge bricks intended for the backs of their heads. And not all have been successful in dodging.

14

The favorite device, however, has been the terrorization of the workers themselves, not only by violence or the threat of violence, but by economic means — by the discharge and secret blacklisting of the leaders in the unionization movement, on trumped-up charges of inefficiency, insubordination, drunkenness, and so on — by cutting off credit at the company store and in private establishments under the influence of the mill management — by carefully planted rumors that the mills were to be closed down and dismantled, as no longer profitable, or of long periods of idleness.

Trickery, too, has been widely resorted to. One much used subterfuge is to refuse to recognize the union as a collective bargaining agency on the claim that its rolls are padded and that it does not in fact represent a majority of the bona-fide employees of the mill; then, while appeal to the National Labor Relations Board is pending, to use anti-union and toadying elements in the mill population to set afoot the psychology that the union is obviously a failure, and that the best thing to do is to get out of it before it collapses utterly and leaves its hapless members exposed to the resentment of the management. It has sometimes worked so well that, by the time the NLRB hearing was held, the mill could really show that the union did not in fact any longer represent the majority of the workers.

It is significant that TWOC has systematically followed a policy of extreme secrecy, both as to its total membership and as to its entry into any particular group of mills, until it has been ready to ask for a NLRB election.

But, despite the great opposition to it, it has had a considerable measure of success to date. Its privately asserted claims to having the greatest number of locals ever established in the South seem to be accurate.

It does not follow, however, that ultimate victory is even near to being within its grasp. So far it has followed a policy of calling few strikes and no large-scale ones. In truth, I am told by its responsible leaders that most of those it has called have been forced by the membership.

These Fabian tactics are of course intelligent in themselves. With the psychology of the workers what I have reported it as being, spade-work is obviously indicated as the proper course for the union for many years to come if it is really to establish itself as a solid agency in the South. But it is far from certain that it will be able to follow such a course through.

For one thing, its policy means that it has not yet been able to raise the general wage level to any considerable extent, though it has had some local successes along that line. The fact is, there has been a widespread tendency on the part of the mills to reduce wages in the upper brackets by way of compensating themselves for the increases in the lower brackets forced by the wage and hour laws.

But, as we know, the Southern worker is an impatient fellow when it comes to paying dues to a union, wants to see swift and spectacular results, is likely to fall away if he doesn't get them. The TWOC has already had bitter experience with these demands and this fickleness — to the point that it has abandoned its early policy of keeping a large force of organizers in the field, and now demands evidence of serious intention and sober understanding that miracles cannot be worked overnight before it will consent to establish a local.

Even so — as what we have seen ominously suggests — it is quite possible that circumstances may develop under which TWOC will find itself faced with a runaway general strike, such as Francis Gorman asserts he was faced with in 1934: with the choice of appearing to order such a strike or of seeing its work fall away into dust.

Another possibility not to be overlooked is that a reactionary Congress may be elected and repeal or emasculate the Wagner Act and the wage and hour laws; and that the mill-owners of the South will seize upon the opportunity for a general offensive against the union.

If either contingency should develop in the next few years, I doubt that the union's chance of victory would be a great deal better than in 1934. Perhaps not at all better. In spite of slow changing, the old pattern is still too powerfully stamped upon the mind of most of the workers to make them able to stand up against the odds they would face.

What those odds are we shall better appreciate when we have looked at what has gone on along the agricultural front.

15

Essentially, the case was of the same sort as that on the industrial and commercial front. Planters and landowners, as certainly as the business community (to which they also often belonged, of course), swung back toward smug assertion of the old standards as their terror dwindled and the sense of security came back.

Hardly had the farm program been launched before the laws had hastily to be amended if the great body of tenants and sharecroppers were to get their share of the benefit payments. Landlords were coolly collecting all payments on their lands and giving the poor whites and Negroes, too ignorant to know what was being done or too cowed by the fear of being deprived of a means of making a living to protest, what they pleased.

This was more true, naturally, of absentee landlords than of those who lived in close contact with their dependents. But absentee landlordism had by now undergone a vast expansion, and was continuing to grow at a great pace. Primarily, that was the natural end-result of the speculation of the twenties. As we have seen, the banks and other money-lenders of the South had been so heavily loaded with land-mortgages when the depression struck that it had speedily become useless to attempt to foreclose and sell because of the glut in the market — which in turn served as a principal factor in the bankruptcy of hundreds of these lenders. But in this wholesale process of bankruptcy the titles and claims of the lenders had of course been transferred to the hands of others, the ultimate creditors. By far the greater part had, in fact, been removed to the North. And even when they remained in the South, it was the usual thing for the holder to reside many states away from the actual site of the land involved.

The result was to bring absentee landlordism of the completely impersonal and harsh type which had already developed in Southern industry to the soil also. As soon as the New Deal policies made the growing of cotton profitable again, the new holders of Southern paper bestirred themselves to foreclose wherever they had not already taken title and, since it was still impossible for them to sell the land at the prices fixed in the twenties, to make it yield the highest possible return. One of two methods was commonly used. If the land was poor, they simply left it to grow up in weeds and scrub pine or to be denuded by the rains into a red, gullied waste, and collected subsidies from the Federal government for " taking it out of production." But if the land was fertile, then they turned to operating it on strictly business lines and, wherever it was possible, on a mass production basis.

Managers, overseers, gang bosses were either sent in from the North or were selected from among the hardest and most ruthless types of Southerners. Mechanization was extensively resorted to, the tractor and gang plow substituted for the old man-and-mule combination. And the tenants and sharecroppers who were still tolerated were dealt with as a sort of inferior machines on their own account — took what they were given, kept their mouths shut about it, or were thrown off the land.

How extensive such holdings were is significantly shown by the fact that, early in 1940, Senator Harry Byrd of Virginia introduced a resolution in the Senate to limit the annual subsidies paid by the AAA to any one " farmer " to $5,000, and raised the figure by stages to $50,000 without ever gaining any support from the Senators from the cotton South, always well aware of the identity of the real powers in their states.

Chiseling on the tenants and sharecroppers attached to such

baronies was not always the work of the owners but often of the managers and other understrappers, to whom the system gave a perfect opportunity. But, by one or the other or both, the practice was, as I say, very usual from the first. And despite the frequent changes in the law, no few of them have known how to go on seizing the great part of the subsidies intended for their dependents; sometimes by reducing them to the status, real or nominal, of mere wage-hands; sometimes by threat of dismissal and black-listing; and sometimes by threat of violence or the police, who, in areas in the Deep South at least, are often pretty completely under the control of the local representatives of the absentees.

But the far-away landlords and their stewards had no monopoly on chiseling. The local absentees (now including those banks and other lenders who had managed to survive the perils of the depression) have been pretty good at it, too; eagerly learning the new tricks of the distant operators, they have themselves been able to show the latter a thing or two. And for their part also, they have known how to go on leaping the not too great hurdles of the law.

And if the absentees were, in the large, the worst of it, it was only a matter of degree. The landlords who lived on close terms with their tenants were often only a little less adept in chiseling and in adjusting themselves to the fluctuating law than the absentees, many times no less. Against that, to be sure, it is to be recalled that now, as always, there were numbers of landlords who in varying measure exhibited higher standards of honor and humanity in dealing with those who worked for them. I wish I might say that they were unquestionably the majority, but I am far from sure that it would be the truth. Circumstances in the South of the period, like those in the years from the Civil War until 1900, operated inevitably to break down rather than build up nice notions of honor, and to call forth the most grasping sort of individualism. More, under the tradition of the South the seizing of benefits intended for the tenants was frequently, in all sorts of landlords, both absentee and resident, not felt as constituting dishonesty at all, but as being simply a part of the natural right of the man of property to claim all revenues over and above what was required to feed and clothe the workmen after the established standard.

But the old complete individualism of economic outlook showed itself in other ways than in mere chiseling on tenants and sharecroppers: in company with the ancient incapacity of the great body of Southerners to examine and analyze a case realistically even when their own fate hinged upon it, the tendency to take the easiest answer as explaining all their ills.

If Southern landowners grasped all possible government benefits for themselves even more avidly, if anything, than the industrialists and commercialists, they were not laggard in joining the latter in denouncing the New Deal in general. At least, this statement is true for nearly all the greater ones, and it has some measure of applicability to even the yeoman farmers, particularly the more solidly established ones. The lesser sort of farmer, indeed, would generally part company with the greater landowners when they demanded the complete destruction of the New Deal, as, with perfect inconsistency, they often did. But they joined eagerly in the chorus of bitter complaint and criticism.

They weren't getting large enough subsidies, continually demanded more — usually got them. And the price of cotton was not nearly high enough.

In fact, it averaged in the vicinity of twelve cents from the end of 1933 until the fall of 1937 — a figure which afforded a neat profit, despite the devaluation of the dollar. But it hung there precariously and only because of the government's determined spending and reduction of acreage; it threatened continually to fall again, and despite brief upward surges, showed no real promise of ever moving up to the twenty-cent level which the World War and the twenties had convinced most of the farmers was the minimum acceptable price.

The basic reason for this was clear enough. The South was losing its foreign market for cotton. It had, in fact, begun to lose it even before the depression set in.

16

To understand the matter, we have to recall what I have before suggested: that there was a great expansion of cotton mills in countries like Japan after 1920 — countries which had not been much industrialized. In 1920 Japan had just 3,814,000 spindles; in 1930 she had 7,072,000; and in 1938 the figure had gone up to 12,550,000, though it is interesting to observe that it fell by a million in 1939. India rose from six and a half million spindles in 1920 to nine million in 1930. China climbed from less than four million to more than seven million in the same decade. And Brazil from a little more than a million to almost three million.

What is important also is that the vast increase in these countries did not at first seriously reduce the number of spindles in the countries which had long furnished the chief export market for Southern cotton. In 1920 the United Kingdom had a little more than fifty-seven million spindles; in 1930 it still had well over fifty-five million.

Here, therefore, was a great new market opened up to Southern cotton in the space of a few years. And it is this that ultimately explains the expansion of Southern cotton acreage in the twenties to which I have already referred, an expansion of over fifteen million acres.

Southern cotton exports averaged between five and six million bales annually in the years 1921–4. But in 1925 and in 1926 they passed eight million bales, and in 1927 they leaped up to 10,926,614 bales.

But now most of the new spindles in the East and South America were employed in making almost (by American standards) unimaginably cheap yarns. That meant that they required cheap cotton, far cheaper than most American cotton could be had. And the operation of the Republican tariffs, in making it always harder for all foreign nations to secure dollars for exchange, made the case of these new mills even more pressing. Naturally, then, they began to look about to encourage new and cheaper sources of supply. And new and cheaper sources of supply promptly arose to meet them. In the production year 1920–1 the total cotton yield of all countries outside the United States was only 6,964,000 bales. In the year 1929–30 it had mounted to 11,535,000; and in 1936–7 it had reached 18,476,000 bales.

The normal effect of this was undoubtedly making itself felt as early as 1928, when Southern exports suddenly tumbled by nearly three and a half million bales. In 1930 the total was well under seven million bales.

By this time something else was happening. Whereas the multiplication of spindles in the East and South America had not greatly affected the old cotton-manufacturing countries of Europe in the twenties, the effect of their competition would be spectacular in the thirties. If the United Kingdom still had 55,207,000 spindles in 1930, in 1938 it would have only 36,322,000.

The South, having expanded its acreage to meet the new demand for cotton created by the growth of mills in Asia and Latin America, now found itself not only losing that new market to new producers of cheaper cotton but also losing its old market because of the competitive power of the new mills. And to complete the circle, countries like England, striving desperately to meet the competition and finding it more and more difficult to lay hand on dollars as the gold of the world increasingly fled to the United States, themselves began to use greater quantities of cheaper cotton coming from other parts of the world than the South.

The year 1932 saw exports of Southern cotton mount again to 8,707,548 bales, and in 1933 they were again only a few hundred thousand bales under that figure. These years were, of course, the worst ones of the world depression — a fact which effectually disposes of any supposition that the original slump in exports was due simply to that depression — but they were also years of exceedingly poor cotton crops in the new cotton-growing countries, and the decrease in their yield almost exactly corresponded to the increase in Southern exports.

In 1934, when world production outside the South shot up by nearly three million bales, the foreign market took only seven and a half million bales of the Southern staple. Next year it absorbed well under five million bales, and in each of the three following years only between five and six million. The South's export market was now actually smaller than it had been in the early twenties. Sales abroad for the four-year period 1935-8, were nearly six hundred thousand bales below those for the period 1921-4.

And in 1939 the bottom dropped out of the export market, with foreign countries buying only 3,326,840 bales of Southern cotton. The outbreak of the war in Europe naturally had a great deal to do with that directly, and even more indirectly. For England, in particular, denied commercial credits in the United States and unable to expand her sales to this country in any considerable measure, inevitably turned to hoarding her dwindling supply of gold for the buying of necessary war materials here; sought cotton (and even more, tobacco) in countries where she could get credits and where she could pay for it by expanding exports on her own account.

To sum it up, the South was losing its export market for cotton — had been progressively losing it for thirteen years — primarily because the staple could be produced more cheaply elsewhere. And secondarily because of the operation of a series of stupid or highly doubtful national policies — the tariffs, the failure to settle the war debts on a realistic basis rather than making political capital of it, the smug encouragement of the flight of the world's gold to these shores — developed long before the New Deal was heard of.

But few people in the South showed any disposition to recognize the facts, and least of all the landowners and their spokesmen. In very large measure the loss of the export market was completely ignored in considering the price of the staple. Fact is, indeed, that the majority of the landowners did not even trouble to know that the market was being lost. But whenever it was taken account of at all, then that also was laid wholly or mainly to the New Deal. In Texas a magazine, the *Texas Weekly,* published and edited by

Peter Molyneux, was even founded, in part at least, to expound this view.

I do not imply that the New Deal was entirely blameless in the premises. A logical case might be made out against it for its failure to go more energetically about changing the policies which were helping to throttle the cotton export market, though it is to be said in its defense that it is doubtful that the people, long fed on falsehood, would have stood for it. But, ironically enough, the chief immediate blame which can, in any view of the matter, be laid to the New Deal resides precisely in the fact that its policies have kept the price of American cotton relatively high. It is quite possible that if the Southern farmers had been left strictly to their own devices after 1932, the loss of the export market would have proceeded a great deal less rapidly. But I do not think that they would have been exactly enthusiastic about a price of, say, four cents a pound.

17

How the stark individualism of the Southern landowners operated against this background of unrealism was to be manifest soon enough.

From the beginning they had hurled bitter epithets at the New Deal, not only on the score of the price of cotton but also on that of the restriction of acreage, which alone made the prevailing price possible. What their demands really came to was that each man should be allowed to plant as he pleased, with the government paying him always better subsidies on all the cotton he produced and at the same time raising the price level!

So intense was the resentment against the quota restrictions, the itch of most men to steal a march on the government and their fellows, that they were not long in devising ways to circumvent them. Fudging on acreage grew continually bolder. And intensive cultivation increasingly displaced the old extensive system. Commercial fertilizers, the use of which had sharply declined at the bottom of the depression, were now poured upon the land more lavishly than ever; in 1937 and 1938 the average was nearly three hundred pounds for every acre planted to cotton in the South. And more and more, whenever it was possible, the local planters took their cue from the baronies of the absentees and turned to mechanization.

The result? In 1932 and 1933, as we have seen, the annual production had been slightly more than thirteen million bales. It fell to less than ten million in 1934. But in 1936 it was back to thirteen million. And then — in 1937, when the farmers took the bit in their teeth and planted four million acres more than in the previous year, the average production per acre rose to two hundred and sixty-seven pounds an acre, more than fifty pounds higher than any previous record, and the total crop reached the staggering total of almost nineteen million bales, very close to two million more than the greatest crops of the past! The total available supply of cotton in the world that year was well over fifty million bales, or about twice the world consumption.

By spending many hundreds of millions more than it had planned for piling up cotton in warehouses, the Federal government succeeded in keeping the bumper crop from playing complete havoc with the economy of the Southern farmer and the South as a whole, which would have been its natural result. Nevertheless, the price did fall to below eight cents a pound, as against the eleven- to fourteen-cent levels which had prevailed since the inauguration of the farm program.

But at any rate this would at least serve to force the Southern landowners to some realistic understanding of their position? Down to date, there has been little sign of any such reaction. A few planters, more yeomen, did indeed begin to show some vague recognition of the guilt of their own assertive individualism in the case, and the collapse served to make awareness of the fact that the foreign cotton market was being lost a little more general. But the predominant effect was simply to redouble the bitterness against the New Deal, as being, presumably by some black magic, responsible for it all.

What incited that bitterness quite as much as the fall in cotton prices was the Works Progress Administration and relief in general.

All along, Southern landowners, like Southern business men and the middle class, had grumbled angrily against all forms of relief as affording a haven for indolent loafers who ought to be turned out to make their own living or starve. That, in part, was less ruthless than it sounds, proceeded quite naturally from the old monadism and the general incapacity to analyze large cases, the tendency to the purely personal; was commonly accompanied by a fiercely sincere conviction that all the people who worked for WPA or who got direct relief, and who were not outright invalids, could really find employment and make their own way if they so much as half tried. But it also had in it much of the South's easy believing what it wanted to believe, and of the same sort of calculation — often conscious, probably more often hidden from the protestant's own awareness by moral indignation — which I have already noted in the case of the industrialists and business men.

One quite conscious factor in their resentment, of course, was the feeling that they were paying the bill, in taxes. In point of fact, most actual farmers and many great landowners paid no income taxes or any Federal taxes of any kind save the hidden ones, of which they were usually only cloudily or not at all conscious. But the tradition inherited from the frontier days still made the very word a red flag to them, and the absentee landlords, business men, and so on who did pay income taxes found it easy to arouse them about it.

But an even more potent factor for their resentment was that WPA and relief interfered with their labor supply.

We have already seen in passing that the depression and the beginning of the New Deal policies had both operated greatly to swell the always existent reservoir of surplus labor in the South. Not only had the collapse of the early thirties resulted in the loss of employment to great armies of tenants and sharecroppers, but also it had wiped out countless thousands of farmers who had been struggling to free their lands from mortgage.

Nor did conditions after the New Deal got into full swing make for rehabilitation. On the contrary. Beginning by still further reducing the employment opportunity for the tenant and sharecropper, cotton curtailment — ultimately a mere reflection of the decline of the foreign market — continuously operated in many ways to make the outlook for the common white who had been born and bred to the soil more and more forbidding.

Its natural tendency, obviously, was to drive the marginal lands and the poorer sort of lands generally — precisely those which the man with little or no capital who was trying to become a farmowner on his own account had found it easiest to acquire — out of cotton-production and increasingly restrict the growing of the staple to the best and higher-priced lands. And since cotton (or tobacco) was traditionally the single money crop of the South, the only one for which local markets were available in most areas, what that meant in practice was that the banks and other masters of capital, sourly remembering their recent experiences and observing realistically enough that farm properties were now dubious risks under the best of circumstances, simply refused any longer even to consider the financing of the purchase of the poorer lands.

Adding to the difficulties of the common white also was the fact that if the poor lands of the South figured less and less in the actual growing of the staple, they were still much in demand by those — planters, established farmers, speculators from the towns — who wanted to collect Federal benefits for fictitiously " taking them out of production." Theoretically, such skullduggery ought not to have been possible under the law, but in view of the fact that the administration of the law was always in the hands of the appointed creatures of the Democratic politicians, it was often quite feasible for the right people; and it could be made very profitable when the lands involved were to be had for little or nothing. Many a poor one-gallus devil whose land had been held of so little account that he had managed to survive the depression now suddenly found his mortgage foreclosed on this account.

As for the better lands — the prices asked for them had come down greatly from the figures of the 1920's; but in general they had not, save in the case of distress offerings, come down to a level in keeping with their real earning capacity. Moreover, distress lands were apt to be available only to those on the inside of the charmed financial circle, and not to the struggling fellow who sought to raise himself to landownership with no more than a shoestring. The banks, hemmed about with the new Federal regulations under which anybody less than a bondholder became a dangerous gamble, were not only uninterested in financing the purchase of the poor lands; they were uninterested in financing the purchase of any kind of lands, save for exceedingly choice clients. And even the Federal farm-loan banks, which offered long terms and which continually had huge foreclosed holdings for sale, were usually inclined to deal only with farmers and planters already solidly established.

Yet more, when a man succeeded in getting his hands on land, the cotton-quota system made it harder than ever for him to get hold of enough cash to meet his payments on it. That was so, even if the administration of the system was completely honest and he received his full acreage allotment under the law. But in fact the politicians who controlled it often took advantage of the ignorance and fears of the small farmers and fudged on their allotments for the benefit of the great holders in their localities. For that matter, many farms held in fee simple were, and are, every year abandoned by their owners for the good reason that they found the quotas assigned them inadequate to meet their annual expenses, as inflated by the Southern farm-credit system.

18

All in all, it was perhaps more difficult than at any time in the history of the South for the landless white — even though of superior ambition and energy — to lift himself out of that estate.

And to grasp the full implications of that, it is necessary to bear in mind that the Southern rural population kept right on, keeps right on, increasing at the rates we have seen. Southern industry continued to grow, of course, once the bottom of the depression was passed, and continues to grow at present. But in no recent year has it provided new jobs for more than about twelve per cent of the new contenders for them provided by population growth alone.

Which means, manifestly, that if the landowners of the South could have availed themselves of the conditions freely and taken full advantage of the glutted labor market, they could — and, in the main, undoubtedly would — have hired workers at rates as low as, or perhaps even lower than, those which had obtained in the worst of the depression, when cotton-pickers had sometimes got as little as twenty cents a hundred pounds.

But here WPA and direct relief came into the equation and canceled out this opportunity, so far as they took up the slack — which, though far from completely, was still sufficient to hold wages fairly close to the minimum standards which had long prevailed in the South generally. In truth, the effect of this often went so far as actually to make it difficult or impossible for the landowners to secure a normal supply of labor even at the old established rates. This for the reason we have previously seen: that poor as was the stipend paid Federal relief clients in the South, it still afforded a more attractive standard of living, or at least one considered so, than that provided by such jobs as hoeing and picking cotton, stemming tobacco, and gathering strawberries, fruit, and truck in season.

Getting on WPA or direct relief had in fact literally become an object of eager ambition, not only for Negroes but for many of the common whites — for most of the landless perhaps, save those who rose from the old yeoman farmer class, and no few of these were inclined to forget their pride and succumb as time went on.

The standard Southern wage for picking cotton is fifty cents a hundred pounds. A strong and active man, trained and toughened to the task from childhood, can pick three hundred pounds or even considerably more in a fourteen-hour day. But the average gathering for men and women is no more than half as much, for children far less. Hoeing cotton, a grueling job, brings a dollar a day at best, usually only seventy-five cents, sometimes only fifty; the day extending from dawn till dark. And the other tasks I have enumerated are paid on a comparable scale, are all back-breaking and long. Finally, every one of these jobs necessarily lasts only a few weeks; and when taken together they nowhere afford employment for more than four or five months in the year.

In contrast, WPA, with its short hours and relatively light tasks, continued round the calendar. And any reluctance to such regular employment which the farm-bred Negroes and poor whites might have had was effectually counterbalanced by the psychological factor that it furnished the generally much coveted opportunity to live in town.

Into every city and hamlet where the Federal agency was established, but especially in the larger places, poured an unending stream of aspirants, to live with relatives, to make their living after any fashion — often including thievery — to endure the greatest hardships, until they could fulfill the residence requirement and get on the rolls.

The slum quarters in the towns, white and Negro, exhibited in these days, and continue to exhibit, a curious spectacle for the South. Once almost deserted in the daytime save for children and old grannies, they swarmed with males and women of work age now. In the morning the crazy porches were sprinkled with direct relief clients or the able-bodied who had not yet got on the WPA list, sunning themselves happily. And in the afternoon, once the brief WPA days was over, they were crowded with active men and women, laughing, sleeping, drinking cheap wine or corn whisky, or dreaming restlessly of violence to relieve the monotony of their leisure. To the great disgust, naturally, of all Southerners of the superior orders, who never troubled to ask themselves how it had come about — but above all to that of the passing landowners.

In 1937, with the harvest season for the bumper crop of cotton, the situation became exceedingly tense. The landowners in many sections found themselves faced with the prospect of seeing their cotton rot in the fields for lack of labor to gather it. So pressing was the danger that in some cases they even offered to pay higher wages than the standard in order to attract pickers from elsewhere — sometimes succeeded, to the disgust and anger of their fellows in the districts from which such labor migrated. And WPA officials sought to meet the need by suspending the stupid rule forbidding the rehiring for six months of anybody who quit his job with the agency, and decreed that those on its rolls must accept employment as cotton-pickers when it was offered, under penalty of being discharged and losing their relief status permanently. Even so, the response was so reluctant that it was not long until the planters were resorting to the old pattern of intimidation and coercion — to forced labor.

At Anderson, South Carolina, a town dominated by bankers and merchants who are mostly themselves also planters or who do the great part of their business with landowners, the old vagrancy laws of the Black Code — originally designed to perpetuate essential slavery — were brought out again, and the chief of police issued an ultimatum to the effect that anybody who could not satisfy him as to his means of support would have to accept a job picking cotton or go to jail and be farmed out to the landowners to pay his board bill. In practice the chief's definition of vagrancy proved flexible enough to include a good many Negroes, as well as some whites, who were neither on relief nor without visible means of support, but who simply preferred to earn their living as handy men in town, barber-shop boys, and so on, rather than toil in the cotton.

From Anderson the practice spread rapidly to other towns in South Carolina, Georgia, and the deep South generally, as well as Tennessee — even found a few imitators in North Carolina. And in many districts threatened with the migration of labor to other places where higher wages were offered, armed patrols began to ride the roads to head off those who were leaving and drive them back to work at the prevailing wage.

I do not imply that the landowners had no case. Obviously, it is an anomaly when crops cannot be gathered or are gathered with difficulty in a country where population far outruns the available number of jobs. It is also true, as we know, that cotton is a crop which at best yields a narrow margin of profit. The cotton-growers are perhaps accurate when they protest that a flat wage of twenty-five cents an hour for labor regardless of efficiency, as has been proposed in Congress, would be an intolerable burden for them. On the other hand, it is only reasonable for farm laborers to expect to have some of the benefits paid to cotton by government passed on to themselves. Even with cotton selling at eight cents, as in 1937, a gathering cost of five dollars for a bale of five hundred pounds might, I think, very well be borne. And such an increase in wages, plus a more flexible administration of the relief agencies, would unquestionably go a long way toward solving the crop-gathering problem.

In the last analysis, however, I am afraid that the clamor against WPA and the high-handed methods sometimes used to get labor have been and are motivated by something more than the legitimate desire of the landowners to get their crops harvested at a price they can afford; that, in many instances, it has in it also an element of itching desire, often less than consciously realized, to enjoy all the natural advantages of a great supply of surplus labor — of the kind of individualism which holds that a man of property has a right to take full advantage of the necessities of other and less happy men.

Nor must I leave the theme without noting that there has long been a prospect of the surplus of labor being expanded to truly overwhelming proportions. As early as 1934 the Rust brothers of Memphis announced that they had built a completely successful cotton-picking machine. The announcement proved premature, and, moreover, the Rusts proved to have a social conscience and seem deliberately to have withheld the machine from mass manufacture until they could see some hope that it would not play havoc with the common whites of the South. But as I write this, they have just announced that they plan to put it into mass production before the end of 1940.

It may be that they are over-optimistic still. But the general history of such machines suggests that the cotton-picker will eventually be perfected, for use in relatively flat country at least — and the greater part of the richer cotton lands of the South are located in just such country. The Rust brothers announce the establishment of a foundation which will turn back a large portion of the profits from the invention for the purpose of retraining and rehabilitating the people dispossessed by it.

But, for all that, it is an ominous machine. For it promises to eliminate most or all of the sharecroppers and a great many of the tenants within a short period, since it overcomes the last and principal barrier to the mechanization of Southern cotton farming. Estimates of the number of people who will thus be deprived of a means of making almost any sort of livelihood range up to two million, far more than any foundation could ever hope to rehabilitate. And in fact the estimates may be too low for the ultimate effect of the picker machine. It seems to me that in the end it is likely to mean the mechanization of Southern cotton farming as a whole and the absorption of most of the good cotton lands of the South into vast mass-production plantations. It is to be remembered that the cultivation of the staple has always naturally tended to the large unit, since it is a bulky cash crop which requires to be processed before it is ready for market, and so can best and most profitably be handled in great quantities. Furthermore, huge mechanized land units are plainly indicated as the easiest way to recovering, so far as it is possible, the foreign market, lost precisely because of the high production costs of the present methods of growing cotton.

And if this analysis is correct, then the Rust machine eventually means the elimination, not only of the sharecroppers and most of the tenants but also of a big part of the Southern yeoman farmers. Considerable numbers of all these classes would of course be reabsorbed by the new mass-production plantations as laborers and machine-operators. But the total number of those fully deprived of a means of earning a living might well reach five million or more.

19

Now, in all this there was tragedy, of course. Immediate and obvious tragedy for the common whites of the rural South; not only in the direct economic and social fact, but also in that the old shiftlessness, the lack of ambition, the willingness to accept bad living conditions and dependence which had always been growing up from the bottom, was now affecting more and more of them, often in levels which had not been greatly touched by it before, and in disquieting numbers of them turning to a conviction, at once whining and demanding, that they were entitled to more and more without any regard to their own productive effort and merely because they existed.

And scarcely less immediate and obvious tragedy for the common whites of the South at large. It was precisely the increasing surplus of labor which made and makes the success of the labor unions in the textile mills so uncertain and virtually assures their defeat in a showdown; for if people are generally reluctant to leave WPA for jobs in the cotton fields, they are often willing and eager to leave for jobs in the mills, which pay more, and have no scruples about playing " scab." And what was true for the textile mills was true, *mutatis mutandis,* for many other trades. One of the bitterest of complaints among unionized and skilled labor in the South, such as brick-masons and painters, is that WPA continually turns loose a flood of people, trained only to the barest modicum of competence in these trades, to take their jobs or enable contractors to beat down their wages by offering to work at dirt-cheap rates.

And beyond this, again, there was the inevitable effect on living conditions of the crowding of the armies of the dispossessed into the slums of the cities.

No less immediate and obvious was the tragedy for the land-

owning classes. Planter and yeoman alike were plainly heading for
disaster in their stubborn failure to try to analyze the situation before them, their smug insistence on assigning most of their troubles
to a man or a set of men in Washington.

But ultimately the tragedy extended to the South as a whole.
Since the whole economy of the region arose mainly from the two
crops of cotton and tobacco (for which the same essential conditions were true), the rapid loss of the foreign market for these
staples was a matter which immediately and directly concerned the
fortunes of virtually everybody in Dixie. And the population and
unemployment problems involved extensive consequences for
everybody, also.

They meant, for one thing, the constant curtailment of the potential and actual productive capacity of the South — less to go around
in the higher circles as well as the lower. They meant that school
costs fell upon the more prosperous classes with inordinate weight.
Despite the fact that Southern schools were still generally the
poorest in the country, the costs relative to total wealth were the
highest for any section, for the good reason that the region, with its
great birthrate, had a relatively greater number of young people of
school age. And now, as the proportion of those who could pay no
direct taxes increased, a greater and greater part of the burden
naturally shifted back upon those who could.

Again, the population and unemployment problems meant, as I
have already noted, a constantly greater crowding of the slums in
the towns. And of Negro slums as well as white. And out of these
slums came consequences which, by the most elementary rule of
common sense, were of the most vital interest to every white man
who lived in the towns, and eventually to every white man in Dixie.

One of them was a notable perpetuation, and even an increase,
of the tendency to private violence, which, like lynching, might
normally have been expected to recede under the conditions of the
town.

In 1935, according to the figures of the uniform crime reports
of the Federal Bureau of Investigation, the eleven former Con-

federate states had a murder-rate of 21.9 per 100,000 people in all towns ranging from less than 10,000 to over 250,000. For 1936 the figure was 22.76, and for 1937 it was 23.23. (Perhaps, however, it should be recorded that it dropped to 20.70 in 1939.)

How did this compare with the rest of the nation? The year 1937 will stand with accuracy for the other years instanced. In 1937 the New England states had a murder-rate of 1.3 per 100,000 people in towns of the same class as those referred to in the South. The rate in the Middle Atlantic states was 3.8, in the North Central group 4.5. The Mountain states had a rate of 4.7, and the Pacific coast of 4.2. That is, the Southern cities were over five times as murderous as those of either the North Central area or the Far West, over six times as those of the Middle Atlantic country, and over eighteen times as those of New England!

The Negro in the slums was the main, though by no means the whole, explanation for this appalling showing. Police reports and maps for cities like Atlanta and Charlotte (the two which had the highest murder-rate for the South) reveal plainly that the murder line follows the location of black slums with great exactness, that most of the criminals and the majority of their victims are found there, and that the greatest incidence of the crime occurs in exactly the slums where unemployment, crowding, squalor, and want are most prevalent.

This does not mean, to be sure, that the slums, and the population and economic problems behind the slums, were alone responsible for the Negro's murder-rate. Violence, as we have seen, has always been a part of the pattern of the South. And of course violence for the Negro as well as for the white man. That would have followed naturally in any case. But we have observed that it was the result of Reconstruction and the economic purposes of the white South that Southern courts had become and largely remain to this day places in which the Negro could count on little consideration — which left him little choice but violence if he were determined to have redress against white men of any power. And there was another side to the matter: the courts were places in which his con-

cerns would be counted as of such little account that he could not
even be reasonably sure of justice as against another Negro, and
in which even the murder of another Negro would be reckoned as
such a venial offense that it was likely to go unpunished if the
criminal had a white man of rank to speak for him, and which in
any case would be almost certain to be set down as second-degree
murder or manslaughter and punished with the lightest sentence.
Often a Negro murderer of another Negro drew no heavier penalty
than that commonly meted out to a chicken-thief. And when in
North Carolina in 1937 such a murderer was actually condemned
to execution and ultimately dispatched, it so startled one editor that
he was moved to investigate and discover that it had been twenty
years since another case of the kind had happened in the state.

But it was the slums created by the population and unemployment situation that, with their close-packed throngs of idle or partly
idle Negroes, afforded the perfect opportunity for the pattern thus
developed to come to full flower.

20

However, as I have indicated, it was not entirely the Negro
slums. Murder among the Southern whites living in the towns was
more frequent than in other parts of the United States. And when
it came to crimes of lesser violence — in which the South held
much the same pre-eminence as in murder — the matter was
plainer. White men and boys appeared in Southern police courts
for cutting and shooting scrapes only a little less frequently than
Negroes. And here again the police records showed clearly the exact
correlation between the slum and these crimes.

The crime bred by the slums did not end with violence, naturally.
I have chosen to emphasize crimes of violence merely because they
fit most closely with the old pattern of the South. But in other
criminal fields the South enjoyed the same unhappy leadership of
the nation. In 1936, for instance, Atlanta had roughly twice as many

cases of burglary and housebreaking, half again as many cases of theft, as Boston. And Atlanta was more typical than not.

The South, in short, was paying an enormous crime bill because of the interaction of its population growth, the increasing unemployment on the land, and the town slums. And not only in the court costs and the loss of property, but also in the risk to human life. No Southern white man of whatever rank could walk the streets of his city with the confidence of safety he would have enjoyed in Boston or even in Chicago. If Negroes generally killed Negroes, they did not always do so — any more than white murderers. And their constant practice in the murder of their own race made it always easier for them to pass over to the murder of the white man who offended them or whose pocketbook they happened to want.

Even more serious, if anything, for Southern white people was the fact that the crowded and hungry slums served as terrible incubators of disease in all Southern towns. Studies and maps prepared by the health departments of such cities as Atlanta, Memphis, Birmingham, New Orleans, and Charlotte show an even more exact correlation between the slums and disease than between the slums and crime. In them are invariably to be found the focal centers and primary distribution points of syphilis, gonorrhea, tuberculosis, and other chronic contagious or infectious diseases. And out of them grow virtually every epidemic of such scourges of childhood as measles, whooping cough, scarlet fever, diphtheria, and colitis, of such scourges of child and adult alike as dysentery and influenza.

And once more it is the Negro slum that is the spearhead of the menace. That in part, perhaps, because sanitary conditions are generally a little worse there than in the white slums, hunger and privation a little more common; but far more because of the close relation between the Negro slum and the more prosperous Southern white people. From these slums thousands of servants pass out every day into the homes of the whites, to cook their food and care for their children. And in estimating this, it is well to bear in mind that a far greater proportion of Southerners than Northerners regularly keep servants, since a Negro servant can be had in Southern towns for anything from two dollars a week up to six or seven. Even many families among the lower middle class regularly employ a servant, in order that the wife may hold a job in commerce or industry.

Thousands of Southern white children and adults, belonging to the classes which do not dwell in slums, die every year because of the slums. And thousands of others suffer the misery and the expense of chronic illness.

But there was more to the consequences of the population and unemployment problems even than this. In the final reckoning they were making a situation a good deal like that which had faced the South in the eighties — a situation which it was quite possible to imagine eventuating in the same life-and-death struggle between the common whites and the Negroes for the means of subsistence which had threatened them. As yet the fact was largely hidden by the hated WPA, which, as matters stood, served more or less effectively to take up the shock. But if it were removed, as so many people in the South wanted, or if the cotton-picking machine worked out as I have suggested, then the issue might well develop with great rapidity.

And in this there was ultimately the same inherent possibility of complete class division and the destruction of Southern unity which had been present in the former case. In fact, the development of class division was not waiting for the development of this issue. The same sullenness and suspicion of their old once-trusted leaders, political and economic, which I have reported as infecting increasing numbers of the workers in the textile mills, was also creeping through the ranks of the sharecroppers and tenants, of laborers generally, and, above all, of the unemployed.

The South was a great way from any developed class break as yet. But it was moving in that direction perhaps more certainly than it had ever done before. The masses were almost as solidly, and quite as blindly and uncritically, for the New Deal as the classes were against it — a fact which many aspiring politicians did not fail to note, some of them grudgingly, but some of them with eager opportunism.

And there was even the outside possibility, which must not be overlooked, that when and if the hour of complete economic crisis arrived, the Southern common whites might not after all fight it out with the Negro, but combine with him. This is, I think, improbable, since it involves the abandonment of the most solidly established tradition and the notion of superiority which the common white himself has always valued most. Nevertheless, it is worth noting that in the Southwest and Tennessee a few of the most desperately driven of the dispossessed white tenants and croppers have actively co-operated with the Negro in the more or less radical Southern Tenant Farmers' Union. And for what it is worth, a prominent and intelligent labor leader in the South tells me that the old fierce reluctance of Southern white labor to belong to the same unions with the blacks shows some signs of abating.

21

But the response of the South as a whole to these considerations was little more adequate than that of the landowners to their own immediate problem. Indeed, its response was generally less adequate than it had been in the eighties when the South came face to face with its first great quandary. For there was now no leadership ready or equipped to carry through anything like so bold a departure as the introduction of industrialism had once been.

Here was the final great tragedy of the South as it stood in 1940 — not that it had no intellectual leadership. In those elements at which we have already looked with some closeness — in its schoolmen, its literary men, its more enlightened editors, and so on — it had the best intellectual leadership it had ever had, the first which really deserved the adjective. The tragedy was that this leadership was almost wholly unarticulated with the body of the South. If the people of the region were not entirely unaffected by what the men who represented the new analytical and inquiring spirit were doing, they were still affected by it only remotely and sporadically.

This was true all along the line. Take the strictly cultural field for example. If the South now had more writers of a literary sort than any other part of the country, it was still overwhelmingly the nation's poorest book-buying area. And this was true not merely with reference to the population as a whole — was not to be explained simply by reference to the presence of the Negroes and the large numbers of poor whites — but strictly with reference to the wealthier classes and to those who had been to college.

A private library of any dimensions was the exception rather than the rule in the big and beautiful houses in the fashionable suburbs, and often when they were found there they represented simply a collection made by some secretary and kept purely for exhibition purposes. The body of business men, including those of high rank, read no book heavier than Dale Carnegie's manuals on how to make more money by false geniality; and perhaps the majority read no book at all. The same often held for their wives and daughters. Many houses in the twenty-thousand-dollar class and up were to be found completely bare of books save for half a dozen disposed as ornaments on a table in the drawing-room.

The South read a good deal more now than in the past, to be sure. But the total number of those who read anything worth reading was still incredibly small. And among those who read, if a few greeted such writers as Thomas Wolfe, Faulkner, and Caldwell with tolerance and even sympathetic understanding, the prevailing attitude toward them was likely to be one of squeamish distaste and shock, of denial that they told the essential truth or any part of it — in many cases, of bitter resentment against them on the ground that they had libeled and misrepresented the South with malicious intent.

It was the measure of something that, after fifteen years of the new spirit in Southern writing, Margaret Mitchell's sentimental novel, *Gone with the Wind,* which had curiously begun by a little offending many Southerners, ended by becoming a sort of new confession of the Southern faith. The scene at Atlanta when the motion picture made from the romance was given its first showing in the nation was one of the most remarkable which America has seen in our time. Primarily, of course, the showing, and its accompaniment of parades and balls, represented a purely commercial scheme arranged by the producers of the picture. But in the event it turned into a high ritual for the reassertion of the legend of the Old South. Atlanta became a city of pilgrimage for people from the entire region. The ceremonies were accompanied by great outbursts of emotion, which bore no relationship to the actual dramatic value of a somewhat dull and thin performance. And later on, when the picture was shown in the other towns of the South, attendance at the theaters took on the definite character of a patriotic act.

In other purely cultural spheres the tale was much the same. Most of the larger Southern towns, for instance, now paid at least perfunctory respect to the kind of music which is usually called classical. Volunteer symphony orchestras or local concert- or chamber-music groups were maintained in some instances. And musical festivals, with important concert and opera artists on the program, were general. But it was noteworthy that Southern radio stations regularly carried fewer " class programs " than those of any other American region. Members of the staff of one of the largest of these stations tell me that this is due wholly to the fact that there is no effective demand for such programs. And what is to the same purpose is that I am told by the largest music dealer in a Southern city of a hundred thousand people, which serves as trading center for a million people, that he has only four customers who regularly buy phonographic-record albums of the more serious composers.

I digress a little, of course. But I have set these matters down as a proper part of the story as a whole, and as leading naturally back to the matters with which we were originally engaged. If Southern people of the ruling orders read the Southern novelists but little and often repudiated their findings when they did read them, they read the studies, such as those emanating from the University of North Carolina Press, which were concerned with the questions directly involved in the cotton-population-unemployment quandary of the South hardly at all. Indeed, they were usually dismissed contemptuously and bitterly as the work of busybody theorists bent on raising disturbing issues which had better not be thought about at all and upsetting conditions which were quite well enough if let alone.

But the core of the tragedy lay deeper than this. It was, after all, not surprising that any body of people should prefer the comforts of complacency and illusion to facing highly unpleasant facts for which the remedy was far from being obvious — least of all that the Southern people, so long trained to believing what they liked to believe, should prefer them.

If, as I have said, the South now had the best intellectual leadership it had ever possessed, it has to be borne in mind that intellectual leaderships are by themselves always helpless. Invariably they are quite incapable of taking their facts and ideas directly to the people, persuading them of their validity, and translating them into action. What is necessary is an active and practical political and economic leadership which is able and willing to serve as a liaison force to these ends. The South simply had no such political and economic leadership, or at least it had far too few men who had been brought under the influence of the new intellectual leadership much to change the result. That is what I meant in saying that there was no articulation between the new intellectual leaders and the body of the South, and it is in this that the tragedy of the South as it stood in 1940 centrally resided.

22

It would not be true to say that in politics the South had no choice save between demagogues of the Right and demagogues of the Left (in their appeal, not their practice, of course). But there would be a good deal of truth in it.

Demagogues in plenty there were, from both sides of the fence.

Cotton Ed Smith, of South Carolina, remained in the Senate as the archetype of the man who served only the planter and industrial interests in his state, while whipping up and delighting the people with attacks on the Negro, appeals to such vague shibboleths as states' rights, and heroic gasconade of every sort. Blease had been retired to private life by a clientele grown at length tired of his bluster. And Huey Long was dead and his gang in prison or on the way to prison. But there was Bilbo, of Mississippi, in the Senate and proposing to solve the problems of the South by deporting all its Negroes to Africa; and Robert Rice Reynolds, of North Carolina, posing as the great champion of the people, but doing nothing for them except attempting to stir them to a crusade of hatred against aliens, of which his state had the smallest proportion in the nation. There was Little Ed Rivers, serving as Governor of Georgia and setting up to be devoted heart and soul to the New Deal and to the service of the masses, but actually serving only his own ambition and trying his best to seize arbitrary power in his state by calling out the militia to enforce high-handed and illegal orders in defiance of the rulings of both state and Federal courts. Old Gene Talmadge had just surged back from eclipse to be elected Rivers's successor. And it was at least not proved that the clean-up in Louisiana was going to result in anything but the restoration of the old Democratic hierarchical system of politics.

But on the higher level the South had men whose integrity, by their lights, was not open to doubt, or but little open to doubt — men of ability. Such men as Carter Glass and Harry Byrd, of Virginia, and Josiah William Bailey, of North Carolina, for example. But neither Glass nor Byrd showed much interest in the fundamental problems of the South, even as they affected their own state. Both called themselves Jeffersonians, but they were clearly far from actually believing in the ideas of the "leveling" Mr. Jefferson. What they believed in, if one is to judge by the record, was a system of state aid to the wealthier classes which should not go quite so far as the high-tariff Republicans wanted to carry it, and which would show more regard for large landowners. As I have indicated, both have bitterly fought all proposals to repeal the poll tax in Virginia, which disfranchises about sixty per cent of the white people of the state in general elections, and with success. Senator Glass grandly ignores the question of tenantry and sharecropping and unemployment altogether. And so far as I am aware, Senator Byrd's sole approach to them is to insist that $1.25 a day is quite adequate pay for the men who pick the apples on his plantations.

In fine, two honest and able examples of the sort of mind which takes it for granted that the interests of the classes to which they belong are the only ones which need to be taken into account in making dispositions for the nation and the South — the kind of mind I have portrayed as being generally bred by the conditions of the South among the upper orders of the region.

Bailey is a somewhat different case. In North Carolina he is generally called a " scholar." He is in fact something less than that, but he is a man with a better background than is usual in a Southern senator. He is much more aware of the fundamental problems of the South than the Glasses and the Byrds. But he is quite as conservative as either of the Virginians when it comes to remedies. Eager to hold power, he plays the Democratic hierarchical game for all it is worth, and directs his efforts mainly to pleasing the conservative large landowners and the industrial and commercial interests in North Carolina. And, fancying himself as a constitutional lawyer, he is always more interested in legalisms than in realities.

More hopeful have been the Bankheads of Alabama. As I need not say, neither the Senator nor the late Speaker of the House could be accused of being Leftist in their proper sympathies. But both have shown a better grasp of the case of the tenant and sharecropper than almost any other Southern politicians, and both have exhibited a consistently wider understanding and sympathy for the masses in general than was usual in their Southern colleagues. Lister Hill, the new Senator from Alabama, shows some signs of sharing their sentiments. And there are perhaps some others.

By and large, however, the scene is pretty barren — is made up on the one hand of honest but complacent Tories and too few men of liberal sympathy to have much practical effect, and on the other of a horde of outright demagogues, either of the Right or of the Left, or men of naturally conservative inclinations and mediocre capacity who pose as New Dealers and Great Liberals because they have found it to be politically useful in winning the vote of the Southern masses.

As for the economic leadership, it can be disposed of quickly. If there is a single business or industrial leader in the South at present who exhibits even as much breadth of view as the men who promoted the Cotton Mill Campaign of the eighties, who has set about to face the quandary in which the South is now placed and to arouse business men in general to the situation, he has escaped my notice. Such is the end-result of the long decay of the feeling of responsibility and honor under the conditions of Progress, the absorption in the ideal of personal profits.

23

The result is that the body of the South has inevitably been confirmed in complacency and illusion. In large part, efforts to call attention to the problems which exist have been treated not only as an unnecessary attempt at trouble-making but as a gross affront to the section. And often the active leaders have been the first to assert it.

Consider, by way of illustration, what happened when President Roosevelt's National Emergency Council released its famous " The Nation's No. 1 Economic Problem " report on the South in 1938. This report was almost entirely based on the findings of Howard Odum and his associates at Chapel Hill and dealt with nothing that was not open to factual proof. And it was received as such by the more intelligent newspapers of the region, but by no means by the majority of the newspapers. Some of them promptly denounced it as an insult to the South; others grumbled that it was high time somebody thought up something pleasant to say about the section. And they won instant support from the political and industrial leaders generally. Most of the Democratic politicians who were formally aligned with the New Deal refrained from publicly attacking the report, but they made their dislike for it amply plain through the private grapevine to business. Senator Bailey, bolder than most, took to the lecture platform to denounce it at Chapel Hill and other Southern points. And the Southern States Industrial Council, an organization made up of many of the most important business men of the South, including some of those who are supposed to be most liberal, assailed it as a pack of falsehoods invented out of Yankee and New Deal malice, with a view to discrediting and crippling Progress in the South.

The consequence was that the full effect of the report was largely lost upon the section, and it has now been pretty thoroughly forgotten by most Southern people.

I do not suggest, of course, that there has been absolutely no attempt to face the problems which confront the South, or that nothing has been done about them. But, outside the schools, they have not anywhere been faced with any fullness and consistency, and what has been done has been pretty much like trying to cure a cancer by an application of rose water.

Consider the agricultural question, to begin with. A few people, like Dr. Clarence Poe, editor of the *Progressive Farmer,* the largest farm paper of the section, have insisted on the obvious necessity of the South re-examining its whole farm structure, with a view to the development of a rational crop system, escape from dependence on the foreign market for cotton and tobacco, and the preservation and extension of the yeoman farmer class. But they have been paid little attention.

On the political front, efforts to meet the problem have mainly taken the form, in measures offered and supported by Cotton Ed Smith, Senator Bailey, and so on, of schemes aimed at trying to recover the foreign market for cotton and tobacco. It has even been soberly proposed that Great Britain be coerced into buying more American tobacco under threat of confiscation of her resources in

this country and the cutting off of her war supplies from the United
States. But the favorite idea has been to allow farmers to grow as
much cotton as they pleased and could, with a Federal subsidy to
be paid on the portion consumed domestically and the rest dumped
abroad at whatever price could be got for it. It is manifestly a
piece of wishful thinking, which in the final analysis simply pro-
poses to give away a large part of the productive capacity of the soil
of the South. In view of the production costs in the East and in
South America, the notion that there is much prospect of American
cotton ever again for any length of time fetching a price abroad
which will yield a profit under present growing conditions, or under
any growing conditions save perhaps those of mechanized, mass-
production farming, is almost certainly a Fata Morgana.

As for the tenant and sharecropper problem, the only attempt
to deal with it is embodied in the Bankhead Law, which provides
for Federal loans to selected landless persons who want to purchase
farms. But the total number of such loans made in the whole nation
in the last three years comes only to 13,000, which of course does not
even begin to scratch the surface. It is altogether probable, indeed,
that the problem is too staggering to be successfully met by any such
simple device as government loans. And, in any case, what is manifestly needed to begin with is a set of conditions in which the man
who is trying to pay for a farm will have a reasonable chance of
succeeding — a combination of land priced with regard to its earning power and not with regard to speculation, a rational agriculture,
and a system of financing the farmer from crop to crop which does
not impose impossible charges upon him.

When we turn to unemployment, we find that, so far as it has
been faced at all (save, of course, in the grumbling and sullen acquiescence of the politicians in appropriations for relief), the result
has been merely to reconfirm the faith in the old conception of
Progress — to bolster the conviction of business men and politicians
that the industrialization of the South must be carried forward at
any cost and on any terms, and that cheap labor must be maintained
as the primary essential condition.

from feeling rather than from thought, an exaggerated individualism and a too narrow concept of social responsibility, attachment to fictions and false values, above all too great attachment to racial values and a tendency to justify cruelty and injustice in the name of those values, sentimentality and a lack of realism — these have been its characteristic vices in the past. And, despite changes for the better, they remain its characteristic vices today.

In the coming days, and probably soon, it is likely to have to prove its capacity for adjustment far beyond what has been true in the past. And in that time I shall hope, as its loyal son, that its virtues will tower over and conquer its faults and have the making of the Southern world to come. But of the future I shall venture no definite prophecies. It would be a brave man who would venture them in any case. It would be a madman who would venture them in face of the forces sweeping over the world in the fateful year of 1940.

INDEX